174/02.CDS.2

174/02.CDS.2

Preprints of the Contributions to the
Stockholm Congress
2-6 June 1975

Conservation
in Archaeology
and the
Applied Arts

Published by
The International Institute for Conservation
of Historic and Artistic Works
608 Grand Buildings, Trafalgar Square, London WC2N 5HN

Editorial work on these papers was done by
David Leigh (Field Archaeology), Anne Moncrieff (Ceramics and Glass),
W. A. Oddy (Metals), Pamela Pratt (Rock Art), and coordinated
by N. S. Brommelle and Perry Smith at the IIC Office.

ISBN 0 9500525 6 6

Contents

TEXTILE CONSERVATION IN SWEDEN. PROBLEMS AND PRACTICE

A. Geijer and A. M. Franzén, Swedish Central Office of National Antiquities (Riksantikvarieämbetet), Storgatan 41, S-114 84 Stockholm, Sweden

1. INTRODUCTION

1.1 Major textile collections in Stockholm

Sweden has a large heritage of ancient textiles, representing many different categories and ages. A great deal of this heritage is to be found in Stockholm. The following particulars may be useful.

The gigantic collections of the Nordic Museum mainly comprise Swedish folk art textiles and costumes as well as other textiles in secular use from the 16th century until recent times. The Royal Armoury (Kungl. Livrustkammaren), housed in the same building, is famous for its splendid ensembles of historic royal garments and accessories. In the Royal Palace, whose art collections are administered by Kungl. Husgeradskammaren, there is a collection of tapestries particularly worthy of notice. Some outstanding furnishing textiles from the 17th and 18th centuries are exhibited by the Nationalmuseum, which also owns a number of rare textiles from Egyptian burial grounds. In the Military Museum (Armémuseum) one can see a representative selection from the remarkable Swedish Collection of Trophies, consisting of flags and banners captured in the field, mostly during the 17th century. Finally mention should be made of the Ethnographical Museum, which, however, is temporarily closed for rebuilding.

A many-sided category is presented by the liturgical vestments and other ecclesiastical textiles which until lately have been preserved in churches all over the country and are sometimes still used for divine service. Quite a number of these date from the Middle Ages, but there is a great deal of interesting material from subsequent periods as well, some of it partly of oriental origin. A number of these garments are now in the custody of the Museum of National Antiquities (Historiska Museet), whose twin institution, the Central Office of National Antiquities (Riksantikvarieämbetet), supervises the care of all the churches in Sweden together with the art treasures in their possession.

Yet another category is made up of textile remains preserved in the soil, most of them unearthed in the course of archaeological excavations. It is only in recent years that these 'archaeological textiles' have really come to be regarded as serious objects of conservation. Sad to say, we know of a great many textile finds that have been destroyed through lack of understanding of the delicate materials involved.

Three of the institutions mentioned above have, since the turn of the century, had textile studios of their own for the conservation of their very extensive collections. The Royal Armoury, the Nordic Museum and the Royal Collections are cases in point. Two museums have established workshops of their own in recent years, while other collections of ancient textiles, here and in the country, have been served by the central textile conservation workshop, whose gradual development we will now turn to consider.

1.2 Development of the Textile Laboratory of the Central Office

The interest in ecclesiastical art and antiquities that began to develop at the turn of the century was, unfortunately, accompanied by many misguided and drastic restorations, causing irreparable damage to many types of art. The fragile textiles which, in Sweden more than most other countries, were still in the possession of individual parish churches were in particularly great danger. To avert this danger, two museum directors in Stockholm — Bernhard Sahlin and Rudolf Cederström — decided, in association with the textile expert Agnes Branting, to start a studio for the special purpose of textile conservation under scholarly control. Supported by a private donor, the venture was inaugurated in 1908 under the name of 'Pietas'. This semi-official workshop subsequently developed into a kind of central institute for textile conservation, documentation and research. It was frequently consulted, above all by churches all over the country but also by museums and institutions lacking textile specialists of their own. The specialized competence thus successively developed was also drawn on by various institutions in other countries. During the 1940s the leader of 'Pietas' (A. Geijer, appointed in 1930) was formally attached to the Museum and Central Office of National Antiquities, which ultimately incorporated the textile studio. Since 1965 the studio has been headed by A. M. Franzén.

From its very inception, 'Pietas' adopted a scientific approach. Objects of major importance were discussed from a variety of standpoints. Each item was photographed before and after conservation and described in detail, a careful record being kept of the measures taken. This annually compiled documentation and its appurtenant index now constitute archives of scientific value and have been the foundation of many publications on the history of textile art. The descriptions have also been of practical benefit in subsequent conservation work.

2. ON THE STATE OF PRESERVATION OF VARIOUS TEXTILES

When deciding on practical measures and conservation methods, it is important to take into account the character of the textile material and its state of preservation in each particular case. The oxygen in the atmosphere affects all organic substances, but to varying degrees. Textile materials are probably more subject than most others to the ageing process, i.e. they weaken, disintegrate and are finally destroyed. However, the speed of this process varies considerably according to the nature of the fibres and the local conditions.

Animal fibres — mainly wool and silk — are more resistant, whereas vegetable fibres are attacked by bacteria of decomposition which flourish in humid environments. Thus flax and cotton rapidly moulder and decay in a damp atmosphere, which explains why these materials are not present in most archaeological finds containing woollen materials. This is also the case in the famous 'deep-frozen' burials in Siberia and in Greenland as well as in the boglands of Northern Central Europe, where objects made of animal fibres, sealed off from the atmosphere and in constant humidity, have been preserved — perhaps also because of the presence of methane. In 'normal' archaeological finds, animal fibres have been conserved owing to the proximity of metallic objects containing copper, which, in contact with moisture, produces salts that act as a disinfectant. But the best possible conditions for the conservation of fragile organic materials are created by a constantly dry climate, such as that of Egypt, where even linen does not decay.

When not buried under soil, silk and other animal fibres react somewhat differently. Silk is very apt to become brittle in a warm atmosphere; as for woollen fabrics, their greatest enemies are moths and other insects, against which very special precautions have to be taken. Linen is 'treacherous', for the humidity of the atmosphere increases the elasticity and strength of a sound thread while, on the other hand, its capacity to assimilate moisture makes the material very prone to infection and decomposition. It is also known that linen fibres deteriorate when the temperature exceeds 80°C.

The common enemy of textiles of all kinds is light, particularly sunlight, although even ordinary daylight and artificial light are harmful to them. The damage caused by the various kinds of light varies according to the nature of the fibres and of the dyes. Moreover, light intensifies the oxidizing process and thus accelerates the destruction of the fibres. The preservation of colours raises an intricate problem. It is difficult to reconcile the need for protection against the harmful effects of light with the legitimate desire of museums to show such objects to the public. Unfortunately the manner of displaying textiles in our museums often constitutes a direct danger to them.

2.1. Preliminaries

Before embarking on any practical operations, the following measures should be considered: careful examination of the object, photography, and measurement. As the composition of a textile unit may be of historical value, its parts should not be removed unnecessarily. Note that seams, joints and other details may have a vital bearing on an attribution of the item. In all cases, the original must be thoroughly investigated and documented before anything is removed. Documentation may be performed successively as work proceeds. The observations and analyses which can then be performed may not be possible later on.

3. CLEANING

The success of a conservation is above all contingent on cleaning being done in the best possible way. This means removing the dirt, i.e. such impurities as may impair the appearance of the textile object and damage the fibres — dirt being defined as everything which does not originally belong to the object and which is caused by natural or industrial pollution.

Of the various methods occurring, we generally prefer water treatment ('wet cleaning'), water being the liquid originally familiar to all natural fibres and always used for their preparation and dyeing, fulling, etc. With delicate and fragmentary material, however, it is essential for all the procedures to be carefully executed in strict compliance with the correct method, thus utilizing the particularly beneficial properties of water. The water should be soft and pure (non-calcareous). Mains water should be tested, and distilled water must always be used for delicate material. If the textile is very dirty, some neutral detergent may be added, but it must be thoroughly rinsed away afterwards. A wide table-basin is needed in which large textiles can be spread out before the water is poured over them, to a depth of some 2-4 cm. Cleaning is performed with a sponge, which is repeatedly and carefully pressed against the textile and the table. The fibres gradually swell, and textiles of various materials which were stiff and brittle in their dry state now become soft and flexible, and a textile that is crumpled and distorted may easily recover its original shape.

Now we proceed to the next stage. Assuming that some of the water has been discharged through an outlet, the remainder is removed with the sponge. At the same time the position of the fabric is adjusted little by little — a delicate, painstaking job. When this procedure is at last complete, the textile is left in situ to dry. The remaining moisture, combined with the surface tension, presses the textile more closely against the bottom of the basin, from which it becomes detached when it has dried. It is particularly important at this stage for the bottom of the basin to be smooth and glossy; glass is an ideal material. The fabric is now smoother and more even than it would be if it had been ironed; another advantage is that this is accomplished without the application of heat, which invariably damages sensitive fibres to a greater or lesser degree.

Water treatment is suitable for all kinds of textile materials. The procedure described here is particularly successful where the treatment of thin fabrics of silk or linen is concerned. Thick, stout fabrics and embroideries usually need to be pinned out on a firm underlay after treatment. In principle the water-treatment method can be used in a very wide variety of cases, ranging, for example, from full-size flags and banners up to about 10 m^2 to tiny archaeological fragments measuring only a few cm^2; in the latter case the sponge is replaced by a small dropping bottle.

Our experience is that water and wet cleaning are generally suitable for all ancient textiles down to fairly recent ages. It is only when dealing with textiles from the 18th century and later that one needs to be on one's guard, e.g. against silk with water-colour paint and certain 19th-century fabrics which might contain details in yarn that is liable to 'bleed' in water. In cases of this kind, use will have to be made of organic solvents — i.e. dry cleaning. No such problem arises, however, where mediaeval textiles are concerned.

It should also be mentioned that ultrasonics have proved to be an excellent means of cleaning delicate archaeological textile fragments.

4. METHODS OF USING AN ADDITIONAL SUPPORT

This support may be either a backing material, or layers of some kind applied on two sides, the object in both cases being to reinforce and protect some textile item, whether in the form of fairly large pieces or more or less fragmentary remains. The techniques used to bind the old and new textile materials together are either textile or chemical in character.

In discussions of textile conservation, some people have asserted that the chemical type of technique is a new method and the only rational one. But this is an oversimplification. Both sewing and glueing have long been in use — since the 19th century, at least — and both have had bad results, though this would hardly justify an absolute condemnation of either.

The various kinds of 'plastics' and the methods for their use which began to appear in the 1950s have prompted serious objections. For one thing, they had the effect of depriving the fabrics of most of their flexibility and, consequently, of their most characteristic appearance. Another thing was that these substances, despite all assurances to the contrary, proved impossible to dissolve in the long run, except perhaps with the aid of solvents which must be considered dangerous to the textile fibres. In reality this means that conservation on these lines is irreversible, thus precluding both corrections and satisfactory analyses at a future date. Moreover, the apparent indispensability of hot ironing in this form of treatment is disturbing. It is only fair to record, however, that the plastic products and methods have been greatly improved, and also that there are situations where some form of glueing is the only possible recourse; this is above all true of some late fabrics of poor quality which are too brittle for sewing. In cases of this kind we have employed plastic methods, reversible conservation being in any case unattainable.

If, however, one is adamant about leaving the door open for future examinations and corrections — in so far as this is possible — we feel that textile methods afford the best opportunities. But in this case one must avoid the mistakes made earlier, above all that of too much sewing. Sewing must be done with fine needles and supple yarn, guided by a light hand, and the stitches must be sparse and fairly long. Very short stitches, retaining only a few threads of the weave, will subject it to strain, finally resulting in breakage. The fact should also be stressed that needlework is flexible to a degree which is hardly possible when applying glueing procedures. The textile working method permits experiments and later corrections, as well as the freedom to choose the kind of supporting fabric that will fill gaps and tears in an aesthetically satisfying manner.

While on the subject of supporting material, a few words may be said concerning what is known as 'crepeline', a French product of pure silk which is virtually transparent. This material was first used for manuscript conservation at the Hof Bibliotek in Vienna, whence R. Cederström introduced it to Sweden during the 1920s. When we started work on the Trophy Collection in 1936, the method of water treatment described above was developed in connection with the technique for the conservation of flags — of which water-treatment is a prerequisite. Here, in general, the more or less fragmentary flag cloth is placed between two layers of crepeline, after which all three layers are sewn together using long, sparse stitches. Most of the sewing thread then comes to rest on the new material, thus sparing the old. Naturally the durability of this extremely thin material has been queried, but adapted in this way it has proved astonishingly resilient in relation to its thinness. This has furthermore been established by systematic tests on flags exhibited in the Armémuseum, some of which were cleaned by the same method as was used earlier on the fragmentary flag [1].

A general rule should be as far as possible to avoid sewing dense stitches in a fragile old textile which might be damaged by the strain thus imposed. Instead, sewing should be concentrated on the new material or, better still, sewing should be avoided altogether. This is in fact possible in many cases when dealing with small pieces (1-2 dm^2 approx.). Using only a few stitches, the textile can be fastened to a solid fabric, e.g. linen, which in turn may be pasted to the back of a passe-partout with a front 'window' framing a sheet of Melinex. A window of this kind will protect the surface of the textile and at the same time facilitate the study of the object. Further conservation may well be unnecessary.

5. IMPREGNATION

Everybody who is familiar with excavated textiles, especially woollens, will have noticed broken strands that have become detached from the weave, which also appears dry and dull. The reason for this must be that the wool has lost its natural oil, lanolin. During the early forties, attempts were made to restore this oil using a solution of 'British Museum leather dressing'. The result was beautiful but transient.

A more serious attempt was made to produce a special preservative for the fibres in 1960, in connection with the conservation of a Coptic tunic belonging to the Museum of Applied Arts in Copenhagen. These experiments were conducted in association with trained chemists, who introduced us to a soluble cellulose product, Modocoll E, an appropriate solution of which was injected into the woven object, which was kept moist for the purpose. The venture was a great success. The large, heavy textile, made entirely of wool and too fragile to be handled, was sufficiently strengthened to permit the insertion (by sewing) of a solid supporting material. The garment, which was unusually complete, looked beautiful after its conservation had been completed in 1961, though we do not know what it looks like today. Being soluble in water, Modocoll seemed a good means of momentarily securing recently unearthed textiles, but perhaps it could also be used as a more long-term preservative [2]. An element of doubt on this point eventually led to experiments using Luviscol, which is also soluble in water. Concerning this, we hope to be able to learn from the experience of others.

REFERENCES

1. Franzén, A. M., Aktuella problem i textilkonservering, 'Fornvännen' (Journal of Swedish Antiquarian Research), 5-6 (1964).
2. Geijer, A., Boström, H. and Axelson, H., Modocoll som prepareringsmedel för textilier (Modocoll as a preservative for textiles), 'Svenska Museer' 1 (1961).

APPENDIX: EXAMPLES OF WORK UNDERTAKEN

1. Between 1871 and 1881, Hj. Stolpe excavated large burial sites on the island of Bjorko in Lake Malaren. He identified the place as the historical Birka, a famous trading centre of the Viking age. The important finds of various kinds remained little known until the early thirties, when the late Holger Arbman started investigations for publishing purposes. A. Geijer was entrusted with the textile remains, then still preserved as they had been found, filled with earth, tucked into small boxes, or attached to bronze objects, the corrosion salts from which had acted as a disinfectant. The task of extracting the textile remains was accomplished with distilled water, soft paint brushes and blotting paper. The following technical types were found: fine woollen fabrics, strips of silk fabric, tablet-woven bands of silk and metal wire, variously worked dress-trimmings of gold and silver wire. Parts of the fragments were mounted on a support, some also protected by glass.
See Geijer, A., 'Birka. III. Die Textilfunde aus den Gräbern', Uppsala, 1938.

2. The Bronze Age mantle from Gerum, dated 1500-1000 B.C., was found during peat-harvesting in a bog in West Sweden. It was delivered to the Historical Museum in 1920; no treatment has been undertaken.
See Post, L.v., Waltertorff, E.v. and Lindqvist, S., 'Bronsåldersmanteln från Gerumsberget', Stockholm, 1925 (German translation).

3. In 1970, the grave of a woman from the early Middle Ages was found beneath the floor of the old parish church of Leksand, in the province of Dalarna. Great blocks of the burial were transferred to Stockholm, where the main part of the excavation could be done indoors. Large and well-preserved woollen fragments were extracted. The work will be published by M. Nockert, who carried out the excavation as well as the conservation and archaeological research work.

4. Burial vestments of Andreas Sunesson, Archbishop of Lund, d. 1228, whose sarcophagus was opened in 1923. The textiles, mainly of silk, were removed to the adjacent museum and there mounted on a supporting fabric.
See Rydbeck, O., Fürst, C. M. and Branting, A., 'Arkebiskop Andreas Sunessons Grav i Lunds Domkyrka', Lund, 1926 (German and French summaries).

5. Refuse finds of textiles from mediaeval Swedish towns, unearthed during building activities. The fragments were filled with mould and clay. When delivered to the Textile Laboratory they were still wet, which made rinsing easier. There were about 1,500 fragments, mainly of wool but also of silk and gold. After water treatment, no impregnation was carried out.
See Geijer, A. and Franzén, A. M., Textile finds from excavations in Swedish towns, 1960-1966, in 'Res Mediaevales', Lund, 1968.

6. Textile fragments from burial grounds in Egypt (Coll. C. J. Lamm, now in the National Museum). After rinsing the textiles, which were mainly in good condition, each fragment was fastened with a few stitches to a piece of linen. This was placed in a passe-partout in which an individual 'window' had been made. There was no glueing directly on the ancient material.
See Lamm, C. J., 'Cotton in Mediaeval Textiles of the Near East', Paris, 1937, and other works.

7. Textile remains from burial grounds in Nubia, excavated by the Joint Scandinavian Archaeological Expedition to Nubia; mainly dated to 350-550. Being in very bad condition, the textiles needed fairly cautious treatment with water. Some fragments were then impregnated with Modocoll. In this connection, systematic analyses of weaving techniques and diagrams were performed.
A catalogue, with descriptive text by I. Bergman and analyses and drawings by K. Adde Johansson, will be published shortly.

8. Chasuble, belonging to the parish church of Styrestad, of Italian velvet with a cross-shaped panel embroidered in gold and multi-coloured silk. The needlework is of Westphalian origin, second half of the 15th century.
See Branting, A. and Lindblom, A., 'Mediaeval Textiles and Embroideries in Sweden', Vol. II, Uppsala, 1932.

9. The 'Golden Gown of Queen Margareta' in the Cathedral of Uppsala. Queen Margareta of Denmark, Norway and Sweden died in 1412. She was buried in the Cathedral of Roskilde, where her robe was shown beside the tomb. There it was captured in 1659 when Denmark was invaded by Swedish troops under King Charles X, who ordered the precious relic to be delivered to Uppsala Cathedral. The robe may have been shown hanging, which might have caused the weave to burst because of the heavy gold. During the 19th century it was forgotten, but was rediscovered in 1907 by A. Branting. In connection with the arrangement of the Vestment Chamber, a kind of conservation was carried out, fortunately conscientiously restrained. When in the 1960s we started thorough investigations and conservation, we found that the reversibility of the earlier treatment was complete.
A monograph by A. M. Franzén and A. Geijer is in preparation. .

10. Two flags from the Trophy Collection, of which about 515 flags and banners have been conserved up to now. The first is a typical case: a Russian flag from about 1700, made of Chinese silk damask, size about 5 m². Conserved between crepeline. The second is a Danish flag, captured in 1676 from the stronghold in Helsingborg. Made of thin woollen material, red and white, size 7 x 17 m. It has been given a backing on one side, of cotton fabric dyed in the two colours of the flag.
See Geijer, A., Conservation of flags in Sweden, 'Studies in Conservation' III (1957).

11. A Coptic tunic, belonging to the Museum of Decorative Art, Copenhagen, gave rise to a new method. The weave of the large and heavy garment was so brittle that it seemed necessary to apply a backing material to the interior of the garment. But if the fragile textile were to endure such a procedure, a strengthening impregnation was essential. After a solution containing Modocoll had been injected into the damp weave, a solid linen fabric could be inserted and fastened to the ancient weave with sparse stitches.
See Franzén, A. M., En koptisk tunika, in 'Rig', Lund, 1961 (English summary).

12. Iranian 'riding coat': burial find from Antinoé, A.D. 350-450 (Musée des Tissus, Lyons). From numerous fragments of a rare woollen fabric a remarkable coat was reconstructed. It had been trimmed with multicoloured silk, of which tiny remains showed the design (which could be identified in other museums), as well as the shape of the trimming pieces. The only way to show what the unique garment had looked like was to make a reconstruction in entirely new materials. (Figures 1-7). An article by A. Geijer is in preparation.

13. A woman's headgear of fine, nicely worked linen, belonging to the Convent of the Order of St. Bridget in Uden, Netherlands, where it is regarded as a relic of St. Bridget of Sweden. The relic was brought to Stockholm by one of the sisters, who was commissioned to ask for conservation and investigation. An apparently later addition was to be removed. A. M. Franzén thinks it is a coif from the 14th century, which may well have been worn by St. Bridget.
See Andersson, A. and Franzén, A. M., 'Birgittareliker inlånade till Historiska museets utställning 'Birgitta och det Heliga landet', 30 November 1973-17 February 1974', Stockholm, 1975.

14. The Aartsbisschoppelijk Museum in Utrecht asked for assistance concerning the investigation and conservation of two very remarkable liturgical vestments brought from the old church of Dokkum, Friesland. They had been revered as relics of St. Boniface, martyred in this church, A.D. 755. As the nature of the interesting textile materials dates them to the 12th century, this was an art-historical problem as well as a rather complicated conservation task.

15. During excavations in the cathedral of Bremen, North Germany, serveral rich burials from the Middle Ages were recently discovered, among them seven tombs containing bishops buried in full canonicals. Already visible remains of silks, gold braids and embroideries seem to date them to the 12th-14th centuries. The excavation leader, wanting our assistance, has asked for permission to transfer the material in blocks to Stockholm. The work has only just begun.

Figure 1.   The contents of the parcel received from Lyon.

Figure 2.   Fragments after water treatment.

Figure 3.   Detail before any conservation procedure.

Figure 4. Front of the coat after conservation. Note traces of the appliquéed trimming.

Figure 5. Back of the coat after conservation.

Figure 6. Making the copy. The patterned Sassanian silk is copied in batik.

Figure 7. The copy from the back.

LES TEXTILES BRODÉS D'OR DANS LES TOMBES PRINCIÈRES D'ÉPOQUE MÉROVINGIENNE À SAINT DENIS

Albert France-Lanord, 11 avenue France-Lanord, 54 Villers-les-Nancy, France

La Basilique de Saint Denis près de Paris est justement célèbre car elle fut le lieu de sépulture de presque tous les rois de France depuis le 8e siècle. L'église actuelle, qui date du 13e siècle, a été édifiée à l'emplacement d'une série d'édifices plus anciens. La première chapelle, construite au 4e siècle, devint le choeur d'une église maintes fois agrandie et embellie. Les noms de Sainte Geneviève, de Dagobert, de Pépin le Bref et de Charlemagne sont liés à l'histoire de ce sanctuaire. Des travaux de recherches importants ont été poursuivis depuis 1938 par le Professeur Sumner McK. Crosby de l'Université de Yale, en vue de préciser l'histoire des édifices successifs. Ces travaux, qui ont entrainé des sondages et des fouilles, ont repris à partir de 1946 et se continuent encore [1, 2].

C'est ainsi que des sondages entrepris en dessous du choeur actuel de l'église ont provoqué la découverte de très nombreuses sépultures mérovingiennes. Les fouilles, dirigées en premier par Edouard Salin, et faites par le personnel du laboratoire d'archéologie des métaux à Nancy en 1953-1954 et 1957, furent ensuites dirigées par M. Michel Fleury, directeur de la circonscription archéologique de Paris, et se poursuivirent jusqu'en 1961. Diverses circonstances m'ayant amené à me spécialiser dans l'étude du matériel archéologique retrouvé dans des sarcophages dégagés du sous-sol d'églises, je me suis occupé de tout le matériel découvert à Saint Denis.

Les sarcophages demeurés dans le sol à l'abri des infiltrations de terre et d'eau présentent des différences considérables avec les sépultures conservées dans la terre. C'est ainsi que les squelettes peuvent être presque totalement décomposés alors que certaines matières organiques sont plus ou moins partiellement conservées.

Le milieu de décomposition très particulier de ces tombes a permis de retrouver en assez grande quantité des restes de textiles, de cuir, de bois et même parfois des restes anatomiques. Une technique de fouilles tout à fait particulière a été mise au point pour permettre d'étudier en laboratoire les restes de toute nature que risquaient d'être détruits au cours d'une fouille hâtive pratiquée in situ.

En 1959 une tombe d'un intérêt particulier a été découverte. Elle renfermait les restes d'une femme parée de très beaux bijoux dont l'identité a été reconnue grâce à un anneau sigillaire. Il s'agissait de la reine Arnegonde, une des femmes de Clotaire, second roi de France, morte vers 570. L'intérêt de cette trouvaille était considérable, car d'une part elle donnait une base solide aux chronologies et que d'autre part l'abondance des textiles et leur état de conservation permettaient pour la première fois d'avoir des éléments valables pour l'histoire du costume. Cette tombe a été étudiée à fond et publiée en 1961 et 1962 [3, 4]. J'ai du reste eu l'occasion d'en parler à Stockholm et dans les universités suédoises en 1963. Depuis j'ai continué a travailler, malgré certaines interruptions, sur les textiles et les restes divers retrouvés à Saint Denis.

Une des particularités de cette nécropole réside dans la très grande quantité de broderies d'or qui ont pu être découvertes. Si des restes semblables ont été parfois retrouvés dans des tombes de cette époque [5], jamais une aussi grande quantité de tissus ornés d'or n'avait pu être mise au jour et étudiée. Actuellement 20 sarcophages contiennent des restes de broderies ou de galons mesurant de quelques centimètres à plusieures mètres. Ceci a posé des problèmes nouveaux, tant pour la fouille que pour la conservation et l'étude.

D'un sarcophage à l'autre, les conditions de conservation sont très variables; il en est de même des conditions de découvertes, car beaucoup de tombes ont été violées dans des temps très reculés. Comme il est très difficile de travailler dans le sous-sol de l'église, les archéologues ont été conduits à effectuer des prélèvements complets de débris retrouvés dans les sarcophages, en glissant sur le fond des plaques d'aluminium et en enlevant ainsi la masse complète qui peut être ensuite radiographiée et disséquée en laboratoire.

D'une manière générale, les textiles sur lesquels les galons ou broderies étaient fixés n'ont pas été conservés. Dans le milieu acide de décomposition dans les sarcophages, les restes de fibres animales — soie, laine, cheveux, poils — laissent souvent des restes bien conservés. Certains fragments d'étoffe mesurent quelques dizaines de décimètres carrés, mais plus souvent quelques centimètres. Parfois une série de préparations microscopique est nécessaire pour déterminer la nature d'un tissu. Les fibres végétales sont infiniment moins bien conservées. La présence de quelques objets métalliques, surtout en cuivre, a pu donner des conditions de conservation privilégiées à quelques morceaux d'étoffe.

Les altérations dues à la décomposition et à l'action des bactéries rendent l'identification des colorants extrèmement aléatoire, d'autant plus que très souvent des processus plus ou moins définis ont été utilisés pour empêcher ou ralentir la décomposition des corps.

On ne traitera ici de ce qui concerne les galons et broderies d'or. Par chance, la sépulture la plus importante, celle de la reine Arnegonde, contenait des broderies remarquables. Elles ont été décétées par la radiographie des restes des mains posées sur le bassin. Il s'agissait de galons brodés d'or qui entouraient le bas des manches. Comme le support textile était totalement décomposé, les fils d'or étaient totalement emmêlés et formaient quatre couches superposées. Il a fallu les dérouler, les redresser et les remettre à plat au moyen d'une série de transpositions sur des supports provisoires. Ces supports étaient constitués par des morceaux de papier de soie enduits de cire d'abeille. Le moyen de consolidation des éléments de broderie et de la masse brune formée de ce qui subsistait du textile était également de la cire, qui était versée goutte à goutte chaude sur les parties à traiter. Après refroidissement partiel, la masse était assez solide pour pouvoir être traitée. Un léger réchauffage était éventuellement nécessaire, en travaillant sur une plaque chauffante. On a pu ainsi dérouler et redresser les fragments de broderie et le mettre à plat sur un support définitif en papier de soie, après enlèvement de l'excès de cire.

De cette façon, après un grand nombre d'heures de travail, deux galons mesurant chacun 35 cm ont été reconstitués. Il s'agit d'une série de rosettes de trois types, faites de fils d'or roulés sur soie, et placées côte à côte, les intervalles étant comblés par des triangles garnis de fils d'or. D'un côté de ce galon il y a une frise de petits triangles opposés, remplis aussi d'un fil spiralé. Tous les fils d'or étaient cousus sur le tissu de soie formant le fond par de très fins points de couture encore visible et eux aussi en soie.

D'autres tombes ont donné des éléments de broderie en quantité très variable d'une sépulture à l'autre. Souvent un galon de 15 à 25 cm garnit le bord d'un voile sur le front. Il est généralement impossible de définir le vêtement sur lequel les galons ou broderies sont disposées, et la seule indication est la localisation par rapport au corps. Une seule tombe a livré plus de 100 g de fils d'or, correspondant à près de 20 m de galon de 5 mm de large. Ces galons étaient disposés le long du corps des épaules et du cou jusqu'à 15 cm en dessous du genou. D'autres éléments complètent les galons: fleurons cousus, décors brochés. L'étoffe qui enveloppait le corps de cette femme était littéralement couverte d'or.

Le premier problème a été d'établir une typologie et de donner une bonne définition des éléments retrouvés, malgré l'absence du textile de support. Les fils d'or appartient à trois types:

1. Fils constitué par une âme de fibres (généralement soie) sur laquelle un mince ruban d'or est enroulé; c'est le fil roulé, caractérisé par son diamètre, la torsion de ruban d'or (généralement S), sa largeur et son épaisseur.

2. Fils d'or cylindriques constitués par un ruban d'or torsadé et passé à la filière; il est caractérisé par son diamètre, le sens de la torsion, la largeur du ruban.

3. Fils d'or plats, formés d'un mince ruban, caractérisé par sa largeur et son épaisseur.

On définit ensuite la mise en oeuvre de ces fils qui peuvent être cousus sur une étoffe: c'est la broderie, ou tissés pour former un galon. Le galon tissé comporte une chaine généralement disparue, le fil d'or constituant la trame. On peut parfois donner le nombre et la dimension des fils de chaine disparus par les ondulations ou les boucles du fil, de même que ces ondulations peuvent aussi permettre de retrouver le décor qui était réalisé par l'alternance des fils de chaine et de trame. Les fils d'or plats sont généralement brochés sur une étoffe qui sert de canevas. Ils ne sont plus à proprement parler des fils de trame ou des éléments de structure d'une étoffe, mais sont intégrés à une étoffe comme on le fait dans une tapisserie. C'est pourquoi je les nomme brochés, réservant le terme de broderie à l'application de fils sur une étoffe au moyen de points de couture. Le décor broché peut former des galons généralement réguliers, définis par les passages au dessus et en dessous du canevas; il peut aussi former des combinaisons géométriques plus ou moins irrégulières et complexes. Une stricte observation de la mise en oeuvre des divers morceaux retrouvés, souvent déplacéces dans la tombe, permet une relative reconstitution des décors. Peut être qu'une nouvelle découverte ou qu'une méthode de fouille encore plus rigoureuse permetrra de pousser encore plus loin les reconstitutions.

Il restait le problème de la conservation de ces broderies tout en permettant leur étude. J'ai adopté un système assez simple, qui consiste à placer les petits fragments côte à côte comme ils étaient sur l'étoffe sur la face adhésive d'un ruban transparent, genre Scotch tape, découpé à la largeur voulue. Ces rubans sont ensuite placés sur une planchette de contre-plaqué garni d'une couche de 2 mm de mousse de plastique, genre klégécel [6], le tout étant recouvert de soie rouge. Ces plaquettes, qui mesurent 26 x 8 cm, permettent de présenter 3 x 25 cm de galons. Elles sont recouvertes d'une plexiglas de 2 mm, fixé sur les bords longitudinaux par des gouttières en plastique transparent. Après quelques années, l'adhésif se dessèche, mais les fils restent parfaitement en place par le serrage. Actuellement les tombes de Saint Denis ont livré 40 plaquettes de galons et broderies, ce qui constitue une collection absolument unique. Le système d'analyse adopté a permis la constitution d'un fichier qui peut servir de référence pour tous les travaux du même genre.

Il faut noter que tous les fils métalliques associés à des textiles qui ont été actuellement retrouvés à Saint Denis sont en or, à l'exclusion d'argent ou d'argent doré. Dans l'étude des textiles remarquables de Birka, Mme Geijer signalait de nombreux galons tissés ou brochés de fils d'argent mais au 10e siècle [7]. Dans des tombes épiscopales du 13e siècle j'ai retrouvé des galons analogues à ceux de Birka, avec emploi de fils d'argent.

Si l'intérêt des broderies d'or de Saint Denis est considérable, celui des textiles mérite d'être également signalé. Dans l'ensemble, les restes sont peu importants en surface, mais très nombreux et souvent bien identifiables. Les tissus de qualité de soie se trouvent dans presque chaque sépulture, accompagnés de lainages aux armures compliquées. Il existait également des galons de laine tissés et des ornements brodés. Dans certains cas, il est possible de déterminer la disposition des étoffes dans la tombe; c'est ainsi qu'il est établi que très souvent les étoffes n'étaient pas disposées comme des vêtements habillant le corps, mais posées pliées en plusieurs épaisseurs sur le corps. Ces étoffes sont accompagnées des accessoires tels qu'aumônières, bourses, boîtes à ouvrages. J'ai dernièrement retrouvé une sorte de perruque placée sur les cheveux sous le voile. Toutes ces recherches nécessitent l'emploi de techniques d'observation et d'étude qui sont généralement inconnues des archéologues. A Saint Denis et ailleurs, j'ai eu aussi fréquemment des restes de fourrures à identifier, ainsi que des cheveux et poils. Si à proprement parler il n'y a pas eu de problèmes de restauration à résoudre, par contre la préservation et la conservation de cet abondant mátériel nécessitera des soins particuliers.

Je voudrais terminer cet exposé par un voeu. Pourrait-on envisager la mise au point d'une méthode de définition et de codification des restes de textiles, en utilisant une terminologie simple qui puisse être utilisée dans différentes langues. Ceci nous conduirait à établir un type de fiche d'identification qui serait d'une grande utilité pour tous ceux qui ont à étudier ou à traiter des textiles anciens, et qui faciliterait beaucoup les publications. Je suis un spécialiste des métaux qui s'est égaré dans les textiles en déroulant des fils d'or, mais je suis plus à l'aise auprès des forgerons que des brodeuses et des couturières. Je pense que mes collègues considéront avec indulgence mon incursion dans leur domaine et que nous pourrons ensemble apporter aux archéologues une aide qui leur est nécessaire.

REFERENCES

1. Crosby, S. McK., 'L'abbaye royale de Saint Denis', Paris, 1953.
2. Formige, J., 'L'abbaye royale de Saint Denis', Paris, 1960.

3. Fleury, M. and France-Lanord, A., Les bijoux mérovingiens d'Arnegonde, 'Art de France' **1** (1961).
4. Fleury, M. and France-Lanord, A., Das Grab des Arnegundis in Saint Denis, 'Germania' **40** (1962). •
5. Crowfoot, G. M., 'The Relics of St Cuthbert. The Braids', Oxford, 1956.
6. Klégécel, fabriqué par la Société Kléber-Colombes, France.
7. Geijer, A., 'Birka. III. Die Textilfunde', Uppsala, 1938.

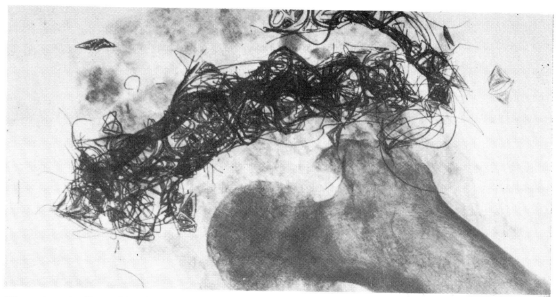

Figure 1.   Radiographie d'un galon brodé d'or de la sépulture d'Arnegonde.

Figure 2.   Un morceau de ce galon remis en état.

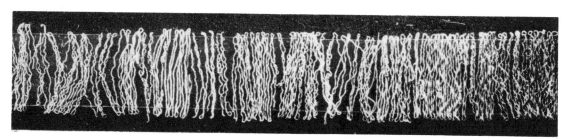

Figure 3.   Fils d'or d'un galon tissé, x 1.5.

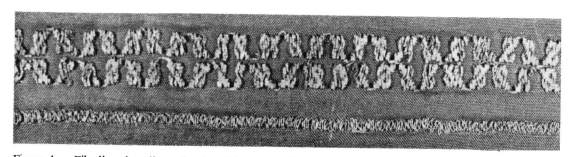

Figure 4.   Fils d'or plats d'un galon broché, en bas très fin galon tissé.

CONSERVATION OF TEXTILES FROM BAMBERG AND SPEYER CATHEDRALS

Sigrid Müller-Christensen, Hermine-Bland-Str. 5, 8 Munich 90, Germany

Since the Institute for Conservation of Textiles was established at the Bavarian National Museum in 1947, several important items of mediaeval textiles from excavations of tombs, and textiles belonging to museums and ecclesiastical treasuries, have been treated there. Amongst these are the textiles from the treasuries of the Cathedrals at Bamberg and Speyer.

At the IIC Delft Conference in 1964 I gave a short report on some of these items. Since then the conservation of the so-called Gunther Tapestry has been finished. Bishop Gunther of Bamberg died in 1065 in Hungaria on the return journey from a pilgrimage to Jerusalem. He had asked to be buried in Bamberg Cathedral. During the restoration of the cathedral in 1830, the tomb was opened and his body was found wrapped in a shroud of silk fabric — a tapestry weave — which since then has been known as the 'Gunther-Tuch'. The history of this tapestry is quite interesting. Immediately after its discovery it was treated by an architect or building expert with some chemicals in order to freshen the colours. The textile appeared badly damaged by the decomposition of the corpse. The French mediaevalist Père Martin was the first to realize the historic and artistic value of the tapestry. When he had solved the puzzle by joining the many fragments, he was happy to find a 'noble' figure of a mounted emperor receiving the homage of two female personifications of cities, although the face of the emperor and the head of his white horse had been destroyed. His reconstruction of the tapestry, published in 1851 in the 'Mélanges d'archéologie' (II, pp. 251-260, pl. XXXIV), has often been reproduced since.

In 1894 the Gunther Tapestry was restored for exhibition in the Bamberg Treasury. In the meantime all the fragments seem to have been completely disarranged. Now they were glued (with isinglass?) on brown chiffon, but back to front. The fragments were not correctly joined, often in the wrong place, e.g. parts of the horse's mane were behind the emperor. The textile also seemed to have been ironed: it had sharp pleats and was askew, pulled in wrong directions. The tapestry was exhibited like this, between two pieces of glass, until 1964. Insect-damage was observed in the original silk as well as in the chiffon. New conservation had to be carried out.

The Gunther Tapestry (220 x 210 cm) is a very fine tapestry weave of silk in brilliant colours. True purple dye has not been used, but natural dyestuffs such as madder, sumac (?), kermes grains, woad and annatto, indigo and weld. Warp: Z, beige, twofold, 22 per cm. Weft: 45 to 70 per cm. There is very little difference between the face and the reverse of the tapestry. On the face one sees colour effects of stamped spots in the ground pattern, and jewels have painted outlines. The reverse is only distinguishable from the face by a few wefts floating free for a short distance.

The magnificent portrait of an emperor, outlined against the ground pattern of flowers, with bejewelled chaplet and carrying a banner, riding on a white horse, may possibly be the pictorial representation of a historic event, the triumph of Basil II after his victory over the Bulgars in 1017. No other silk tapestry of this quality and size, from the first half of the 11th century has, as far as I know, been preserved till the present day.

In preparation for the conservation, nearly 200 fragments were photographed, carefully examined, and notes of the state of preservation were made. The tapestry was spread out on a glass-topped table. Fortunately it was possible to remove the glued chiffon, partly dry, partly after a treatment with distilled water. Cleaning with distilled water followed, and the fabric was straightened out while still wet. When dried, the fragments were arranged in their proper places with the greatest exactness and then removed from the glass-topped table to a board of plywood covered with felt, and fixed with sparse stitching with fine, coloured silk threads. A special colourless glass protects the face of the tapestry.

I should like to add two other examples of textile conservation in order to show that in every case one must come to an individual decision, on the basis of the material facts. Besides the liturgical vestments from the tomb of Pope Clemens II (died 1047) in Bamberg Cathedral, we found a veil concealing his head. It is a Hispano-Moresque, very fine, woven fabric of white silk with a Cufic inscription. Because of its good preservation only a partial support of crepeline was found necessary.

Another veil used as a sudarium has been preserved from the tomb of the emperor Henry III (died 1056) in Speyer Cathedral. Henry III was crowned by Pope Clemens in Rome, 1046. Even though the veil now consists of many fragments, it is a very important example of what was originally a large embroidery in silk on a very delicate weave. It is surely Islamic work. After its excavation in 1900, the competent expert Wolfgang M. Schmid made a reconstruction of the pattern, but all the fragments were placed in disorder between glasses. For the exhibition of all the textiles from the princely sepulchres in the Cathedral at Speyer, the fragments of the veil were cleaned and mounted according to the reconstruction, between two layers of crepeline, by sewing. It is now on display, back-lit to show the texture of the weaving and embroidery (the light being under frosted glass and some distance from the veil).

REFERENCES

Grabar, A., La soie byzantine de l'éveque Gunther à la cathédrale de Bamberg, 'Münchner Jahrbuch der bildenden Kunst' III (1966), 7 et seq.

Beckwith, J., 'The Art of Constantinople', London, 1961, pp. 98 et seq.

Müller-Christensen, S., Beobachtungen zum Bamberger Gunthertuch, 'Münchner Jahrbuch der bildenden Kunst' III (1966), 9 et seq.

Beckwith, J., 'Early Christian Byzantine Art', Harmondsworth, 1970, p. 100.

Müller-Christensen, S., 'Das Grab des Papstes Clemens II im Dom zu Bamberg', Munich, 1960, p. 54.
Müller-Christensen, S., Die Gräber im Königschor, Textilien, in Kubach, H. E. and Haas, W., 'Der Dom zu Speyer', Munich, 1972, p. 942.

CONSERVATION OF A PERUVIAN PARACAS NECROPOLIS MANTLE

Pat Reeves, Los Angeles County Museum of Art, Los Angeles, California, USA.

1. INTRODUCTION

A Paracas Necropolis mantle is a heavily embroidered, untailored, rectangular outer garment dating from 300 BC to AD 300. The mantle discussed here is in the collection of Mr Alfred C. Glassell, Jr, of Houston, Texas.

The conservation of the Glassell mantle consisted of:
1. Study of the textile
2. Removal from old backing
3. Steaming and blocking
4. Mending and attaching to a new backing material
5. Sewing to a mounting fabric stretched on a wood strainer

2. DESCRIPTION OF THE TEXTILE

The mantle consists of three separate loom widths, sewn together lengthwise. The central width is woven of two-ply black alpaca wool, Z spun and S doubled. The average yarn count per inch (2.5 cm) is 22 warps by 22 wefts. In stretched areas, the count is 20 warp and 20 weft per inch (2.5 cm); in more compressed areas, 24 warp and 24 weft. The other two loom products forming the borders of the garment are of a pale green cotton yarn with an average count of 32 warps by 32 wefts per inch (2.5 cm). This cotton yarn is also a two-ply, Z spun and S doubled. The embroidery yarn is two-ply alpaca wool in seven dyed colours. The embroidery is applied in a sloping stem stitch over four yarns and back under two. The embroidery stitch is consistent in length on both the lower thread count field and the higher count borders. This creates finer and more densely covered borders. The measurements before blocking were:

Total width at left	4' 3"	(129.5 cm)
Total width at right	4' 3"	(129.5 cm)
Length at top*	9' 9"	(297.2 cm)
Length at bottom	9' 11½"	(303.5 cm)
Central woollen loom width at left	3' 3"	(99.1 cm)
Central woollen loom width at right	3' 3"	(99.1 cm)

The borders averaged 5¾ inches (14.6 cm) in width at the top and 5½ inches (14.0 cm) at the bottom.

The two long borders are solidly embroidered, both background and design motif. The central portion is a checkerboard pattern of 49 rectangles placed in five rows.

The length of the fringe (much of which is missing) averages 1¼ inches (3.2 cm) and employs six of the embroidery colours in addition to a red (which also forms the background of the borders) which serves as a divider between the colours.

The design motif, in both the borders and on the central field, consists of two figures, the 'predator' and the 'captive'.** The predator wears a cat-like face mask, and an elaborate head dress from which four snake-like appendages issue. The captive, whose body is clutched by the claws of the predator, is also masked and also has an elaborate head dress. He carries weapons in each hand and has human hands and feet, unlike the animal-like talons of the predator.

3. CONDITION OF THE TEXTILE BEFORE CONSERVATION

When the mantle was received by the conservator it was loosely sewn to a black fabric and the borders were both sewn and glued to a purple cotton material.

Much of the embroidery and the base fabric were missing in the upper right hand corner. The upper left corner has missing base fabric but most of the embroidery stitches remained; they were quite dry, brittle and in complete disorder.

The embroidery in the field was fairly intact except for certain areas of dark yarn which had rotted away. The black wool base fabric of the field was very fragile and had disintegrated in several areas. In some areas it was totally missing.

The lower border was in much better condition than the upper border. However, the left end of the lower border was in poor condition, the base fabric having disintegrated, and the embroidery yarns which remained having become dry, brittle and much disarranged.

The adhesive used to secure the borders to the purple cotton fabric appeared to be a type of 'white glue'. It was so desiccated that it no longer adhered the embroidery threads to the cotton backing. The extreme left and right portions of the black wool field had also been secured with the same white glue.

---

*As far as design is concerned, Paracas mantles have no 'top' or 'bottom'. What is referred to as the top is the point where the embroidery begins; identification of the so-called top is based on research that seems to indicate that the work progressed in a clockwise direction.

**An iconographic study of the Glassell mantle is being prepared by Helen Pinon Wells, Curator of the Fred Harvey Fine Arts Collection, Heard Museum, Phoenix, Arizona.

4. CONSERVATION

After thorough study and analysis — preliminary study and analysis of an art object before conservation are of vital importance — the first step in the conservation of the mantle, removal of the old backing material, was begun. Because the adhesive had dried and was no longer clinging to the textile, it was only necessary to clip each holding stitch and remove them with forceps.

The fragility of the embroidered borders necessitated the use of a nylon tulle, placed on the face of them; the borders could then be turned over onto a smooth cardboard. Next, the stitches were clipped and pulled out from the back, and the purple cotton fabric removed. Another piece of nylon tulle was then placed on the underside of the borders and basted through the textile to the piece of tulle on the face of it. Thus protected, the borders could be turned face up.

Guide lines, with heavy thread, were set up vertically and horizontally in the centre of the mantle, horizontally at the junctures of the borders and field, and horizontally at the edge of the knit stem stitch which covered the joining of the fringe to the borders. Preliminary steaming and blocking followed. After steaming and blocking, the guide-line threads were removed, and the mantle covered with acid-free tissue paper and a fine cotton sheeting. The mantle was rolled, again wrapped in the tissue paper and sheeting, and removed from the work table.

A black cotton material of suitable texture (which had been washed and ironed) was placed on the work table to go under the black wool field of the mantle. A cotton material was dyed to match the red of the borders, then washed and ironed; two strips of appropriate length and width were placed on each side of the black cotton material. Thread guide-lines were set up to ensure that the joins of the three pieces of cotton fabric would fall accurately, red for border, black for field, and red for border. The three pieces were then sewn together.

The four edges of the cotton lining (red, black, red) were thumb-tacked to the worktable to provide an even tension. The thumb-tacks were used beyond the area where the mantle would lie. The mantle was then unrolled onto the lining. Again, guide lines were set up at the centre of the mantle (vertically and horizontally), where borders meet the field, and on the four outside edges. A steaming and blocking process was repeated three times.

The field was then invisibly sewn to the lining with black thread. Each figure on the field was encircled by such stitching, and all necessary mending on the field was done.

The sewing-down and mending of the borders required a great amount of time because of the fragile condition of the textile. Where designs were intact, they were sewn only enough to secure them and protect them. In very serious areas where base fabric was missing, the embroidery yarns of each design were steamed and blocked at least once before mending commenced. It was necessary to block some of the designs as many as three or four times.

To serve as an aid in reconstructing extremely damaged areas, a tracing of one complete border design was made on waxed paper. This was convenient because the transparent waxed paper could be turned over for the design in reverse.

Mending of the embroidery was done in many coloured threads to conform with the colours of the original embroidery. Only in one area, where the threads were too brittle to withstand a needle, crepeline (a strong, almost invisible, square-count French silk) was used to cover the embroidery. Crepeline was closely sewn around the outside of the design; the extending edges were frayed away. Later, the crepeline was coloured with a wax pastel pencil to match the colours of the embroidery. The knit stem border was securely sewn down. The fringe was steamed and arranged in proper colour sequences.†

When the frame for the mantle had been selected and the dimensions were known, a wooden strainer was made. After a cotton velvet backing fabric had been spread out and thoroughly steamed to allow for shrinkage, then seamed in the centre, the fabric was stretched and thumbtacked to the strainer. It was then released, and stretched and thumb-tacked three times. Following this procedure, the velvet was stapled to the strainer.

The mantle was unrolled on the stretched velvet, and guide lines established for accurate adjustments. Excess lining was cut off, leaving a narrow margin to turn under the knit stem border, allowing the fringe to lie on the velvet. The mantle was sewn down to the velvet at intervals of 8in (20 cm) in both directions. The knit stem border was sewn down, and the fringe again adjusted and sewn down.

Diluted black acrylic paint was applied to areas on the field which remained white in colour from the old adhesive, toning the stains without leaving a glossy surface. Analysis of the 'white glue' was found to be impossible. It could not be dissolved in water, Picrin, amyl acetate, or toluene. Consultation with other conservators resulted in the decision to mask the glue stains with acrylic paint.

When the conservation of the textile was completed, it was covered with glassine paper and packed in a well-padded crate for the trip to its owner in Houston, Texas. The frame and the plexiglass were packed in a separate padded crate for shipment.

The conservator travelled to Houston to oversee the framing process. The wood strainer (supporting the stretched velvet on which the mantle was mounted) was screwed to the frame. The mantle was protected with UV No. 1 plexiglass, separated from the textile one-half inch (1.3 cm). A washed piece of cotton flannel fabric was stapled to the back of the frame to serve as a dust and moisture barrier.

Conservation of this textile required 553 hours, exclusive of the time required for the trip to Houston and the work done there.

---

†Analyses of colour sequences in Paracas fringes are discussed in the author's article, Conservation and mounting of a Peruvian Paracas mantle, 'Curator' XI (1968), 108-122.

REFERENCES

Bird, J. and Bellinger, L., 'Paracas Fabrics and Nazca Needlework', Textile Museum, Washington, D.C., 1954.

Bird, J., The conservation of large embroidered Paracas mantles from Peru, 'Curator' **XI** (1968), 95-107.

Gayton, A. H., The cultural significance of Peruvian textiles: production, function, aesthetics, in Rowe, J. H. and Menzel, D., 'Peruvian Archaeology, Selected Readings', University of California, Berkeley, 1967, p. 275-292; reprinted from Kroeber, 'Anthropological Papers', **25** (1961), 111-128.

D'Harcourt, R., 'Textiles of Ancient Peru and Their Techniques', University of Washington Press, Seattle and London, 1974.

Stafford, C., 'Paracas Embroideries', J. J. Augustin, New York City, 1941.

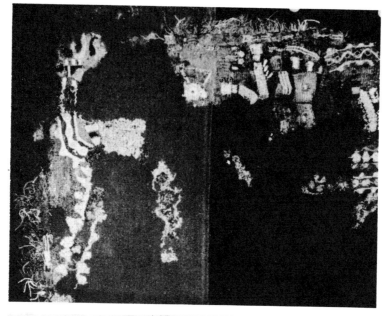

Figure 1.   Paracas necropolis mantle, belonging to Mr Alfred C. Glassell Jr.
(a) Upper right corner before removal of old backing fabric
(b) Upper right corner after removal of old backing fabric
(c) Upper right corner after mending to new backing fabric

24

Figure 2. Paracas necropolis mantle, belonging to Mr Alfred C. Glassell Jr. After completion of conservation work.

NOUVELLES EXCAVATIONS DES SEPULCRES DES VII-IX SIECLES AU CAUCASE SEPTENTRIONAL ET LE PROBLEME DE DATATION DE QUELQUES GROUPES DE SOIERIES ANCIENNES

A. A. Jeroussalemskaja, Musée de l'Ermitage, Leningrad 191065, USSR

1. INTRODUCTION

Le Musée de l'Ermitage possède une grande collection de soieries du Haut Moyen Age découvertes au Caucase Septentrional à la fin du siècle passé et au début du nôtre [1]. A présent elle est considérablement complétée — tout d'abord grâce aux trouvailles des expéditions de l'Ermitage (tombeau de Mochtchevaja Balka, la haute Bolchaja Laba, à l'altitude plus de 1500 m).

Les présentes soieries nouvelles, dont quelques-unes sont uniques, ont porté le nombre d'echantillons de soie du VII-IX siècles provenant du Caucase Septentrional plus qu'au 300 exemplaires. Ils méritent l'attention vu les aspects différents:

1. Au point de vue purement historique — pour toutes sortes de problème de la 'route de la soie', dont un chemin de detour liant la Méditerranée avec l'Extrême Orient et avec l'Asie Centrale peut être reconstruit dans ces régions-ci, à travers des côtes occidenteaux du Caucase [2].

2. Pour l'étude des tribus locales — celles des adyghéen et des alannes (par example, pour une reconstitution total du costume, pour une définition de l'influence de la mode occidentale et celle de l'Orient, etc).

3. Pour l'histoire proprement dite du tissage de soieries, pour d'étude des textiles de cette époque.

Le présent rapport n'attire pas l'attention vers les deux premiers aspects. En ce qui concerne le troisième — soi-disant 'textile' — même celui-ci ne serait pas traité d'une manière exhaustive. Je n'y suppose qu'analyser de près seulement un sujet: celui de la précision des datations de certaines anciennes soieries (byzantines, égyptiennes iraniennes, sogdiennes) sous le jour de nouvelles données archéologiques. Comme on le sait, le problème de la datation est un des plus aigus pour les historiens du textile ancien puisque les trouvailles des soieries fermement documentées ne sont que très rares.

C'est pour cela que le résultat le plus important de derniers travaux au Caucase du Nord consiste en mise en évidence des complexes archéologiques, dans certains cas datés d'une manière très précise, comportant des tissus caractéristiques (voir Section 2).

Nos collections d'autrefois, par exellence, ne permettaient que donner une datation archéologique sommaire des monuments sans aucune distribution des pièces par les sépultures isolées.

Ensuite le nombre des cas qui font possible de synchroniser des diverses soieries est augmenté — quand on les trouve cousues ensemble dans les mêmes vêtements (voir Section 3).

2. LES TROUVAILLES DES COMPLEXES ARCHÉOLOGIQUES DATÉS

Les objets d'inventaire funéraire des sépulcres caucasiens du Nord (Mochtchevaja Balka, Hassaüt, Echkackon [3]) où les soieries se sont conservées sont datés de toute évidence des VII-IX siècles et se rapportent à la culture soi-disant 'alanno-saltove' (Figure 1). Le plus ancien est le sépulcre du Vercknij-Chir-Ürt [4] qui avait fourni aussi un certain nombre des soieries. La datation y est fixée à l'aide des monnaies byzantines du VII siècle et des intailles sassanides de l'époque tardive, ainsi que par des formes caractéristiques de la céramique et des objets métalliques: c'est la deuxième moitié du VII siècle (non postérieure au début du VIII siècle).

De cette façon d'abord il suit de là la première confirmation que la date 'la plus postérieure' de toutes datations possibles de certaines soieries du Haut Moyen Age, représentées tant par des séries que par des spécimens uniques, qui provoque jusqu'à nos jours des discussions, est considérée comme la plus postérieure qu'elle soit en vérité (H. Wentzel, P. du Bourguet, parfois D. King) [5]. Tout les soieries trouvées dans les sépulcres énumérés en tout cas ne peuvent être dater d'une époque plus tardive que le IX siècle. De plus, il faut aussi prendre en considération le caractère réitératif de leur utilisation, en plupart des cas, et assez souvent leur usure ainsi qu'une intervalle temporelle, qui sans aucun doute devait séparer le moment de leur confection de celui où elles se sont trouvées dans les régions perdues du Caucase Septentrional et ensuite dans les sépulcres des tribus locales. C'est pourquoi il est à considérer la limite la plus haute de ces soieries probablement comme le milieu du IX siècle. Donc la plus grande partie de tissus de Mochtchevaja Balka et de Hassaüt (ainsi que par conséquent des tissus analogues des trouvailles européennes) doit être du VIII siècle, dans certains cas — de la limite des VII-VIII siècles.

Cela se rapporte, en particulier, aux tissus très célèbres dans l'histoire de la soierie du Haut Moyen Age, comme:

1. Le tissu vert aux simourghs [6] (Figure 4): un cafetan, trouvé dans Mochtchevaja Balka, à mon avis, est daté de la limite des VIII-IX siècles (la datation est confirmée par trouvaille dans la cathédrale de St. Remi à Reims) [7]. Une datation tout-à-fait pareille est portée à tout le groupe des soieries 'rouges' et 'vertes' aux simourghs.

2. Deux soieries bleues byzantines aux exploits de chasse de Bahram Gour [8] utilisées réitérativement: celle 'au coup de Bahram' (le parement d'une manche) pour laquelle on se réfère à la limite des VII-VIII siècles, l'autre — 'à la chasse aux lions de Bahram', complétant en petit fragment le cafetan précité aux simourghs (Figure 4) — à la deuxième moitié du VIII siècle.

3. Un tissu en soie rouge 'aux coqs', trouvé en 1973, d'un type nouveau (une partie de cafetan) dont l'analogie la plus proche est la soierie aux pégases du Musée de Vatican. La datation — la limite des VIII-IX siècles.

4. Une soierie rouge aux boues et aux archares, un petit sac, trouvé dans un complexe datant de la fin du VIII – début du IX siècle (Figure 2). Le type des images et de la bordure des médaillons le rapporte, d'un côté aux soieries 'syro-alexandrines', de l'autre – aux illustres soieries d'Aachen – bleues 'à la quadrige' et rouges 'aux canards', ce qui précise la datation de celles-ci comme le VIII siècle.

5. Une série des soieries 'de chasse' syro-alexandrines, dont la bordure des médaillons est formée d'une guirlande de lotus: par liaison avec la soierie citée dans le no.2 – 'au coup de Bahram Gour' – et avec les exemples du no.4, cette série laisse apparaître comme une datation la fin VII-VIII siècles.

6. Les soieries sogdiennes à la bordure de lotus, imitants les précédentes – la soie à 'la Sacrifice d'Abraham' [9] (la manche de Mochtchevaja Balka) et la soie 'aux chevaux' (fragment du Musée de Berlin) remontent à la même datation.

7. La datation sommaire dans les mêmes limites est raportée aussi au célèbre tissu byzantin bleu 'aux coqs' (de la région de Kislovodsk), ainsi qu'à la série des échantillons analogues (Paris, Lyon, Grenoble, Londres, Berlin, Barcélone, New York).

Le nombre d'exemples de cette sorte peut être augmenté.

La deuxième confirmation possible à argumenter par l'archéologie, concerne la plus 'antérieure datation' (la date la plus 'basse') non seulement pour les soieries évoquées ci-dessus, mais aussi pour les autres variétés de soierie du Haut Moyen Age, celles qui sont moins connues (et même celles parfois qui sont fixées pour la première fois).

Quant aux soieries des complexes funéraires de Hassaüt et de Mochtchevaja Balka, leur datation ne peut être admise qu'étant d'une époque antérieure du milieu du VII siècle, maximum. Tout cela est d'une importance aussi pour quelques tissus susnommés. Par ailleurs avec une tendence dont nous avons parlé – de les dater d'une époque assez postérieure, d'autre côté, il est possible d'y trouver une attribution ancienne traditionelle – 'VI siècle' ou tout au mieux 'VI-VII siècles' (par exemple, pour la soie verte aux simourghs) [10]. Une pareille datation parait surtout importante – terminus post quem – pour deux groupes fort connus des soieries égyptiennes, importées en deux occasions – d'Antinoë (les sépulcres – Hassaüt, Mochtchevaja Balka) et deux autres – de Panopolis-Ackmin (Mochtchevaja Balka, Vercknij-Chir-Ürt). Les soieries de l'Antinoë (du même type que celles trouvées au Caucase du Nord – Figure 3a) étaient autrefois rapportées, par excellence, à en juger par les traits stylistiques, à une époque la plus ancienne, aux IV-V ou bien aux V-VI siècles [11]. Leur combinaison avec d'autres tissus et des objets d'inventaire funéraire des sépulcres du Caucase Septentrional – leur entourage – exclut complétement l'admission d'une datation si ancienne.

La datation plausible des soieries de cette sorte – une époque apparement non antérieure au milieu du VII siècle – est confirmée indirectement aussi par la trouvaille d'un fragment de l'Antinoë dans un château Sogdien au mont Moug (mis à bas en 733).

La soierie confectionée à l'ancien Panopolis-Ackmin était trouvée – dans un état bien usé – dans le sépulture féminine de Mochtchevaja Balka (elle ornait la couvre-chef et le bandeau). Ce complexe funéraire riche contenant une quantité d'ornéments et de tissus caractéristiques est daté affirmativement du VIII siècle, pas avant. Une trouvaillé absolument identique (Figure 3b) était faite récemment en Astana (Hsintsiang). Elle était accompagnée d'un document du 643. Dans le sépulture se trouvait une autre soierie de même provénance (Figure 3c) dont une variante très proche était découverte dans le plus ancien des sépulcres cités – Vercknij-Chir-Ürt – dans un complexe de la limite des VII-VIII siécles (Figure 3d). Ainsi ce groupe des soieries de l'Ackmin trouvé au Caucase du Nord, doit être daté probablement d'une époque non plus ancienne que le milieu du VII siècle. Une telle datation est approuvée encore par la réproduction de tissus similaires aux monuments synchrones (un relief sassanide du milieu du VII siècle de Taq-i-Bustan, des fresques de l'Asie Centrale de la même période de Balalyk-Tepé) [12].

Enfin, pour la première fois les données nouvelles de l'archéologie permettent d'attribuer une série différente des soieries (du type 'samit', 'samit brochés', 'damassés' etc.), auparavant inconnues ou bien connues d'après les collections d'autres musées, mais ne possedenat pas des données quelconques à les dater. Certaines d'elles contiennent dans leurs dessins les motifs ornementaux, qui permettent de les lier avec d'autres soieries, plus illustres. Celles-ci en étaient apparement le prototype – le fait qui à son tour permet dans une certaine mesure d'en corriger les datations. A titre d'extempie on peur alléguer:

1. Une soierie sogdienne du VIII siècle, réproduisant – en qualité du motif essentiel – le motif supplémentaire de la célèbre soierie byzantine (de Ravenne) aux lionnes [13]. De cette manière sa datation du IX-X siècles indiquée dans les éditions probablement doit etre exclue; elle plaide en faveur du VIII siècle.

2. Une soie sogdienne aux 'doubles axes', traitant aussi en qualité d'un motif essentiel le motif supplémentaire de certains tissus iraniens, y compris la soie 'aux simourghs'. Les tissus aux doubles axes de Mochtchevaja Balka sont souvent fixés dans les complexes portant une date ferme du VIII siècle. Y compris, par exemple, la sépulture d'enfant aux objets de toilette du type de l'ancienne époque alanne et aux monnaies byzantines de Leon III et de Constantin (717-745) (Figure 1).

3. SYNCHRONISATION DES SOIERIES DE DIVERS TYPES

Je n'attire pas ici l'attention aux synchronisations du textile ancien, qui soient possible sur la base des confrontations stylistiques, ainsi que de leurs colorants et de leur technique. Il n'y aurait que question de l'existence commune des soieries différentes pendant une même époque, qu'on établit en définitive de leur trouvaille dans un même sépulture, ou bien, de plus, de ce qu'elles sont cousues ensemble encore à l'époque ancienne. Evidemment, surtout, quand il s'agit de l'incorporation de petits fragments (Figure 4), certaines hésitations sont possibles (dans les bornes de quelques périodes de dix ans, et bien sûr, non cent ans) à propos des datations de la confection des tissus qui étaient trouvés ensemble. En tout cas, il faut toujours prendre en considération l'état de leur conservation, ainsi que la manière de leur utilisation.

La synchronisation pour les tissus de Mocht. Balka (voir Section 3)

Sogdiennes	Chinoises	Iraniennes	Byzantines	Dates absolus
Double-axes ('medaillons de perles') Figure 1; Sacrifice d'Abraham ('med. de lotus') ref.9				Complexe funéraire du VIII-IX ss. (Figure 1)
Double-axes Figure 1; Rosette à 8 pétales ('med. des perles') ref.12, Fig.4-2	Damassé polychrome broché ('petits rombes')			Indications des monnaies de Leon III et Constantin (717-745)
Double-axes Figure 1; Motif geometrique ('med. de la spirale') ref.12, Fig.3-2; Cheveux ('medaillons florales') ref.12, Fig.7; Visages geometrisées	Damassé monochrome ('petits rombes')	Rang des lions (ТГ ∋ X, (1966))		Complexe archéologique que près de Tchefjabinsk du VIII-IX ss.
Double-axes Figure 1.; Rosette à 8 pétales ('med des perles') ref.12, Fig.4-2; [Motif supplementaire — cf 'simourgh tissù de St. Leu ref.7]		Simourgh ('med. des perles') Fig.4, ref.7	'Chasse aux lions de Bahram Gour' Fig.4*	1. Complexe du VIII-IX ss. (Figure 2) 2. Date St. Leu — l'année 835.
	Rang de motifs florales stylisées**		Boucs et archares Figure 2	Complexe du VIII-IX ss. (Figure 2)
	Rang des lotus geometrisées (bord d'un 'zandanijì l' classique) ref.12, Fig.2		'Filet' rombique de rosettes florales — d'Antinoé	Complexe du VIII-IX ss. t.a.q. pour tissu analogique d'Asie Central — 733

Notes
* cf. Falke, I, Fig.107
** cf. 'Touen-Houang', 'P. Pelliot's Mission', v.13, NEO.3663
† cf. Falke, I, Fig.35, 36

La table représente les plus importants rangs horizontaux d'une telle synchronisation. Le cumule de ces rangs (grâce à leur convergence dans quelques points) ramène, parfois, encore à l'apparition des dates absolus: quand il est possible d'établir la datation ferme de trouvaille, pour quelques chaînons du rang. Celle-ci, de cette manière, peut être passée pour une datation terminus ante quem, non seulement pour un tissu quelconque, mais pour tout un grand groupe de ce range — surtout, quand les chaînons pareils peuvent être contrôlés par plusieurs points de cette sorte.

REFERENCES

1. Bibliographie — dans : Jeroussalemskaja, A., O severokavkazskom chelkovom puti v rannem srednevekov'e (De la route de la soie par le Caucase Septentrional au début du Moyen-Age), 'Sovetskaja Arheologija' **2** (1967), 56;

   Jeroussalimskaja, A. A., Trois soieries byzantines anciennes decouvertes au Caucase Septentrional, 'Bulletin de liaison du CIETA' 24 (1966), 16-18.
2. Jeroussalemskaja, A., ibid, 70-73.
3. Kouznetzov, V. et Rounicht, A., Pogrebenie alanskogo droujinnika **XI** v.(Un sépulture d'un guerrier alannien du IX siècle.). 'Sovetskaja Arheologija' **3** (1974), 196-203.
4. Une partie des tissus sont à l'instant dans l'Ermitage; le compte-rendu préliminaire de ces excavations — voir dans 'Materialy po archeologii Dagestana' (Matériaux archéologiques de Dagestan) **2** (1964).
5. Wentzel, H. Das byzantinische Erbe der Ottonischen Kaiser, 'Aachener Kunstblätter' **43** (1972), 11-96; du Bourguet, P., 'Catalogue de tissus coptes', Louvre, Paris, 1965; King, D., Patterned silk in the Carolingian Empire, 'Bulletin de liaison du CIETA' **23** (1966), 48-49.
6. Jeroussalemskaja, A., Novaja nahodka tak nasyvaemogo sassanidskogo chelka s senmurvami (Une trouvaille nouvelle de la soierie aux simourghes soi-disante sasanidée), 'Soobtchtenija Gosundarstvennogo Ermitaga' **34** (1972), 11-15.
7. Dupont, J., Guicherd, F. et Vial, G., Le linceul de Saint-Remi. Coussin d'Aupais, 'Bulletin de liaison du CIETA' **15** (1962), 38-50.
8. Jeroussalemskaja, A., Le tissu de soie 'au Bahram Gour' du sépulcre de Mochtchevaja Balka, 'Trudy Gosundarstvennogo Ermitaga. Kultura i iskusstvo narodov vostoka' **5** (1961), 40-50. Il y a longtemps que la datation de cette soierie trop antérieurée est rejetée, à ce moment on la date à l'habitude du IX siècle; un communiqué à ce sujet — voir Vial, G., Le squaire de Saint-Calais, 'Bulletin de liaison du CIETA' **20** (1964), 30.
9. Jeroussalimskaja, A., K voprossou o svjazjah Sogda s Visantiej i Egiptom (Au sujet des liaisons du Caucase Septentrional avec Byzance et Égypte), 'Narody Asii i Afriki' **3** (1967), 119-129.
10. Volbach, W. F., 'Il Ressuto nell'Arte Antica', Milano, 1966, pp.50-52.
11. Falke, O., 'Kunstgeschichte der Seidenweberei', Berlin, 1913, Vol. 1, pp.33-39; Pfister, R., La décoration des étoffes d'Antinoë, 'Revue des Arts Asiatiques' **4** (1928), 215-243; Pfister, R., Le rôle de l'Iran dans les textiles d'Antinoë, 'Ars Islamica' (1948); voir aussi: Geijer, A., A silk from Antinoë, 'Orientalia Suecana' **12** (1963), 22-34.
12. A ce sujet — voir: Jeroussalemskaja, A., K slojeniju skoly hudojesvennogo chelkotkachtestva v Sogde A propos de la formation d'un centre de soierie en Sogde), 'Srednja Asija iIran', 1972, 34-35.
13. Réproduction en couleur — cf. Volbach, W. F., ibid., 139.
14. Je ne parle pas ici d'un fragment de soie à simourgh decouvert dans le sépulture du Phylipe de Shvabe (XIII siècle): cette soierie est tissé par une technique 'lampas' dans une autre époque; Müller-Christensen, S., Kubach, H. et Stein, G., Der Dom zu Speyer, 'Die Kunstdenkmäler von Rheinland-Platz' **5** (1972), 962-1511.

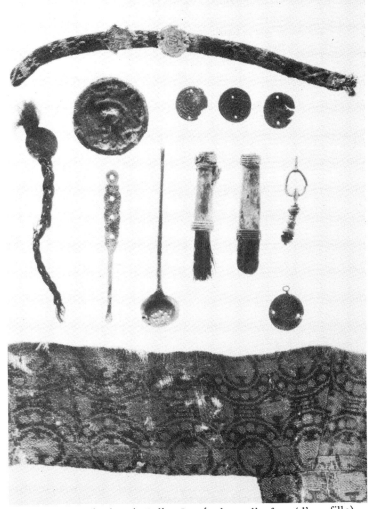

Figure 1.   Mochtchevaja Balka. La sépulture d'enfant (d'une fille).

Figure 2.   Mochtchevaja Balka. La sépulture no.37.

Figure 3. Les soieries égyptiennes importées — trouvées au Caucase du Nord (a, b, d) et en Astana (b, c).
  a. Hassaüt (d'Antinoë)
  b. Mochtchevaja Balka et Astana
  b, c. Astana (avec un document du 643) (d'Ackmin)
  d. Vercknij Chir-Ürt (d'Ackmin)

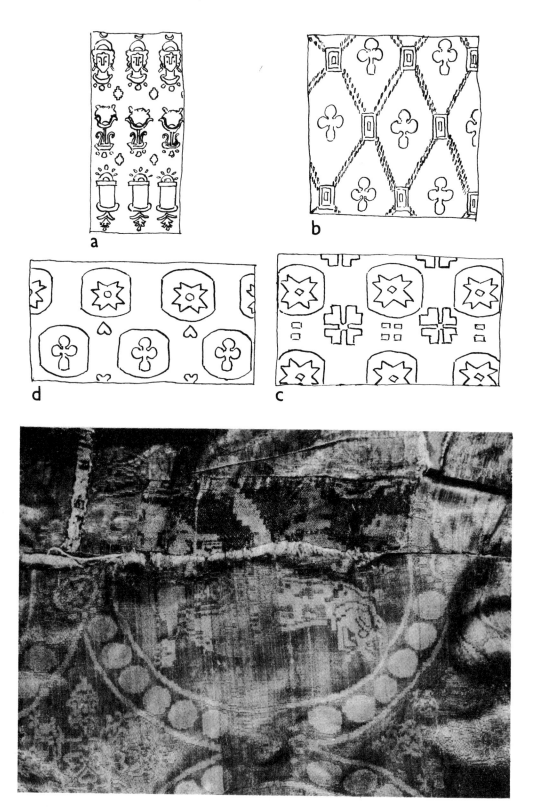

a

b

d

c

Figure 4. Mochtchevaja Balka. Tissu 'aux simourghs' avec un petit fragment de soierie 'à la chasse de Bahram Gour'.

PRESERVATION OF THE 'WASA' SAILS

Sven Bengtsson, Statens Sjöhistoriska Museum-Wasavarvet, Djurgårdsbrunnsvägen 24, 115 27 Stockholm, Sweden

1. INTRODUCTION

The royal warship 'Wasa' capsized and sank in the middle of Stockholm harbour when she had just started her maiden voyage on 10 August 1628. After unsuccessful salvage attempts she was gradually forgotten, until rediscovered in the 1950s. In 1961 she was raised with the aid of modern salvage techniques and the excavation and preservation of her vast hull and its contents could begin. The great number and variety of objects not only made a valuable contribution to the history of shipbuilding, monumental art and the knowledge of life on board a ship in those times; it also presented many problems of preservation of the different materials that made up the big find. Existing methods had to be tested and adapted to the special needs, and in most cases entirely new methods had to be developed. One example was the preservation of the sails.

When the excavation reached the orlop deck, the sail-locker was discovered. It contained two big heaps of badly deteriorated sailcloth and ropes. From the different dimensions of the ropes it could be established that the heaps consisted of several sails, at first believed to be spare sails. The heaps were removed from the ship by pulling sheet iron underneath them and transferring them into boxes which were taken ashore to the preservation laboratory. The bigger of the heaps had to be cut in two parts due to the narrowness of the ship's hatches. At the laboratory the boxes were stored in water tanks awaiting the unfolding of the sail fragments.

2. UNFOLDING

The very fragile condition of the cloth and ropes made it imperative that all operations were carried out under water. The sail heaps were moved from their boxes into shallow, plastic-clad wooden baths, which were filled with water until the heaps were covered. Sodium pyrophosphate was added (some 4 kilos to 1600 litres of water) to loosen the mud and clay which covered the surface of the heaps. The clay could then be removed by careful underwater brushing and a simple hose siphon. After several changes of water, the uppermost layer could be photographed. A transparent drawing film was laid over 1:5 scale enlargements of these photos, and all visible ropes and other parts of sail were drawn on the film. The parts were numbered with markers tied to the ropes and removed from the heap. The next layer was then cleaned, photographed and drawn, and this continued right down to the bottom layer.

The sail parts removed from the heaps were put into a bath-tub and soaked in a 1% solution of oxalic acid and water. The sails, like all finds on board the 'Wasa', were impregnated with iron deposits from rusted iron objects. The oxalic acid dissolved the rust and the rust-bound clay and made the unfolding of the cloth fragments easier. After washing in running water, the sail parts were moved to the unfurling tray, consisting of a frame 10 cm high on a 2 x 4 m base, covered with plastic foil. Here the fragments were stretched out on a netting, temporarily fixed with lead weights, measured and drawn. Details of special interest were photographed. The tray was then emptied of water, the weights removed and the sailcloth covered with gauze. The net, the sail and the gauze were rolled up together for the drying treatment.

3. DRYING

The vegetable fibres of the material were so corroded by the long immersion that they could not stand immediate drying. The surface tension of the water would pull them together, causing an irreversible collapse. The cloth would have become flat as paper and the ropes thinned and shrunk. Instead, it was decided to use alcohol-xylene extraction of the water. The rolls of net and sail were first put into a 50% solution of alcohol in water, then in two successive baths of pure alcohol. The water was deemed to be extracted by then, so the rolls were moved to a xylene bath, which was also changed once. The time in each bath was usually about 24 hours. Due to the low surface tension of the xylene, the fragments could be unrolled and allowed to dry without shrinkage.

4. PRESERVATION

The dry cloth was very brittle and light, crumbling when touched. It still had many wrinkles and tears, which could not be straightened out in the present state. It was evident that the material had to be mounted and protected for the future in some way. Existing methods of textile preservation were tested but ruled out because of the extreme brittleness of the fibres. A suitable method for preserving the 'Wasa' sails should have these characteristics:

1. An inert backing with good tensile strength in all directions.
2. The backing ought to be transparent, to allow the cloth to be studied from the rear.
3. Each fibre should adhere to the support.
4. The front side of the fibres should be protected.
5. The method should be reversible, i.e. the substance used should be soluble without too much danger to the sail fragments.
6. The material used should protect the fibres against UV-light.

In collaboration with the Institute of Polymer Technology at the Royal University of Technology in Stockholm, a method was worked out which answered all these requirements. It consists of a backing of glass fibre cloth, treated with a copolymer of plastic so that it becomes a clear sheet, on which the sail is fixed with a water emulsion of the plastic. The polymer has the same refractive index as glass, which means that the glass fibre cloth is rendered invisible by the treatment.

4.1 Preparation of the plastic
The plastic consists of a copolymer of styrene, 2-ethylhexyl acrylate and isobutyl acrylate. The monomers are freed of inhibitors and mixed with toluene in a retort. The viscosity of the plastic can be varied by changing the proportions of the acrylates. The mixture is heated under agitation in an oxygen-free nitrogen atmosphere. Cymolhydroperoxide is added as a catalyzing agent at equal intervals during the reaction, which goes on for about 30 hours. The vapour from the boiling toluene is continuously reclaimed by using a reflux condenser, so there is no loss of solvent. When the reaction is finished, the mixture is allowed to cool to room temperature and the nitrogen flow is cut off. As it is impractical to run 30 hours in a row, the reaction is interrupted at night by stopping the heating and agitation. The following morning the mixture is reheated and the agitation resumed. The nitrogen flow remains on all the time to ensure that no air enters the system. For detailed instructions, see appendix.

4.2 Preparation of the backing
The close-weave glass fibre fabric is stretched with springholders on a frame, constructed from standard scaffolding pipes and joints. The width of the fabric is 1.5 m, and 2.0 m are unrolled each time, which gives the sheets a standard size of 3 m^2. The stock copolymer solution is diluted with toluene (4 parts polymer, 1 part toluene) and is applied on the glass cloth with paintbrushes until the texture of the cloth has disappeared, usually five times on the front side and three times on the back. The whole sheet can be turned over to facilitate the painting of the back.

4.3 Mounting of the sail fragments
By stretching string underneath the now transparent sheet, the position of the sailcloth, seams and boltropes is marked according to the reconstruction drawings of the sails, based on the earlier measurings of the fragments. The rectangles of the standard sheets are superimposed on the drawings. The dried sail pieces belonging to the sheet in question are laid out on the sheet. Parts overlapping the edges are cut off and saved for the adjoining sheet.

The mounting emulsion is produced from the stock polymer, distilled water and an emulsifier, as described in the appendix. The sailcloth is soaked with the emulsion, sprayed from simple plastic spraying bottles. When wet, the cloth is easily stretched out on the backing. The seams and boltropes are straightened out along the string markings, the wrinkles are smoothed and any tears are joined. The boltropes are sewn to the backing as they are too heavy to be fixed with the emulsion only. A second protective layer of emulsion is brushed on when the first has dried.

When the sail has dried the plastic has both stuck the fibres to the support and surrounded them with a protective film. It has not actually wetted the fibres, however, with the result that the cloth has a fairly dry appearance. White spots of emulsion on the transparent backing are made to disappear by heating them with a hair-drier. A wooden lath is stapled to the upper edge of the sheet, which is cut away from the frame and hung vertically in a temporary store room. Every second sheet is covered with plastic foil to prevent the sheets adhering to each other. Before transferring to a more permanent store, the sheets are photographed and 1:10 enlargements of the photos are put together to form a composite picture of the whole, restored sail. In the same way the sheets themselves might be joined together some time in the future when a new 'Wasa' museum can offer big enough exhibition space.

5. IDENTIFICATION OF THE SAILS
During the unfolding of the remnants of sail many interesting observations could be made concerning the work of the 17th century sailmaker. Knots, splices, seams and other technical details were examined, and as the work progressed, the way of cutting out the cloths, sewing them together to form sails, putting the boltropes, clews and cringles on, and finally folding and packing in the sail-locker, was revealed. Also the different sails could be identified.

When the 'Wasa' capsized and sank she carried four sails on her mast, according to contemporary documents: the foresail, the fore and main topsails and the mizzen. These have, of course, completely disappeared during the centuries. Apart from the mizzen bonnet and two sails for the long boat, the sail-locker contained six sails belonging to the ship: spritsail, spritsail topsail, fore and main topgallants, mainsail and mizzen topsail. Together with the four lost sails they add up to a complete set of ten sails, with an estimated area of about 1200 m^2. The recovered sails represented a half of this, originally about 600 m^2. Of course, the area actually recovered varied from sail to sail, from the almost complete fore topgallant to others where almost only the boltropes had survived. The better preserved sails are reconstructed by the method described. In the case of those where most of the cloth is missing, as many fragments as possible are laid out on each sheet, but according to a certain system, in order to save time and space. When the work is finished, the total number of sheets will be over 140, i.e. about 450 m^2 of glass fibre cloth have been treated with the plastic to support the oldest known sails in the world.

The method of preservation described here has, as mentioned, been tailored especially to the needs of this vast mass of textiles in the worst possible state. But it might also be possible to apply the method, directly or with modifications, to protect and preserve other fragile textiles.

APPENDIX

Instructions for preparing 5 kilos of the stock copolymer solution, used in the preservation of the 'Wasa' sails.

Ingredients
500 g 2-ethylhexyl acrylate
440 g isobutyl acrylate
1060 g styrene
46.5 ml cymolhydroperoxide ($C_9H_{12}O_2$, 80%)
3000 g toluene

Cleaning of the monomers
The inhibitors in the monomers are removed by shaking each monomer in a separating funnel together with a solution of 5% NaOH and 20% NaCl, 20 parts solution to 100 parts monomer. The solution is changed twice. The monomers are then washed three times with distilled water and dried over calcium chloride.

Producing the copolymer
The inhibitor-free monomers are mixed in a retort with 1722 g toluene. The retort is heated under agitation and a flow of oxygen-free nitrogen. When the temperature has reached 100°C, the adding of cymolhydroperoxide is started. It is added by means of an injection syringe, hourly. The amount is 1.5 ml for the first two hours, then 2.0 ml for the next three hours, and finally 2.5 ml is injected per hour until the process has continued for 14 hours, when 2.5 ml is injected every second hour until all cymolhydroperoxide is added.

The 1278 g toluene is added to the retort in three parts, the first after 2.5 hours' reaction time (432 g) and the rest at three-hour intervals (432 and 414 g). Four hours after the last injection, the heating and agitation is turned off. When the retort has cooled to room temperature, the flow of nitrogen is cut and the copolymer is ready for use.

The total reaction time is about 29 hours, divided into four working days, as the heating and agitation is shut off at night and resumed the following morning. The flow of nitrogen and cooling water is maintained all the time.

Preparation of the emulsion
500 g of the stock polymer solution is vaporized under vacuum from most of the toluene, until the remainder weighs 320 g. 12 g emulsifier (Berol EMU) is mixed with 1200 g water. Some 300 g of this is poured into the thick polymer and shaken to form a thick emulsion, which is poured into the rest of the water solution under heavy agitation with a high speed 'Polytron' emulgating tool. The agitation should continue for about 20 minutes. The temperature during this process should not exceed 20°C.

PROBLEMS AND ETHICS OF THE RESTORATION OF POTTERY

H. W. M. Hodges, Queen's University, Kingston, Ontario, Canada

The conservation and restoration of ceramics are not subjects that have figured prominently in the pages of 'Studies in Conservation' over the past years, while H. J. Plenderleith devoted only seven pages of text to the entire subject in the first edition of 'The Conservation of Antiquities and Works of Art' [1]. One could thus be forgiven for supposing that there exist few real problems in this field, an attitude which gains considerable support from two widely held and popular beliefs. The first of these is that pottery 'has the essential quality of lastingness: any properly fired ware is indestructible in ordinary conditions' [2]; while the second is that 'building up a pot from broken sherds needs patience and dexterity rather than any special knowledge' [3]. These attitudes, here voiced by archaeologists, seem to be equally subscribed to by many conservators. The fact that ceramics do survive under the majority of natural environments, and continue to survive without undue obvious damage under many laboratory treatments, has encouraged the use of processes that in the case of any other material would be considered totally inadmissable. Thus one is enjoined thoroughly to dry out pottery before washing it; to impregnate it with a consolidant before removing superficial dirt, and to dry it in an oven at a temperature which is not specified. Harder pottery may be scrubbed with a nail-brush to remove dirt, while incrustations of lime are to be removed by soaking it in dilute citric acid, followed by several rinsings in clean water [4]. As to restoring pottery, advice may come in the form of entire volumes [5] or as sections of handbooks [6]. In either case what is largely discussed is technique, and too often the ethics of restoration are relegated to a single passage which may be paraphrased as a choice between making the restored parts discernable or not, as the case may be.

Two decades ago, when most of the works just referred to were first written, far less was being asked of ceramics than is the case today. At that time, the shape and style of pottery, its techniques of production and decoration were essentially the only features considered either by archaeologists or art historians, and provided that the visible material evidence was left intact, what was done by way of conservation or restoration mattered little. The ever increasing use of chemical and physical methods for examining bodies and glazes, and the introduction of methods of dating by thermoluminescence (TL) have imposed a new set of criteria upon the conservator who must ask himself what is the precise effect of any treatment he may devise upon the ceramics he is supposedly conserving. Thus even the most time-honoured and bland of processes, the removal of highly soluble salts by prolonged soaking in changes of water, is not beyond criticism if conducted with excessive zeal. Certainly the soluble salts will be removed, and so to an extent will other less soluble materials that may well be a part of the original composition of the body, as for example calcium carbonate [7]. The removal of surface incrustations with dilute acids can be even more damaging. Since these deposits were normally laid down from solutions, and since the pottery may well be porous, the probability is that the incrustations lie not only on the surface but also in the interstices. An acid treatment aimed at cleaning the surface may achieve only that end, leaving a mass of extraneous material in the pores to confuse subsequent analysis. Equally, the acid may remove not only the incrustation on the surface and in the interstices, but also acid-soluble components of the body, again confusing any analytical results. To complain that the analyst should not be examining ceramics that have been so treated (as indeed he should not) ignores the fact that he may be unaware that it has been carried out, especially where laboratory records and object have become separated. The same objections can be raised to the more violent forms of cosmetic treatment such as the removal of layers of decayed glaze with hydrofluoric acid [8]. Briefly, the analyst is entitled to know whether what he is looking at is original or whether it has been 'improved' by the removal of some unspecified part of it. The remedy lies in a more careful scrutiny of pottery before it is given any treatment whatever, and perhaps a less extensive use of cosmetic treatments, even at the risk of leaving at least some of the pottery in a less-than-perfect state.

Most conservators are aware that the phenomena on which TL dating methods are based are destroyed by excessive heating. The matter need not be laboured here save to point out that enthusiastic drying, especially with hot air blowers where very high local temperatures may result, and the use of heat to solidify thermo-setting resins, can quite accidentally achieve the same damage as deliberate heating. As things stand, those involved with TL dating techniques are rightly suspicious of ceramics that have been through a conservator's hands: ideally they should not have to be.

When it comes to consolidating and mending broken pottery most conservators subscribe, in theory, to the principle of reversibility, supposing that if an adhesive has a known solvent it can, if need be, at some later date be removed. In practice such a removal is very difficult to achieve, but this in itself does not justify the use of resins that are known to become insoluble in time. Those who are concerned with the restoration of archaeological ceramics are perhaps more conscious of this problem than others, and it is sometimes argued that in the case of historically well-dated ceramic objects the removal of repair materials will not arise. The same view could have been argued by archaeological conservators about all their processes a quarter of a century ago. However enticing some of the newly developed resins may seem, one wonders whether their wide-scale application today will appear quite so justifiable when IIC celebrates its fiftieth anniversary. Indeed, today the conservator and the manufacturer of adhesives seem to be in direct conflict. Unlike durability and the ability to resist detergents, reversibility is not a strong selling feature for an adhesive. With an ever increasing range of polyester and epoxide resins from which to choose, so does the temptation to use them become stronger. One can only hope that they lack the stability claimed for them by their manufacturers.

The development in recent years of historical archaeology, by which is meant the excavation of historically recent sites, has had the result that one is now faced with the remains of vessels, better examples of which already grace our museum shelves. In many cases such pottery will be in a deplorable condition from the point of view of both physical damage and chemical change. Lead-glazed vessels, especially those originally coated with raw glazes, tend to suffer greatly if buried under anaerobic conditions where sulphur-using bacteria thrive. In extreme cases the whole surface may become totally blackened due to the formation of lead sulphide. By cautious refiring and the addition, if need be, of further small quantities of raw glaze materials, such wares can be brought back to something approaching their original condition. The results can be most dramatic, but one needs to ask whether this kind of exercise is one in which conservators should indulge. The question must be put because it is technically possible to restore nearly all the ceramics from historical sites to a condition close to that of the pottery in fine art collections, although it would be a very time-consuming and expensive process.

The standard of restoration adopted or, if one prefers, the degree of deception practiced by restorers, as already noted, is a subject that receives scant attention, despite the fact that it is fundamental to the whole process of restoring pottery. It would, in fact, appear that there exist only two valid reasons for restoring pottery, and those reasons need to be considered if good restorations are to result. First, there are many occasions when it becomes necessary to display a number of sherds in a more intelligible form. If the fragments are to make any impact on the viewer some kind of reconstruction is essential, despite the fact that the sherds may represent only a small part of the entire vessel. Such restorations are no more than a technique for displaying otherwise meaningless fragments, and their intention is only to allow the viewer to relate the sherds to the type of vessel from which they came, no attempt being made closely to simulate the original vessel in the reconstructed parts. This class of restoration has to be carried out more commonly by restorers of archaeological ceramics, for obvious reasons, than by others, and has a very close parallel in the style of restoration often forced upon those dealing with severely damaged mural paintings.

The second reason for restoring ceramics needs very precise statement. It is to present the original craftsman's work in a form in which it will communicate to the viewer, as nearly as possible, what that craftsman intended to communicate in the first place. This does not say, and does not imply, the restoration of ceramics in appearance and form to their first perfection, let alone does it aim at repairs that are unidentifiable [9]. It means, rather, the rigid application of the code of ethics drawn up in the Murray Pease Report [10]. It further demands that missing pieces should be restored in such a way that they neither distract nor give the immediate impression of being restorations. Again for obvious reasons this style of restoration is most commonly practised by conservators dealing with fine art collections, and has a close parallel in the kind of work done by restorers of oil paintings.

Unfortunately the custodians of collections seldom appear to recognize that both types of restoration are perfectly valid, and that they could, and should, co-exist in any museum. Instead one sees the application of blanket regulations enforcing one or the other style, regardless of specific cases, throughout an entire collection. Hence, in a museum in which the custodian is an archaeologist, one may see superb pieces of pottery made hideous because a few missing sherds have been left in glaring contrast. Equally, one sees in some fine art collections carefully disguised restorations that transcend all rational and ethical limits. In short, the decision as to which type of restoration should be adopted should not depend upon whether a vessel is old or recent, has been buried or not, is in a predominantly archaeological or fine art museum, nor yet upon the whims of a custodian, but upon its own merits. Such decisions demand more of conservators than mere patience and dexterity.

REFERENCES

1. Plenderleith, H. J., 'The Conservation of Antiquities and Works of Art', Oxford, 1956.
2. Hawkes, J. and Hawkes, C., 'Prehistoric Britain', London, 1949, p. 162.
3. Atkinson, R. J. C., 'Field Archaeology', London, 1946, p. 214.
4. Atkinson, R. J. C., 'Field Archaeology', London, 1946, pp. 214-5.
   Plenderleith, H. J., 'The Conservation of Antiquities and Works of Art', London, 1956, pp. 326-7.
   Wheeler, Sir M., 'Archaeology from the Earth', London, 1956, pp. 185-7.
5. Parsons, C. S. M. and Curl, F. H., 'China Mending and Restoration', London, 1963.
   Pond, T., 'Repairing and Restoring China', Toronto, 1974.
6. Gedye, I., Pottery and glass, in 'The Conservation of Cultural Property', UNESCO, Paris, 1968, pp. 109-114.
   Guldbeck, P. E., 'The Care of Historical Collections', Nashville, 1972, pp. 126-130.
7. Freeth, S. J., A chemical study of some bronze age sherds, 'Archaeometry' 10 (1967), 110-111.
8. Plenderleith, H. J., 'The Conservation of Antiquities and Works of Art', Oxford, 1956, p. 329.
9. Parsons, C. S. M. and Curl, F. H., 'China Mending and Restoration', London, 1963, p.20.
10. Pease, M., 'The Murray Pease Report', New York, 1968, p. 56.

RESTORATION OF CERAMICS

J. Larney, Victoria and Albert Museum, London SW7, England

Restoration of ceramic objects in the field of the decorative arts differs from that in archaeology in requiring such skills as modelling and the careful imitation of decorative embellishments that can only come from long training and practice, preferably with a background of experience in creative work. However, the practical details of materials and techniques can be written down, and the more detail the better, even though the reader may modify them to his own purposes. I described the methods used at the Victoria and Albert Museum in 1971 [1], and have recently followed this with a book containing much more information [2].

This paper summarizes some of the principal features of our present methods together with a detailed description of our recent experience with assemblies of ceramic tile panels, which it is hoped will be helpful to ceramic restorers confronted with similar problems.

Most of the ceramic objects that undergo conservation at the museum are those that have been previously repaired, where adhesives and fillings used are showing signs of breaking down or have already parted and where the overpainted areas have discoloured badly. Objects that have been riveted are also taken apart and repaired again by more modern methods.

Before any treatment is begun, each object must be closely examined and all damage noted down. Special care must be taken to examine the glaze for signs of flaking or unfired decoration or gilding which could easily be lost. An ultra violet lamp is used to reveal the extent of old repairs hidden by overpainting. The old adhesives most commonly met with are animal and cellulosic glues, rubber-based adhesives, shellac, and, more recently, epoxy resins. The first two are easily removed with warm water and acetone. Toluene, turpentine or a paint stripper such as Nitromors will deal with rubber adhesives. Shellac can become almost insoluble with age and often presents problems, but it can be broken down with either a 50/50 mixture of ammonia and industrial methylated spirits or Nitromors. Epoxy resins can also be broken down with Nitromors, but this can often take some days if the repair is comparatively old. An earthenware object repaired with shellac should be pre-soaked in water before applying Nitromors, otherwise a purple stain which can develop could be drawn in under the glaze if the body of the ceramic is dry. The discolouration is then virtually impossible to remove.

Rivets and dowels, of both brass and iron, are commonly found as a past method of repair, and these are always removed. Some rivets can be pulled out easily with pliers if the area is first soaked with warm water applied with cotton wool swabs, but they often require sawing through. This is done by carefully sawing across the centre of the rivet with a small hacksaw blade, taking care not to damage the glaze (Figure 1). When sawn through, each half of the rivet can be gently turned and then extracted. Rust stains left by iron rivets can be removed or greatly reduced by a local application of Jenolite, and stains from copper or brass will respond to treatment with ammonia. Ingrained dirt on worn glazes, or on the type of biscuit porcelain known as parian ware, can be removed by using Solvol Autosol with a stiff bristle brush, and wiping over afterwards with white spirit or acetone. Broader stains, which occur more often on porous-bodied ceramics such as earthenwares, can be treated with the Sepiolite pack method [1]. Very stubborn stains and discolourations may be removable with hydrogen peroxide.

All break edges must be absolutely clean before bonding takes place; if not, a perfect join will be spoiled by discolouration. Even slight grease marks from the fingers could spoil the bond and to ensure cleanliness, acetone should be used to wipe each edge. As Sellotape is used for holding the pieces together, a careful check of the adhesion of the glaze to the body should be made at this stage to see that no damage can be caused when the tape is finally pulled off. There is often danger of enamel design and gilding being removed when taking off the tape. If there are any signs of this happening or if one is in doubt, the Sellotape should be swabbed off with white spirit, and in this way any possible damage can be avoided.

Where an object is large, as for example a charger, and is only broken into two or three pieces, a sand box in conjunction with retort stands and clamps can be used for added support. The Sellotape is applied as normal and the object is balanced in the sand box whilst the adhesive is setting (Figure 2). Sellotape must always be applied in a systematic fashion, moving from the back to the front of the object, while making sure that the tensioning is always even. The choice of the adhesive for bonding is determined by the object, the body, the dimensions, and the stresses and strains likely to be involved. The harder-bodied ceramics like porcelains and stonewares are generally bonded with an epoxy resin such as Araldite AY103/HY951. Earthenwares and other porous-bodied ceramics are usually bonded with a polyvinyl acetate emulsion, or Sintolit, a fast-setting polyester resin. When set, any excess adhesive is removed from the surface of the ceramic with a sharp blade. Missing areas and chips along the break edges are then filled with an appropriate filler. In the case of earthenwares and of terracottas this would usually be Polyfilla, either plain or with pigment added to give the filling approximately the same colour as the ceramic body. Adding colour to the filling can often help the retouching process where the colour of the body shows through the glaze. The Polyfilla should always be mixed to a fairly stiff consistency which will make it much easier to handle. Pigments are added before mixing with the water, and as the Polyfilla will dry considerably lighter than it looks when in its wet state, a sufficient quantity must be introduced and well ground in. Judging the amount of pigment required becomes much easier with practice. When rubbed down, the surface of the filling can often be pitted due to air bubbles that have been trapped during the mixing, and a second layer may be required. If a very smooth surface is required, a new commercial product, Fine Surface Polyfilla, can be applied as the final layer, and this will provide a beautifully smooth ground ready for retouching.

Araldite AY103/HY951 is the resin generally used for fillings on porcelains and stonewares and all hard-bodied ceramics. A white pigment, titanium dioxide, is ground into the resin to produce a white base, and into this either barytes or Kaolin powder is mixed to the consistency of a stiff putty. This must be firm rather than sticky, and one should be able to work it in the fingers, with a dusting of dry Kaolin powder, or roll it out. A little unpigmented Araldite should be applied to the surrounding edges of the area to be filled to ensure a good bond between the body of the ceramic and the putty. It is worth achieving as much accuracy as possible with the filling at this stage, thus avoiding extra grinding and rubbing down later. The finish of a filling is crucial — the slightest discrepancy on the surface will show up under the retouch. As with Polyfilla, the initial rubbing down may reveal pin-holes, and a second layer of putty will then be required. Wet-and-dry silicone carbide paper, from a medium coarse to a very fine grade, is used to rub the fillings down, taking care not to abrade the surrounding glaze. One must keep re-filling and rubbing down until the perfect surface is achieved.

The same Araldite putty can be used for modelling missing limbs such as hands. Here the restorer must be able to model to a very high standard and to adapt his style to the object upon which he is working. Hands and other limbs must, of course, correspond in proportion and structure with the appropriate features of the object. The surface coating will fill in a lot of detailed modelling, so it must be remembered to make allowance for this by over-emphasizing such details. Where a whole or part of a limb is missing, a dowel or supporting armature will be needed upon which to build the basic shape. On a very small figure, where only fingers are missing, it may not be possible to drill dowel holes. In this case, a block of Araldite putty is applied to the break edge, keeping it within the perimeter of the outline. When this is at the rubbery stage, wires cut to size can be inserted in position (Figure 3). Fuse wire can be used where a hand is very tiny, and it is also advisable to dip the ends of each wire into neat Araldite before inserting, to ensure a strong bond. Once the main block has set hard, another application of Araldite putty can be layered on and the fingers approximately shaped in. Building the fingers up in several thin layers is the preferable method to use. This will avoid too much rubbing down where, although there are supporting dowels, the fingers are still relatively delicate. A very fine abrasive paper cut in narrow strips is used to surface the made-up fingers ready for retouching (Figures 4 and 5).

Missing petals, leaves and flowers often need replacing. There are several ways of doing this. Half petals are usually built up directly on the flowers, using Plasticine as a support. Where whole petals or even flowers are missing, there are usually others of the same character on the object, from which to make copies. One of the easiest methods of making leaves, for example, is to make up some Araldite putty and roll it out like pastry on a sheet of glass or silicone paper dusted with Kaolin powder. When it is of the correct thickness, the shape is cut out with a sharp scalpel dipped in industrial methylated spirits to ensure a clean edge. Lines and other indentations can be made with a modelling tool at this stage, and the shape is left to set hard. If the leaves need to be curved, this can be done when the putty is at the rubbery stage just prior to setting. For some flowers, the putty is rolled out and cut to a curved strip, with the outer edge cut in six or so petal shapes. The whole strip is then rolled up, and the petals opened outwards from the centre to their desired angles with a modelling tool. Any trimming or surfacing is done when the Araldite putty has set hard. Individual petals can be made and allowed to set hard, then all assembled together and set into a pad of putty. This can already be seated in position on the object or can be free-standing, and bonded on when the whole unit has set hard.

Press moulds can be made with either Plasticine, dusted with French chalk, or Paribar, but this method is usually only successful where the shape to be copied is simple and has no undercuts. Where the flower or leaf is more complicated, and there are identical ones on the object, rubber latex or silicone moulds can be taken and casts made in epoxy resin.

Retouching, the last process, is perhaps the most difficult. Its success depends to a very large extent on the accuracy and quality of the work that has gone before. As mentioned previously, there is no hope of covering up mistakes with a layer of retouch, for they will only become more obvious. The retouching medium itself should be easy to apply and should ideally be non-discolouring, clear, and hard enough to rub down and polish. The closest we have found to these specifications is a polyurethane. It is moderately easy to apply by both brush and spray-gun. As one can obtain as good a result with this cold-curing resin, it seems unnecessary to subject objects to the temperature that most stoving enamels require. A full range of artists' dry pigments of the best quality will be required. These must be finely ground and should mix easily into any medium. All equipment for retouching must be impeccably clean and it is preferable to carry out the operation in as dust-free a room as possible, otherwise small particles in the air will settle on the retouch and impair the result. The pigments must be ground into the medium with a spatula or palette knife before being applied by brush or spray-gun. This must be done with particular care if a spray gun is used, because the slightest particle will clog up the nozzle and cause the spray to splatter or be uneven. It is better to build up the retouch by layers, each one being rubbed down, when hardened, with a very fine abrasive paper. It is advisable to allow a full 24 hours between each coat of polyurethane (type P.U. 11) whenever possible, ensuring that it is fully cured and hard enough to rub down. The P.U. 11 has, in itself, a sufficiently gloss finish; if not overloaded with pigment, it will retain this quality, and an additional coating of clear resin will not always be necessary. Solvol Autosol can be used to produce a final polish. If a matt finish is required, a matting agent can be introduced into the medium either before the pigment is added or afterwards. For large background areas where it would be difficult to achieve an even coating by brush, the P.U. 11 can be applied with a spray gun. When using the spray gun, one must take care that the retouch does not overlap onto the glaze itself. Most spray guns can be adjusted to produce a very fine line, thus minimizing the amount of paint that might travel onto the surrounding glaze. Producing a lustre effect is one of the most difficult processes, but there are now on the market reflective colours which, when mixed with the medium, do give a good lustre effect. These colours can be used either in combination with pigments and medium or with the medium alone, and will produce iridescent films. Experiments with these colours are still in progress, and the results are encouraging.

BACKING A PANEL OF TILES

The situation often arises where it is necessary to back a set of tiles so that they can be displayed as a panel forming a decorative composition. In the past, many different methods have been employed to attach tiles to wooden backings. This was often done with copper wires running through the tiles to the wood, or even by merely plastering them down. Eventually the old repairs begin to break down and discolour, and the tiles become loose and unsafe. At this stage, full restoration and re-backing is required. This means that all the tiles must be removed from the old backing, individually repaired and then assembled on a new support. An expanding polyurethane foam, supplied by Strand Glass, was selected as the backing material, being light and rigid and unaffected by humidity. Also it would stick to the tiles so that no adhesive would be required.

The first step in the process, before dismantling, is to number the individual tiles in sequence. The panel of tiles is then laid face down on a protective layer of foam rubber and the old backing is removed. Each tile is thoroughly cleaned and all the old plaster or cement is chipped away from the edges. Old wires and hooks are taken out and any old fillings and repairs removed. Broken tiles that have been badly stuck together are taken apart and the break edges are thoroughly cleaned, ready for re-bonding. As the majority of the tiles involved are earthenware, the adhesive used is Sintolit, which has the added advantage of being fast-setting, so that the pieces can be held together in position whilst curing. Each tile should have its number re-written on its back with a Chinagraph pencil. This will make it possible to check that they are in their correct positions when laid face down for backing. If the number is always written in the top right hand corner, it will also ensure that the tiles are the right way up. Large panels should be divided up into smaller units for backing and then joined together, each section being no more than about 90 cm x 120 cm in size. It is also as well to make a chart on squared paper at this stage, which will show the numbering of the tiles in the panel as a whole and for each individual section. The sequence of numbers for each unit can then be easily checked. Having cleaned and rebonded all the tiles and divided them up into smaller units, one section is taken and placed face down on a sheet of polyethylene on a flat surface. It must be ensured that the surface is perfectly level, for the tiles will take up a curve or any unevenness. It may seem unnecessary to mention this, but having taken one section and laid it out face up, the tiles must be turned over. Starting with the top row as an example, the numbers would run, from left to right, one to, say, nine. When turned over face down for backing they will read, again from left to right, nine to one, and so on. When they have all been turned over, a wooden frame is clamped round the tiles, making sure that the polyethylene sheeting is drawn up between the outer edge of the tiles and inside the frame (Figure 6). This will prevent the foam from sticking to the wood. The frame should allow for the depth of the tiles themselves plus 2 cm for the foam backing. These measurements will obviously depend on the size of the panel as a whole and the strength and rigidity of the backing required. However, one generally requires the thickness of the foam to be at least twice that of the tiles. The spaces between each of the tiles and the inner edge of the frame are filled in with Polyfilla, which is mixed to a stiff putty consistency and pressed well into the gaps with a spatula (Figure 7). By doing this, the polyurethane foam will be prevented from creeping down between the gaps and forcing the tiles out of line. The Polyfilla should be given plenty of time to dry out completely. A sheet of expanded aluminium mesh is cut to fit within the frame, but leaving a small margin all round. This mesh is incorporated as an added reinforcement. Wooden blocks are cut and placed on top of the mesh, one in each corner of the frame and at regular intervals down the sides, with one or two in the centre. These can be stapled to the mesh quite easily and thus not pushed out of position by the foam. The reason for the blocks is to prevent the mesh from rising to the surface and also to provide keys for the sections to be linked together. For the latter reason, it is important that the positioning of the blocks is the same on each section of the panel. These blocks also provide solid areas into which the outer frame can be screwed. Heavy sheets of glass, large enough to cover the width of a section, should be prepared by covering with polyethylene sheeting. These will be needed to lay across the frame to keep the surface of the foam level. The polyethylene sheeting is to prevent the foam from sticking to the glass. Three or four heavy weights will also be required to hold the glass down. The Strand Glass polyurethane expands to approximately 20 times its original volume when allowed to expand naturally. When restricted, as it will be in this case, the final volume is reduced by about a third, and one must calculate on this basis roughly how much to pour at a time. The catalyst and resin are mixed in equal proportions. Disposable paper cartons, specially made for measuring out resins, are available from Strand Glass, and these, being marked in units by volume, are ideal for mixing the foam in. The two components of the foam are measured out in separate containers and then poured together, stirred vigorously with a palette knife for no more than 20 seconds and immediately poured onto the tiles at one end of the section (Figure 8). The foam will start to rise within a few seconds of being poured, and the sheet of glass must at once be placed across the frame to keep the surface level and to force the foam to travel along the top of the tiles and through the mesh. The weight of the glass has to be reinforced with the heavy weights to prevent the foam from pushing upwards. As the foam, once mixed, starts to expand very rapidly, it is essential to have another person standing by to help with the glass and the weights. The whole operation only takes about two minutes so help must be on hand, for if the foam gets out of control, it does cause a great deal of mess. Although the complete expansion of the foam only takes a few minutes, the glass and weights should be left in place for at least two hours before the start of the next pouring operation. It should be explained that, owing to the limited amounts that can be handled at one time, several pourings are needed to complete each section. Before the next pour, the polyethylene cover on the glass must be checked for any tears and if necessary recovered. The next pouring can then follow, using the same procedure as before, until the whole section is filled. The completed section should be left under weights for 24 hours. After this time, the weights and glass are removed and the wooden frame unclamped and taken away. When the panel is turned over, the protective sheet of polyethylene is removed and any excess foam round the edges can be sawn or filed off. The sections should be kept flat or leaning up against a solid support, otherwise warping could occur. When the section is face up, a check is made to see that the tiles are in their correct positions, and any foam that may have managed to squeeze through is cut away with a sharp blade. Polyfilla is used for filling-in where required, both on and in between the tiles. Silicone carbide paper is used to rub down the fillings and it may be necessary to refill some areas where correction is needed. When the fillings are finally surfaced, all the sections are linked together and assembled in the frame. The gaps in between the sections are filled in with Polyfilla as before (Figure 9). The panel should be thoroughly brushed over before retouching, to be sure there are no loose particles which will spoil the surface of the paint. The polyurethane P.U.11 with dry pigments is used for the retouching. The fillings on the tiles are retouched as perfectly as possible and the lines in between are painted in a neutral ground colour (Figure 10).

ACKNOWLEDGEMENT

The photographs are reproduced by kind permission of Barrie and Jenkins, 24 Highbury Crescent, London N5 1RX.

REFERENCES

1. Larney, J., Ceramic restoration in the Victoria and Albert Museum, 'Studies in Conservation', **16** (1971), 69-82.
2. Larney, J., 'Restoring Ceramics', Barrie & Jenkins, London, 1975.

APPENDIX: MATERIALS USED

Araldite AY103/HY951. Ciba-Geigy Ltd, Duxford, Cambridge, England.
Artists' Dry Pigments. Winsor and Newton, Rathbone Place, London W1.
Barytes Powder, Grade 1. Barium Chemicals, Widnes, Lancashire, England.
Jenolite. A. Duckham Ltd, Jenolite Works, Rusham Rd, Egham, Surrey, England.
Kaolin Powder. Available from most chemists.
Nitromors (water washable). Wilcot Parent Co., Alexandra Park, Fishponds, Bristol, England.
Paribar. Available from dental suppliers.
Plasticine. From artists' materials or craft shops.
Polyfilla.   }   Polycell Products, Broadwater Rd,
Polyfilla Fine Surface. }   Welwyn Garden City, Herts, England.
Polyurethane P.U.11. Furniglas Ltd, 136/8 Great North Road, Hatfield, Herts, England.
Polyvinyl Acetate Emulsion (DMC2). Harlow Chemical Co. Ltd, Temple Fields, Harlow, Essex, England.
Polyurethane Foam. Strand Glass Ltd, Brentford Trading Estate, Brentford, Middx, England.
Reflective Colours. Cornelius Chemicals Ltd, Ibex House, Minories, London EC3.
Sellotape. Sellotape Products, Borehamwood, Herts, England.
Sepiolite 100 Mesh. Berk Ltd, Abbey Mills Chemicals, London E15.
Solvol Autosol. Solvol Lubricants Ltd, Reginald Sq, London SE8.
Solvents. Hopkins and Williams, Freshwater Rd, Chadwell Heath, Essex, England.

Figure 1. Plate, showing rivets being sawn through.   Figure 2. Plate Sellotaped together.

 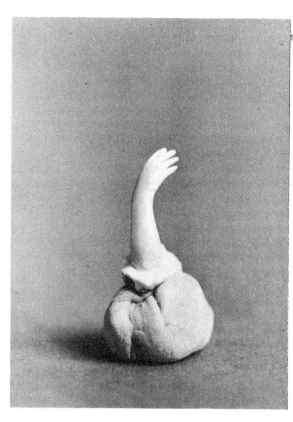

Figure 3. Block of Araldite putty with wires inserted for fingers.

Figure 4. Hand and fingers modelled and surfaced ready for retouch.

Figure 5. Completed restoration of hand. The arm has been bonded onto the figure with Araldite. Polyurethane P.U.11 has been used for retouching.

Figure 6.   Tiles face down on polyethylene sheet. Wooden frame clamped round.

Figure 7.   Gaps between tiles being filled in with Polyfilla.

Figure 8.   Polyurethane foam being poured onto tiles. Section has already been partly backed.

45

Figure 9.   Panel after backing. Polyfilla fillings ready-surfaced for colouring-in.

Figure 10.   Completed panel. Retouched with polyurethane P.U.11 and dry pigments.

THE EFFECT OF DETERGENTS ON PORCELAIN

P. Rado, The Worcester Royal Porcelain Co. Ltd, Worcester WR1 2NE, England

1. INTRODUCTION

The term 'porcelain' may mean different things to different people. European industrial ceramists usually associate the word with the type of porcelain made on the continent of Europe and, incidentally, ancient China, viz. 'hard porcelain', often referred to as 'true porcelain'. The technologist in the USA defines the term porcelain on the basis of use: 'A glazed or unglazed vitreous ceramic whiteware used for technical purposes, e.g. Electrical Porcelain', as opposed to 'china' which is the same material, but used for domestic purposes [1]. However, the US art connoisseur and archaeologist share the European meaning.

In the context of this paper the expression 'porcelain' comprises a ceramic product, used for tableware and ornamental ware, which is white and translucent. This definition does not only include hard porcelain but also bone china* and translucent vitreous china, e.g. the so-called American Household China. These products are almost invariably glazed and the effect of detergents is therefore confined to the glaze (more correctly the decoration on the glaze) as distinct from the 'body', the interior part of the ware.

2. THE STRUCTURE OF GLASSES AND GLAZES

The glaze is a thin layer of glass fused to the body. In his classical work on glass structure, Zachariasen [2] found that 'the atoms in glass must form an extended three-dimensional network ... which ... is not periodic and symmetrical as in crystals'. There are a number of compounds which can form glasses. These are termed 'network formers'. Those of practical importance for ceramic glazes are silica and boric oxide. With both oxides the structural units are joined together at their corners by shared oxygen ions to form an irregular three-dimensional network. Fused or vitreous silica and fused boric oxide are the simplest glasses. Fused silica consists of tetrahedra and is strong, whereas fused boric oxide, being made up of only triangles, is weak.

However, neither of these fused oxides would be of any use as a glaze because fused silica has too high a melting point (above $1700^\circ C$) and fused boric oxide by itself is soluble in water. Nevertheless, silica is the basis of all ceramic glazes and boric oxide is present in practically all glazes other than those for hard porcelain. To cause them to melt at a reasonably low temperature, their structure is modified by so-called 'network modifiers'. Amongst these are the larger cations, e.g. alkalis and alkaline earths. Certain cations, such as sodium, cause gaps in the network of the glass (Figure 1). This weakens the glass structure and causes devitrification or poor chemical resistance. However, if another cation, say calcium, is introduced in addition to sodium, the gap or gaps in the structure are closed and a much stronger bond is produced.

Glaze compositions are usually presented as chemical formulae, viz.

$$RO . R_2O_3 . RO_2$$

where RO represents the sum (taken arbitrarily as unity) of basic or monovalent and divalent oxides, such as alkalis and alkaline earths, R_2O_3 the neutral or trivalent oxide alumina and RO_2 the acidic oxides, silica and boron oxide (although Singer [3] moved boric oxide to the trivalent column). The network formers are thus in the third column, the network modifiers in the first column and alumina in the centre acts as a 'network co-former'.

The bases (network modifiers) invariably have a fluxing action and thus tend to reduce the firing temperature required to produce the glassy effect; the smaller the cation, the greater the fluxing power. Their fluxing effect in decreasing order is as follows: lithia — lead oxide — soda — potash — baria — lime — strontia — magnesia — zinc oxide.

Regarding the acidic oxides (network formers), boric oxide also acts as a flux — indeed, a strong flux — whereas silica, as already indicated, increases the melting temperature; so does the neutral (network co-former) alumina, at least in most cases.

Typical glaze formulae are given in Table 1.

Table 1 Typical glaze formulae

Formula		Firing Temperature
1. 0.7 CaO 0.3 K_2O	$Al_2O_3 . 10 SiO_2$	$1400 - 1440^\circ C$
2. 0.3 PbO 0.1 MgO 0.4 CaO 0.1 K_2O 0.1 Na_2O	$0.3 Al_2O_3$ { 3.0 SiO_2 0.4 B_2O_3 }	$1080 - 1120^\circ C$
3. 0.7 PbO 0.3 Na_2O	. { 0.9 SiO_2 0.6 B_2O_3 }	$700^\circ C$

*Art connoisseurs dislike the expression 'china' and even refer to bone china as 'bone porcelain'.

Glaze No. 1 is designed for hard porcelain having very high alumina and silica contents and being free from the oxides of lead and boron, thus demanding a very high temperature, the highest of all glazes.

Glaze No. 2 is suitable for bone china or vitreous china, a relatively low firing temperature being required to 'mature' the glaze. Note the great number of fluxes (the higher the number of fluxing constituents, the greater the fluxing effect) and the much smaller amounts of alumina and silica compared with glaze No. 1.

Formula 3 is not really used as a glaze at all. Containing very high amounts of the most powerful fluxing oxides, a very low amount of silica and no alumina, it serves as a flux for colours applied to the glazed and fired porcelain.

The question arises: what is the reason for the big difference in glaze composition for hard porcelain as opposed to other types of porcelain? The answer is given by the historical development of the two types of porcelain. The governing factor determining glaze composition — and thus, also, firing temperature of glaze — is thermal match between body and glaze.

The hard porcelain body has a low thermal expansion (coefficient of expansion approximately 4×10^{-6}) and therefore requires a suitably low thermal expansion glaze. Bone china and vitreous china bodies have high thermal expansions (coefficient of expansion approximately $7 - 9 \times 10^{-6}$), twice that of hard porcelain, and thus need a high thermal expansion glaze.

The higher the silica and alumina contents, the more strongly bonded the glaze becomes. This implies a higher firing temperature, a lower expansion but also an increase in durability, both mechanical (as in increased resistance to scratching) and chemical. The latter, the greater resistance to attack by corrosive chemicals, is of some importance with regard to the effect of detergents on porcelain. (Hard porcelain deserves to be so-called because of the great hardness of its glaze; its body is far more brittle than that of bone china.)

3. COLOURED STAINS

Colour on porcelain and ceramics generally is provided by metal oxides, as shown in Table 2.

Table 2. Oxides of metals used for colouring

Metal	Colour
Cobalt	Blue — violet
Chromium	Green
	Pink if prepared with other metals, e.g. tin
Iron	Brown — red
Copper	Green — turquoise
	Red if colloidal and fired in reducing atmospheres
Uranium	Yellow — orange — red
(depleted)	Black under reducing atmospheres
Vanadium	Yellow — green — blue according to varying amounts of zirconium compounds
Tin	White
	Yellow with vanadium compounds
Manganese	Brown
	Black with compounds of iron, cobalt and chromium
Selenium	Red (with cadmium)
Gold	Pink (in colloidal condition as chloride)

The metallic oxides are finely mixed with fillers, such as quartz, china clay and alumina, if applied under the glaze. If they are used on the glaze, fluxes similar to the one shown as Formula 3 in Table 1 are added; in that case an extra firing in the range $750°C - 900°C$ is required. The noble metals, gold and silver, are applied in the same way as on-glaze metal oxide stains.

4. TYPES OF DECORATION

The simplest form of decoration is the glaze itself. There are self-glazing types of porcelain bodies, such as the now obsolete Parian and dense Cordierite which, on a limited scale, is used for cooking ware. The glaze can be white (colourless) or coloured; also, the normally white body can be coloured. In addition to the two traditional ways of applying decoration already referred to, viz. either under or on the glaze, there is now a third method which is becoming more and more popular: 'in-glaze' application. The colour is applied on the glaze but the ware is then fired to a temperature sufficiently high for the decoration to sink well into the glaze. The three methods of applying decoration are shown schematically in Figure 2.

4.1 Under-glaze

The decoration is applied to the unglazed body, the piece is glazed, and decoration + glaze — and in the case of hard porcelain, also body — are fired in one glazing fire. It will be seen that with both hard porcelain and other types of porcelain there is no 'movement' of the decoration.

4.2 In-glaze

The decoration is applied to the glazed and fired piece, which is re-fired at a temperature which can be as high as the first glazing firing. Figure 2 shows that the decoration sinks into the glaze, more so with the 'soft' glazes on bone china and vitreous china than with hard porcelain. Certain special decorations, e.g. the famous cobalt blues on hard porcelain, used to be re-fired at 1400°C so that the decoration sank as deep into the glaze as it does with bone china, etc.

4.3 On-glaze ('over-glaze' in USA)

As with in-glaze, the decoration is put on the glazed and fired piece but then fired to a very much lower temperature (different coloured stains requiring different temperatures, so that some pieces have to have several on-glaze firings). It will be seen that, on hard porcelain, the decoration hardly moves whereas with other porcelains it sinks partly into the glaze, almost like an in-glaze colour on hard porcelain.

4.4 The merits of the various methods

It should be stressed that the positions of the layers as shown in Figure 2 are somewhat idealized; there are several intermediate positions. Movement of colour is more pronounced with the 'soft' glaze on bone china, etc.

Under-glaze decoration seems the simplest but it is comparatively rare because the colour palette is very small. With higher temperatures, the staining metal oxides tend to become unstable, and the higher the temperature, the more restricted the colour choice. The great majority of decorations have been applied on-glaze, practically all colours of the spectrum being available. The glazes on bone china and vitreous china have the advantage of softening (onset of melting) at temperatures at which on-glaze colours are fired and therefore allow the colours to become firmly united with the glaze. The glaze on hard porcelain remains rigid at on-glaze decorating temperatures. This sometimes causes on-glaze decoration on porcelain to be 'dry', instead of 'glossy'.

Recalling the effect of glass composition on durability, it will be realized that on-glaze stains with their powerful fluxes will be weak if exposed to chemical attack. Therefore more refractory stains have been developed which, at high temperatures, will sink into the glaze and thus be protected by it.

Great strides have recently been made in enlarging the colour range in regard to porcelain for temperatures well in excess of the normal on-glaze region. This has been achieved in conjunction with work on very fast firing and the coloured stains developed for in-glaze application will retain their colour shade only under very fast firing conditions, viz. one hour compared with the conventional 8-24 hours.

5. DETERGENTS AND AUTOMATIC DISH-WASHING MACHINES

The well-known chemist and ceramist J. W. Mellor [4] was the first to treat the subject of the effect of detergents on ceramics comprehensively and, in his inimitable way, did so extremely fully. He listed five factors determining the efficiency of the cleansing agent:

1. Temperature and concentration.
2. Emulsifying power, viz. the capacity of holding dirt, oil and grease in suspension.
3. Saponification power, i.e. the speed with which the detergent forms soluble soaps with fatty materials.
4. Tendency to prevent formation of adherent and insoluble substances which inhibit the action of the cleansing agent.
5. Non-corrosive effect on the vessel being cleaned.

Dale and Francis [5] added to these the effect of agitation. Mellor [4] also reports the composition of some of the first detergents on the market, viz:

Type 1	72% soap
(Persil)	15½% sodium carbonate
	10% sodium perborate
	2½% sodium silicate
Type 2	67% sodium phosphate
(IMI)	25% sodium carbonate
	5% sodium silicate
	3% water
Type 3	Mainly sodium metaphosphate which produces a soluble stable complex with calcium and magnesium
(Calgon)	salts. This is important in the case of hard water containing calcium and magnesium salts which may otherwise produce insoluble soaps adhering as films on the surface of the ware in washing machines.

Some of the latest types of detergents contain larger amounts of silicates and a great number are based on complex phosphates such as tripolyphosphates, orthophosphates and pyrophosphates [6, 7].

It is again Mellor [4] who describes the chemistry and general mechanism of the attack by detergents on ceramics in great detail. Oel [8] has dealt with the chemistry of attack and uses the amount of silica dissolved (in the decoration) as a criterion of attack.

According to another source [9] the theory of glass structure as applied to the attack on on-glaze decoration by various chemical compounds predicts that glass surfaces can be protected from alkaline attack by certain cations which are preferentially adsorbed on the glass surface and retard its breakdown. Experiments proved that a small amount (2 – 2½%) of sodium aluminate (or aluminium salt) in the wash solution greatly reduces the deterioration of on-glaze colours. This has been confirmed more recently by Gray et al [10].

Sharratt and Francis [11] conclude that the alkalis in detergents seem to attack the flux rather than the pigment; the loss of gloss thus produced makes the ware more prone to marking by cutlery, usually referred to as 'silver marking'.

As far as washing machines are concerned, Mellor [4] describes two types: in the 'rotating brush' type the deterioration is mainly due to mechanical wear. This kind of machine has been superseded by the more effective and less harmful 'spray' type. Schlüter [12], who gives a comprehensive account of more recent dish-washing machines, differentiates between the 'vortex' and 'jet' systems. In describing the washing-up programme, he concentrates on factors like mechanical effect, temperature, time and chemical action, which have a greater impact on decoration than composition of water, hygiene and economic operation.

The need for two agents in automatic dish-washers is stressed by Wedell [13] and Gray et al [10], one for washing, the other for rinsing. The purpose of rinsing agents is to ensure efficient draining of the ware without droplet formation. They contain low-foam, non-ionic surfactants to which organic acids are sometimes added, i.e. combinations of ethylene oxide and polymerized propylene. Even with the best rinse aids, the last remaining liquid leaves an infinitesimally thin film which dries on the ware. Such deposits have been proved harmless to health.

Kraft [14] is the latest of the many researchers who have investigated the effect in automatic dish-washers of various detergents on the market. Gray et al [10] discuss in depth the role of detergents in dish-washing machines. Kohl [15] stresses the need for the detergent manufacturers to produce effective detergents which do not attack on-glaze colours on porcelain.

6. METHODS OF TESTING

Most tests in use [9, 11, 16, 17] involve immersion under standard conditions of concentration and temperature of test solution, and duration of immersion, and are aimed at simulating a number of washings which would amount to reasonable usage. Sometimes straight cycling tests in automatic dish-washers are used. Results are expressed in arbitrary figures denoting degree of wear.

Harth [18] has developed a system of evaluation which differentiates between type of attack and intensity of attack; this is claimed to be more meaningful than the usual single classifications.

Lohmeyer [17, 19, 20] has introduced a system using a spectral photometer which measures complementary wavelengths and thus gives results in precise figures.

Relatively little has been published in America on testing methods apart from the 'FB-2C' test [16]. This allows results to be obtained quickly and shows good correlation with actual automatic dish-washer performance. Otrhalek and Bacon [16] who developed this test draw attention to the fact that (as with practically all other methods) testing is done on clean surfaces unsoiled by food residues which are thought to have a protective influence. (This has been stressed also by other authors [18, 10].)

In Britain, test procedures laid down by the British Ceramic Research Association are used; they are based on principles similar to those in USA and Germany. This organization regularly tests detergents available on the market in Britain and other countries. It has been shown that some washing agents are changed in composition without change in name and are thus liable to pass from a harmless to a harmful detergent. In order to prevent such occurrences, the Association is seeking to conclude agreements with detergent manufacturers whereby 'product approval' is given for the use of a detergent which passes the test procedure laid down; the manufacturer of the detergent guarantees that its formulation will not be changed unless the new composition has been proved harmless by the Association. Product Approval has been given for the following detergents: Freedom and Kenwood Freedom, Hygleam, Bio-gleam, C66, Bio-66 and Colston [9].

7.   THE EFFECT OF VARIOUS FACTORS ON THE RESISTANCE OF PORCELAIN DECORATION

Two points should be borne in mind:

1. Porcelain glazes, including the 'soft' glazes on bone china, are usually not visibly attacked by washing agents (although they may be covered by a film). Nevertheless, in recent investigations of glaze surfaces (presumably of bone china type) attacked by a strong detergent, the scanning electron microscope revealed a layer of loosely adhering flakes [9]. When these flakes were removed, a second, more adherent but badly cracked layer was noticed. However, in the present context we are concerned with attack visible to the naked eye.

2. Coloured stains under the glaze or in the glaze are unlikely to be attacked because they are protected by the glaze.

For these reasons the discussion of factors influencing the resistance of porcelain colours is confined to on-glaze decoration.

7.1 Body

It seems absurd to think that body composition could affect on-glaze durability. There is, however, evidence of ion migration from body to glaze and vice versa [9]. Mainly alkali ions are affected and there is a strong possibility that these ions migrate from the body to the surface of the glaze thus affecting the structure of the coloured stain, making it more resistant or possibly less resistant.

7.2 Glaze

Mellor [4] states that wear in rotating brush dish-washers is perhaps more pronounced with hard porcelain than it is with bone china or earthenware because of more intimate coalescence of the softer glaze with on-glaze colours. As has been shown, on-glaze decoration on the 'soft' glaze moves partly into the glaze and is thus afforded greater protection than on hard porcelain.

However, one might argue that, even if the coloured stain is protected by the 'soft' glaze, the flux in the glaze may have weakened the glaze at the site of the colour to such an extent that the apparent advantage of intimate coalescence is nullified.

According to theory, the higher silica content of the hard porcelain glaze should indeed lead to better durability. In the range of bone china glazes, a higher silica content definitely caused better resistance against acid attack, but no such clear-cut effect was noted with alkalis and thus detergents [9].

Alkalis and alkaline earths in glazes have a deleterious effect on durability [9]. This could be predicted from the random network hypothesis in connexion with the mechanism of alkali attack on a glass [9]. Migration of sodium ions from glaze to colour has been positively established by the use of radio-active isotopes [9]. This and the reverse migration afford the most likely explanation of the phenomena observed [9].

Viscosity of the glaze at the maximum firing temperature, or the temperature of the glazing fire itself, had no influence on the resistance of on-glaze colours against detergent attack [9].

7.3 Coloured stains

There are few literature references of practical value in connexion with the effect of composition on the lead-borax-soda-silica combinations which form the basic flux formulae of ceramic pigments. Small additions of boric oxide have a beneficial influence but, beyond a certain amount, boric oxide causes a sharp drop in durability. Increasing amounts of lead oxide added to a sodium tri-silicate glass cause a rapid increase in resistance [5].

Regarding pigments, comprehensive surveys are given by Dale and Francis [5] and also by Sharratt and Francis [11], who found different durabilities with the same colours prepared by different manufacturers, green, black and orange colours being most readily attacked. According to Kraft [14] the resistance of colours to detergents decreased in the following order: red, grey, light green, blue, yellow and dark green.

Firing temperature of coloured stains present as on-glaze decoration has a profound effect on durability. Generally, the higher the firing temperature and the greater the 'heat work' (which signifies the combined effect of time and temperature) the better the durability [11] since this causes stronger bonding. The presence of glaze vapours, oils, sulphurous and other gases in the on-glaze kiln atmosphere can affect resistance too [11].

Thickness of layer of coloured stain also influences durability, thicker coats giving better resistance, especially as far as gold bands are concerned [9]. Gold is very resistant to detergents [18]. Different methods of applying on-glaze coloured stains, viz. hand painting, silk screen printing, lithography, etc., can be responsible for different thicknesses.

7.4 Type of washing: hand v. machine

As with textiles, hand washing is kinder to on-glaze decoration than machine washing. Moreover some automatic dish-washers are more vicious than others.

7.5 Type of detergent

Individual makes of detergents have been investigated by a number of authors [9, 14, 16].

There is some controversy about the role of phosphates in detergents. Mellor [4] points to the beneficial use of Calgon (sodium (hexa-)meta-phosphate) in removing films from the surface of the ware, formed in dish-washers as a result of calcium and magnesium salts in hard water. Pils [6] showed that tripolyphosphate was practically harmless. Sales [7], however, points out that attack increases with increasing content of tripoly-phosphates, orthophosphates and pyrophosphates. According to Lohmeyer [21] polyphosphates are less aggressive than corrosive alkalis.

Complex phosphates which have a sequestering action are more liable to attack the decoration than are simple phosphates. Alkalinity seems to have little influence in determining corrosive action [9]. Gray et al. [10] refer to tests where detergents with higher pH (i.e. 11.1) were more effective than those with lower pH in removing laboratory-prepared 'soil' consisting mainly of cooked egg, cooked cereal, milk and margarine; however, the higher pH product is thought to cause more damage to decoration.

Soaps attack colours strongly whereas most synthetic detergents are harmless, the carboxyl group being responsible for the attack, pH not being a major factor [9]. This is in line with findings by Pils [6] who established that detergents of high alkalinity and intense cleansing action need not necessarily be specially aggressive as regards decoration.

Gray et al. [10] stress that the presence of sodium silicate in the detergent contributes to the protection of fine china against over-glaze damage. Nevertheless they also mention that in certain cases silica in the washing agent can produce a film on the ware washed in an automatic dish-washer. Such films are particularly difficult to remove, only hydrofluoric acid being effective [9].

Lohmeyer [19] reports that washing agents can increase the gloss of on-glaze colours.

7.6 Detergent concentration

The majority of investigators point out that the concentration of the detergent has no, or only a minor effect. However, Gray et al. [10] stress the need to use the prescribed measure of detergent in automatic dish-washers, as insufficient amounts lead to the formation of undesirable films on the ware. The concentration should be between 0.25 and 0.75%. It depends on the hardness of the water and is much less with soft or 'softened' water.

7.7 Temperature of washing

All authors without exception emphasize the marked effect of washing temperature which overrides all other factors involved in the washing process. The higher the temperature, the worse the attack. At temperatures above or even approaching 70°C very severe damage can occur.

Thermal shock due to very rapid changes from hot to cold in the washing cycle can also have a strongly corrosive action [7]. Agitation prevents temperature gradients [16].

7.8 Hardness of water

This is not regarded as of importance by a number of investigators. Mellor [4], as mentioned, points to the harmful effects of calcium and magnesium salts in the water which are overcome by Calgon. Wedell [13] recommends the softening of hard water by an ion exchanger. In many dish-washers, ion exchangers are part of the outfit. Lohmeyer [19] emphasizes that only softened or neutral water should be used, on no account tap water.

Water pressure in dish-washers is of no influence [19].

7.9 Cycling of washing

The longer the porcelain is exposed to the action of the detergent, the worse the attack. Dish-washers with cycles that include two washes, separated by a rinse, usually give superior performance as far as protection of on-glaze decoration is concerned [10].

8. CONCLUSIONS

1. Despite the more strongly bonded structure of the hard porcelain glaze, there is no clear-cut evidence of superior resistance to detergent attack of on-glaze decoration on hard porcelain compared with bone china, etc. The greater durability of the porcelain glaze is, apparently, counterbalanced by the lack of close union between glaze and coloured stain.
2. Only on-glaze colours are seriously affected by detergents.
3. Machine washing is more harmful than hand washing.
4. The temperature of the detergent solution is the most decisive factor in determining the resistance of on-glaze decoration. The lower the temperature, the less the risk of attack. 60 °C should on no account be exceeded.
5. Some detergents are more harmful than others. A harmless detergent may become harmful if its formulation (though not its name) is changed. Detergents of the same name produced in different countries may have different effects.
6. Greater co-operation is called for between the manufacturers of ceramic colours, of porcelain, of detergents and of automatic dish-washers, although some considerable progress has already been achieved. Perhaps the most significant step forward in protection has been the procedure arranged between detergent makers and the British Ceramic Research Association which guarantees a stable — harmless — formulation for the detergent. Another example is the fruitful co-operation between colour manufacturer, potter and kiln builder which led to an extended range of fast-fired in-glaze colours protected by the glaze against detergents.
7. As far as conservation of porcelains of historic and artistic merit is concerned, it need hardly be stressed that such pieces should not be washed in washing machines but by hand in an approved detergent, leaving them in the detergent solution for the shortest time possible and, above all, to use just warm, not hot water.

ACKNOWLEDGEMENTS

The author is indebted to Mr A. Dinsdale, Director of Research, The British Ceramic Research Association, for allowing him to make use of the Association's findings. He would like to thank Mr R. Steven, Managing Director, and Mr R. T. George, Technical Director, The Worcester Royal Porcelain Company Ltd, for their interest and encouragement.

REFERENCES

1. Dodd, A. E., 'Dictionary of Ceramics', George Newnes, London, 1964.
2. Zachariasen, H., The atomic arrangement in glass, 'J. Amer. Chem. Soc.', 54 (1932), 3841.
3. Singer, F., Concerning the position of boron in the glaze formula, 'Trans. Amer. Ceram. Soc.', 12 (1910).
4. Mellor, J. W., The durability of pottery frits, glazes, glasses and enamels in service, 'Trans. (Brit.) Ceram. Soc.', 34 (1935), 113-190.
5. Dale, A. J. and Francis, M., The durability of on-glaze decoration, 'Trans. Brit. Ceram. Soc.', 41 (1942), 245-256.
6. Pils, S., The wear of porcelain colours in industrial and domestic dish-washers, 'Ber. Deut. Keram. Ges.', 45 (1968), 281-285.
7. Sales, H., Attack on ceramic colours, 'Ber. Deut. Keram. Ges.', 45 (1968), 298-301.
8. Oel, H. J., Investigation on the leaching of glazes and enamels, 'Ber. Deut. Keram. Ges.', 45 (1968), 305-309.
9. British ceramic Research Association, private communications (Franklin, C. E. L., Tindall, J. A., Dinsdale, A., Ruddlesden, S. N., and Smith, T. A.).
10. Gray, F. W., Richter, V. J., and Odioso, R. C., The role of detergent in automatic dish-washing performance, 'J. Amer. Oil Chem. Soc.', 44 (1967), 725-727.
11. Sharratt, E. and Francis, M., The durability of on-glaze decoration (Part II), 'Trans. Brit. Ceram. Soc.', 42 (1943), 171-182.
12. Schlüter H., Domestic dish-washing machines, 'Ber. Deut. Keram. Ges.', 45 (1968), 275-280.
13. Wedell, H., Washing and rinsing agents for machine washing, 'Ber. Deut. Keram. Ges.', 45 (1968), 286-291.
14. Kraft, W., Surface attack on porcelain decoration by detergents in domestic dish-washing machines, 'Sprechsaal', 106 (1973), 7-12.
15. Kohl, H., The behaviour of decorated table-ware in household dish-washers, 'Ber. Deut. Keram. Ges.', 45 (1968), 273-274.

16. Otrhalek, J. V. and Bacon, L. R., A method for testing the interaction of over-glaze decorations with detergent solutions, 'Bull. Amer. Ceram. Soc.', 35 (1956), 438-444.

17. Lohmeyer, S., Measuring damage to decoration on porcelain surfaces, 'Ber. Deut. Keram. Ges.', 45 (1968), 25-26.

18. Harth, R., The stability of porcelain colours in domestic dish-washers, 'Ber. Deut. Keram. Ges.', 45 (1968), 302-304.

19. Lohmeyer, S., Behaviour of porcelain colours in washing tests, 'Ber. Deut. Keram. Ges.', 45 (1968), 292-297.

20. Lohmeyer, S., Optical changes in porcelain decorations due to machine washing, 'Ber. Deut. Keram. Ges', 46 (1969), 129-137.

21. Lohmeyer, S., The effect of washing agents on porcelain, glass and silver, 'Ber. Deut. Keram. Ges.', 49 (1972), 307-310.

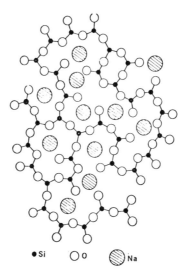

Figure 1.   The structure of soda-silica glass

$\bullet$ Si $\bigcirc$ O $\oslash$ Na

Figure 2.   Methods of applying decoration.

Firing	Under-glaze	In-glaze		On-glaze	
	Glaze & decoration combined	Glaze °C	Decor.	Glaze °C	Decor.
Hard porcelain	1400°C	1400	1250	1400	850
Bone china etc.	1100°C	1100	1100	1100	800

Layers

Decoration ▭
Glaze ▨
Body ▧

	Under-glaze	In-glaze	On-glaze
before Decorating fire			
after Decorating fire			
Hard porcelain			
Bone china etc.			

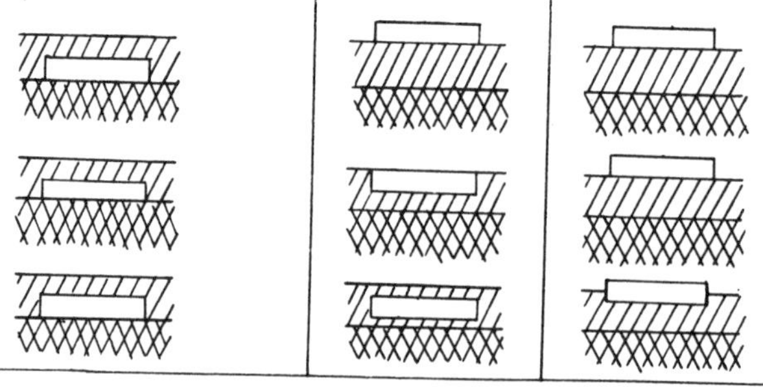

THE RESTORATION OF COARSE ARCHAEOLOGICAL CERAMICS

E. T. G. Mibach, Conservation Division, National Historic Parks and Sites, Parks Canada, Dept. INA, 1570 Liverpool Ct., Ottawa KIA OH4, Ontario, Canada.

1.   INTRODUCTION

Before a pot reaches restoration, the stage to be described in this paper, it is assumed that it will have received careful conservation treatment in the field and laboratory to remove encrustations, salts and stains, without damaging the basic constituents of the pot (e.g. lime temper) or delicate decoration. Patches of the surface will not be missing in tape-shaped rectangles, and it will not have received treatment which might prejudice future analysis, such as destruction of content residues, or overheating (above about $100^{\circ}C$) or radiography which could affect thermo-luminescence dating. For TL a sample is generally best preserved damp in its earth matrix. It will also have been consolidated if necessary, with a suitable material on the surface or in depth.

The reader is referred to Dowman [1], Gedye [2] and Larney [3] as basic texts.

2.   MENDING

This is generally best carried out by starting at the base of the pot (or a. the top if there is no base), and building up one sherd at a time. It will be easier to find the correct sherd if they have been sorted out on the bench by position (rims, bellies, bases), orientation (from inner throw lines and other clues), and colour variations. The result of yielding to the temptation to build up two or three large pieces is usually that the accumulated errors in each section make perfect joining impossible. Each successive sherd is tested to be sure that it fits perfectly and does not need further cleaning, and that it will not 'lock out' a sherd to be added later. Sherds must never be filed down to fit in. If the edge of the ceramic is friable enough to need consolidation, it is often advisable to consolidate all the fragments, rather than the edges only, since this may result in a new break at the interface of the consolidated and untreated zones. The needs of each pot must be judged individually.

Sufficient, but not excessive adhesive is applied lightly to the centre of the broken edge on both sherds. They are then joined, 'wiggled' slightly to settle them, and dried in equilibrium in a box of fine, clean sand. The mend is judged satisfactory if the edge of a fingernail can be drawn across the join in either direction with no sensation.

In cases where the pot has sprung, or where many supporting pieces are missing, padded clamps, string bindings, and other devices may be required.

3.   GAP-FILLING WITH PLASTER

The use of plaster is an art which requires experience. A.J.K. dough can also be extremely useful by itself, or to build a supporting framework for plaster reconstructions. The advantages of plaster are that it is inexpensive, quick and easy to make up, and heavy enough to act as a counter-balance when half of a heavy pot is missing. The filled area can be sculptured precisely to irregular shapes following the lines of the extant portions. The disadvantages of plaster, 'ghosting' (traces of plaster left in surface irregularities) and fragility, can largely be overcome by proper working techniques. Plaster is not recommended when the finished product will be incorrectly handled.

'Ghosting' can be minimized by careful workmanship, by using pre-tinted plaster, and by the application of a coat of PVA solution to the surface around the area filled. This is removed afterwards by careful rolling with a solvent-soaked swab. Plaster can be strengthened by mixing it up with very dilute PVA emulsion instead of with plain water.

Other materials can be added to plaster to make it more plastic or to change its colour. These additives must not exceed a total of 25-30% dry weight, or the plaster will be weakened. Plasticizing materials include kaolin, barium sulphate, calcium carbonate, non-bake modelling clay, carboxymethyl cellulose, Polyfilla, marble powder, and gum arabic. Standard recipes can be drawn up after experimentation with local materials to determine working properties and degrees of shrinkage.

Pre-coloured plaster is easier to work with than white plaster: precision of form is easier if the colour contrast between pot and plaster is minimized, final painting may be avoided or lessened (particularly on cracks where neatness is difficult), and any scratches received in the future will not show up so glaringly. Powdered earth pigments may be used to colour plaster, but the colours used by building construction firms to tint cement are far less expensive and have greater tinting power, so that smaller amounts can be used. Dilute PVA emulsion should be used with bone and lamp blacks, as these are especially weakening. The final effect of standard colour recipes can be tested rapidly by mixing a small amount, spreading it on a piece of semi-absorbent paper and pressing this to dry on the side of a tungsten table lamp, which is also used to provide raking light for refinishing.

The main disadvantage of pre-coloured plaster is that if new plaster must be added to already set plaster, even of the same recipe, the colour will not be the same at the join. This can only be overcome by carefully sculpting down the entire plaster area to precisely the same shape, but 2 mm lower than the final surface, and using one batch of plaster to cover the entire area.

Successful plaster working depends on thorough mixing, precise application, and refinishing when the plaster has set, but is still damp.

1. Prepare a support for the area to be filled by pressing flat, smooth, talc-dusted plasticine, or a sheet of dental wax which has been softened in hot water and trimmed to shape, against the inside of the extant part of the pot. If possible, this should be done diametrically opposite the missing area to reproduce any irregularities of

shape produced during manufacture. Plasticine is useful if the support shape must be created ex novo, but dental wax gives a less easily deformed shape, and is likely to drop out at a critical moment.

2. Attach the support inside the pot by pressing the perimeter of the plasticine against the pot (being careful not to deform it or push it into the area to be filled), or by attaching the wax form on the inside with masking tape.

3. Wet the fracture surfaces with water (if the ceramic has not been made impermeable by consolidation), so that the ceramic will not draw water from the plaster. PVA emulsion can be used if additional strength seems necessary.

4. Sift dry plaster into water until the plaster forms a cone-shaped mound protruding slightly above the surface of the water. (The author has always done this the other way round, using a medium-sized enema bulb as a conveniently balanced and controllable water dispenser. This method makes it easier to judge the amount of dry plaster needed, but does not work for everyone.) Mixing is most conveniently done in a shallow half-soccer-ball. Hold the container in the palm of one hand and mix the plaster into the water with a plaster spatula, gently at first to avoid bubbles, then by crushing the mixture against the bottom with a sideways motion. When the plaster no longer feels gritty and has begun to set, it is applied first around the edges of the gap and then in the middle until the entire area is slightly proud.

Any manipulation of the plaster after it has set past creamy consistency will weaken it. This may be compensated by using PVA emulsion in the water, if putty consistency is needed, but this is never as satisfactory.

5. When the plaster has set but is still damp, use a straight-sided, toothed plaster tool, held perpendicular to the surface, to cut the filled area to its final shape. This is more easily controlled than a straight blade.

6. While the plaster is still damp, remove finishing marks and perfect the shape of the filled area with moistened medium grade 'wet or dry' emery paper, followed by fine grade. Do not use excessive water or pressure. Manual sensitivity is critical at this point: hand and wrist should be used as a sensitive but rigid template.

7. Any small hollows or pockmarks can be filled at this point by using some of the damp, slaked plaster used for the gap filling. Small amounts can be crushed into a little more water and applied with a fine paint brush. If a new batch of plaster is mixed and added on, the old plaster will absorb water from the new, causing a difference in colour and making the new plaster much harder. Finishing will wear away the softer plaster around the new area, leaving bumps and valleys. It is usually easier to remove an insufficiently filled area and start again, than to patch.

8. Final surface texturing to match a coarse surface is best done while the plaster is damp. Smooth finishing is done dry with fine emery paper, avoiding dust. At no time must tools or emery paper touch the original ceramic.

9. Cracks can be filled with coloured plaster, acrylic putty, or Polyfilla. They should be trimmed while damp.

4.   RECONSTRUCTION OF SMALL AND MEDIUM-SIZED POTS

There are many ways of reconstructing pots of which large areas are missing. Variations of gap-filling may be used, with papier maché or A.J.K. dough lattices; one of the easiest ways is to use a clay inner form.

This is done by first using geometric drawing techniques to construct a full-scale cross-sectional drawing of the complete pot, based on the sherds present and comparable pots. The assistance of an archaeologist or curator should be sought for this; if there are not enough critical pieces, or if a nearly identical pot is not known, it may be better to reinforce those mends which are possible, and leave it at that. When the drawing is complete, it is used to make a template in masonite of the inner surface of the pot.

Clay is centred and roughly shaped to correspond to the inside of the pot, upside down, on a turntable or potter's wheel. The mended fragments are tried in position, and clay is added or subtracted to conform to irregularities of shape. The fragments are now placed in position (some previously unidentified sherds may now find a home); tiny balls of clay are used to tilt or level.

Plaster is then used as in gap-filling to complete the missing areas.

If the vessel has no undercuts at the mouth, and if it is felt that the clay form is so accurate that little interior refinishing will be required, the clay may simply be allowed to dry and free itself from the pot as it shrinks. If the vessel is narrow-mouthed, or if interior refinishing will be necessary, the clay should be scooped out while damp.

Plasticine can also be used, but it is more difficult to work with and to clean off.

Odd-shaped areas to be added can be modelled, moulded, cast and attached, or can be built up around a core (e.g. of A.J.K. dough) with plaster or epoxy putty, thus avoiding the need for wire armatures.

5.   RECONSTRUCTION USING POLYSTYRENE INNER FORM AND POLYESTER PASTE

This method of restoration, which was devised by Mr B. V. Arthur,[*] is normally only employed when the pot is either massive in size with few fragments remaining, or when the pot is smaller but has only one or two disjointed fragments. It is based on the use of layers of polystyrene foam sheet to make the inner form.

A full-size archaeological drawing of the pot is first prepared, as in Section 4. On this, horizontal lines are drawn across the pot from one inside contour to the other, at one or two inch intervals, according to the thickness of foam sheet available. From the length of these lines the diameter of each individual circular layer of polystyrene is calculated. If one has a polystyrene cutter with a tilting head, it may be possible to cut the circles to the largest diameter of each layer. These are then glued one on top of the other to resemble the interior shape

*Chief, Conservation Division, National Historic Parks and Sites Branch, Ottawa, Ontario, Canada.

of the pot. If the edges have been cut vertically to the largest diameter, it will be necessary to trim down the edges with a knife and heated spatula. If they have been cut to the minimum diameter of each layer, it will be necessary to fill in the angles between one layer and the next with plaster or similar material. This has, in fact, some advantages, as one can give the inner form a slightly more characteristic irregular shape than would be possible by cutting alone.

When the plaster on the polystyrene has dried thoroughly, a sealant coat of brown shellac or other suitable varnish should be applied. The fragments of the pot can then be sorted and positioned on the contoured form. It may be possible, by examining the contour of each fragment, to fit it in an approximate position. The individual fragments are held in place by bent pins pushed into the foam down the edge of each sherd. It may be necessary to fill some of the small gaps between neighbouring sherds with plaster. This should certainly be considered when the pottery is very friable, as the plaster is perhaps more easily removed than polyester paste. (In the case of a much harder body, it may be considered permissible to butt the polyester paste right up against the fragment.)

Reinforcement should now be placed around the inner form. This can be plastic mesh, galvanized wire net, or aluminium rod or tube, whose diameter is not more than half the thickness of the sherds. This reinforcement should be bent around the entire exposed surface of the form, and between the individual fragments. It should occupy no more than half the depth of the sherds.

At this stage the polyester paste may be applied. (Most of the commercial automobile body filler pastes have proved satisfactory for this use, and are more convenient than making one's own.) The paste should be applied all over the form, covering the reinforcing material. It should still be left lower than the outer surface of the original sherds. It will help if the polyester paste is not made too smooth, as it will be necessary to apply the finishing plaster over this layer. Two or three days should now be allowed for the polyester paste to set. It is essential that it be allowed to cure thoroughly before the finishing plaster is applied.

Immediately before the plaster is applied to the polyester resin, a priming coat of PVA emulsion should be applied, as plaster will not adhere directly to the polyester. The plaster finishing layer is applied in the conventional manner, covering all of the polyester and bringing the restoration up to the level of the existing fragments.

It now only remains to remove the core from the interior of the pot. This may be achieved by cutting with a hot spatula, or, if all else fails, acetone can be poured carefully into the pot to reduce the polystyrene to a 'gooey' mass.

It is of course possible to debate these methods of restoration on the grounds of fidelity to the original, but they may be the only means of showing the public, in a conventional display, what the pot may have looked like before it was broken, since it is possible by these methods to reconstruct an entire pot when very few individual sherds are in actual contact with each other.

6. FINISHING

The ethics and aesthetics of degrees of imitation of the original depend largely on individual opinion and the use for which the finished pot is intended. The author's personal opinion is that the 'six feet—six inches' rule is a good one, i.e. that restoration should not be noticeable at a viewing distance of six feet, but should be clearly distinguishable at six inches. It should be remembered that the idea of reconstruction is to present an idea of the pot as it once was, and that restoration should not distract from the object by presenting a visual pattern of contrasting geometric shapes which have nothing to do with the object.

In many cases, pre-tinted reintegrations (a shade lighter, not darker, than the base colour, so as not to create an optical 'hole') may be sufficient. If painting is required, acrylic paints, or dry pigments in Acryloid B72, are to be preferred to casein, oil, or water-colour paints. Test colours should be matched after drying. Glossy paints can be adjusted with a matting agent such as aerogel silica; variations in colour tone can be stippled in over the base colour; texture can be added with pigments and glue. Final adjustment can be made by rubbing on pastel colours or dry pigments with a finger.

ACKNOWLEDGEMENTS
The author would like to thank Mr B. V. Arthur, Miss Virginia Greene, Mr C. E. S. Hett, Prof H. W. M. Hodges, Miss Barbara Keyser, Mr J. C. McCawley, Mr R. M. Organ, and Mrs J. Wight for their very kind assistance.

REFERENCES
1. Dowman, E., 'Conservation in Field Archaeology', Methuen & Co. Ltd., London, 1970.
2. Gedye, I., Pottery and glass, in 'The Conservation of Cultural Property', UNESCO, 1968, pp. 109-113.
3. Larney, J., Ceramic restoration in the Victoria and Albert Museum, 'Studies in Conservation' 16 (1971), 69-82.
4. Wilson, W. and Forshee, B. W., 'Preservation of documents by lamination', National Bureau of Standards Monograph 5, Washington, D.C., 1959.

Other references:
Clark, C. D., 'Molding and Casting', John D. Lucas Company, Baltimore, Maryland.
Feller, R. L., Stolow, N. and Jones, E. H., 'On Picture Varnishes and Their Solvents', revised ed., Press of Case Western Reserve University, Cleveland and London, 1971.
Greene, V., 'Reconstruction of pottery using A.J.K. dough', paper presented to the IIC-United Kingdom Group.

Nimmo, B. A. F. and Prescott, A. G., Molding, casting and electrotyping, in 'Conservation of Cultural Property', UNESCO, 1968, pp. 95-108.

Torraca, G. (ed.), Synthetic materials used in the conservation of cultural property, in 'Conservation of Cultural Property', UNESCO, 1968.

Skeist, I., 'Handbook of Adhesives', Van Nostrand Reinhold Co., New York, 1962.

APPENDIX: ADHESIVES AND OTHER SUPPLIES FOR CERAMIC RESTORATION

A wide range of adhesives is used in conservation laboratories for different aspects of ceramic restoration. Ideally, a standard adhesive should satisfy several criteria: correct degrees of plasticity and viscosity for the work in hand, physical and chemical stability, rapid drying, reversibility. This last will affect the ease of removal of any excess adhesive, but reversibility itself will often depend on the type and condition of the individual pot.

NATURAL ADHESIVES

SHELLAC

Strong; darkens and embrittles with age, becomes very difficult to remove; thick — often remains as a visible layer between joins; use of flame may singe pot or prejudice TL dating.

ANIMAL GLUES

Yellow; inconvenient to use; shrink; tend to embrittle in time.

CELLULOSIC SOLUTIONS

HMG (cellulose nitrate)   adhesive
In general use: experience has shown it to be useful, durable, and lastingly reversible.
Supplier: Marcel Guest
                    Collyhurst
                    Manchester 9, England

AMBROID (cellulose nitrate)   adhesive
Does not stick very well; amber colour may remain visible.
Supplier: Ambroid Inc.
                    Boston, Massachusetts, USA

DUCO (cellulose nitrate?)   adhesive
Dries quickly, also breaks down quickly; may exert contractile forces. Deficient in plasticizer?

UHU HART (blue tube)   cellulose adhesive
Model makers' glue; very strong (has been used to mend an iron cauldron); quick-drying; ageing characteristics unknown.
Available from hobby shops.

HOME-MADE CELLULOSIC FORMULATIONS

As with consolidants, solvent combinations can be varied according to resin solubility, working characteristics desired, and ambient temperature and relative humidity.

CELLULOID (cellulose nitrate)   adhesive
See Dowman [1] p. 71. Dissolve celluloid in acetone and amyl acetate (1:1), add dibutyl phthalate 0.5—1% v/v.

MOTORCYCLE WINDSHIELDS   adhesive
Cut up and dissolve in acetone and alcohol. For emergency field use when no other supplies are available. Adhesion poor.

CELLULOSE DI-ACETATE   adhesive
Less adherent than cellulose nitrates, but may be more stable; ethyl acetate is a good solvent. Suggested by Mr R. M. Organ* (with note that additive plasticizers tend to be lost in time). Use di-acetate, not mono-acetate; triphenyl phosphate (5%) or dimethyl phthalate (20%) are recommended in this case rather than dibutyl phthalate. Incorporation of an acid acceptor (magnesium acetate 0.5%) is suggested, as is addition of a U.V. absorber (resorcinol benzoate or Tinuvin T). [4]

PVA SOLUTIONS

BAKELITE AYAF   consolidant; adhesive
BAKELITE AYAT   adhesive (somewhat brittle if used alone)
We have used the following with some success: 25% w/v PVA resin (equal parts AYAF and AYAT); 63% v/v methanol; 8% v/v ethyl acetate; 4% v/v acetone.

*Chief, Conservation-Analytical Laboratory, Smithsonian Institution, Washington, D.C., U.S.A.

Supplier: Union Carbide Corp., Chemicals and Plastics
                                           270 Park Avenue
                                           New York, N.Y. 10017, USA

UHU (yellow tube)   adhesive
Mixture of different grades of PVA, or may be cellulose nitrate, depending on country of manufacture; good
working characteristics; stable.
Available from hobby shops.

MOWILITH 60   adhesive
Supplier: Canadian Hoechst Ltd
                                           40 Lesmill Road
                                           Don Mills, Ontario, Canada
or: Farbwerke Hoechst AG
                                           45 Bruningstrasse
                                           Frankfurt am Main, West Germany

VINAVIL K60   adhesive
Make thick stock in industrial methylated spirits (powder dissolves easily) and dilute with same as needed.
Particularly useful degree of plasticity.
Supplier: Montecatini Edison SpA
                                           Via F. Turati 18
                                           Milan, Italy

PVA EMULSIONS ('WHITE GLUES')

Often used for convenience, especially on porous ceramics. Formulae subject to change without notice; tend to
give way in damp climates or storage. Form better optical bridge across cracks than solvent glues.

RESISTOL 850   adhesive
Starch included in formulation; almost impossible to reverse on fragile ceramics.

ELMER'S GLUE-ALL   adhesive
It appears that the formula has been changed; this may now become irreversible.   Available in hobby shops

LE PAGES BONDFAST   adhesive
Not very strong; very flexible (sherds tend to sag); durability unknown.

BULLDOG GRIP WHITE GLUE   adhesive, consolidant
Good working characteristics; dibutyl phthalate plasticizer; information on other additives not available, but
implication is that it should be fairly stable.
Supplier: Canadian Adhesives
                                           420 Marien
                                           Montreal East, P. Q., Canada

PROMATCO A1023   adhesive, consolidant
Vinyl acetate homopolymer; plasticized with dibutyl phthalate; 63% solids; 16,000-18,000 cps viscosity
emulsion; pH 5.6; protective colloid, stabilizing agents, detoxicants added. Preliminary experiences very
promising; high strength adhesive, excellent ageing characteristics claimed. Ivory coloured paste: can be diluted or
used full-strength (e.g. with Japanese tissue fibres as reinforcement). Will redissolve in cold water.
Supplier: Process Materials Corp.
                                           Carlstadt, New Jersey 07072, USA

EASTMAN 910   adhesive
Cyanoacrylate; appears to break down fairly rapidly; useful, like epoxies, in dots to hold heavy ceramics in place
while other glues set.
Supplier: Eastman Chemical Prod. Inc., Chemicals Division
                                           Kingsport, Tennessee 37662, USA
or: Armstrong Cork Co.
                                           Kingsbury
                                           London NW9, England

GE SILICONE RUBBER ADHESIVE
May remain too flexible; difficult to remove (requires hot water and force); primarily useful for modern wares
which find their way into the laboratory; will withstand dish-washers.
Supplier: Canadian General Electric Ltd
                                           Chemical and Metallurgical Section
                                           1025 Lansdowne Avenue
                                           Toronto, Ontario M6H B2G, Canada

EPOXY RESINS

Usually reversible by swelling in methylene dichloride, if pot geometry allows this; can be used where high strength is required (e.g. handles) to avoid need for dowelling, or with filler as putty.

ARALDITE AY 103 with HARDENER AY 951 or AY 956
Supplier: Ciba (A.R.L.)
                                             Duxford
                                             Cambridge, England

EPO-TEK 301
Supplier: Epoxy Technology Inc.
                                             65 Grove Street
                                             Watertown, Massachusetts 02172, USA

DEVCON 5-MINUTE EPOXY
LE PAGES 5-MINUTE EPOXY
Results not entirely predictable.

EPOXY PUTTY   modelling material
Convenient two-part paste system; excellent working characteristics.
Supplier: Ralph E. Bautz (Manufacturer's Representative)
                                             143 Tilford Road
                                             Somerdale, New Jersey 08083, USA

POLYESTER RESINS

Can be excellent on heavy pots or where there are gaps between joins; filled versions shrink less. May discolour slightly.

AKEMI TRANSPARENT   adhesive
AKEMI ORIGINAL (filled)   filler
Supplier: Jaeger and Condino Inc.
                                             P.O. Box 592, 35-44 61st Street
                                             Woodside, New York 11377, USA

SINTOLIT TRANSPARENT STRAW   adhesive
SINTOLIT FILLED   filler
Supplier: 4114 Fifth Avenue
                                             Brooklyn, New York 11232, USA
or: A. Pisani and Co.
                                             Carrara Wharf, Ranelagh Gardens
                                             London SW6, England

CAR BODY FILLER   filler
Distributed nationwide in Canada by Canadian Tire Corp.

BONDAFILLA   filler
Supplier: Bondaglas
                                             55 South End
                                             Croydon, Surrey, England

OTHER MATERIALS

DENTAL WAX (toughened)
Available from dental suppliers or: Amalgamated Dental Co.
                                             132 St Patrick Street
                                             Toronto 2B, Ontario, Canada

PLASTICINE   modelling and moulding
Available from art supply or hobby stores.

ACRYLIC MODELLING PASTE   filler
Considerable shrinkage; may be useful for stuccoing cracks.
Available from art supply stores.

POLYFILLA   filler
Calcium sulphate plus cellulose powder. Useful additive to plaster.
Available from hardware stores or: Niagara Chemicals,
                                          Burlington, Ontario, Canada

DENTAL PLASTER (calcium sulphate)
Available from dental suppliers.

MOULDING PLASTER (calcium sulphate)
Available at less cost from construction firms.

STAYBRITE COLOURS
Colours intended for tinting concrete; used with plaster.
Supplier: W. R. Grace and Co. of Canada Ltd
                                          Construction Products Division
                                          Toronto, Ontario, Canada
                                          (branches in Montreal and Edmonton)

GRUMBACHER POWDERED EARTH PIGMENTS
For tinting fillers and for final retouching.
Available from art supply stores or: M. Grumbacher Inc.
                                          New York, N. Y. 10001, USA
or: M. Grumbacher Inc.
                                          723 King Street
                                          Toronto 213, Ontario, Canada

HYPLAR ACRYLIC COLOURS
For retouching.
Available from art supply stores or from Grumbacher.

THE CONSERVATION OF CERAMICS FROM MARINE ARCHAEOLOGICAL SOURCES

J. Olive and C. Pearson, Department of Material Conservation and Restoration, Fremantle Branch, Western Australian Museum, Finnerty Street, Fremantle, W.A. 6160, Australia

1. INTRODUCTION

The Maritime Archaeology Department of the Western Australian Museum has an active excavation programme, which for the past five years has centred around two Dutch East Indiaman wrecks, the 'Batavia', 1629, [1, 2] and the 'Vergulde Draeck', 1656 [3]. A large number of wrecks from the colonial period (1829-1900) have also been recorded or excavated.

A fair proportion of the artifacts recovered from the wrecks are ceramic materials, including a large amount of stoneware and earthenware as well as a few fragments of Chinese porcelain. The most typical ware recovered is the 'Bellarmine flagon' (Figure 1) of salt-glazed stoneware; 27 were found intact from the 'Vergulde Draeck' and 12 from the 'Batavia'. This paper will discuss our experiences of the problems with both on-site and laboratory conservation that occur with these ceramic artifacts recovered from the sea.

2. ON-SITE CONSERVATION

Due to the isolated position of some of the wrecks lying off the Western Australian Coast, many of the recovered artifacts have to remain on site for up to four months. It is essential that during this storage they are kept in a stable environment. For ceramics, this is simple as they can be kept wet by total immersion in seawater (fresh water being at a premium) to which is added Panicide (20 p.p.m.) to prevent fungus growing. It is essential that the ceramics are not allowed to dry out because the salts which have penetrated the body and glaze of the artifacts will crystallize out and tend to cause mechanical damage.

Any excessive amounts of concretion can be removed by mechanical measures; however, final cleaning is left until full laboratory facilities are available.

One of the problems for the marine archaeologist is the assembly of sherds to determine the type and style of the object and, more important, to check whether all pieces are present. Attempts at using sand baths and clay supports have not proved very successful and the simplest method is to use a temporary adhesive. A nitrocellulose adhesive, which is readily reversible, was first used for this work but proved to be very unsatisfactory. As the ceramic must be kept wet during this work there is a reaction between the water and adhesive creating a white opaque product which was difficult to remove. Also, as the adhesive shrank considerably on drying, the edges of the joined pieces were damaged; the more fragile the ceramic body, the greater the extent of damage. Thus a once-simple break might be changed to a delicate filling and restoration task.

The most satisfactory adhesive for this work is a proprietary PVA adhesive, UHU (manufactured by UHU-Werk H.u.M. Fischer GmbH., D-758 Buhl, Baden, West Germany). This will adhere to wet sherds and does not shrink appreciably on drying. As it retains some slight flexibility it does not cause mechanical damage to the joints. UHU is readily soluble in acetone.

This process can be applied to the three main types of ware found on the wrecks, i.e. earthenware, stoneware and porcelain. Great care, however, must be taken with the earthenware, such as terracotta and majolica ware, as these sometimes have very soft bodies and fragile glazes, and excessive handling will cause damage.

For transportation to the Conservation Laboratory the ceramic artifacts are individually wrapped in polythene to retain a humid environment which will prevent salt crystallization.

3. LABORATORY CONSERVATION

3.1 Storage

As the ceramic objects invariably arrive in large batches, they again have to be stored prior to treatment. In this case, however, the storage can be used to commence the cleaning process by slowly reducing the salt content of the storage solution. It is important that this is not carried out too rapidly by the immediate use of deionized water, as the osmotic pressures set up might cause damage to susceptible glazes. The salt water is therefore gradually diluted during storage until tap water can be used, usually requiring a four-week period. The conductivity of the solution is reduced by this process from 50,000 μmhos to 1,000 μmhos approximately.

3.2 Removal of concretion

Coral growth is prolific in the warm waters off the Western Australian coast and most sherds recovered are coated with some form of encrustation (Figure 2). Those which have lain in close proximity to iron objects are iron-stained and any surrounding concretion is heavily impregnated with iron corrosion products. In the case of earthenwares, this iron-rich concretion is often stronger than the ceramic itself.

The easiest method of removing these concretions is by acid treatment; however, there is always the danger of damaging either the body or glaze. A number of experiments have been conducted to determine whether ceramic materials can withstand chemical cleaning processes. Fragments of two Bellarmine flagons were analyzed by X-ray diffraction techniques before and after cleaning by immersion in dilute acid solutions.

The body of the untreated samples contained as the major phase α-quartz (SiO_2), α-cristoballite (SiO_2) and mullite ($3Al_2O_3.2SiO_2$). There was no evidence of iron or its oxides/hydroxides in the ceramic body. However, the glazes contained α-quartz as the major component with minor phases of magnetite and lepidocrocite ($\gamma Fe_2O_3.H_2O$), the presence of iron being the important factor. Some samples were iron-stained and these stains and the concretions were analyzed to reveal lepidocrocite and calcite ($CaCO_3$).

These analyses indicate that although the bodies of the ceramics are quite stable, being composed of chemically stable silicates, the glazes do contain iron oxides which would be susceptible to dissolution by acid treatment. These are lepidocrocite and magnetite, of which the latter would be formed in the reducing atmosphere of the salt-glaze firing. The iron stain/concretion, essentially calcium carbonate and iron oxides, could be removed chemically. The analyses indicate, however, that it would be very difficult to carry out chemical cleaning with acid solutions without damaging the underlying glaze.

Experiments were carried out with the ceramic samples to test the effect of dilute acid treatments. The samples were immersed in 10% hydrochloric acid solution until all gas evolution ceased, in order to remove all calcareous deposits. The duration of this immersion was approximately one hour. The solutions turned yellow, indicative of the dissolution of iron oxides. This occurred even with samples which apparently had no surface iron-staining. The samples were next washed in tap water and then immersed in a 10% solution of oxalic acid for 17 hours to remove iron stains.

Examination of the surfaces of the ceramic samples by stereomicroscope before and after treatment revealed that:

1. All iron staining was not removed from the surface of the ceramics, although they did appear much cleaner and the original colours of the glazes became more evident.
2. Ceramic samples with no iron stain were apparently cleaner but this was due to the lepidocrocite being dissolved from the glaze, making it lighter in colour.
3. Friable glazes were damaged by the acid treatment which caused severe exfoliation.
4. There was no change in the fresh broken surface of a ceramic sample before and after treatment, which was as expected from the analyses of the ceramic bodies.

These results show that hydrochloric and oxalic acid treatments, although removing calcareous concretions, tend to dissolve iron oxides from the glazes of the ceramics and increase their tendency to exfoliation. Such treatments are therefore not recommended for cleaning stoneware with iron-containing glazes. Earthenwares, particularly terracottas, are far more prone to deterioration by acid treatments, as the body is much softer than stoneware and generally has a high iron content.

One of the most useful chemicals for cleaning ceramics is ethylenediaminetetra-acetic acid (EDTA). The choice of the salt, e.g. di-sodium, or tetra-sodium, determines the pH: the lower the valency the lower the pH. Iron is most soluble at pH 4, the calcium salts at pH 13. Therefore a 5% solution of the tetra-sodium salt of EDTA. (pH 11.5) can be used for removing calcareous concretions without seriously affecting the iron content of the ceramic. In many cases, iron oxides which are bound in with the calcium salts will be removed when the latter are taken into solution.

Water-softening chemicals such as sodium hexametaphosphate (Calgon) are unsuitable for earthenwares, as the body is softened more readily than the calcareous deposit. They are of use in the final cleaning of stonewares when small particles of concretion need to be removed from abraded glaze areas.

Chemical treatments using dilute hydrochloric and oxalic acids cannot therefore be used for cleaning calcareous deposits from stonewares or earthenwares which contain iron oxides in the ceramic bodies or glazes. They can be used for stonewares and porcelain which are free from iron oxides, and results to date have been very satisfactory.

· Our experience has shown that the safest and most satisfactory cleaning techniques are manual. Most calcareous concretion can be removed easily when wet by scraping with a scalpel or similar implement. If the concretion is allowed to dry, however, it becomes much harder, probably by reaction with atmospheric carbon dioxide to form calcium carbonate in a manner analogous to the function of lime in mortar.

In the case of large or very hard pieces of concretion on friable material, a dental burr is used to reduce it to such proportions that it can safely be removed by scraping. Even very friable earthenwares with fragile majolica glazes have been successfully cleaned with such techniques.

3.3 Removal of salt contamination

During storage, the conductivity of the storage solution is slowly reduced to approximately 1,000 μmhos. The ceramics must then be washed further to remove all salt contamination, otherwise salts crystallizing out can damage glazes (Figures 3a & b).

For this stage of the washing process, deionized water with a conductivity of 50 μmhos is used. There are three methods of salt removal: static immersion, flow-through immersion, and agitation-dispersion.

The static immersion process, where artifacts are simply placed in sealed containers of water, is quite slow. Pockets of relatively high conductivity are to be found in the solution immediately surrounding the artifacts; thus the osmotic pressure differential is low and the salt is removed at a slow rate. This technique is used for very friable objects and those with flaking glazes.

The flow-through immersion technique used by Jedrzejewska [4] is more efficient, but very wasteful of deionized water. A much more efficient method, suitable for most of the ceramic artifacts recovered which are in a sound condition, is the agitation-dispersion process. A gentle agitation is effected, which maintains a homogeneous conductivity throughout the solution. Thus an optimum osmotic pressure differential is maintained, which removes the salt at a faster rate.

An apparatus has been devised which suitably agitates the solution in a gentle manner. Old washing-machines of the twin-tub impeller variety can be cheaply and easily modified to suit the requirements. A perspex baffle with several holes drilled in it is placed in front of the impeller and a gentle but uniform agitation of the water results. The 'spin tub' can also be adapted by removing the spin basket and blocking the resultant hole. The pump outlet tube is extended and placed in the tub, which serves to recycle the water. The machine works best on a half-hour on, hour off cycle. Sturdy plastic-mesh bags are used to contain the sherds and ensure that adequate circulation is possible.

With such apparatus the time taken to bring the conductivity down to an acceptable level, about 150 μmhos or less, is reduced from months to weeks. Generally, four weekly changes of water are sufficient. An added advantage is that less deionized water is used. Once the salts have been removed the ceramics are allowed to dry.

3.4 Stain removal

At this stage, any stain removal which is necessary is carried out. This is only attempted if the offending stain is a serious disfigurement, obscuring glaze details, or if its removal is necessary for stabilization. It would be pointless to remove every bit of iron stain from every sherd when their assembly is unlikely. Iron oxide stains are removed from wet stoneware by local application of 10% oxalic acid by means of cotton buds. In this way one has control over the reaction, to ensure that no damage is caused. For large stains one must ensure that the piece is well soaked in deionized water, and then cotton wool pads saturated with oxalic acid are applied.

To date we have not been successful in devising a treatment to remove iron stain safely from stoneware and earthenware ceramics which contain iron oxides in the body or glazes. Localized treatment with oxalic acid is partly successful; however, great caution must be exercised during this process.

Following iron-stain removal, the ceramics are returned to the wash tank where they remain until a neutral pH is obtained.

For the black iron-sulphide stains which are frequently found, and for organic stains, hydrogen peroxide at a strength of 10 or 25 volumes is used, depending on the severity of the stain. Several earthenware majolica apothecary jars, which were so badly stained that they appeared quite black, were treated in 25 vol. hydrogen peroxide for up to 36 hours, after which time the original colours could be seen (Figures 4a & b). There is no need for rinsing after hydrogen peroxide treatment.

After being allowed to dry out, the ceramics are assembled and the surfaces consolidated where necessary. As the techniques [5, 6] for these processes are well known, they will be mentioned only briefly.

3.5 Surface consolidation

Some ceramic artifacts suffer from friability or from flaking glazes. In these cases consolidation is necessary. Of the many consolidants available, PVA dissolved in acetone and ethyl acetate, and soluble nylon, are preferred. These can be either brushed or sprayed on, or, if complete impregnation is necessary, objects can be immersed in PVA.

Soluble nylon has the advantage that it is comparatively permeable and other reagents may penetrate its film. It can therefore be used to consolidate a flaking glaze before commencing the desalination process, to ensure that the glaze is not damaged. It has been used with success on some majolica ware apothecary jars, prior to washing and removal of sulphide stains (see section 3.4).

Where glaze fragments have broken away from the ceramic body they are reattached with PVA.

3.6 Repair of broken ceramics

Assembly of broken ceramics, where practicable, follows cleaning and consolidation procedures. It is rare to find all the sherds of a pot, and often only a few pieces are recovered. A sand box is used for holding the sherds during assembly and repair.

For earthenwares, PVA dissolved in acetone and ethyl acetate, or a proprietary PVA adhesive such as UHU, is used. For stoneware and porcelain, epoxy resins are used if all fragments are present. If not, reversible adhesives must be used, as there is always the possibility that the missing fragment will be recovered on a future expedition.

4. CONCLUSION

Ceramic artifacts survive well under the sea, their biggest dangers being from physical damage. Unless correct procedures are carried out when they are recovered, to desalinate and clean the ceramics effectively, then disintegration of the bodies and glazes of the artifacts may result. The necessity of always keeping ceramic objects wet cannot be over-emphasized. Desalination techniques are the most important of the conservation processes for ceramics from the sea and if these are carried out efficiently there will be little likelihood of the artifacts deteriorating further.

The removal of concretion by mechanical means is recommended in preference to the use of chemicals. Iron stains, however, are still causing a problem which will require further research.

REFERENCES

1. Bateson, C., 'Australian Shipwrecks. Vol 1. 1622-1850', Reed, Melbourne, 1972.
2. Edwards, H., 'Islands of Angry Ghosts', Hodder and Stoughton, London, 1966.
3. Green, J., The loss of the Dutch East Indiaman 'Vergulde Draeck' 1656, 'Int. J. Naut. Archaeol. and Underwater Archaeol' 2 (1973) 267-289.
4. Jedrzejewska, H., Removal of soluble salts from stone, in 'Conservation of Stone and Wooden Objects', IIC, London, 1970.
5. Larney, J., Ceramic restoration in the Victoria and Albert Museum, 'Studies in Conservation' 16 (1971) 69-82.
6. Plenderleith, H. J. and Werner, A. E. A., 'The Conservation of Antiquities and Works of Art', Oxford University Press, 1971.

Figure 1. Bellarmine Flagon. Salt-glazed stoneware, with underglaze iron oxide slip and splashes of cobalt blue.

Figure 2. Bellarmine Flagon as recovered, showing coral encrustation.

Figure 3a.   Colonial porcelain plate showing flaking glaze due to salt crystallization.

Figure 3b.   Reverse side of plate

Figure 4a. Majolica ware sherds after salt removal.

Figure 4b. Same group of sherds after bleaching with hydrogen peroxide.

ROCK PAINTING IN SRI LANKA

R.H. de Silva, Archaeological Department, Colombo, Sri Lanka

1. INTRODUCTION

This paper is divided into two parts, the first section being devoted to a description in general terms of the rock paintings in Sri Lanka and the second being an account of the causes of deterioration and the measures taken to protect them.

Over two hundred wall paintings on rock, in caves, in shrines, and a few in secular buildings have come down to us through the centuries, and it is a part of the function of the Archaeological Department to conserve these pictorial relics of a past civilization. The results of the laboratory investigation of representative specimens of Sinhalese wall paintings, dating from the earliest historical period in the country (Anuradhapura period, 3rd century B.C. to 11th century A.D.) to the 18th century (Kandy period), will be assembled to give a picture of the technique of ancient wall painting in Sri Lanka and its changes through a period of about 1500 years till the dawn of modern times, marked by the arrival of the British in the island. The general technique of Sinhalese wall painting has invariably been some kind of tempera. No evidence is available to support the view expressed in some quarters that true fresco painting was practised in Sri Lanka. Dhanapala [1, 2] argued that the paintings in the 5th century A.D. fortress at Sigiriya were carried out in the buon fresco technique. These arguments were refuted by De Silva [3].

2. TECHNIQUE

2.1 Anuradhapura Period (3rd century B.C. to 11th century A.D.)

The Mahavamsa [4], which embodies the history of the Sinhalese race from its legendary origin in the 6th century B.C. to the advent of the British in the closing stages of the 18th century, contains much information on the social conditions in the country at different periods of its history. It is apparent from these records that a developed art of painting was practised in Sri Lanka from very early historical times. The first reference to wall painting is in the description of the Jataka (stories of previous births of the Buddha) painted in the relic chamber of the Ruvanvali dagoba, built by Dutthagamani (161-137 B.C.) in Anuradhapura, the first capital of Sri Lanka, and all but completed before his death [5].

The materials and technique employed in the execution of the earliest paintings will first be described. Paintings that are extant are to be found on the most durable support, rock, which served as the walls and ceilings of shrines and buildings. The surface of the support was artificially roughened to give a key to the adherence of the first layer of ground. This technique is observed in the support exposed by the loss of wall paintings at Sigiriya. The ground that is laid on the rough surface of the support has, in general, an appreciable thickness (2.5 cm), but there were occasions when the ground in certain rock paintings was laid as a very thin coating on supports that were not provided with a key (Royal Pleasure Gardens in Anuradhapura, Vessagiriya, Gonagolla, Mihintale).

In the beginning, the inert material that formed the ground consisted of a dark brown-red ferruginous clay with the admixture of sand, vegetable fibres (straw) and rice husks; even fragments of leaves are known to have been mixed in the ground of the paintings at Sigiriya. In addition to these organic materials, which would have served to consolidate the ground, a binding medium was used which on drying would have imparted strength to the whole ground. This binding medium has been shown to be a mixture (properly called an emulsion) of a plant gum and a drying oil [6]. On the ferruginous clay ground there was laid a very thin coating or wash of lime as the preparation for the painting. This technique of laying the ground is exemplified by the fragmentary remains of rock painting on the exposed roof of the main cave shrine at Dambulla, Central Province, where pre-Christian Brahmi inscriptions are indited below the brow of the cave. A similar technique was adopted for the ground at a site known as Potgalkanda, a forest-clad hill close to the village of Kandalama, situated between Dambulla and Sigiriya.

At Hindagala, Kandy District, Central Province, in a large cave shrine, a very thin white coating composed of clay in place of the usual lime was laid on the ferruginous clay ground. Apart from the composition of this wash, the method of laying the ground was similar to that obtaining at Dambulla (exposed paintings). The final wash was trowelled to receive the paints.

The next development in the technique of laying the ground was the use of lime, mixed with clay and sand, to give thicker grounds than mere washes, retaining the admixture of vegetable fibres in both the ferruginous clay layer and the superposed lime-based ground. More than one layer of lime-based ground was used in a painting. The surface of each layer of the ground was left irregular to provide a key for the next layer. On the surface of the clay ground there was a concentration of rice husks to provide a further key for the next layer of lime-clay-sand ground. The application of a wash of lime was retained.

The following changes in the technique of laying the ground took place at about the same time:

1. A decline in the use of an initial layer of brownish clay ground.
2. Decline in the admixture of vegetable fibres in the ground containing lime.
3. Decrease in the number of layers of ground.

The final changes in the technique of laying the ground in the Anuradhapura period were the following:
1. The brown-red coloured clay ground was abandoned.
2. The thickness of the lime-based ground was decreased.
3. Occasionally, a very thin coating or wash of lime was used as the ground.

During the Anuradhapura period, the binding medium used in the ground was usually an emulsion of a plant gum and a drying oil. On one or two occasions the binding medium in the ground consisted only of a plant gum.

The pigments commonly employed were lime for the white colour, red ochre, yellow ochre, terre verte, and carbon for black. Mixtures of red ochre and carbon black produced brownish colours. The rare blue pigment lapis lazuli (natural ultramarine) was found in three paintings of this period. This mineral has not been reported as occurring in Sri Lanka. The paint medium, like the binding medium in the ground, was usually an emulsion of a plant gum and a drying oil. In a few paintings the binding medium was found to consist of a plant gum only.

2.2 Polonnoruva Period (11th to 13th century A.D.)

An arbitrary division is made in considering the technique of painting in this period. This is only an historical period, named after the second capital of Sri Lanka, and the paintings falling into this period are considered separately. However, there is no essential difference in the methods and materials of wall painting between the late Anuradhapura period and the Polonnoruva period. In addition to rock supports there survive a few paintings with brick walls as support. Multiple grounds are abandoned, and the single layer of ground consists of a mixture of lime-clay-sand superposed by a wash of more or less pure lime, the surface of which was trowelled. The binding medium in the ground consists of a plant gum and a drying oil, though in a few instances evidence for the use of a drying oil was not forthcoming.

The pigments used did not differ from those used in Anuradhapura times, but the blue lapis lazuli was absent from the palette. The paint medium in two paintings of this period consisted of a plant gum and a drying oil (Dedigama dagoba relic chamber and Tiwanka image house, Polonnoruva) and a plant gum only was found in one painting (Vijaya Bahu's palace). The wall paintings in the relic chamber of the dagoba at Dedigama, Kegalle District, are unusual in technique and do not find a counterpart anywhere else in Sri Lanka. The ground was of powdered brick mixed with a plant gum and was given a superficial coating of a white clay. The pigments used were a black colour (containing iron and silica) and iron ochre. This is the second instance (exposed paintings on the ceiling of the large cave at Hindagala, Kandy District, being the first) of a white clay being utilized before the Kandy period in the final coating laid in preparation for the paints.

2.3 Gampola Period (14th century A.D.)

The painting of the type in the shrine room of the Buddhist temple at Gadaladeniya, Kandy District, is important as marking the latest painting at present known in which a ground of lime-clay-sand similar to grounds found in Polonnoruva period paintings was used. The white coating laid in preparation for the paints is hydrous magnesite, a mineral found in the Kandy District. The binding medium in the ground consists of an emulsion of a plant gum and a drying oil. The binding medium in the paint layer, however, was found to be only a plant gum.

The changes that took place during this period were the following;
1. The introduction of a small quantity of cotton fibres in the ground.
2. The introduction of hydrous magnesite for the thin white coating laid on the ground in preparation for painting.
3. The introduction of cinnabar, a bright red pigment.

2.4 Kandy Period (18th century A.D.)

The paintings belonging to this period have distinctive features which enable them to be distinguished from the paintings of the preceding periods. They are:
1. The use of a light-coloured (grey, buff, off-white) clay with fine grains of sand and admixed cotton fibres for the ground.
2. The ground is generally only a few mm thick.
3. The final coating laid on the ground and trowelled to receive the paints consists of a white clay or hydrous magnesite.
4. The pigments used are clay or hydrous magnesite for the white colour, carbon, red ochre, cinnabar, orpiment (arsenic sulphide) for the yellow colour.

There is no change in the nature of the binding medium in the ground, which is an emulsion of a plant gum and a drying oil, or a plant gum only. The paint medium, too, is either an emulsion of a plant gum and a drying oil or consists of a plant gum only. In certain paintings a preservative coating was given to specific areas. Where this was applied on gum tempera paintings, the demarcation line is easily observable and, in a few instances, dried tears of the resin are present on the painted surface.

3. PRESERVATION

It is appropriate to place on record here the measures that have been taken for the preservation of rock and wall paintings in Sri Lanka.

Much of the conservation work on rock paintings has been done in Sigiriya, a short-lived 5th century A.D. capital, where there are famous paintings of female figures in a secular setting. For the first time in 1900, action was taken by the Archaeological Department to protect the Sigiriya paintings. The edges of the broken ground were pointed. There was further damage done to the ground by an insect known as the mason bee which bores holes and removes the clay ground material from within for the purpose of building nests. These holes were blocked by repairs to the ground using plaster of Paris, and the repaired areas were retouched. A few years later, a wire netting was fixed at the periphery of the paintings gallery to prevent the swallows that abound in the region from making their nests in the gallery and thus damaging the paintings.

In 1907 the Archaeological Commissioner reported two rock paintings existing in the central shrine at Galvihara, Polonnoruva. The paintings within the cave had been photographed in 1871; at which time the walls and ceiling were still adorned. But 35 years later they had disappeared. In 1921, in an effort to preserve the paint layer, beeswax was applied on the paintings in the Tiwanka image house (Northern temple in Polonnoruva). The government sought the services of the Archaeological Chemist in India in 1943, for a few months, and urgent first-aid was rendered at Sigiriya. This same officer returned to the island in 1947 and undertook conservation work on the paintings in Polonnoruva, at Hindagala, Kandy District, and in Pulligoda, North Central Province. He used polyvinyl acetate of varying strengths dissolved in toluene, both to consolidate the ground and as a preservative coating for the paint layer. Two years later a scientific officer was selected and sent to India for training in the conservation of cultural property with special emphasis on rock paintings. Since 1967, Mr L. Maranzi, an Italian restorer, has been in Sri Lanka on four assignments in the restoration of rock paintings. Among the paintings restored by the Archaeological Department with the advice and assistance of Mr Maranzi were those in Sigiriya, Degaldoruva, Hindagala and Suriyagoda (outer wall), Tiwanka image house and Vessagiriya in the North Central Province, Sailabimbarama and Kumarakanda in the Western Province, Aramanapola in the Sabaragamuva Province, Mulkirigala in the Southern Province. The paintings from the relic chambers of the Mahiyangana dagoba, Central Province, and the Mihintale dagoba, North Central Province, which had been transferred two decades before to the Anuradhapura Museum, were also restored.

One guiding principle in the preservation of rock paintings that has been followed here in the recent past should be set down. Whereas the aim of the measures taken to preserve rock paintings was formerly limited to their conservation, we have recently introduced an acceptable minimal measure of restoration in the treatment of rock paintings.

In order to protect rock paintings in the environment in which they are found, a prerequisite is the determination of the causes as well as the manifestations of deterioration. For this purpose visual, physical and chemical examination of the work of art is advisable.

The primary cause of deterioration of rock paintings, as indeed of all cultural property in Sri Lanka, is almost invariably the environment, that is the hot and humid climate of the island. The consequent effects, which now become secondary causes of deterioration, are a lack of adhesion between two or more of the layers that constitute the rock painting. Other secondary causes are the deposition of extraneous matter on the surface of the painting and the formation of microbiological growths on and within the painting.

The measures taken to conserve rock paintings that are affected by these agencies are designed to remove the causes of deterioration, and if that is not possible, to alleviate the symptoms periodically. If a painting cannot be preserved in situ, action is taken, as a last resort, to transfer and mount the rock painting in a different place where the environmental conditions are more suited to their continued preservation.

Numerous viharas of the Kandy period which have been declared protected monuments are living Buddhist monuments. The lighting of candles and oil lamps and the burning of incense, which are expressions of the piety of devotees, have surely led to the deterioration of rock paintings in privately owned ancient monuments of this period. The problem in the conservation of such paintings is the removal of soot.

For the proper conservation of rock paintings, a prime need is full documentation of the paintings existing in the country. The historical background and previous treatment, if any, should be recorded. Having regard to the dearth of trained conservators in the country, the priorities in the conservation programme should be laid down. Before the painting itself is afforded any conservation treatment, the architectural aspects of the monument concerned, of which the painting forms an integral part, should be studied, and any inadequacies (for example, leaking roofs) should be remedied. Only then can the conservation of the painting be taken in hand with care and confidence.

REFERENCES

1. Dhanapala, D. B., A short note on the technique of the Sigiriya pictures, 'University of Ceylon Review', 2 (1944), 64-67.
2. Dhanapala, D. B., 'The Story of Sinhalese Paintings', Ceylon, 1957.
3. De Silva, R. H., The evolution of the technique of Sinhalese wall painting and comparison with Indian painting methods, 'Ancient Ceylon', 1 (1971), 90-104.
4. Geiger, W., (translator), 'Mahavamsa', Colombo, 1960.
5. 'Mahavamsa', ch. XXX, v. 88.
6. De Silva, R. H., 'The evolution of the technique of Sinhalese wall painting', D. Phil. thesis (unpublished), Oxford University, 1962.

Figure 1. Tiwanka image house, Polonnoruva, after conservation and before restoration.

Figure 2. Tiwarka image house, Polonnoruv after restoration.

Figure 3. Mihintale dagoba relic chamber, partially cleaned.

Figure 4. Degaldoruva painting, upper layer before conservation.

Figure 5. Degaldoruva painting, after partial cleaning. Dark rectangles are uncleaned areas of soot. Smaller rectangles are lower layer of tempera painting exposed by removal of upper oil painting.

PRESERVATION AND PROTECTION OF ROCK ART IN LESOTHO

L. G. A. Smits, University of Botswana, Lesotho and Swaziland, Roma, Lesotho, Southern Africa

1. INTRODUCTION

Lesotho is one of the richest rock art regions in the world. Some 500 sites with more than 10,000 paintings have already been located. The total number of sites is estimated at several thousand, the number of paintings around 100,000. Though the art reflects the culture and interests of hunting groups, the age of the paintings — and thus the identity of the artists — has not been fully established. It is known, however, that the latest paintings dating from the 19th century were created by the Baroa or Mountain Bushmen, the former inhabitants of Lesotho. Lesotho's rock paintings are a good (though depressing) example of the urgency and complexity of the problems now facing us in the protection and preservation of this irreplaceable treasure of a vanished culture.

2. THE IMPORTANCE OF LESOTHO'S ROCK PAINTINGS

The paintings are of considerable value historically, artistically and economically. Each one is important to the archaeologist and art historian as a source of information. Much is waiting to be learned from and about this art form. Research is only just starting and future workers will need all possible information in order to study styles, motifs, distributions and meanings of the paintings, as well as the culture of the makers. The number of paintings is limited, the artists are extinct. Every painting is thus important and worth preserving, as it may provide essential information for understanding the overall pattern.

Many of Lesotho's rock paintings are artistically superb in their use of colour, foreshortening and design. Several sites represent an untapped economic asset in a country which is among the 20 least developed nations of the world. Their tourist potential can be developed with relatively small investment, creating sorely needed employment and raising per capita income at the local level.

3. DANGERS THREATENING LESOTHO'S ROCK ART

As in other rock art regions, Lesotho's paintings are seriously threatened. It is estimated that of all the rock paintings which have existed in South Africa not more than 20% remain clearly visible [1].

The actual state of preservation of a set of paintings is determined by

1. Characteristics of the specific paintings
   a. the age of the paintings;
   b. the painting technique employed: a thick coating of paint on the rock, or a thin film which has penetrated into the rock;
   c. the condition of the binding medium, probably albumen-based. This has sometimes disintegrated, leaving the pigments — mainly natural ochres, all apparently of mineral origin — in a powdery condition, especially the whites;
   d. the quality of the rock surface: in Lesotho the paint is applied directly to the porous sandstones, which are more or less friable.
2. Exposure to environmental hazards
   a. sun, rain, wind and frost at altitudes of 1500–2000 m are a cause of fading, weathering and flaking;
   b. deposits of dust, salt, lime and silicates, partly resulting from evaporation of moisture coming through the porous rock;
   c. dripping rainwater, seepage of groundwater from behind, often together with fungi, lichen, bacterial growth, etc.
   d. droppings of birds and rock rabbits, bees' nests, insect eggs and the like, and rubbing by plant growth and wild animals.
3. Human interference and vandalism, responsible for the accelerated deterioration of the rock paintings
   a. sites are used as stables for cattle, sheep and goats, which lick the salty surface and rub against the walls (grease!);
   b. herdboys shelter against rain and cold. They light fires (soot!), scratch or redraw the paintings with charcoal or stones and use them as targets, throwing dung or stones;
   c. sites are occupied by initiation schools, who, it is said, remove and use the red paints;
   d. visitors dampen the paintings with dirty water, using branches and handkerchiefs, in an attempt to heighten their colours. This causes abrasion and leaves clay, salt and lime deposits through evaporation;
   e. visitors scratch their names on the paintings;
   f. a panel has been 'improved' with oil paint;
   g. paintings have been chipped out and removed to private collections and museums. Others have been damaged in the attempt.

4. TECHNICAL PROBLEMS OF PRESERVATION

If action is not taken, neither the rock surface nor the paintings will last for long. However, several ways seem open to prevent, counteract or at least postpone the ill effects of nature, human interference and vandalism. One side of the problem is technical: which preservation methods are suitable for Lesotho's paintings to prevent further damage and restore them to at least a part of their former glory?

Construction of a lean-to roof has the obvious disadvantage of reducing the light in the shelter. The excavation of inverted V-shaped drains on the slopes above the shelter may speed up and divert the run-off, thus reducing the trickling of rainwater over the paintings as well as the volume of groundwater behind them. It does not, however, prevent it [2]. In addition it is often simply impossible. Cementing the cracks and fissures seems useful as it decreases the seepage of groundwater and also strengthens the rockface, reducing the danger of rockfalls. Sites can be regularly cleared of weeds, branches of nearby trees can be cut and dust can be removed from the paintings. Technical advice is needed, however, on whether and how to remove specific deposits such as salt, lime and silicate, which often form a natural protective layer over the paintings. A film of lime which fogs the paintings becomes transparent when dampened slightly with distilled or de-ionized water. If this layer is to be removed, should a 5% solution of hydrochloric acid be used? And what is to be done with the salt and silicate deposits?

Phenyl mercurials, 1% formalin, 10% formaldehyde and peroxide have been recommended against fungi, lichen and bacterial growth. It has been suggested that droppings, grease, oil-paint and even soot can be removed by first applying a solvent — benzene, toluene, xylene, carbon tetrachloride, ethylenedichloride, trichlorethylene, perchlorethylene — and subsequently loosening the remains with absorbent clay such as sepiolite or atapulcite. However, which of the many recommendations should be selected?

Where the binding medium has disintegrated, the use of an albumen-containing base has been advised, as has polymethylmethacrylate Paraloid B72. Strengthening of the sandstone through injection of silicates has been suggested in cases of crumbling and flaking of the rockface, though some judge stone preservatives almost useless. Protection of the painted surfaces (some are larger than 30 m²) by an artificial covering has often been advised as a solution to most of our problems.

However, any preservative applied to rock paintings should never seal the rockface. The rock has to breathe, moisture has to evaporate, for water will always penetrate behind the paint layer and if trapped there will ultimately cause the peeling of an impermeable coating, taking along the adhering rock and destroying the very paintings it was intended to protect. In addition, protective coatings must not yellow or darken nor crack and chip with age. A gloss changing the appearance of the paintings is also undesirable, and the preservative should form a film that can be redissolved if necessary [3].

A number of experiments with coatings on rock paintings have been done. Apart from some disastrous ones with linseed oil and shellac tried long ago in the Pomongwe Cave, Zimbabwe (Rhodesia), and in the Bloemfontein Museum, Republic of South Africa, the following may be mentioned:

1. parts of major panels in the Tassili, Algeria, have been treated with a preservative (personal observation);
2. B. D. Malan applied a silicone preparation to paintings in the Mushroom Hill and Brotherton's Caves in the Cathedral Peak area, Republic of South Africa, in 1959. He reports that after one year the effects of the treatment had to some extent been lost where the paintings are exposed to full sun (personal communication);
3. C. K. Cooke experimented between 1955-1965 in Zimbabwe (Rhodesia) and achieved the best results with 'water-soluble polyvinylacetate clear varnish' (correspondence);
4. P. Duncan treated parts of the Botšabelo site, Lesotho, in 1951 with methacrylate resins and polyvinyl acetate in colourless solutions and emulsions of varying thickness. He reported that the best results were achieved with Bedacryl L (PVA) and that in 1957 only thickly applied films had possibly yellowed slightly (correspondence, personal observation);

However, sealing of the rockface, gloss, and swelling when damp, do not seem to make the above materials a perfect solution to all our problems.

Another substance, Calaton CB from ICI, a chemically modified nylon polymer, has been recommended. It can be sprayed on, is permeable to water vapour, can be redissolved and has a matt appearance. It has been used in conservation as a consolidant for friable surfaces and as an adhesive for the reattachment of areas of flaking paint on a fragment of tempera wall-painting.

What is obviously and urgently needed, however, is not only specialized technical advice on the various materials available, but also definite approval and authorization from our scientists enabling local organizations to select and take the responsibility for the application of a particular treatment for specific rock painting problems.

5. THE PROTECTION OF LESOTHO'S ROCK PAINTINGS

Although some paintings have proved to be extremely resistant even under extreme circumstances, none will survive a determined onslaught by man. Protection against human interference and vandalism is far more difficult than that against natural deterioration. It is not a technical problem but one of ignorance, lack of interest and greed.

1. Legislation and education: in Lesotho the necessary legislation protecting rock paintings has been in force for nearly 35 years, but it has not halted interference and vandalism in the least. Educating the public through schools, press and radio is very important — in Lesotho reference is made to rock art in the primary school syllabus — but many instances show that education does not prevent individuals from damaging the very paintings they come to visit. Legislation and education should therefore never be regarded as substitutes for other forms of protection.
2. Publicity and fencing: information on the location of unprotected or insufficiently protected sites should not be released in any form whatsoever to the general public. The better known sites suffer most from defacement by visitors. In Namibia (S.W. Africa), the famous 'White Lady of the Brandberg' has paid for the publicity accorded to her by providing a target for rifle-shooting [4]. Protection of rock paintings only by means of bars or fences is a futile exercise. Visitors and souvenir hunters go to extraordinary lengths to

get at paintings thus protected. Experience has shown that in the absence of a resident caretaker, fences, etc, are deliberately cut and removed and the site left as exposed as it was before these obstructions were erected [2]. In the Republic of South Africa, a shelter unwisely provided with a signboard in addition to an iron grille has had the iron bars forced apart with a car jack and some of the paintings defaced [4].

3. Removal of the paintings: in view of the vast number of painting sites and the cost of adequate protection in situ, removal by experts of rock paintings, especially isolated ones, and their storage in a central place open to research workers and the general public seems unavoidable if we want to save them for posterity. Some argue, however, that this extreme measure should only be taken where there is a direct danger of destruction, e.g. through road or dam building. This dilemma may be solved, though, if the scientists can approve the application of a relatively cheap protective film to all our painting sites!

REFERENCES

1. Wilcox, A. R., A scheme for the preservation and recording of the prehistoric art of South Africa, 'South African Museums Association Bulletin' 6 (1956), 194-197.
2. Van Riet Lowe, C. Preservation of prehistoric rock paintings and petroglyphs, 'South African Museums Association Bulletin' 3 (1946), 435-443.
3. Gettens, R. J., Principles in the conservation of mural paintings, in 'Essays on Archaeological Methods', Museum of Anthropology, Ann Arbor, 1951.
4. Goodwin, A. J. H., Prehistoric paintings: preservation and perpetration, 'South African Archaeological Bulletin' 11 (1956), 73-76.

CONSERVATION REQUIREMENTS OF AN ABORIGINAL ENGRAVING SITE AT PORT HEDLAND, PILBARA, WESTERN AUSTRALIA

J. D. Clarke, Department of Material Conservation and Restoration, Fremantle Branch, Western Australian Museum, Finnerty Street, Fremantle, W.A. 6160, Australia

1. INTRODUCTION

A research project to investigate the conservation of aboriginal rock art in Western Australia is being financed by the Australian Institute of Aboriginal Studies and conducted by the Department of Material Conservation and Restoration of the Western Australian Museum. As part of this project, engraving sites on a poorly cemented coastal limestone (calcarenite) outcrop have been studied to determine the type and causes of deterioration, and the requirements for conservation. Possible conservation techniques are now being tested in the laboratory and under field conditions.

The site is well known and has been reported by various investigators in natural history and anthropology [1-6]. The site is one of a number in the general area, some of which, in the past, have been destroyed by the development of a port, town site, and industrial area for the export of iron ore, salt and other mineral products. The present sites have been defaced by vandals as well as eroded by natural weathering processes accelerated by industrial development in recent years. The site studied is classified as a Protected Area under the Aboriginal Heritage Act of Western Australia and the land is vested in the Aboriginal Lands Trust.

The site is in the township of Port Hedland, situated on the north west coast of the Pilbara region of Western Australia.

The position of the site is Lat. 20°15′.5″ Long. 118°30′20″

National Grid Reference is SF 50-4, *125, 457.*

2. ROCK ART DESCRIPTION

The engravings were made by unknown aboriginal people in the time before European settlement in 1864. The technique used was to remove selectively a portion of the surface of the exposed rock to create representations of spirit figures, animals and animal tracks, weapons and other objects [6]. While exact knowledge of the technique used is not available, it can be inferred that various methods were used, based on friction, in the form of abraded grooves and scratching, rotation in the form of drilled pits, and combinations where a series of drilled pits have been joined by an abraded groove. Percussion-based methods such as pecking were probably used [6], but are difficult to identify on the rapidly weathering surface. The mechanical properties of the rock (see below) make it relatively easy to engrave the surface with even the simplest of tools. Much of the drilling and scratching could have been done with the shell of the pelecypod (Anadara Sp.) which was also a food source. Whole and broken shells litter the surface of the site, and McCarthy [6] has reproduced engraved lines using Anadara shells.

The depth of the engravings varies with the method and degree of erosion. Some are quite deep (8 mm) while others are so shallow and faint that positive identification is not possible. A transect sample average of positively identified engravings is 3 mm. The width of the engraved line varies from 30 mm in large abraded outline figures to 3 mm in some finely scratched areas, with an average of 10 mm. The drilled pits are usually 10 to 15 mm in diameter and up to a maximum of 10 mm deep.

The overall dimensions vary from small designs about 20 cm long up to large animal outlines several metres long. The site studied has engravings distributed irregularly over a low ridge 1700 m by 100 m. The main concentration is restricted to an area of 360 m by 30 m.

The artists have in many cases incorporated natural features of the rock, such as solution holes, into the engraving [6]. Shown in Figure 2 are typical engravings.

3. CLIMATE

The climate is arid, but is modified by the coastal position. The mean daily maximum is 31.7°C and the minimum is 20.4°C. The area is frost-free but very hot in summer, the maximum recorded temperature being 47.7°C. Thermal radiation temperature in late spring at midday was 69°C.

Rainfall is variable due to irregular cyclonic disturbances in late summer. The average annual rainfall is 277 mm, the minimum recorded 32 mm and maximum 1019 mm. There is an annual average of 27 wet days. The annual evaporation rate is 2480 mm, and although the average relative humidity is 55%, it is usually much higher in summer (60% to 90%). Coastal fogs and dews occur occasionally throughout the year. Winds are predominantly westerly in winter and easterly in summer.

4. GEOMORPHOLOGY AND GEOLOGY

The engravings have been made upon the near horizontal, flat surface of a low ridge. The ridge has a rounded profile rising to a maximum height of 11 m above sea level and 5 m above the surrounding tidal mud flats, mangrove swamps and low-lying alluvial flats, some of which have been infilled for industrial sites.

The ridge is composed of calcarenite [7], known locally as the Bosscut Formation [8], which is correlated with the Coastal Limestone, a common rock unit occurring along the Western Australian coast and regarded as lithified Pleistocene calcareous coastal sand dunes, beach and offshore bar deposits.

The rock at the site is poorly bedded and appears to have been an offshore bar-type deposit. The rock is subject to differential weathering with the inter-grain cement being preferentially removed first, allowing th granular material to come loose. Solution pipes and channels have developed and small cavities in the rock ar lined with layers of secondary calcium carbonate. Jointing appears to be very irregular; the areas used fo engravings are controlled by large flat joints which may in fact represent original bedding planes. The areas with close-space joints have collected sufficient soil in the joint planes to support minor vegetation (mainly nativ grasses) or are covered with rock scree and only very rarely have engravings. In some cases, large flat engravec areas have broken up so that the surface is littered with detached limestone blocks up to 40 cm long, some stil showing a portion of an engraving.

Samples of the rock have been examined in the laboratory in preparation for conservation work. Chemica analysis of a sample (PHO6) showed that 84.2% was soluble in 5 M HCl, the insoluble residue consisting of wel rounded silica (SiO_2) sand grains and 5% opaque minerals, mainly iron oxides.

Partial analysis gave the results shown in Table 1.

Table 1   Partial analysis of rock sample PH06

Component	Weight %	Comments
$CaCO_3$	79.20	as calcite in oolites and cement
$MgCo_3$	0.88	as magnesite or dolomite
Fe_2O_3	0.75	as iron oxide particles
Al_2O_3	0.80	as clay minerals
SiO_3	17.80	as sand grains
MnO	0.01	
Na_2O	0.20	
SO_4^{-2}	30 ppm	as salts, halite and gypsum
Cl^-	2000 ppm	
Total	99.64	

The rock has been examined in thin section and can be seen to consist of loosely cemented oolites [7]. The oolites are composite particles of near spherical shape with diameters of 0.3 to 1.0 mm. They have a quartz or carbonate sand core around which concentric layers of carbonate have built up (Figure 1). These oolites are held together with a finely crystalline calcite ($CaCO_3$) cement. The cement does not fill the inter-grain space and the rock has a porosity of 15% to 20%. As most of the pores are interconnected, this makes the rock permeable.

The average permeability coefficient of 1.4×10^{-6} metre/sec was obtained, using a Ruska Permeameter, from 25 x 20 x 20 mm test samples cut from fresh rock.

The incomplete nature of the cement and high carbonate content make the rock mechanically weak, The uniaxial compressive strength of a 39 x 40 x 76.7 mm block of homogeneous fresh rock was 11.3 Mpa (Mega Pascale). Failure occurred within the cement and at the oolite/cement boundary. A Los Angeles abrasion test [20] on a 5000 gm sample gave a loss of 75% of the sample through a 10 B.S. screen. This value is extremely high and indicates that the rock has very little abrasion resistance. The surface of a naturally weathered rock is coloured 5 YR 6/2 on the Munsell Soil Color Chart [19]. The freshly broken surface ranges from 7.5 YR 7/4 to 10 YR 8/3. The darker surface colour is due to the oxidation of iron minerals which form relatively insoluble films on surface exposed portions of the rock. This film can easily be removed by abrasion. There is no weathered profile or alteration zone developed due to the rapid rate of erosion and porous nature of the rock.

5.   SITE DETERIORATION

The chemical and physical properties of the rock, which made it easy for the aborigines to engrave, also mean that the site is rapidly eroded by natural weathering processes and subject to damage by human activities.

5.1 Damage by natural processes
5.1.1. Solution weathering

The calcium carbonate (calcite) component of the rock is soluble in water, so that rain falling on the site will dissolve the calcite and remove it in solution, thereby lowering the surface of the outcrop. This has a number of effects on the engravings. First, the fine details, such as pecked or scratched areas, are attacked and are either destroyed or become unrecognizable. The larger grooves become wider and have a much flatter profile, gradually merging with the rock surface. Some very large grooves act as channel-ways for run-off and become distorted and enlarged (Figure 2). The solubility of the calcite in rain water depends mainly upon the pH of the water. Winkler [9] has discussed the process and produced a number of tables and graphs on which the following discussion is based.

The actual rate of solution weathering is not known. However, a solubility of 30 mg/1 appears to be a reasonable approximation for the period before industrialization (pre-1960). The North American surface reduction rates quoted by Winkler [9] are for the temperate North American climate. The higher temperatures at Port Hedland will lower the solubility rate. The Port Hedland calcarenite, however, is much more porous than the North American limestones and marbles, and therefore presents a larger surface area, effectively increasing the reactivity and solubility. Laboratory tests have also shown that the inter-oolite cement is much more reactive than the oolites themselves, due to its finely crystalline porous nature. This means that the cement is preferentially removed, leaving the oolites unattached, so they can easily be removed by mechanical processes, such as wind or flowing water, before they are removed in solution. Thus, for every gram lost by solution weathering, another gram will be lost by mechanical processes, effectively doubling the surface reduction rate. It is difficult to convert solubility to surface reduction rate for a given site except on a bulk scale, as there are a large number of variables including the heterogeneous nature of the rock, run-off which tends to erode unevenly forming channel-ways and solution pipes, the deposition of secondary carbonate by saturated waters being heated or evaporated, and the effects of other erosive agencies. An overall rate of 1 mm/100 years is possible before industrialization. The present rate is estimated to be over 2 mm/100 years. An example of solution weathering is shown in Figure 2.

5.1.2 Salt weathering

Salts crystallizing from solution within a porous rock mass have been discussed by various authors [10, 11], and can result in rapid disintegration of a rock mass by direct crystal growth pressure, hydration pressures, and pressure due to differential expansion rates for the salt and rock. The proximity of the Port Hedland site to the sea and the vast excess of evaporation over rainfall leads to a build up of halite (NaCl) and gypsum ($CaSO_4.2H_2O$) in the rocks and soil.

Direct evidence of salt weathering is not visible on the site but is obvious on nearby areas where the same rock is close to the high water mark. Laboratory experiments in which 5 x 2 cm samples were alternated daily between sea water immersion and air dry conditions, resulted in the rock disintegrating in 20 days. Many of the solution pipes and 'pot holes' on the site have probably been initiated by salt weathering and later modified by solution weathering.

5.1.3 Mechanical weathering

The physical action of wind and water on the site is only secondary to solution and salt weathering. Once these processes have destroyed the cement, wind and water will remove the loose material. The mechanical strength and low profile of the ridges would prevent any serious primary wind or water erosion.

5.1.4 Vegetation

The engravings are generally on the larger bare rock surfaces. However, in some cases grass has established itself in cracks and joints and is assisting in the breakup of engraved surfaces. It also helps retain soil which in turn retains water, salt and humic acids which attack the rock.

5.2 Damage by human processes

5.2.1 Rubbish

The site has accumulated a large quantity of rubbish. The aborigines left large quantities of shells (Anadara), and in more recent years various people have left broken bottles, vehicle parts, metal cans, rubber products, and other 'European' rubbish. Besides the visual effect, the rubbish, when left, can become cemented to the surface, stain the surface, or leave a stencil-type impression by 'preserving' the rock surface.

5.2.2 Vandalism

Deliberate vandalism is very common on the site due to its proximity to a population centre. Two forms are present and are probably the work of children. Painted names, initials and lines have been placed on the site, often directly over engravings, mostly using aerosol spray packs of gloss enamel type paint. Engraved names, initials and figures have been made using sharp objects such as nails or broken glass. These are usually in close proximity to the aboriginal engraving but rarely overlap.

5.2.3 Pollution

The results of industrial pollution in the last 10 years have probably been more serious than the combined effects of all other forms of damage in the previous 100 years. The site can be compared with other sites in the area which are not affected by industrial pollution due to the prevailing wind pattern. The most obvious effect is the deposition of iron ore dust from the nearby stock piles, railway, processing plant and ship loaders. The dust has changed the surface colour from 5 YR 6/2 to 5 YR 3/2 [19]. It tends to settle preferentially in the grooves of the engravings, and depressions in the rock surface. Microscopic examination has shown it to be silt- and clay-sized particles of hematite (Fe_2O_3) with a generally flat micaceous habit. Not only does the dust destroy the visual appearance of the site but by settling in the engraved grooves it is 'protecting' them from further erosion which, with increased erosion on the margins, causes a faster rate of engraving loss, shown in Figures 2a and b.

The more serious effects of pollution are not so obvious, as they represent extensions of natural processes. The industrial complex, which includes internal combustion engines, diesel-powered electricity generation, and pelletizing plants, has modified the atmosphere. Large quantities of CO_2, SO_2 and NO_2 are released into the atmosphere causing a large drop in the pH of the precipitation which results in a greatly increased rate of solution weathering, and introduces additional salts such as sulphates into the weathering system. The effects of industrialization on natural building stone have been well documented [9], and the same principles apply to natural outcrops.

Comparison of McCarthy's photographs [6], taken in 1958 before major development, and the same figures today shows a dramatic change. The engravings have lost their sharp outline and much of their detail. In some there are whole sections missing, which would have required the removal of several millimetres of rock.

5.2.4 Attrition

The effects of people walking over engravings have been documented [6]. The rocks' poor abrasion resistanc means that the surface-exposed oolites are easily dislodged by peoples' feet and this process quickly destroys a engraving by selectively removing the higher portions. At the time of McCarthy's visit (1958), the area was used a an aboriginal reserve and the people living there crossed the ridge to use a well. They have since been moved t other housing areas and the site is now visited only by a small number of people who come to examine th engravings.

6. SITE CONSERVATION

The studies to date have shown why the site is deteriorating. To prevent or at least slow down the deterioratior an integrated programme will be necessary. Some steps can be taken immediately to protect the site, wherea others will require careful laboratory study and testing before they can be used on the site. The conservatior programme which is now under way is as follows:

Stage 1. A section of 20,000 m², containing the majority of the engraving, is to be fenced with a security-typ wire mesh. This will include an entrance/shelter in which information about the site will be displayed. This fence while visually offensive, is necessary to prevent further acts of vandalism. When the fence is complete, th enclosed area will be thoroughly cleared of all rubbish and any vegetation which interferes with drainage. Th existing vandalism will then be removed or obscured. The paint is very difficult to remove, as available pain removers soften the paint film but the pigment stays in the pore spaces of the rock. As the paint often overlie engravings, the use of wire brushes or similar scouring agents could further damage the engraving. Trials usin various paint removers have shown that a 50/50 mixture of cellosolve acetate and acetone on a cotton-wool swa is the most effective way to destroy and partly remove aerosol spray enamel paint films. Engraved-type vandalisn is to be removed by chipping the area to destroy the image and treating the chipped area with dilute HCl to creat a surface texture matching the surrounding rock. Where the offending engraving is close to or overlies an origina aboriginal engraving it will be filled after careful clearing with a cement made of crushed calcarnite and a sma quantity of white Portland cement.

It has been found in Western Australia that if a rock art site is cleaned up, the existing vandalism removed, an informative advisory signs erected, it has a much greater probability of staying that way than a damaged unmarked site.

The problem of iron ore dust build-up is both serious and difficult to solve. A large amount can be washed of with water, but this will also remove some of the rock at the same time. However, on a small section of the sit which was cleared of rubbish in 1971 by W.A. Museum personnel, the build-up of dust has been much slower presumably due to the rain being able to wash the cleared surface more effectively. Laboratory and field test have shown that a 5% EDTA (tetra-sodium salt of ethylenediaminetetra-acetic acid) solution in water is ver effective and removes all the iron ore dust by complexing the iron oxide and keeping it in solution. It can then b washed off with a minimum of water, still preserving the natural surface colour of the rock. The problem with it use is that EDTA is also a complexing agent for calcium [12] and it may damage the limestone. Tests on sma samples, however, have shown no damage. Two areas of 0.5 m² have been treated at the site with no effect on th rock, but will be watched in case there is any delayed damage before the use of EDTA is recommended for th whole site. Further tests are being arranged using other salts of EDTA.

As there are no compulsory dust or pollution emission controls on the industries in the area, the surface woul need to be cleaned every two or three years. For this to be carried out without damage to the site over a period o time, it will be necessary to stabilize and protect the existing surface (see Stage 2 for a discussion of possibl treatments).

It is envisaged that, once the site is fenced and cleaned, it will attract an increasing number of visitors and, a the rock has such low abrasion resistance, suitable pathways will have to be marked out so that people do no walk on engraved areas. The site will need to be watched carefully. As the number of visitors increases, th pathways may become abraded and form grooves which will act as channelways. Also, the surface layer of rock may break up due to its low load-carrying capacity, allowing up-slope blocks to move and destroy the engravings To prevent this, pathways could be marked out using a protective matting such as a conveyor belting, which would prevent abrasion and also help to distribute the load more evenly.

Stage 2. If a longer term view of site conservation is taken, it is obvious that major problems will still exist at the end of Stage 1. These are due to the chemical composition and physical structure of the rock and, unless the surface zone of the rock is altered to a more stable chemical and physical composition, the effects of natural weathering, accelerated by industrial pollution, will destroy the site in a few decades.

There are a number of possible treatments being investigated to protect the rock from solution weathering and salt weathering. They will need to be tested in the laboratory, under accelerated weathering conditions, and in the field before deciding which, if any, is the most suitable and feasible for the site.

One 'solution' would be to roof the area, which would keep the rock dry, preventing weathering to a large extent, and also dust contamination. The cost of 20,000 m² of roof in an area prone to cyclones would be very high and would also destroy the character of an open-air aboriginal site by enclosing it in a European-type building.

There have been a number of successful impregnation techniques developed and reported in recent years. Gauri [13] and Domaslowski [14] have both used epoxy resins to impregnate rocks used in statuary. Trials on small samples, using some of the methods described, have been carried out. The 4 cm² samples were all completely penetrated by the resin (Araldite D and hardener HY-956) using both Epoxide No. 8 and xylene to lower viscosity, and using xylene as the solvent. The ease of penetration was due to the high permeability. Upon hardening, the samples were only slightly discoloured and had a slightly waxy finish where large amounts of resin were absorbed into the rock. The samples were tested for compressive strength and showed only a slight increase in the samples with heavy resin impregnation (11.8 Mpa untreated, 12.8 Mpa treated with 25% epoxy/xylene mixture). Abrasion resistance was greatly increased, and there was no effect of salt weathering on the treated sample, whereas the untreated sample had almost completely decomposed when both samples were alternated between sea water and dry conditions.

While it appears that epoxy resins can impart the necessary physical properties to rock, there are several problems associated with their use in open sites. They break down with time due to the disruption of their molecular structure by ultra-violet radiation [15] and they are weathered by polluted atmospheres. Richon [16] reports that even specially formulated resins used as electrical insulators have shown some effects after 30 years' exposure. Gauri [17] has also shown that the chemical reactivity to SO^2 of epoxy-treated carbonate rocks can be increased in certain cases. Tests on treated samples as outlined above have shown that they are still subject to attack by weak acid solutions. While tests will continue on various resins, monomers and polymers, their own weathering appears to be a real problem, and at best they can give only short-term protection in an exposed, polluted site, subject to high ultra-violet radiation levels.

Winkler [9] noted the use of sodium fluoride (NaF) to improve the weathering properties of carbonate rocks by converting the more reactive calcite ($CaCO_3$) to fluorite (CaF_2) which is practically insoluble. Tests using 2 cm cubes have given disappointing results. Mechanical strength remains the same, chemical properties are not improved, and even after three weeks' immersion in a concentrated NaF solution, very little of the $CaCO_3$ was converted to CaF_2. The use of barium hydroxide ($Ba(OH)_2$) has been reported [9], especially in limestones subject to SO_2 attack, where it reacts to form $BaSO_4$ ($Ba(OH)_2$) which is practically insoluble. Tests using 2 cm cubes and larger 4 cm^2 x 7 cm blocks have shown that the mechanical strength is slightly increased and significant barium is exchanged for calcium, to increase the density. Exposure tests have yet to be carried out with these specimens.

The other technique yet to be investigated is cement grouting, a technique used in engineering geology to improve rock properties. A cement slurry is pumped into the rock mass at low pressure, usually through a series of holes drilled into the rock. The slurry works its way through the pores, cracks and joints in the rock mass and, upon setting, binds the whole mass together by forming a series of interlocking crystal structures. The degree of injection can be controlled by the pumping pressure, and, if required, the rock can be made completely impermeable. The cement slurry can be varied in composition so as to be chemically and physically compatible with the rock mass. Commercially available Portland cement is well suited to limestone as it contains calcium, silicates, aluminates and ferrates, which, with the addition of water, form a gel of hydrous compounds and set, by crystallizing, into an interlocking network which will bond chemically with the calcite particles in the rock. The cement slurry can be modified by various additives. Gypsum ($CaSO_4.2H_2O$), will slow the setting rate, and ground mineral matter, such as blast furnace slag or limestone, will control the physical properties of the cement such as strength (which should be similar to the rock if uneven stresses and cracking are to be avoided), porosity and chemical reactivity. Zvorykin [18] discusses cement injection as used in Russia to preserve masonry, especially the use of additives. There are, however, problems with cement grouting a large site; the process is irreversible and must be right the first time. While conservators have often rejected irreversible processes, in rock art conservation where the site is exposed to harsh variable conditions, reversible processes, while highly desirable, are probably going to be unobtainable and we will be forced to use irreversible processes or lose the rock art altogether. With adequate testing, especially in accelerated weathering units, it should be possible to use a process with confidence in its durability and a full understanding of its chemical and physical effects. Cement grouts are attacked by natural weathering processes and also by polluted atmosphere and water. The weathering rates are, however, very low if the cement has been carefully formulated for its environment. By filling all the permeable channel-ways down to the size-limit of the slurry particles with a virtually insoluble, inert material not affected by heat or ultra-violet radiation, the problems of salt weathering are greatly reduced. Solution weathering will only affect the exposed carbonate grains, and the rock will shed much of the rain-fall before it has time to react. The cost of cement grouting is favourable due to the low cost of the slurry compared to organic resins, although the test work is probably more expensive and the injection process requires skilled operators and the hire of equipment. Special precautions are also needed to preserve the engraved surface in its original condition.

7. CONCLUSION

With man's present technology and understanding, he cannot prevent exposed rocks from weathering and destroying rock art on their surface. He can, however, influence the rate of weathering by changing the environment or the compositon of the rock. As weathering is a dynamic system which modifies the rock's chemical and physical composition, to bring it to equilibrium with its environment, the conservator must be aware of the total system before attempting to alter any part of it. There are sites in Western Australia which are in close harmony with their environment, and they have and will survive for thousands of years. Others, like the Port Hedland site, are far from equilibrium, due partly to man's influence on their environment, and unless we strive to correct the balance they will soon be lost forever. Although investigations to date have produced techniques which will satisfactorily clean and protect the site, extensive research is required before a treatment can be recommended which will chemically and physically preserve the site for posterity.

REFERENCES

1. Cleland, J. B. and Giles, H. M., A scientific trip to the north coast of Western Australia, 'J. West. Aust. nat Hist. Soc.' **II** (1909), 45-63.
2. Campbell, W. D., Description of some rock carvings at Port Hedland, 'J. West. Aust. nat. Hist. Soc.' **II** (1911), 102-109.
3. Basedow, H., 'The Australian Aboriginal', F. W. Preece and Sons, Adelaide, 1925.
4. Davidson, D. S., Aboriginal Australian and Tasmanian rock carvings and paintings, 'Mem. Am. phil. Soc.' **5** (1936).
5. Davidson, D. S., Notes on the pictographs and petroglyphs of Western Australia, 'Proc. Am. phil. Soc.' **96** (1952), 76-117.
6. McCarthy, F. D., The rock engravings at Port Hedland, Northwestern Australia, 'Kroeber Anthrop. Soc Paper' Nos. 26-29 (1962-63), 1-74.
7. Pettijohn, F. J., 'Sedimentary Rocks', Harper and Bros., New York, 1957.
8. Low, G. H. and Noldart, A. J., 'Port Hedland 1:250,000 Geological Series', Geo. Survey of West. Aust. 1960-61.
9. Winkler, E. M., 'Stone: Properties, Durability in Man's Environment' Springer-Verlag, Vienna, New York, 1973.
10. Winkler, E. M., Decay of stone, in 'Conservation of Stone and Wooden Objects', IIC, London, 1970.
11. Cook, R. U. and Smalley, I. J., Salt weathering in deserts, 'Nature' **220** (1968), 1226-7.
12. Keller, W. D., 'Principles of Chemical Weathering', Lucas Bros. Publishers, Columbia, 1968.
13. Gauri, K. L., Improved impregnation technique for the preservation of stone statuary, 'Nature' **228** (1970), 82.
14. Domaslowski, W., Consolidation of stone objects with epoxy resins, 'Monumentum' **IV** (1973), 51-64.
15. Winslow, F. H., Polymers under the weather, 'S.P.E. Journal' **28** (1972), 19-24.
16. Richon, E., 'Outdoor Electrical Insulators Made from Cycloaliphatic Araldite Epoxy Resins', CIBA Ltd, Basle, 1968.
17. Gauri, K., Efficiency of epoxy resins as stone preservatives, 'Studies in Conservation' **19** (1974), 100-101.
18. Zvorykin, N., Consolidation des monuments d'architecture par injection dans les maronneries, 'Monumentum' **II** (1968), 74-81.
19. 'Munsell Soil Color Charts', Munsell Color Company Inc., Baltimore, 1954.
20. Severinghaus, N., 'Crushed Rocks, Industrial Minerals and Rocks', The American Institute of Mining, Metallurgical and Petroleum Engineers, New York, 1960, p. 28.

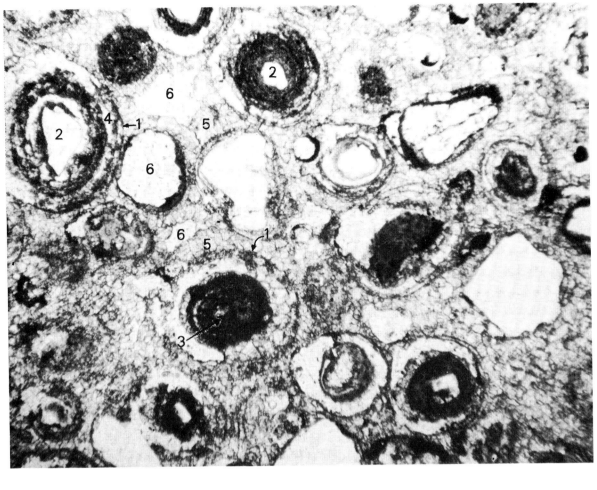

Scale in mm

0   0·5   1·0

Figure 1.   Photomicrograph of a thin section of the Port Hedland calcarenite, polarized light, scale in mm, showing the relationship of the various components. Oolites (1) made up of quartz sand cores (2) and rare carbonate sand cores(3), with concentrically deposited layers of carbonate (4). The inter-oolite cement (5) is finely crystalline calcite, with numerous voids (6).

Figure 2a.   An early photograph taken about 1901 showing a deeply engraved representation of a large marine mammal (dugong) with associated shallower engravings representing barbed spear heads, a snake, animal tracks and other indeterminate objects. Scale similar to Figure 2b. From Western Australian Museum Collection.

Figure 2b.   A photograph taken in 1974 of the same engravings as Figure 2a, clearly showing the extent of deterioration. The shallower engravings have been virtually weathered away, while the depth and profile of the deep engraving have changed considerably. The surface texture of the rock has also been smoothed due to the deposition of iron ore dust (darker areas) in depressions and erosion of higher material only. Scale is 20 cm.

Figure 2a.

Figure 2b.

AN INVESTIGATION OF THE NATURAL DETERIORATION OF ROCK PAINTINGS IN CANADA

J. M. Taylor, R. M. Myers and I. N. M. Wainwright, Canadian Conservation Institute,
National Museums of Canada, Ottawa, Ontario K1A OM8, Canada

1. INTRODUCTION

It is evident that nature is slowly weathering away the many rock painting sites in Canada and that conservation techniques are required to prevent the loss of these valuable sources of history. As a first step in an effort to conserve the sites, studies are in progress at the Canadian Conservation Institute to determine the causes of natural deterioration. The project, which is performed in cooperation with members of the Canadian Rock Art Research Association [1], the Anthropology Department of Trent University and the various authorities responsible for the sites, involves both examination of the paintings in the field and laboratory study of samples removed from the sites. So far it has been established that groundwater seepage, surface exfoliation and biological growths are the main causes of decay. The object of this paper is to outline the project and to discuss the results achieved.

2. ROCK PAINTING SITES IN CANADA

The vast majority of the hundreds of pictograph sites located across the country [2, 3, 4, 5] have been painted with red ochre on granitic cliffs or boulders. Few, if any, are found on limestone or sandstone. In the Great Lakes or Precambrian Shield area the paintings are often found along the shorelines of the numerous lakes and rivers, while those in the valley areas of the Rocky Mountains are located along old Indian trails. With the exception of the Agawa Bay Site in Ontario and those in which such post-contact subjects as the horse and rifle are depicted, the ages of the paintings are not known [6].

Unlike cave paintings which are sheltered from the weather, Canadian sites are fully exposed to wind, rain, seepage, biological growths, to freeze and thaw cycles during the cold winters and warm summers and, in the case of shoreline sites, to wave splash. All of these elements contribute to the natural deterioration of rock by the process known as rock weathering.

3. FIELD WORK

Nine sites in the Shield region and ten in the Similkameen Valley area of British Columbia were selected for study. Collectively these sites are representative of many found across the country. In the most exciting part of the work, the sites have been visited by canoe, snowshoe, ski-plane and camper truck.

At each site colour and black-and-white photographs of the paintings and surrounding area were made including detailed close-up shots of the painted areas. Next, the sites were thoroughly examined to determine the condition of both the paintings and surrounding rock and to gain some insight into the factors which could be contributing to decay. These observations are recorded in a 'Site Condition Report'. Finally, for laboratory study, samples were removed from the sites. These included small pigmented rock chips from the paintings for pigment and cross-section analysis, samples of lichen or algae growing on the paintings, specimens of groundwater seepage and larger sections of the surrounding non-painted rock for geological analysis.

Additionally, efforts are being made to locate old dated photographs of the sites which may exist in the albums of local residents, archaeological records, or in the files of geological survey crews who may have worked in the site area years ago. As will be seen from Figure 2, these photographs are very useful in determining the causes of deterioration and in displaying the need for conservation treatment.

4. LABORATORY WORK

As discussed in detail in earlier papers [7, 8] the emphasis in our laboratory work has been focused primarily on examinations of samples removed from the sites to investigate the nature of the bonding of pigment, and surface deterioration. For this purpose the samples are embedded in polyester resin, cross-sectioned and examined using both light microscopy and a scanning electron microscope (SEM) equipped with an energy dispersive X-ray analyser (EDX). X-ray diffraction is used to analyse the pigments and to determine, with petrographic analysis, the rock type. Atomic absorption analysis is used to analyse groundwater seepage samples.

5. RESULTS

The combined results of our field and laboratory investigations have shown that the flow of groundwater seepage over a pictograph, the exfoliation or spalling of the rock surface, and biological growths such as lichen and algae are the three main causes of deterioration of the sites. The effect of each, of course, varies from site to site. However, one or more of these agents were commonly observed at the sites, eroding the paintings, in some cases slowly, in others quickly.

6. EFFECT OF GROUNDWATER SEEPAGE

At sites on vertical rock faces, during certain times of the year, it is common to observe groundwater seeping from cracks in the rock and flowing down over the paintings. Similar observations can be made at almost any rock cliff. Seepage flow occurs during the spring thaw and after a heavy rain but at other times it stops and the rock surface is dry. Our SEM examinations of the samples removed from the sites have shown that this is one of the more subtle yet common causes of deterioration.

Groundwater typically contains small amounts of such elements as K, Ca, Na, Si and Al which have been leached from minerals as it flows through the soil and the cracks in the rock interior. The atomic absorption analysis of samples collected at the Agawa site shows the presence of these elements in parts per million concentrations. As the groundwater seeps down the rock face some evaporation occurs and the less soluble ions, Si, Al and to some extent Ca, precipitate to form an insoluble mineral deposit 'skin' on the surface of the rock. At sites which receive considerable seepage, a white deposit is evident. However, normally the deposit layer is thin, transparent and often invisible on the rock surface.

This has an important effect on the structure of paintings exposed to seepage. Long before the paintings were made, a thin deposit layer had formed on the rock surfaces. When an artist arrived at such a site, the pigment was applied to the deposit, rather than directly to the rock surface. Subsequently, due to seepage, a deposit has continued to form over the pigment layer. As a result, a four-layer cross-section structure is formed.

This is illustrated in the SEM photomicrograph of a sample, removed from a painting at the Agawa Bay Site, in Figure 1a. The cross-section shows (a) the rock base, (b) the deposit formed before the painting was made, (c) the pigment layer, and (d) the surface deposit formed subsequently. This structure is typical of samples removed from sites exposed to seepage. In some cases the four-layer structure can be observed using a light microscope. However, with many, the higher magnification of SEM is required.

The elemental composition of this sample is shown in the SEM-EDX line analysis in Figure 1b. The scans show that the deposit layers above and below the pigment contain Si and Al, that the pigment contains Fe, and that the section of the rock base contains K, Al and Si, from which a feldspar ($K Al Si_3O_8$) may be inferred. By X-ray diffraction, the pigments analysed to date have all been found to be hematite (Fe_2O_3) and the mineral deposits amorphous. At some sites, calcium carbonate ($CaCO_3$) is also present in the deposit.

Considering the consequence of seepage and deposit formation, a number of factors are evident. First, somewhat paradoxically, the deposit contributes to both the preservation and the deterioration of the paintings. The deposit layer over the paintings acts as a natural protective coating. It holds the pigment in place and protects it from erosion by wind and rain. However, as the layer thickness increases, it gradually obscures the paintings from view.

Secondly, the minute crack observed in the photomicrograph between the rock surface and deposit (e) shows that this bond is vulnerable. Probably due to different rates of thermal expansion, minute segments of the deposit, with attached pigment, loosen and fall away from the rock as shown by the missing segment (f). This 'deposit fallout' explains the slow and gradual loss of pigment from the paintings.

Finally, the continuing deposit formation over the pictographs suggests a method of dating. In theory, by measuring the deposit thickness and determining the current rate of deposition, one could calculate the age of a painting. For this it would have to be assumed that the annual rate of seepage flow had not been altered by such events as new crack formations in the rock since the paintings were made. This is a large and risky assumption.

For conservation, as a first approach, it is apparent that a method of preventing the flow of seepage over the paintings is required. While we have yet to experiment, one possibility is the use of a small gutter attached to the rock above the paintings to catch the flow and divert it away. Also, at the sites where a thick mineral deposit has formed over the paintings, it would be quite possible to restore them somewhat by carefully dissolving away some of the excess deposit.

7. EXFOLIATION

The loss of the surface layer of rock from the paintings was the most obvious form of deterioration observed. At four* of the 19 sites examined, it was found that thin plates of surface rock had fallen away from the rock base and as a result large fragments of the paintings were missing. On remaining areas the rock surface was loosely attached to the base and will eventually fall away as well. In some cases, detritus from the paintings was found on the ground below.

This is a process known as exfoliation or spalling and is caused by frost action on the rock surface. As the outer layer of rock expands and contracts with changing temperature, thin cracks develop just below and parallel to the surface. Moisture penetrates into the cracks and with subsequent freezing and expansion the cracks widen, and gradually thin laminations of surface rock, in the order of 5 to 10 mm thick, loosen and fall away.

Our examinations to date tend to indicate that exfoliation is not as common a problem as seepage or biological growths. Apparently some igneous rock surfaces are more susceptible than others. There was little visible evidence of exfoliation at 15 of the sites. The surfaces were hard and sound and in general the paintings were in much better condition than those on the four exfoliating sites. However, compared to seepage and biological growths, exfoliation can result in the relatively quick loss of the entire surface layer of a rock face and should be regarded as the most serious form of deterioration.

An excellent illustration of the durability of paintings on a solid rock surface, as opposed to those on exfoliating rock, was found in examining two sites on Horwood Lake, Ontario, which had been exposed to accelerated weathering conditions. The paintings are located on two shoreline rock faces and are separated by a distance of only 8 metres. Due to the construction of a dam on the lake approximately 45 years ago, both sites have been submerged during the summer and exposed during fall and winter when the lake is drained. This annual

*Sites at Lac Wapizagonke, Quebec, Horwood and Dryberry Lakes, Ontario and Hedley Cave, British Columbia.

cycle of wetting, drying and freezing would be expected to accelerate the decay of both sites. One of the sites was photographed by C. G. Riley and D. M. Delahey on a canoe trip in 1922 before the dam was built (Figure 2a). On inspection in 1974 it was found that the paintings, except for a few traces, had disappeared (Figure 2b). The rock surface was loose and exfoliating, including the few fragments of remaining paintings. Significantly, the paintings on the second site were essentially intact. The rock surface was solid and not exfoliating. Also, a mineral deposit formation over the paintings had helped to prevent the pigment from being leached away.

For conservation, there is probably not much that can be done practically to control exfoliation. Instead, it would perhaps be preferable to attempt to salvage the paintings by removing the loose fragments as they exfoliate over the years. Eventually the pictograph could be reassembled for display in a safe location.

8. BIOLOGICAL GROWTHS

Lichen and algae were also found encroaching on the paintings at some of the sites. In addition to defacing the paintings, it is evident that these growths accelerate the rate of decay. The pigment intensity on areas where growth occurs is often considerably less than on lichen-free areas. Considering the conservation aspect alone, the growths should be removed from the sites. However, there is a possibility that lichenometry can be used to estimate a minimum age for the paintings [9, 10]. In theory, by measuring the growth rate of a species on a painting over a period of years, one would be able to calculate the date it started growing. The painting would be at least that old and this would be valuable information to archaeologists. Therefore, if lichenometry is feasible, dating attempts should be made before lichen is removed from the paintings.

To obtain more definite information on these aspects, studies are currently in progress in the laboratory to examine the effects of biological growths on the paintings, to determine if lichen dating is practical and to develop safe methods of removal.

9. CONCLUSIONS

It has been demonstrated that seepage, exfoliation and biological growths are the major causes of deterioration of pictographs on vertical igneous rock faces in Canada. Of the three, while seepage and biological growths are observed more frequently, exfoliation is the most pernicious form.

ACKNOWLEDGEMENTS

The authors wish to acknowledge the support and encouragement of the Director of the Canadian Conservation Institute, Dr N. Stolow, Mr Selwyn Dewdney for his continuing interest and advice, and Mr T. Jones for locating copies of the 1922 Horwood Lake Site photographs. The assistance of the Ministry of Natural Resources at Chapleau, Ontario, the Archaeological Sites Advisory Board of British Columbia and the members of the Upper Similkameen Band during our site visits is gratefully acknowledged.

REFERENCES

1. For information, contact Mr S. Dewdney, 27 Erie Avenue, London, Ontario, Canada.
2. Dewdney, S. and Kidd, K. E., 'Indian Rock Paintings of the Great Lakes', University of Toronto Press, revised edition, Toronto, 1967.
3. Corner, J., 'Pictographs (Indian Rock Paintings) in the Interior of British Columbia', Wayside Press, Vernon, 1968.
4. Pohorecky, Z. S. and Jones, T., Aboriginal pictographs on Kipahigan Lake in Precambrian Shield of Saskatchewan and Manitoba, 'The Musk-Ox', 2 (1967).
5. Keenlyside, D., 'Rock art of the Great Plains', unpublished report, Department of Archaeology, University of Calgary (1968).
6. Dewdney, S., 'Dating Rock Art in the Canadian Shield Region', Royal Ontario Museum, Art and Archaeology, Occasional Paper 24, University of Toronto Press, Toronto, 1970.
7. Taylor, J. M., Myers, R. M. and Wainwright, I. N. M., Scientific studies of Indian rock paintings in Canada, 'Bulletin of the American Institute for Conservation', 14 (1974), 28-43.
8. Myers, R. M. and Taylor, J. M., An investigation of natural deterioration of aboriginal rock paintings by scanning electron microscopy and X-ray microanalysis, in 'Proceedings of the Microbeam Analysis Society', 9th annual conference (1974), 16a − 16c.
9. Reference 3, p.14.
10. Reference 6, p.24.

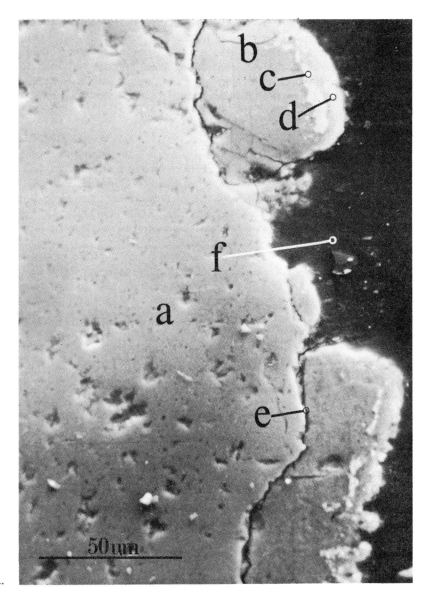

Figure 1a.

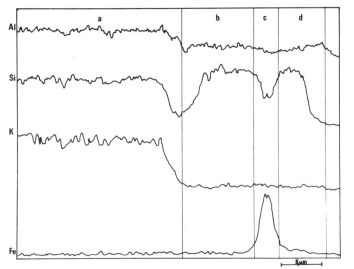

Figure 1b.

Figures 1a and b. SEM cross-section photomicrograph and EDX element line scan of a sample from a painting at the Agawa Site: (a) rock base (b) deposit under-layer (c) pigment (d) surface deposit (e) crack (f) missing fragment.

Figure 2a. Photograph of a site on Horwood Lake, Ontario, made in 1922 by C. G. Riley and D. M. Delahey.

Figure 2b. Photograph of the Horwood site in 1974 showing that the paintings have disappeared.

THE CONSERVATION OF STAINED GLASS

John Lowe, West Dean College, West Dean, Chichester, Sussex, England

'You find in the churches of Poitiers and Brittany an infinite number of panes of glass which are incised outside by the injury of time, and the glass-makers say that it is the moon that has done this, but they will pardon me — it is the damp and rain which have melted part of the salt of the glass.' (Bernard Palissy)

1. INTRODUCTION

Stained glass windows were originally made to serve a double purpose. They are designed as works of art to please the eye, and they are also made to serve as part of the fabric of a building, to withstand wind and weather and to keep out the rain. In talking about the restoration of stained glass it is important to remember this double function, for the problems that face a restorer who has to return a sound and weatherproof window to its place in a church or any other building are to some extent different to those involved in restoring stained glass shown under the artificial and much safer conditions of a museum collection. In a museum, glass is protected from such destructive elements as wind and rain, from impurities in the air and lichenous growths, and from great variations in temperature. Because of this, the museum restorer enjoys a greater freedom than the outside restorer, and can use techniques which would be quite unsuitable or which have not yet been proved satisfactory for outside work.

This paper is intended to set down only the general features of practical restoration. Its purpose is to provide a background to the subject for specialists in other fields of conservation who are nevertheless interested in the problems and differences of opinion manifest in the Congress material.

2. THE TECHNIQUE OF GLASS PAINTING

In all forms of conservation, it is obvious that the restorer should have a knowledge of how a work of art was originally made. In fact the craft of glass-painting is comparatively simple and, with one or two important exceptions, its methods have changed remarkably little since the German monk, Theophilus, described them in the 11th or 12th century.

The most important change of all occurred in the first half of the 16th century with the introduction of translucent enamels, and it is essential to understand the difference between stained glass windows and painted glass. Throughout the Middle Ages, stained glass windows were composed of pieces of white and coloured glass, cut to fit the basic design or cartoon and held together in a framework of leads. At this period, with the exception of the black enamel painting and the silver-yellow stain mentioned below, all the colour came from the glass itself, which was coloured in its manufacture by adding different metallic oxides to white glass. These coloured glasses are called pot metals; the colour runs through the whole thickness of the glass and is as permanent as the glass itself.

Certain colours, however, and particularly ruby, were so dense in tone that they would not transmit light sufficiently. The mediaeval glass-maker overcame this by producing sheets of white glass that had a thin skin of the densely toned glass on one side. This is called flashed glass; in the manufacture, a bulb of white molten glass was dipped in a pot of molten ruby, or whatever colour was being flashed, so that when the coated bulb was blown into a cylinder and flattened out it produced a sheet of glass that was coloured on one side, the greater thickness of the glass being white. The process of flashing is described by Theophilus and is found in the earliest existing windows. Flashed ruby is by far the commonest, but blue and other colours are sometimes found. It is worth noting that the flash tended to get thinner as the Middle Ages advanced, and that the flashed or coloured side of the sheet is almost invariably found on the inner face of the window.

The original necessity of flashing dense colours was frequently turned to advantage by the mediaeval glazier. By abrading off the thin layer of coloured flash he could obtain both white and colour on one sheet of glass. For example, if a figure had a ruby tunic trimmed with white cuffs, instead of having to cut and lead on extra pieces of white glass for the cuffs, the glazier abraded the area of the cuff from a piece of flashed ruby. In heraldry, with intricate charges on coloured grounds, this technique was particularly useful, especially as all the gold charges could be obtained by painting the white abraded areas with yellow stain.

The most fundamental and important change in the history of stained glass occurred in the 16th century with the introduction of painting with translucent-coloured enamels on white glass. These enamels were made by mixing a flux of highly fusible lead glass with various metallic oxides which coloured the flux. With this type of enamel the oxide was dissolved in the flux by strong heat, staining it to the required colour. The enamel was therefore merely a highly fusible coloured glass ground to a fine powder, which, mixed with a suitable medium, could be applied to the glass as a paint. On being fired onto the sheet of white glass it regained the transparency it had partially lost through being powdered, and became a thin coat of transparent coloured glass upon the surface to which it had been applied.

This important change in technique was closely related to a fundamental change in the attitude to glass-painting at the time of the Renaissance. Following the increased realism of 15th century stained glass, the 16th century glass-painter tried more and more to achieve the effects of easel-painting, until we find that in the 17th and 18th centuries the leading, which had played so important a part in the design of a mediaeval window, was merely used to hold large squares or rectangles of white glass together, and the whole surface was treated like a canvas. By the late 16th century, translucent enamels were available in a wide range of colours, and their total adoption was perhaps accelerated by the increasing difficulty of obtaining coloured glass, for wars and political unrest in Europe gradually brought the glass-making areas of Lorraine and elsewhere to ruin. At first one find coloured enamels used together with coloured glass, but by the middle of the 17th century, enamel painting predominated and coloured glass was not fully used again until the revival of mediaeval-style stained glass in the first half of the 19th century.

Returning for a moment to mediaeval glass, there were two enamels used by glass-painters at that time, and indeed later, in association with white glass and pot-metals. The first of these was the opaque black or dark brown enamel which was used for painting all the main outlines or trace lines, the washed tones and the shading on the glass. This opaque enamel was made from a flux of highly fusible green lead glass mixed with copper or iron oxide. The use of these oxides varied at different periods, which explains the changes in colour from a full black to a somewhat reddish brown. The ingredients of this opaque enamel were ground and mixed together cold, and not under heat as with the translucent enamels. The glass-painter mixed the ground powder with water and a binder such as gum or a vegetable oil to make it flow and adhere to the glass, and applied it to the glass with a brush. After the painting was completed, the pieces of glass were fired, the flux of lead glass melting and fusing the enamel on the surface of the window.

The second colouring agent in glass-painting was the silver-yellow stain. At about the beginning of the 14th century, the glass-painter discovered that if he applied silver, in a suitable chemical combination, to white glass and fired it, the silver stained the glass yellow. This stain actually penetrates the glass in the process of firing and is not merely fused on the surface as the enamels are. According to the quantity of silver used, the intensity of firing and the number of applications, the fired stain varies in colour from a pale yellow to a deep orange and finally red. It is always applied to the back or outside of the glass, as there must be no other painting on the surface that receives the stain. It is also worth noting that old potash glass takes the silver stain more easily than modern soda glass, and that different qualities of glass will cause the stain to give different tones.

In modern glass-painting and in restoration work this stain is obtained from silver chloride. The mediaeval practice appears to have been to cut some silver into small pieces or to use it in thin sheets, and to burn it with sulphur in a crucible, which converted it into a sulphide. This was finely ground and mixed with an earthy vehicle such as pipeclay which made the stain manageable in painting. Yellow stain in mediaeval glass was usually painted on white glass and was chiefly used to touch up details of figure and canopy work or grisaille ground patterns, but in later times it was painted on coloured glass in order to change the tint of a piece, or part of a piece. For instance, using blue glass and yellow stain, a green hill and the sky could be painted on one piece of glass. In figure painting, both hair and face could be painted on one piece of glass, and decorated borders to white robes were frequently stained yellow. In the 15th and 16th centuries, many small panels and roundels were painted in grisaille on a single piece of glass, and details were touched in with yellow stain. Yellow stain was also used in combination with enamel painted glass of the 17th and 18th centuries.

These then are the various sources of colour in a stained glass window. This lengthy description of them is needed because different kinds of windows demand different types of restoration, and one can only fully understand the various techniques of conservation when one knows the nature of the original materials.

3. CLEANING

In the conservation of stained glass, obviously cleaning is the commonest and most fundamental part of the restorer's work, though the nature of the cleaning will vary considerably from one piece of glass to another depending on the condition of the particular panel and the kind of dirt, corrosion or whatever it may be which has to be removed. Before any cleaning is undertaken, however superficial, it is essential to make a thorough examination of the panel. The condition of the leading should be sound enough to support the glass while it is being cleaned. If there are any cracks or breaks in the glass one must be certain that they will not be enlarged and the glass further fractured during cleaning. Last and most important of all, the condition of all enamel painting should be thoroughly examined, both the opaque black or brown enamel of the trace lines and shading, and, if it is a piece of later glass, the translucent coloured enamels. It is worth noting that though enamels of all kinds are nearly always painted on the inner side of the window, one does very occasionally find enamel painting on the outside of the glass, and one should always watch out for such exceptional cases.

If both the structure of the panel and the enamel painting are completely sound, cleaning may proceed without any special precautions. Needless to say only the expert is qualified to judge the state of the enamel painting and to advise on the cleaning of the painted side.

For straightforward washing of a window to remove superficial dirt, which can be undertaken with the glass still in the window or in the studio, one should use a detergent in water. Of those commonly available, non-ionic detergents such as Lissapol N are believed to be among the safest. Distilled water is ideal, but a soft water will do perfectly well. The windows should be washed with a soft chamois leather, but if dirt around the leading is difficult to remove, a soft brush can also be used. When the glass is clean, all traces of detergent should be carefully washed off with clean water and the window thoroughly dried with a polishing duster. If there are any cracks in the glass, every care should be taken to keep these free of soap or water as it will not be possible to dry them. This also applies to any parts of the window that have been plated — that is where a badly fractured section of the glass has been repaired and supported by putting a piece of clear glass cut to the same shape on either side of the broken piece, the two plates held in position in the leads — for if moisture is allowed to get under the plating, condensation will start and will attack both glass and enamel painting.

This simple treatment is quite satisfactory for cleaning off light dirt, and is particularly suitable for cleaning windows which have to be treated in position. For greasy dirt from an urban atmosphere a slightly more potent treatment is needed. This should only be used by an expert, and should preferably be done when the glass can be laid flat and the cleaning fluid kept under complete control. In this case, the glass is cleaned with distilled water containing about 5% ammonia. The proportion of ammonia will vary slightly according to the condition of the panel. It is important that the ammonia should not be left on the glass for too long, and that after each section of the panel has been cleaned it should be thoroughly washed with distilled water and dried. Given time, the ammonia could attack the enamel painting, and every trace must be removed.

4. DETERIORATION AND DECAY

Up to now, we have been talking about the cleaning of stained glass that is in sound condition. We must now consider two of the main problems of stained glass conservation, the deterioration of enamel painting, and the various forms of decay that occur in the glass itself. When either of these conditions is found, more elaborate precautions are necessary during cleaning, and additional treatment is needed to prevent further deterioration.

All enamels consist of finely ground glass, so that in theory, when the enamels are fired on the sheet glass of the window, they should fuse onto it, becoming a permanent part of it. If, in fact, the firing of the enamel painting is correctly done, this is so and the enamel should never move. However, much old glass-painting was imperfectly fired, and a complete fusion between enamel and glass never took place. Sooner or later, this half-fused enamel will be attacked by dirt, lichenous growths or by condensation caused by moisture and variations of temperature, which will cause the enamel painting to lift away from the surface of the glass and to flake off. This has nothing to do with the age of the glass. The enamel painting on many 13th century panels is in much sounder condition than that of some much later glass. With well-fired panels the trace lines usually have a slightly glossy surface. Bad firing leaves the lines looking matt and rather dry.

Once enamel has started to lift and peel off, the painting must be treated with extreme care. Unfortunately, there is little one can do to save those parts which have already started to flake, and these loose bits will inevitably come off, however carefully cleaning is carried out. But if one is forced to remove loose enamel, and particularly trace lines, it is essential that the missing part of the line should be marked so that, if the principles of a particular workshop permit, it can be touched in after the panel has been cleaned. Luckily, one often finds that where part of a trace line has flaked off, a small part still remains, leaving a shadow of the line on the glass which can be followed in repainting. One must also remember that wherever part of the enamel has come away, it will leave a 'raw edge' which will be especially vulnerable if carelessly handled.

Therefore, in cleaning glass where the enamel shows any weakness, though it is still permissible to use the ammonia solution, this should be carefully dabbed on with cotton wool swabs and wiping avoided, and the panel must afterwards be completely dried, for the presence of moisture is more likely than anything else to cause further deterioration.

Once the panel is clean and dry, it is desirable to find some adhesive treatment that will hold any loose enamel in place and also check any further tendency of the enamel to lift.

It is not the purpose of this article to probe deeply into the necessary properties of such an adhesive, nor those of overall lacquers, which may be used to attempt to check the corrosion described below. It may be briefly stated, however, that an adhesive or lacquer should be water-white and remain so under the conditions of exposure whether internally in a museum or externally, as it were, in a church. It should also be itself invisible or nearly so in situ. It hardly needs to be said that the material should stick and go on sticking to the glass. A lacquer applied overall can, if its physical properties are appropriate, be expected to improve the appearance of superficially corroded glass by quenching the diffusion of light reflection from the surface. Whether the general principle of applying lacquer in this way is technically sound is beyond the scope of this paper.

Two perceptibly different types of decay are found on stained glass, though they may both arise from the same causes. The first condition we call simply corrosion. Here the whole surface of a piece of glass starts to decay, the glass turns opaque and appears black in transmitted light, and the whole surface is covered with a layer of fine powder or flaking scales. This condition can appear on either side of the glass. The second form of decay is called pitting and is more commonly found on the outer face of the glass. Here the break-up of the structure of the glass appears as a number of small holes or pits which, as they increase in number and size, join together to form craters on the surface of the glass. Occasionally the pits are so deep that they penetrate right through the glass. Where corrosion or pitting is found in a window, it is normally limited to certain areas, and one frequently finds that one particular colour has been most seriously affected while other parts of the window are perfectly sound.

It is beyond the scope of this paper to probe the causes of corrosion except to say that it is common ground that the composition of the glass is the primary factor rendering some glasses inherently more susceptible to adverse conditions than others.

Corrosion attacks the painted areas of windows in different ways, and its relation to the black enamel painting produces certain phenomena which are not easy to understand. Usually, the black enamel, either as trace lines or shading, protects the glass it covers, while the surrounding areas of unpainted glass are severely corroded, leaving the painted glass untouched and standing up in relief. Sometimes, however, corrosion forms on the outside of the glass, exactly over those areas which are painted on the inner side, the extent of the corrosion corresponding with the thickness or thinness of the enamel painting. Finally, it should be noted that areas of glass covered by yellow stain are invariable freer from corrosion, than areas without stain.

5. CORROSION REMOVAL

The question of whether or not it is technically or aesthetically desirable to remove some or all of the corrosion from the glass is not one to be decided in this paper. The following notes proceed on the assumption that a decision to do so has been made. That being so, there is a double problem of removing the corrosion and then of replacing the polished surface of the glass, both to restore its translucency and, if it is to return to its position in a church, to make sure that surface imperfections are not left to collect rain and dirt which might promote further decay.

Until fairly recently, corroded glass was treated with a solution of hydrochloric or hydrofluoric acid after the loose flakes of corrosion had been scraped off with a knife. It was essential in this method that the acid solution should not be left in contact with the glass for a moment longer than necessary, and that the acid should be neutralized immediately the corrosion had been removed. The acid could not be used on any painted areas of glass, owing to the danger of removing the enamel, so that its use was largely confined to the back of the glass. Another disadvantage of this treatment was that it gave the surface a slightly frosted appearance.

Later various types of abrasives were used, a process which was first evolved by Mr Dennis King. Mr King devised a machine based on those used for making lenses, where a revolving spindle was fixed submerged in a tank of water (necessary to keep the glass cool during grinding), to which he could attach a variety of abrasive wheels, specially shaped to deal with the irregular shape and surface of each piece of glass, which in this case was removed from the leading for cleaning.

On a smaller scale, a small dental hand-drill could be used. One major advantage of the drill was that it enabled one to work on any corroded part of a panel without removing the glass from the leading. The panel was laid flat on a table, the corroded area under treatment was kept flooded with water, and the corrosion abraded off, first with fine carborundum wheels and later polished with wooden and leather wheels and rouge powder of varying abrasive strengths until the surface of the glass was again polished.

While there was no doubt that this abrasive treatment was a most successful method of restoring the colour to corroded glass, its dangers were fully realized. It was always thought of very much as a last resort. One had to face the fact that though the immediate results were most spectacular, in re-polishing one was removing a part of the total thickness of the glass. Providing the glass never decayed again this did not matter. But the very fact that a window had corroded so badly that it had made such drastic treatment necessary did indicate that that particular glass was especially liable to decay and that at some time in the future it might need to be freed from corrosion again.

The treatment of pitting was similar to that of corrosion. Formerly the affected areas were treated with acid, but later each pit was cleaned out with the drill and a small metal dental burr, again flooding the area with water to prevent the glass heating and cracking. Acid treatment, however, was still used when working on thin or brittle glass which would not stand the pressure and vibration of drilling. After the pits had been cleaned, the level of the glass could be restored by dripping a suitably coloured resin into each hole.

Further refinements of the abrasive method have been made possible by the successive appearance on the market of two instruments. The first of these, the 'Cavitron', a dental tool with a probe which is excited to vibrate at ultrasonic frequencies, disperses the crust by the 'cavitation' produced in a thin film of water between the surfaces of probe and glass. The second, the air-abrasive tool, is now so familiar in conservation work that its application for this particular purpose need not be described. These methods have still to be followed by polishing if the reasons for so doing are regarded as important.

6. RESTORATION

The loss of painting is found in two different forms. In the first case, either some or all of the enamel painting has worn away, but the original glass, be it white or coloured, is still there. In the second case, not only the painting has gone but also the original glass, and there is either a hole in the panel, or the missing glass has been replaced with an intrusive piece. The intrusive glass may be of roughly the same date as the panel, or a much later piece of glass inserted during some previous restoration. It is not unusual in cleaning old glass to find that what looked like a convincing mediaeval head turns out to be a piece of restorer's cold (i.e. unfired) painting. This comes off immediately in cleaning and one is left with a bright piece of white glass in the middle of the panel.

The desirability of repainting and replacing missing parts, and its extent and style if it is to be done at all, is outside the terms of this paper.

When it is done, irrespective of the extent to which the restorer is required to imitate the original, there are two problems. The first problem is that of retouching an original piece. It can be regarded as a principle that a technique involving refiring should not be used. Whereas some old glass could be safely refired under some conditions, there is no certain way of knowing a priori when it will be safe. This being so, a cold method using transparent pigments in a stable medium is unavoidable. Whereas the related fields of the retouching of paintings and ceramics make a range of materials easily available for museum conditions, those of a church greatly increase the problems of durability. Even in the museum, the greater light dosage of exhibited glass than that normal for paintings requires a better light-stability for both pigments and media.

The second problem, that of replacing missing pieces, is technically simpler. Replacement pieces can be painted and fired by known and satisfactory methods. It is essential to mark the new pieces with a diamond cutter with a signature and date to avoid future confusion.

7. RELEADING

Finally, releading must be considered. Pure lead is practically indestructible, but the leading of windows seldom lasts for ever, for the weight of the glass causes it to stretch and in time the soldered joints weaken and crack open. Roughly speaking, the leads in a window will last for about a hundred years. It is obviously most important that the leading should be sound, for glass is heavy and weak leading puts the whole window in danger.

Normally, releading is perfectly straightforward. First, a rubbing is taken from the panel to mark the position of the leads. Then the old leading is removed and if there are any breaks in the glass, they are now repaired. The pieces of glass are then laid on the tracing ready for releading. When the old leading is removed, one occasionally finds that very small pieces of glass have at some time been lost, and that past glaziers have filled these gaps with small plugs of lead. Such plugging, or the addition of a number of strap leads, may have slightly moved the glass from its original place in the design; for example, a head is no longer at quite the right angle to the body, or a detail of costume has become misplaced. Before releading, such pieces can be re-adjusted and the fragments of missing glass built up with an epoxy resin, which can be coloured to the right tone.

The leading was an integral part of the design in mediaeval stained glass, forming the main outline of the drawing, so that the leading often varies in thickness according to its place in the design. Wherever possible, these variations in thickness should be followed in releading. Often, in previous restorations, lead of a uniform thickness will have replaced the varied leads of the original glazing, so that the modern restorer will have to be guided by his knowledge and feeling for design in replacing them with leads of varying thickness, a task that again demands a thorough knowledge of old glass.

PROBLEMS AND POTENTIALITIES IN THE CONSERVATION OF VITREOUS MATERIALS

Anne Moncrieff, Victoria and Albert Museum, London SW7, England

1. INTRODUCTION

This paper will review some of the present methods used in the conservation of vitreous materials, the problems, and the prospects for future developments. It is based on the author's experience in the Victoria and Albert Museum, London, and for this reason mainly concerns decorative art conservation. Archaeological problems are the subject of papers in this volume by Mibach, and Olive and Pearson.

The subjects of cleaning, repair and restoration will form the first half of the paper, the second part being concerned with the problem of providing protection for objects which are deteriorating in museum conditions or which are exposed to weathering.

2. CLEANING

There are three main methods of cleaning vitreous materials: mechanical, chemical and ultrasonic. All these methods are used on both glass and ceramic objects.

Mechanical cleaning by hand, using scalpels, knives, needles, glass-fibre brushes, emery paper, and the more severe treatment of grinding on a grinding wheel, has been used to remove deposits from the surface of glass and ceramic objects. These encrustations may arise from extraneous matter deposited on the surface, during a period when the object was buried, for example, or during weathering, and may also be corrosion layers formed when the object itself deteriorates due to atmospheric attack, e.g. the gypsum and syngenite crust on stained glass.

A more recent development in mechanical cleaning has been the use of the air abrasive equipment [2]. Like all the other mechanical methods, this needs skill and care on the part of the operator to select the best abrasive powder and the appropriate air pressure for the particular job, and to manipulate the jet in such a way as to cause the least possible damage. Glass can be damaged by the air abrasive, as it can by most mechanical treatments, but in skilled hands it is not damaged, especially if the treatment stops just short of complete removal of all the deposit. With experience, it is possible to clean up to a line of paint without altering the thickness of that line, but paint and enamel can be protected from abrasion during the cleaning treatment by a coat of rubber latex.

The British Glass Industry Research Association (BGIRA) [4] is carrying out experiments to find out whether the crust formed by natural weathering has any protective value in reducing the rate of further attack, or, in other words, whether removal of the crust exposes the glass to more vigorous attack. Results so far suggest that the crust is not protective. Air abrasive cleaning affected the results on a simulated ancient glass but did not reduce the durability of an ancient sample. Grinding and polishing of the sample doubled the resistance to this sort of weathering, probably by reducing the total effective surface and maybe also by the removal of some alkali in the surface of the glass, from the heating during grinding.

Chemical cleaning uses three main types of material: acids, water, perhaps with detergents, and sequestering or chelating agents. Acids are all potentially damaging to vitreous materials but have been used safely, with care and some experience of their effects. It is sometimes believed that glass is resistant to all acids except hydrofluoric acid, but some mediaeval glasses have been found to be soluble in hydrocholric and nitric acids [1, 5, 6]. Hydrofluoric acid has been used to clean stained glass; the etching of the surface produces a kind of chemical polishing by removing the pitted surface, thus giving better light transmission. But this is a deliberate and intentional destruction of original material and is only done when the design on the window is otherwise completely obscured. In similar circumstances, the mechanical grinding method can be used to restore transparency. This also removes original material but may be preferable to hydrofluoric acid, if the glass is strong enough to stand grinding, because acid etching may remove alkali from the underlying glass.

Even water and detergents are not always harmless. Prolonged washing and soaking may be needed to remove harmful soluble salts from objects recovered from the sea, or from such objects as drug jars and floor and wall tiles. Unfortunately it may also remove the slightly soluble glaze and body components, thereby affecting future chemical analysis results and possibly also the durability of the material (see also the paper by Hodges in this volume). The water should be tested frequently to ensure that soaking is not continued beyond what is necessary to remove the damaging salts. Chemical analysis could be useful in such cases in identifying those ceramics and glazes likely to contain soluble, or slightly soluble material in their original composition. Objects of this kind, not heavily impregnated, could then be stabilized by keeping them in constant humidity conditions rather than submitting them to the hazards of soaking. The effect of detergents on porcelain is the subject of a paper by Rado in this volume. An example of detergents damaging stained glass by dissolving the fired-on paint has been reported by Newton [1]. Also an experiment at the Victoria and Albert Museum has shown that some commercial detergents, probably those containing sodium polyphosphate, will remove or fade the colour from lustre designs on ceramics.

Sodium polyphosphate (Calgon), sodium thiosulphate, polyphosphoric acid and ethylene diamine tetramine (EDTA) solutions and pastes are useful in removing deposits of calcium salts on ceramics and stained glass, but they will remove calcium, potassium and even other metal ions if used to excess [1, 5, 7]. Hydrogen peroxide will bleach out organic stains but will not remove iron stains, which are similar in appearance to the organic ones. Chlorine-containing bleaches such as sodium hypochlorite can be effective but may leave soluble salts behind to cause trouble later unless thoroughly rinsed out.

There is still need for more work on cleaning. For example, the problem of removing iron stains from ceramics has not been solved; corrosion products can still not be removed completely from pitted stained glass without removing the surface of the object.

Ultrasonic cleaning is applied by means of a dental cleaning tool (Cavitron) [8] or in an ultrasonic bath. Like all cleaning methods, skill and experience are required to use this method safely, but it has been found to be the most effective method for cleaning pitted stained glass [7]. The York Glaziers Trust has made a study of the use of ultrasonic bath cleaning on stained glass and has found it effective and safe if the paint has been well-fired. Unfired overpainting is removed by this cleaning [1].

Laser cleaning is the subject of a paper by Asmus in this volume. Although very expensive to purchase, laser may be able to do cleaning, without damage, that cannot be done by any other method.

3. REPAIR

At present, epoxy-based adhesives are commonly used for vitreous materials. Also used are polyvinyl acetate and butyrate, cyanoacrylates, and silicones.

The problem is that the epoxies yellow with age. Some are better than others in this respect, but they have the advantage of strong adhesion which is fairly resistant to water. However, it has recently been found that on prolonged exposure to moisture, as, for example, with stained glass exposed externally, the bond will fail. This problem can be solved by pretreating the glass surfaces with a siloxane before applying the epoxy adhesive [10]. The refractive index of the adhesive rarely matches that of the glass, so the breaks remain visible. With vessel glass, where the breaks are very apparent, this detracts from appreciation of the object. Minnesota 3M Research Ltd [11] have developed an adhesive which has the same refractive index as plate glass windows and will fill cracks in such windows, making the crack invisible. It is not so effective with broken, as distinct from cracked glass, because the breaks need to be very carefully fitted and held together, and the gap between them very small if it is to work. Unfortunately the refractive index of vessel glass in a museum display may vary considerably from one object to another. There is a possibility that a range of adhesives of different refractive index could be formulated, so that the adhesive could be matched to the glass. This would be very interesting for museum work.

Epoxy adhesives, although shrinking very little on curing, can exert enough force to damage the surface by removing splinters or flakes of glass when the adhesive is cleaned off or if it pulls away on ageing. This has been reported [14] and also seen at the Victoria and Albert Museum. Epoxies are not the only adhesives that will do this. Animal glue will have the same effect [27]. For this reason, and because of the yellowing, all surplus adhesive should be removed from the surface of the glass before it has finally dried or cured, and labels should not be stuck onto glass objects. Werner [15] reports an incident where a label caused moisture to be retained on the surface, inducing crizzling of an unstable glass. Damage to the surface by adhesives is worrying and needs study. I have not been able to produce the effect under experimental conditions with modern glass. It probably only occurs when the surface layer of the glass is under tension, perhaps due to alkali depletion of the surface layer and the formation of a hydrogen glass (see Reference 1 for an explanation of this type of deterioration). It would be necessary to produce a sensitive glass for use in selecting adhesives, if any, which are free from this risk.

Polyvinyl alcohol and polyvinyl butyral are not sufficiently water-resistant for use outdoors and therefore can only be used for museum work. They do not have the bond-strength of epoxies, but are more easily reversible and have better light-fastness than most epoxies.

Cold-setting acrylics, such as are used in dentistry, may have uses in ceramic and glass repair [12]. At present they are very expensive. Many act as fillers rather than adhesives and will thus fill gaps undercut to hold them but will not stick two pieces together. Development is active in this field and some of the new products will certainly find a place in conservation work.

Cyanoacrylates are only useful, at present, for breaks which can be fitted together very exactly, and where the surfaces to be bonded are clean and not at all porous. When the conditions are right, they give a strong bond and have the advantage of being very quick-setting, so that the pieces can be held together and there is no need for strapping and waiting. The bond is reversible, but only after long soaking in solvent. They are more difficult to remove than most epoxies.

Silicone-based adhesives have been tested by Bettembourg [13] and have given good results on accelerated weathering tests when used on stained glass. They may replace epoxies for outdoor use.

Many adhesives require heating to give a strong bond quickly. Damage to vessel glass by heating has been reported by Bimson and Werner, and the Corning Glass Museum [16], and should therefore never be permitted in museum work. It is, however, possible that heating up to 250°C or even higher does not cause damage to stained glass [4] and that adhesives requiring heating could be useful for this material. One alternative to heat-curing might be to use adhesives which are cured by ultra-violet radiation. Opticon UV57 [17] is one of these. Tests at the Victoria and Albert Museum on Opticon were disappointing in that it did not make the break more invisible than epoxy and was too fluid to fill gaps or hold pieces together, so that strapping was still needed; it did not give a strong bond. This result did not justify its use, bearing in mind also the disadvantage of its high cost and short shelf-life, even when kept in a refrigerator. It may be that our sample, after flying from America, was not in good condition when we tested it. The short shelf-life suggests that it would be advisable to use material of this type manufactured in the country where it is to be used.

Flaking glaze on ceramics is reattached with adhesives and consolidants. At the Victoria and Albert Museum we have not found one which will reattach a flaking glaze and hold it firmly when the composition of the glaze is such that it is a bad fit for the body and has become distorted on detachment from the body as a result of compressive forces. If the adhesive, such as an epoxy, forms bonds strong enough to hold the springing glaze, then it is also of a type that penetrates the body of the ceramic, causing an unsightly dark, wet-looking patch. Inorganic types of adhesive, such as silicates or silanes, which cross-link to form a silica-type network with only a few organic bonds, might be free from this defect, but they might be insufficiently flexible and will be irreversible. Flaking black paint (which is a fired-on enamel) and other enamels on glass can also be difficult to fix, as can Limoges enamels on copper where the glass surface is flaking. The points already made about adhesives damaging the surface are particularly important here. The adhesive must be a cure and not a cause of the problem.

4. RESTORATION

The ethics of restoration in the field of pottery is the subject of a paper by Hodges in this volume, so I shall not discuss this matter. If one is required to make a restoration involving imitation of the original design then there are problems with the medium to be used. Pigments of good light-fastness are available to match most colours. The colour change after a period of time is almost always due to yellowing of the medium. Acrylics, polyvinyl acetates, polyurethanes and epoxies are often used. The two-pack polyurethanes are better for colour retention than the one-pack type, and better than most epoxies. Cold-cure acrylics are also good, but the two-component systems which must be mixed together immediately before use are not liked by restorers, because they begin to set during use and are difficult to mix accurately in small quantities. One-pack polyurethanes usually yellow on ageing, but some are satisfactory for many years of museum exposure. Acrylics and polyvinyl acetates are good for colour retention but cannot be rubbed down, partly due to their thermoplastic nature. Also, unless they change on drying out to a less soluble form, building up a thickness by successive coats may be a problem, the underlayers softening too much from the solvent in subsequent layers. It is possible that an acrylic rejected by picture restorers because of crosslinking might be successful in this field. If the degree of crosslinking were sufficient to give some hardness but stopped short of brittleness and did not further crosslink on ageing, it should still be removable on vitreous materials where strong solvents can be used without damage.

New materials are constantly appearing on the market, some of which may be useful for this work. Indeed, there are so many that it is difficult for any one organization to test them all, and more exchange of information on tests and results by different Conservation Departments could save time and prevent good new materials from being missed. There is no really satisfactory synthetic plastic material to replace missing pieces of stained glass. At the Victoria and Albert Museum some years ago, epoxy resins with soluble dyes were used for repair work, but they have not stood the test of time. The bright lighting needed to display this glass in a museum is a very severe test of a synthetic resin's light-fastness. Conservators are wisely using glass of a suitable colour to make replacements until a completely reliable material is found.

5. PROTECTION FROM DETERIORATION

The use of surface treatments to protect vitreous materials from further deterioration is necessary where they are exposed to the weather. Stained glass in churches and cathedrals, if it is to remain in its original position in the window spaces, unprotected from the weather, has only a limited life. Only 20 more years has been predicted for some of the glass at Canterbury Cathedral [36].

There are three possible methods of dealing with this problem, all three based on isolating the glass from the environment. One is to move the glass a little further into the building and provide external glazing in the original position. One form of this is known as isothermal glazing [1, 5, 6, 14, 18, 19]. Another method is to provide a protective coating of an inorganic or organic material [1]. The third is to place the ancient glass with new glass, on one or both sides, either with an air space between the ancient glass and the plating, or with the ancient glass embedded in a synthetic resin inside the plating — a lamination process, such as that used at Cologne [20].

Another case of deterioration of vitreous materials where protection is needed is that of the so-called 'glass disease' where the glass is of an intrinsically unstable composition. In moist conditions, it deteriorates, forming a layer of alkaline salts which, being deliquescent, absorb moisture, forming alkaline solutions which further attack the glass [21]. There are two possible methods of protection in such cases. At present, such glass is kept in constant humidity conditions, usually at about 40% relative humidity. An alternative would be to apply a protective organic or inorganic coating to prevent moisture reaching the glass. Limoges enamels on copper sometimes show similar deterioration; flaking glazes on some ceramics may have the same cause. A third possibility would be to alter the glass composition towards a more stable state. This has been done. Newton [1] quotes an American patent where the alkali atoms of the surface layer are replaced by fluorine. Sulphur dioxide has also been used in a similar way [22, 23]. These treatments were on modern glass and may not be possible on ancient glass where the surface has already been altered by weathering. The risks of damage to art objects by such drastic treatments are considerable. Surface appearance is so important that almost any alteration of refractive index or colour is unacceptable. Also, there is no evidence that such a surface treatment would be sufficient to protect the underlying layers from attack by moisture. Stresses between the surface layer and interior, where the interior is a frail ancient glass of unstable composition, might cause failure after many years, even if the treatment itself did not cause stresses which destroyed the object. However, although at present this does not seem a likely possibility, it should not be completely ruled out. It seems certain that the decay is due to the glass composition, so the obvious way to cure it is to alter that composition, other methods being less radical but more in the nature of palliatives.

Another potential treatment might be the use of lasers to revitrify the surface, as discussed by Asmus in his paper in this volume. This might be possible but, if the surface is depleted of alkali and has formed a hydrogen glass, it is difficult to see how the original composition could be regained. Even so, when the original composition of the glass is unstable, this might be an advantage. There is a risk of creating stresses which in glass manufacture would be removed by annealing. This solution is not normally possible because annealing temperatures might break or distort the shape or appearance of the object. It is an exciting idea and worthy of further study, although the risks of such treatment would have to be carefully evaluated before applying it to an art object.

101

Taking the possible methods of protection separately:

5.1 Isothermal glazing

This is fully described by Newton in the Corpus Vitrearum Medii Aevi Newsletters[19] where the example which are at present in use are detailed. It is also the subject of a paper by Newton in this volume, so it would be superfluous to go into detail here. It is safer than the other methods in that it leaves the glass in reasonably dry air and not in contact with a synthetic resin or inorganic coating, whose long-term effect on the glass is not known. It will certainly retard the deterioration of the glass. Whether it will completely stop all decay, we cannot know at present. The necessary information on the effects of air pollutants found indoors on the decay of glass is not available, but the relatively good condition of glass in museums without air-conditioning shows that these effects are small. Isothermal glazing is expensive but not as expensive as the Cologne type of lamination.

5.2 Coatings
5.2.1 Organic coatings

The easiest and cheapest way to protect glass would be to spray it with an organic resin coating. However, the effectiveness of such treatments, at present, is very much in doubt. Most plastics are permeable to moisture. Even the best in this respect will permit a few molecules to pass which, over a long period of time, could be sufficient to cause decay, so that the coating would only retard decay, not prevent it. More worrying is the possibility that moisture penetrating the film would be trapped against the surface of the glass and, by dissolving alkali from it, create an even more dangerous condition than that of untreated glass, where moisture on the surface will evaporate at the next dry spell or, in the case of stained glass outdoors, be washed away, together with dissolved alkali, by rain [15]. Indeed, one theory is that repeated washing of glass removes the damaging alkaline solution without the need for other treatments. This might be so for relatively stable glass but, for an inherently unstable one, is unlikely to be sufficient.

To be successful, a coating would have to be readily adherent, water-resistant, and unaltered by ageing. Polyvinyl chloride, polymethyl methacrylate and thermo-plastic acrylics, polyurethanes, polyvinyl fluoride and siliconized polyesters have been suggested [33] and some are being tested at the British Glass Industry Research Association (BGIRA) [23] and by the Victoria and Albert Museum. Bettembourg has had some good results on artificial weathering with a polyurethane-based coating [24]. The problems of having to use accelerated weathering and the difficulty of predicting from this the durability in practice, and the differences in behaviour on modern glass and on ancient glass of different compositions, are described by Newton in his paper to the International Congress on Glass [25]. In addition to the possibility of moisture penetration through the coating there is the disadvantage that, if adhesion between the glass and the coating does fail, it does not fail uniformly. There have also been examples of applied coatings taking off the black enamel in separating from the glass [14, 27]. The black enamel and the unpainted surface of the glass may be disturbed by shrinkage of the coating during drying or during subsequent crosslinking [26] (see also Section 3). These are difficult to simulate on modern glass for testing purposes. Newton, Bettembourg and Frodl-Kraft have made glasses of composition similar to unstable mediaeval glass to use for testing [33]. It may be necessary also to weather the glass before treatment to form a hydrogen glass layer under tension on the surface (see Newton [1] for a description of the breakdown of glass) because it is probable that such a layer would require very little additional tension to pull it away from the underlying glass. Both tests outdoors in natural conditions and accelerated tests will be necessary to examine the effects of a number of interacting factors. For example, a soft flexible film might be thought best because it might exert less tension on the surface, but we have found on testing coatings for stone that they pick up a lot of dirt and retain it even after washing. If they were to be used on glass, they would have to be frequently replaced. All coatings, inorganic or organic, can only be effective if applied to clean neutral surfaces and this is difficult to achieve on weathered glass surfaces. Removal of all the corrosion would be difficult without also removing much of the painted detail. There is often pitting, and it is possible that salts remaining in these pits might cause the coating to fail. Also, coatings prevent a proper inspection of the original surface. This is a problem which affects the art historical assessment and for this reason, as well as for the reason of possible failure of the coating material, the ideal coating should be removable. However, in the desperate situation of much stained glass today, protection is essential. Isothermal glazing, where it is possible, has an advantage over coatings in that there is no interference with the original glass.

5.2.2 Inorganic coatings

The application of inorganic coatings from solution or by radio frequency sputtering and vacuum deposition have been used in the optical, electronic and metal industries and are a possible method of protecting glass [1, 29]. All these processes are expensive and at present require heating to about 250°C either during application or to fuse the applied coating. This might make them unsafe to use on art objects. The experiments of Bimson and Werner and the Corning Glass Museum [1, 16], mentioned above, show that this would indeed be dangerous for vessel glass, but treatments involving heating were used on stained glass in the early part of this century with no apparent damage [1, 4, 31]. If a heat treatment is included in the cycle, the glass must be very carefully cleaned. Traces of iron, etc., will cause staining of the glass and the protective layer. Some experiments being carried out by and for the BGIRA should be mentioned. An easily fusible borosilicate glass has been shown to give protection to glass of poor durability [28]; radio frequency sputtering using Corning 7070 glass gave a coating that failed to adhere to simulated mediaeval glass [28, 33]; vacuum deposition of a silica-rich glassy layer a few millimetres thick was predicted to give protection against moisture and has shown good results on modern glass [1, 32, 34]. Silica, zirconium oxide, and titanium oxide coatings can be formed by dipping the glass in solutions of the metal chlorides and then heating to fuse the coating [31]. There is a suggestion that, on glass of poor durability, potassium or sodium chloride crystals might be formed on the glass and produce defects in the coatings [35]. This is being investigated. Schröder has found that treated vessel glasses show no change after 20 years in a museum atmosphere [1, 35]. All these coatings, it is said, could be formulated so as to have the same refractive index as the glass, and not alter its appearance. They would not change the colour provided that the glass could be cleaned thoroughly without damage before the treatment was applied. They are probably irreversible, so need even more thorough testing before being used on art objects than do organic coatings, which can be removed.

5.3 Plating and lamination

Plating of the type in which an air-gap is left between the plating glass and the ancient glass has been used for a long time to protect badly broken stained glass, especially the heads of figures where strap leads would interfere with the design. This has the advantage that there is no synthetic substance in contact with the glass but, unless the putty and lead provide a complete seal, there is a slow interchange of air with the atmosphere, allowing the entry of air pollutants, gases, dirt and moisture. The main danger is that condensation may occur and, being unable to evaporate, cause damage. In the Victoria and Albert Museum, such plating has been removed after 20 years in a museum atmosphere. There is dust inside the plating, probably from the putty which dries out in the museum, and there is evidence of damage where adhesives which were used to fix the plating have pulled away the surface of the glass. There are deposits on the glass but it is not yet known whether these are due to the glazing or to the museum atmosphere, in which case they would be present even if the glass had never been glazed. Removal of the plating of a head at Canterbury, which had been plated and exposed to the weather for 30 years, showed that there had been no deterioration of the modern glass. This might suggest that condensation in plating is not so damaging as was feared. It may be that the mediaeval glass has been not damaged but protected in this case. Much more evidence is needed and Newton in his report of these results has asked for any information on relevant experiences. There will always be a need for this or the 'Cologne process' to be used for very fragile or much-broken glass, to provide the necessary extra support until, and maybe even when, adhesives are developed that are absolutely reliable.

The Cologne lamination process is described in the paper by Wolff in this volume, so I shall not go into detail here. The protection is given by the cover glass and not the organic resin sheet, which only acts as an embedding protection for the ancient glass. There is no danger of moisture penetration, unless the cover glass is broken, provided that the bond between the ancient glass, acrylic sheet and cover glass, together with the lead and putty, is sufficient to prevent moisture from getting in and working along the interface. Twenty years' experience suggests that this is so, for there has been no damage by water penetration. The reversibility of the process has been tested and found to be good. The process is expensive and requires a skilled team of workers to carry it out effectively on a large scale. It is effective on glass with many breaks and on very thin ancient glass which would not be strong enough to remain in an isothermal glazing situation without support.

6. CONCLUSION

This is a personal view of the problems and potentialities in the field of conservation of vitreous enamels. It is supplemented most valuably by the practical experience and theoretical studies given in the papers in this section of the present volume, whether or not I have mentioned them individually.

REFERENCES

Summaries of the references given, along with many others, can be found in the excellent bibliography by Professor R. G. Newton [1].

1. Newton, R. G., 'The Deterioration and Conservation of Painted Glass: A Critical Bibliography and Three Research Papers', Oxford University Press for the British Academy, 1974.
2. Gibson, B. M., The use of the airbrasive process for cleaning ethnological material, 'Studies in Conservation' 14 (1969).
3. Larney, J., Ceramic restoration at the Victoria and Albert Museum, 'Studies in Conservation' 16 (1971).
4. Newton, R. G., 'CVMA [Corpus Vitrearum Medii Aevi] Newsletter' No. 12, 10 January 1975, University of York.
5. CVMA Technical Committee, Answers to the questionnaire on the conservation of windows, 7th Conference, Florence, 2-16 October 1970.
6. Frenzel, G., Umweltgefahren bedrohen mittelalterliche Glasmalerei, 'Kirche u. Kunste' 49 (1971), 58-60.
7. Bettembourg, J. M., 'Nettoyage par voie chimique et par ultrasons des verres de vitraux', compte rendu du 8e colloque du CVMA, York, 25-27 September 1972, 47pp.
8. Hempel, K. F. B., The restoration of two marble statues by Antonio Corradini, 'Studies in Conservation' 14 (1969), 126-131.
9. Frodl-Kraft, E., Restaurierung und Erforschung. 1. Die Sud Rose von Maria Strassengel, 'OZKD' 21 (1967), 192-197.
10. Explosives Research and Development Establishment, How they saved the Churchill window, 'Plastics and Rubber Weekly' (1973), 12.
11. Minnesota 3M Research Ltd, Pinnacles, Harlow, Essex CM19 5AE, England.
12. Hussong, I. and Wihr, R., Ein Wichtiger Forschritt im Nachbilden und Ergänzen antiker Gläser, 'Trierer Zeitschrift' 23 (1954), 231-238.
13. Bettembourg, J. M., 'La restauration de vitraux brisés. Veillissement acceléré de collés', typescript dated 3.11.72., 8pp.

14. Hahnloser, H., 'Restaurationsbericht von Konrad Vetter, Bern, betrschreiben von Hans Acker, 1441. Sow Beil und Burgdorf', compte rendu, 8e colloque du CVMA, York, 25-27 September 1972.

15. Werner, A. E. A., The care of glass in museums, 'Museum News', Technical Supplement No. 13 (1966) 45-99.

16. Bimson, M. and Werner, A. E. A., The danger of heating glass, 'J. of Glass Studies' VI (1964), 148-150.

17. Opticon UV57. Opticon Chemical, P.O. Box 2445, Palo Verdes Peninsula, California 90274, USA.
    Brinch Madsen, H., A new product for mending glass, 'Studies in Conservation' 17 (1972), 131-132.

18. Bacher, E., Exterior protective glazing, 'OZKD' 27 (1973), 66-68.

19. Newton, R. G., 'CVMA Newsletter' No. 8, 6 May 1974; No. 9, 30 July 1974; No. 10, 16 September 1974.

20. Jacobi, R., Ein Konservierungsverfahren für mittelalterliche Glasfenser auf der Basis der moderne Sicherheitsglastechnik, 'Glas-, Email-, Keramo-Technik' 22 (1971), 172-174.

21. Werner, A. E. A., Problems in the conservation of glass, in 'Ann.1e Congrès des Journées Internationales d Verre', Liege, 1958, pp. 189-205.

22. Brockway Glass Company Inc., 'Corrosion retarding fluorine treatment of glass surfaces', U.S. Patent Nc 3, 314, 772, 18 April 1967.

23. Newton, R. G., 'CVMA Newsletter' No. 5, 12 October 1973.

24. Bettembourg, J. M., 'Protection des verres de vitraux contre les agents atmosphériques. Etude de films d résines synthétiques', Laboratoire de Recherche des Monuments Historiques, typescript, September 1974, pp.

25. Newton, R. G., 'A problem arising from the weathering of poorly durable glasses', 10th Internationa Congress on Glass, Kyoto, Japan.

26. Frodl-Kraft, E. and Frenzel, G., 'OZKD' 17 (1963), 93-114.

27. McGrath, R., Frost, A. C. and Beckett, H. E., 'Glass in Architecture and Decoration', Architectural Press 1961.

28. 'CVMA Newsletter' No. 5, 12 October 1973.

29. Weinig, S., 'Applications of sputtering — past, present and future', Materials Research Corporation, USA NATO Conference on Coatings, London, 1972.

30. Brackley, G., Lawson, K. and Satchell, D. W., 'Integral covers for silicon solar cells', Photovoltaics Specialist Conference, 2-4 May 1972, Maryland, U.S.A.

31. Frodl-Kraft, E., 'Das Problem der Schwarzlot — Sicherung an mittelalterlichen Glasmalden', Austria Institute for Artistic Research of the Ministry of Ancient Monuments, Vienna, 1963.

32. Linsley, G. F., 'A possible method of conserving ancient glass', compte rendu du 8e colloque du CVMA York, 25-27 September 1972, p. 51.

33. 'CVMA Newsletter' Nos. 2 and 3, 30 April 1973.

34. Hammond, V. J., private comments to Professor Newton, June 1973; reported in [1].

35. Schröder, H. and Kaufmann, R., Schutzschichten für alte Gläser, in Schott, E., (ed.), 'Beiträge zu Angewandten Glasforschung', Stuttgart, 1959, pp. 355-361.

36. Cole, F. W., 'The state of "Adam Delving"', compte rendu du 8e colloque du CVMA, Canterbury, 3(September 1972, pp. 31-32.

MEDIAEVAL STAINED GLASS CORROSION – CONSERVATION – RESTORATION

Eva Frodl-Kraft, Bundesdenkmalamt, Hofburg, 1010 Vienna, Austria

The question of the best and the least harmful methods of conservation and restoration for mediaeval stained glass cannot be answered in isolation. It must rather be dealt with in connection with those processes of corrosion which necessitate restoration. In order to predict the consequences of restoration, one must first of all know how the mediaeval glass and its painting react under certain environmental conditions.

Whereas the chemical aspects of the process of corrosion are already known to a considerable extent [1], most of the physical aspects are still rather mysterious. Why and under what circumstances do relatively uniform, powdery weathering crusts form in one case, individual pits in another, and compact, hard, shiny, yet opaque layers in a third — and are these different types of weathering, to some extent at least, no more than phases of a single, continuous process (Figure 2c)? For example, individual pits, in groups, may eventually make up a more or less homogeneous weathering crust, but the formation of such a crust need not necessarily be preceded by discrete pit formation. Black paint usually protects the glass against weathering, though the reverse may occur in individual cases. Similarly, the elevated leads no doubt protect the adjacent glass; but on the other hand they also facilitate the accumulation of rain or condensed moisture, which intensifies the process of corrosion in these areas (Figure 2c).

In any case, the few precise studies that have so far been carried out over periods of several years have shown that weathering, once it has attacked the entire outer surface of the glass and led to the formation of crusts, proceeds according to a certain, steady rhythm: as soon as the compact top crust has reached a certain thickness, it begins to exfoliate and gradually uncovers the crusts underneath and finally the glass surface with its powdery coating. Now the formation of crusts sets in once more on this permeable and porous surface; weathering and crust formation inevitably bring about a reduction of the glass substance, which is quite considerable in some cases (Figure 3). Of course the rate of progress of the phases of new formation and erosion is variable; it depends on the properties of the glass and the painting, on the one hand, and the atmospheric conditions and the location of the glass on the other. Thus, in one and the same panel, the corrosion and erosion may be speeded up or slowed down by environmental changes alone.

However, chemistry and experience have shown that the existence of water, above all of accumulated moisture, is the most important factor initiating and sustaining all processes of weathering. A current series of experiments at the University of Zurich, which has not yet been completed [2], is intended to provide accurate information on the level of atmospheric relative humidity which is necessary in order to initiate a process of weathering in mediaeval glass (approximately 33% according to the present state of research). In other words, in an exceptionally dry atmosphere, chemical weathering of glass does not normally occur. Of course this has no effect on mechanical erosion. Obviously there is a striking conflict between glass, calling for the lowest possible atmospheric humidity, and wood, which indicates one of the difficulties arising in the air-conditioning of churches which have wooden furniture as well as mediaeval stained glass windows.

One may conclude that, from the viewpoint of mere conservation, the most favourable solution would be to remove the original stained glass windows from the churches, replace them by copies, and keep the originals under museum conditions. This may, in fact, be necessary in special cases; however, one must bear in mind that keeping stained glass in museums does not necessarily guarantee the best possible conservation. It is by no means sufficient to eliminate moisture; the climatic conditions must be calculated accurately whether the glass is in a museum or in a church.

This may be illustrated by an exceptional case. It does not call for general conclusions but it demonstrates that ensuring a dry atmosphere is by no means enough if the temperature is disregarded. In the 18th century, a sacristy was attached to the Gothic side choir of St. Michael's Church in Vienna, in such a way that its attic enclosed the upper part of the choir windows. One of the windows had retained the mediaeval stained glass in the tracery, but it was plastered on the side facing the interior of the church. The extreme temperature fluctuations in the low, unventilated attic and the fact that the layer of mortar completely prevented any temperature equalization between that room and the interior of the church have led to a weathering of the outer surface of the glass, which hardly ever occurs under 'natural' conditions. Although the outer surface is smooth and appears to be unaffected by the weather, the glass has nevertheless (even after removal of the inner layer of mortar) lost its transparency almost completely; it has become opaque. A micro-section shows that true devitrification, that is, a decomposition of the interior of the glass, has occurred, the optical effect of which can hardly be improved by cleaning the surface [3].

In this case, exceptional conditions have affected the glass much more severely than any attack of the weather could have done during the same period of time. Generally, however, under the 'natural' conditions to which the stained glass windows have been exposed ever since they were fitted in their places, the attack of water, enriched with pollutants, above all sulphur, constitutes the greatest danger.

Although our outline description of natural conditions and the processes of corrosion is bound to be rather superficial, the primary measures of conservation, intended to halt or at least to retard weathering, are clearly indicated under these circumstances. The glass surface, mainly the outside of the glass, must be protected against the attack of moisture, it must be kept permanently dry and, in addition, must be protected against mechanical erosion and against strong temperature fluctuations. The question of whether or not the weathering crusts are to be left on the glass is not yet touched upon in connection with this primary objective. Provided the glass can be kept dry, it is irrelevant whether its surface is more or less bare or covered by weathering crusts.

However, this question arises as soon as a decision is made on the protective method to be applied. Basically, there are two methods: the coating of the outer surface of the glass and isothermal protective glazing. At present the first method, coating with synthetic resin, is being tested in Austria, but it is not used in practice. It can only be applied on a fairly smooth surface and thus requires the removal of weathering crusts and all loose particles. This is a kind of direct interference with the glass substance which is considered unjustified by Austrian conservators except in special cases.

As regards the second method, isothermal protective glazing, experience has proved that it offers the best possible protection against further weathering, above all if the inner surface of the glass is slightly heated [1,4]. Apart from the fact that work is carried out on the basis of empirical data which have not yet been verified by exact calculations, the disadvantages of this method, which leaves the original surface itself untouched, are of an aesthetic nature. Optical problems arise in the interior of the church, as the mediaeval stained glass windows have to be removed from their original position in the glazing grooves and re-hung inside the building without being tightly fitted in the stonework, so that air can circulate freely. Whereas relatively easy solutions to these problems can usually be found in the interior, the outside appearance of the church is severely impaired, particularly in the case of large windows, so that doubts may be cast on the benefit of the method itself. In any case, it is painful to replace the vivid surface of the stained glass window with its beautiful lead network by the rigidity of reflective, rectangular areas. Compromises can be made even here — for example, protective glazing made of hexagons (Figure 2a) — but these are compromises not only with regard to aesthetics but also with regard to conservation, as it is quite obvious that the protection against the inflow of air from outside is more effective with large individual panes of glass and simple lead-lines, especially if a solid glass is chosen.

Wherever it has been possible to keep exact records on the progress of corrosion and decomposition of the glass over a certain period of time, it has become evident that matters are proceeding at a frightening speed (Figure 3). There must not be any more delays; protective measures have to be taken immediately. From this point of view it may be justifiable to put up with the aesthetic disadvantages of isothermal glazing, considering its great advantage of leaving the original substance of the mediaeval stained glass window completely untouched. In practice, however, measures of restoration affecting the stained glass itself, depending on its state of preservation, will be necessary whenever the method of protective external glazing is applied. Usually the mechanical durability of the stained glass as well as its artistic appearance have been impaired in the course of time.

If the mediaeval lead network still exists, and fortunately such instances are not too rare in Austria, one will certainly try to preserve or to mend it for reasons of conservation as well as aesthetics. Tests of tensile and compression strength have clearly shown that the mediaeval lead profiles are definitely superior to modern profiles with thin cores and broad flanges as far as resistance against wind pressure is concerned [1, no. 46]. The bulging panels of the famous West Windows at Chartres Cathedral with their modern leading, which are being restored at present, jake it quite obvious that modern profiles are mechanically unsuited, in particular for large panels (Figure 1).

Broken glass fragments are not linked by lead but cemented edge-to-edge, for which a silicone adhesive, tested at the Laboratoire des Monuments Historiques in Paris, has proved most useful [1, no. 8]. If the glass is broken into several pieces, leaded cover glasses are fixed on both sides without being glued onto the original glass. The cover glasses rest on it without any intermediate layer; if the surface of the original glass is not completely smooth, the cover glasses are made from moulds thereof. This method of preserving fragmented pieces has been applied for almost three decades in Austria and in spite of all the valid theoretical arguments raised against it, damage to the original through the penetration of dust or moisture has not been detected anywhere [5, no. 10].

The most difficult task within the whole range of technical preservation is the fixing of loose black paint. There is no practical experience available in Austria.

In addition to the numerous practical difficulties of restoration, serious questions of principle arise when it is attempted to restore the distorted or damaged artistic appearance of mediaeval stained glass. The sponsor of the work, as well as the restorer, may all too easily succumb to the idea that by restoration they can re-create the original artistic appearance — just as if the weathering crusts were no more than a veil, after the removal of which the stained glass would present itself in its original colour composition and luminosity. But this hardly ever happens; a panel of stained glass consists of a large number of individual pieces of glass which — according to their different colouring — differ with regard to their chemical composition as well as their physical properties. Therefore they have reacted in different ways to the same outside influences, so that the different states of preservation in one panel of stained glass are as numerous as the individual pieces or types of glass (Figure 2b-e). Frequently there are even more variations of the state of preservation, because weathering and ageing have not progressed evenly on the whole surface of one and the same piece of glass. Whereas in some areas the transparency is reduced by the formation of more or less thick weathering crusts, it may even be increased in other areas where the paint or the flashing has weathered away and the original shadings have got lost; more than that, when the modelling and shading have already weathered away, they may turn into their opposites if the base glass, to which they have offered protection for such a long time, is less weathered than the surrounding glass and now appears as a light area.

There is not just one state of preservation of stained glass, but a whole complex of states of preservation, each of them being related to the original state in a completely different way. Wherever the formation of weathering crusts has led — or rather, appears to have led — to an increase in substance, their removal may to some extent restore the original appearance — though again, in many cases, this only appears to be so. This is particularly true for crusts covering parts of the surface, which impair the clarity of outlines and shades or make them completely indiscernible; their removal is a true benefit (Figure 4d, f). In other instances, however, where genuine substance, no matter if it is painting or glass, has simply disappeared, the restorer, trying to reconstruct the original on the basis of existing traces, goes beyond the limits of the conservator's work and enters into the province of re-creation.

In any case, one should bear in mind that although measures such as cleaning, i.e. the removal of weathering

106

crusts, may balance the appearance to some extent by restoring the transparency of the badly weathered areas and adjusting them to the less weathered ones, they are far from regaining the original artistic appearance.

REFERENCES

1. Newton, R. G., The deterioration and conservation of painted glass: a critical bibliography and three research papers, 'Corpus Vitrearum Great Britain, Occasional Papers I', London, 1974 (published for the British Academy by Oxford University Press).
2. Ferrazzini, J. C., paper on the conservation of the stained glass of Regensburg Cathedral, read on the occasion of the Colloquium of the Fachgutachterkommission in Regensburg, 22 November 1974.
3. Bacher, E., Ein mittelalterlicher Glasmalerei - Fund in der Wiener Michaelerkirche, 'Österreichische Zeitschrift für Kunst und Denkmalpflege' **XXVIII** (1974), 210-12.
4. Bacher, E., Aussenschutzverglasung, 'Österreichische Zeitschrift für Kunst und Denkmalpflege' **XXVII** (1973), 66-68.
5. Newton, R. G. (ed.), 'News Letters' 1 (December 1972)—13 (February 1975), Technical Sub-Committee of the British Committee of the Corpus Vitrearum Medii Aevi (Department of Physics, University of York).

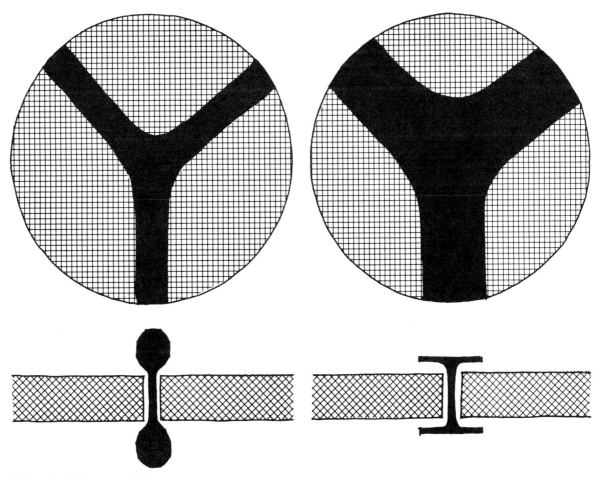

Figure 1. Enlargement X4.

Figure 2.

a. St. Walpurgis Church, Styria, choir window, isothermal protective glazing, hexagonal pattern.

b. St. Walpurgis Church, Styria, St. Agatha panel from choir window before restoration.

c. St. Walpurgis Church, Styria, St. Agatha panel, external surface before restoration. The state of preservation varies from almost perfect condition (green glass surface appearing black) to a more or less homogeneous crust (appearing white).

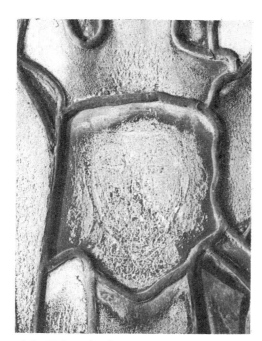

d. St. Walpurgis Church, Styria, St. Katharina panel, external surface of the face. The parts of the face adjacent to the raised leads were to some extent protected by them against running water and are therefore less corroded than the central area. Here individual pits are found as well as pits forming lines which follow the external paint.

e. St. Walpurgis Church, Styria, St. Ursula panel, external surface, detail, in the centre green dress. The black shading, especially in the lower part, is more affected by corrosion than the glass itself.

Figure 3. Magdalen Church, Judenburg, Styria, Presentation in the Temple.

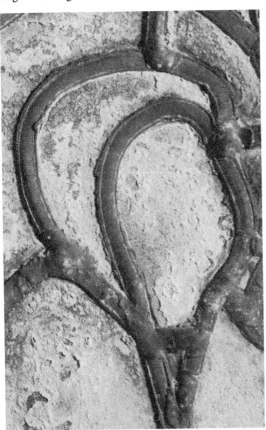

a. The Virgin's head, external surface in 1963.

b. Detail, Mary with the Child, state of preservation in 1963.

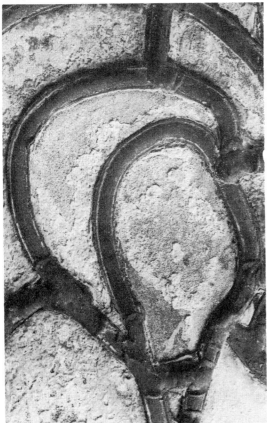

c. The Virgin's head, external surface in 1973. In the course of ten years the white corrosion crust has partly weathered away (cf. the face), a process which in 1963 had just started (cf. the veil above the face).

d. Same detail, state of preservation in 1973. In some parts transparency has increased, whereas in others it has diminished since 1963.

Figure 4.

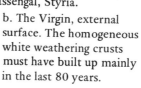

Pilgrimage Church, Maria Strassengal, Styria.

a. Visitation panel from choir window; in situ until 1975. The Virgin. Loss of transparency in consequence of massive weathering.

b. The Virgin, external surface. The homogeneous white weathering crusts must have built up mainly in the last 80 years.

Graz, Landesmuseum Joanneum, panel from Maria Strassengel taken out in 1894.

c. Detail, St. Wolfgang, external surface. Almost perfect state of preservation; the panel has never undergone cleaning.

d. Detail, St. Wolfgang. Almost original colour and transparency.

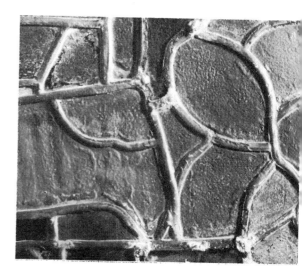

Waasenkirche, Leoben, Styria.

e. Detail from choir window, external surface before cleaning. The thick black crusts, which have already vanished on the central parts of the glass, have survived adjacent to the leads, rendering the contours illegible.

f. Same detail after cleaning. By removing the crusts not only the transparency but also the clarity of the outlines was improved.

all photographs: Osterr. Bundesdenkmalamt, Vienna.

CONSERVATION OF MEDIAEVAL WINDOWS (ISOTHERMAL GLAZING)

R. G. Newton, Department of Physics, University of York, YO1 5DD, England

1. INTRODUCTION

The main cause of deterioration of window glass is persistent moisture. Free-flowing rain need not harm glass and the frequent washing of windows with water prevents them from deteriorating because the alkaline products of ion-exchange, between the glass and water, are washed away. If moisture is trapped in dirty deposits on the outside of the window, or if condensation occurs frequently on the inside (without any washing), the glass will rapidly be etched. For example, if the seal of a sealed double-glazing unit breaks down, then the two interior-facing faces of the glass (faces nos 2 and 3, counting from the outside) can become permanently etched in as little as four years.

An outside protective glazing will prevent pigeon-droppings from reaching the window, and will stop rain from moistening any deposits on, or cracks in, the glass, but condensation can occur if the interspace is nominally sealed (it can never remain completely sealed). A better scheme is to allow air from inside the building to pass freely through the interspace and this is called 'isothermal' glazing because the aim is to produce nearly equal temperatures on both faces of the stained glass, so that condensation shall not occur.

2. TYPES OF PROTECTIVE GLAZING

There has been much confusion in the use of terminology, and I recommend the following:

1. The term 'double glazing' should no longer be used in connection with stained glass because it is an architectural term for glazings intended to protect the occupants of the building from cold, noise and 'steaming-up' of the glass, and the air space between the panes is intended to be permanently sealed.

2. The term 'external protective glazing' should be used where an external shield of glass or plastics material is employed to protect the mediaeval glass against the weather, pigeon droppings, and damage by stones, etc. The space between the two panels should not be sealed but should be ventilated to the outside so that any moisture which may collect in the space can dry out when the sun shines and warms both the air in the space and the stained glass.

A special case of (1) exists at Lindena (see item 2.3 below) where the mediaeval glass has been moved into the building but it is not ventilated to the inside. Thus it is not 'isothermal' glazing because there will be a temperature drop across the glass.

3. 'Isothermal' glazing is essentially a system intended to protect mediaeval glass from contact with both forms of moisture (rain and condensation) at all times. It is generally used with heated buildings (see the Table) and corresponds to placing the ancient glass in a 'museum-type atmosphere', where little or no further deterioration is likely to occur because the glass is kept dry. This type of glazing consists of removing the ancient glass from the glazing grooves and re-hanging it inside the heated building in such a way that the warm air in the building can pass both sides of the ancient glass. Modern glass is placed in the glazing grooves. The fact that the warm air in the building can reach both sides of the stained glass means that the temperature can be nearly the same on each side; we have isothermal (= equal temperature) conditions. It is probable that the system can also be used with an unheated building, provided a wide enough ventilated gap exists between the two panels. The system is known as the 'Swiss system' because it was first used in Switzerland in 1945 [1], although Professor Marchini re-invented it in Florence at the end of 1969 [2] and the system which he uses is noticeably different from that in use in Austria, Germany and Switzerland. There are also claims that it was first used in a church in Lindena (Brandenburg) in 1897 [3], but this seems to have been a special kind of external protective glazing [4].

2.1 Advantages and disadvantages of external glazing
2.1.1 Addition of modern glass to the outside of the glazing groove

The first advantage of using modern glass on the outside is to protect the ancient glass against damage by weather, stones, pigeon droppings, etc. There seems little doubt that some protection of the ancient glass against corrosion is provided because the glass at Lindena is still in good condition after 75 years. It also seems that some of the windows in Nuremberg which have been cleaned, but were left unprotected, have deteriorated again [3].

If the ancient glass is left in the glazing grooves, the external glazing should be ventilated to the outside so that any condensation in the space between the glazings can dry out [5, 6]. Nevertheless on cold nights some condensation will occur on the mediaeval glass and some damage by the water must be assumed to occur while the glass is wet and especially during the drying out. An additional reason for ventilating the cavity is to avoid buckling of the mediaeval glass due to expansion of the air in the cavity when the sun shines.

If the modern glass is hung to the outside of the glazing groove there will be loss of the architectural and aesthetic value of the Gothic moulding of the mullions. Some architects regard this loss as being serious, particularly in strong sunlight, but it would not occur if an isothermal glazing system were used. Dr Beranrd Feilden, the architect to York Minster, points out that the depth of a window in its reveal is of fundamental importance to the appearance of a building and designers consider this carefully because it can give either an impression of flatness or of sculptural relief, indicating either a thin wall or a thick one. Any changes in the apparent depth of the reveal are material alterations and it must not be tampered with if the principles of conservation in its general sense are to be respected.

A disadvantage which is common to both external protective glazing, and isothermal glazing, is the harsh nature of the flat modern glass on the outside of the building with its tendency to produce reflections of the sky or of the surrounding buildings. In extreme cases this effect makes the cathedral resemble a shopfront. These reflections can largely be removed by dividing the glass with lead-lines, because the different pieces then cease to be exactly parallel, or the surface of the glass could be etched or sand-blasted with an attractive design.

In the Great East Window at York Minster there is a space some 65 mm wide between the two sets of glazings and the external protective glazing has been disrupted by diamond leading. This provides a satisfactory appearance from the outside of the building but in strong sunlight the straight diagonal lines of the diamond glazing can produce an aesthetically unpleasant effect when viewed from the inside. A thin diffusing screen could be hung between the two glazings, as is now being done at Ingoldstadt [7].

Some exterior protective glazings at York Minster have been leaded in such a manner that the main lead-lines of the design of the mediaeval glass are followed by lead-lines on the outer glass. In this case, however, the two panels are soldered together at the edges, so that the space between the two pieces of glass is only about 3 mm and any displacement of the shadow of the outer leading, relative to the leading of the mediaeval glass, is quite negligible. This arrangement would not be suitable for 'isothermal' glazing because there must be a clear space through which the air from the building can move.

2.1.2 Isothermal glazing, the modern glass being placed in the glazing groove, and the ancient glass moved inwards

The big advantage of this system is that the mediaeval glass does not become wet. Mr R. E. Lacy, of the Building Research Establishment, has done some calculations of the frequency with which condensation is likely to occur on the mediaeval glass, during the winter months, for three types of 'external glazing' [8]. The calculations were carried out for windows of three types: A, external protective glazing; B, 'isothermal' glazing and C, a sealed double-glazed window, as if they had been installed in King's College Chapel, Cambridge, with an interior temperature on average 7°C above the exterior temperature. Subsequently [9] he repeated the calculations for the conditions in York Minster, with an interior temperature assumed to be constant at 15°C in winter. These are D, for single-glazed windows and A* for one with an outer rainshield. He has calculated the percentage of the time, for different months of the year, when condensation might be expected to occur on the ancient glass. The figures are given in the Table below.

The disadvantages of isothermal glazing are the cost (see Section 2.2) and the fact that the modern glass on the outside needs to be treated in some way to reduce the 'shop front effect', described above, by disrupting the flat surfaces with suitable lead-lines. One of the ways of doing this, without producing aesthetically unpleasant effects when viewed from the inside, is to insert the diffusing screen between the mediaeval glass and the external leaded glass mentioned above [7]. This increases the weight to be supported on the cross bars, and by the mullions, and also makes the assembly more complicated. The extent to which reflections are a problem depends much on the surroundings of the building. With many cathedrals in England there is a wide area surrounding the building but as Bacher [10] remarks, the two Steier churches already treated by the Austrians are so hemmed in by surrounding buildings that the reflections are not serious. At Prato Cathedral near Florence, however, the television aerials on neighbouring buildings can be seen reflected in the outer glazing on the East Window [11].

Estimated frequency of condensation (percentage of all hours) on inner leaf of
double windows in churches, with three different arrangements

Month	Outer rain-shield of modern glass		B: ancient glass free-standing within church	C: sealed double-window	D: single-glazed windows in the heated building
	A	A*			
January	22	2	6	14	15
February	23	1	3	12	18
March	16	1	3	11	15
April	7	1	1	3	10
October	11	1	2	7	25
November	16	2	3	10	18
December	22	2	6	15	18

Mr Lacy comments that the figures in column B are probably all zero and that the values listed may represent occasions when the air in the building became saturated, or nearly so. As can be seen from the column A*, the figures become much smaller for a heated building.

Other, more sophisticated, ways might be found for avoiding the reflections, such as to fire-on matt designs which simulate the appearance of mediaeval windows but which need not cast hard shadows on the ancient glass, and this is being studied in Austria. Any treatment, however, still further increases the cost of the installation.

The isothermal glazing system depends on the use of heated air (or at least a building which is warmer than the external environment) to equalize the temperatures on each side of the ancient glass. If the building is not heated, tubular electric heaters could be placed on the sills; heating wires are being strung across the interspace in a German experiment [7].

Another, apparently minor, difficulty with isothermal systems arises from the displacement of the mediaeval glass further into the building. The tapering of the mullions, and the sloping of the reveals, means that the panels no longer fill the space. Light can shine around the sides, over the top, and under the bottom unless the panels are fitted with wider edges, and the lancets with 'skirts', etc. The difficulty can be overcome but the additional frames, edges, skirts, etc. add to the expense. Dr Bernard Feilden remarks that the alteration of the depth of the internal reveal is of less importance than when it occurs outside the building, because the inside is more likely to be viewed with a limited field of vision and the distortion of the designer's intentions is much less; moreover it is less likely to be seen in the sharp relief of sunshine and shadow.

Another disadvantage of the isothermal system, with its circulation of air, is that dust and dirt can be carried into the interspace, but the mediaeval windows in Austria, Germany and Switzerland can be taken down relatively easily for cleaning by unscrewing the nuts. Security measures are adopted to ensure that the nuts cannot be removed by thieves.

2.2 Mechanics of isothermal systems

It seems that only two engineering-type drawings of isothermal systems have yet been published, one by Bacher [10] and one by Hahnloser [12]. The former uses a gap of 60-85 mm and the latter does not give any figures. Dr Frenzel used gaps of 20 mm to 50 mm in the Lorenzkirche at Nürnberg. Nowhere is the optimum gap discussed from the point of view of achieving equal temperatures but experiments carried out at the British Glass Industry Research Association in Sheffield, and supported by the Department of the Environment, have shown that with a gap of 80 mm the air from the building flows down the interspace with velocities up to 1 m/s, depending on the temperature difference; there is also much turbulence. Bacher's paper [10] gives an excellent amount of detail about the way that the isothermal glazing system is installed in Austria. In Marchini's system [2] in the churches of Or San Michele and Santa Croce in Florence, and in Prato Cathedral, there are quite small openings (e.g. 45 cm^2) at the top and the bottom of the lancets [11].

Little has been published about the costs of installing either external protective glazing or isothermal glazing. Some figures quoted by Dr Frodl-Kraft [13] were 9750 Austrian Schillings per m^2 (say 1350 DM/m^2 or £15 per ft^2) for installing isothermal glazing at the Leechkirche in Graz, and Dr Frenzel [14] has quoted 60 DM/m^2 for the extra cost of arranging for the free flow of air around the mediaeval glass. There seem to be discrepancies between these figures and more detailed costings are needed. In the systems described by Bacher and Hahnloser, the mediaeval panels are held in place on the cross-bar by means of nuts on screwed bolts but the latest system in Berne Minster uses a neat device with rotatable cups [1].

2.3 The glazing at Lindena Church

I am greatly indebted to Professor Maercker of Halle in the DDR [4] for some up-to-date information about Lindena, which shows that the installation is not isothermal, yet it is also not a simple external weather shield.

Lindena is a little village, lying about half way between Berlin and Dresden, close to the small town of Kirchain-Dobrilugk, at about 51°38'N and 13°34'E. Dr Maercker visited it in 1969 and again in January 1974. This painted window is a small lancet on the north side of the apse and it was restored in 1897 by Oidtmann in the Rhineland and put behind external protective glazing. No doubt the primary object was to protect the mediaeval window, which is rather near the ground, from damage by stones, etc.

In 1974 the window made the same impression on Dr Maercker as it did in 1969. The wooden surround (1897) to the external protective glazing, which is at the original position of the mediaeval glass, seems to Dr Maercker to be not now tight enough to prevent some circulation of the external air although, in 1969, he seemed to think that there was no entry of air from the outside.

The painted glass, from the middle of the 13th century, is apparently in good condition on both sides and the painting on the outside is still clearly visible. The frame for the mediaeval glass is placed some 60 to 80 mm behind the original position of the window. It, and the stabilizing saddle-bars of 1897, are still secure in the reveal and, as far as Dr Maercker could observe, no air from inside the church can enter the space between the glazings.

Dr Maercker remarks that the window has needed no maintenance since 1897 although the mediaeval panels, with their leading of 1897, have bent a little. He says he does not know of any 13th century window in the DDR which is in such a good state of preservation as regards both the glass and the paintwork. He attributes this to the protection afforded by the external protective glazing, even though there was probably no ventilation of the cavity for the first few decades. This would seem to be a case where a nominally-sealed cavity gives adequate protection for 75 years but it would be interesting to know whether the 13th century glass happened to have a particularly durable composition, such as that possessed by the piece of pink 12th century glass from York Minster [15].

REFERENCES

1. Addy, I., Report to the Radcliffe Trust Scheme for the Crafts on a visit to certain European stained gla restoration workshops, churches and cathedrals, with particular reference to isothermal systems, May 197
2. Marchini, G., Proceedings of the VIIth Colloquium of the Corpus Vitrearum Medii Aevi, Florence 197 p. 42.
3. Frenzel, G., Umweltgefahren bedrohen mittelalterliche Glasmalerei, 'Kirche u. Kunst' 49 (1971), 58-60.
4. Maercker, K. J., private communication, 7 February 1974.
5. Pilkington Brothers Ltd, Condensation on windows, 'Glass and Windows Bulletin No.1', 3-6.
6. Diamant, R. M. E., 'The Internal Environment of Dwellings', Hutchinson International, 60 and 104.
7. Frenzel, G., private communication, 26 November 1974.
8. Lacy, R. E., 'Estimates of the frequency of condensation on the windows of a large church or cathedra unpublished report from the Building Research Establishment, 12 March 1973.
9. Lacy, R. E., 'Condensation on windows of York Minster', unpublished report from the Building Resear Establishment, 13 February 1974.
10. Bacher, E., Aussenschutzverglasung, 'OZKD' 27 (1973), 66-68.
11. Newton, R. G., personal observation, 10 May 1974.
12. Hahnloser, H., 'Restaurationsbericht von Konrad Vetter, Bern, betr. Schreiben von Hans Acker, 1441, sow Biel u. Burgdorf', paper for the 8th Colloquium of the Corpus Vitrearum Medii Aevi at York, 15 p typescript and 16 photographs.
13. Frodl-Kraft, E., private communication, 23 March 1973.
14. Frenzel, G., private communication, July 1972.
15. Hedges, R. and Newton, R. G., Use of the 'isoprobe' for studying the chemical composition of some 12 century glass from York Minster, in 'The Deterioration and Conservation of Painted Glass', Oxfor University Press, 1974, pp. 79-93.

THE CONSERVATION OF MEDIAEVAL STAINED GLASS ACCORDING TO THE JACOBI METHOD OF LAMINATION USED AT COLOGNE*

Arnold Wolff, Architect to Cologne Cathedral, Dombauverwaltung, 5 Köln 1, Roncalliplatz 2, West Germany

1. INTRODUCTION

In spite of its fragility, glass is considered today to be one of the most permanent materials that exist. No one imagines that it can be corroded by air pollution. People are generally surprised when one mentions the weathering of mediaeval stained glass paintings and the great need for their preservation. As it happens, the corrosion of ancient stained glass has taken on horrifying dimensions during the last decades. If we do not find effective methods of protection soon, the whole still relatively plentiful amount of mediaeval glass will be completely ruined. Thus some of the most magnificent products of mediaeval culture would only be preserved in photographs of mostly poor quality.

2. THE WINDOWS OF THE KINGS IN COLOGNE CATHEDRAL CHOIR

In the fifteen 17.15 m high Gothic clerestory windows of Cologne Cathedral choir, we find one of the most important groups of mediaeval stained glass windows in Europe. Forty-eight figures of Kings, surmounted by high Gothic architectural canopies, are arranged around the scene of the Adoration of the Three Magi in the central window. The glass above the figures is filled with a rich variety of diaper patterns and, in the tracery lights, with glowing colours which filter and transform the light, creating an impression of infinitely high space. Neither in their total area nor in their artistic quality (with the exception of Koenigsfelden) is there any work of early 14th century stained glass to compare with this series of Kings, created about 1310.

Unique also is their degree of completeness. More than 95% of the glass and the whole of the leading holding the pieces of coloured glass together date from the time of their origin. In shocking contrast to this is the very poor state of their preservation. The originally 4–6 mm thick glass pieces have been reduced by corrosion through air pollution to a thickness of only 2.0–0.8 mm. At the same time, the fired-on black paint has been destroyed almost completely on the outside, and on the inside up to about 50%. Even worse are the innumerable cracks. The constant wind pressure, the removal of the windows on two occasions during the world wars, and the supersonic bangs of jet aircraft between 1955 and 1965, have broken almost every single piece of glass. Two to three cracks are the rule, but 20 or even up to 40 cracks in one piece are not infrequent. This means that one square metre of glass, which on average contains about 350 pieces, has broken into from 800 to over 1000 fragments. Added to this is the great amount of dirt that has accumulated as a result of the weathering. The product of this corrosion, the so-called 'belemnite', forms a 1–2 mm thick whitish layer on the outside of the glass, and this retains the dampness for a long time. Therefore it increases the absorption of dirt and dust, as well as of destructive chemicals of every sort, e.g. chloride, fluoride and, above all, sulphur dioxide. At the same time, the transparency of the windows is much reduced, so that some colours fade into an indefinable brown. Although most of the belemnite was removed from all the glass surfaces in 1948, there is a thick crust on most of the panes again now.

In the face of these devastating circumstances, all traditional methods of conservation were bound to fail. Until now, the ultimate method of saving windows consisted of putting an outer, protective layer of laminated glass or perspex outside, in front of the old glass panels hanging at a distance of 8–10 cm inside. But even this method is now impossible, for the single glass panels cannot be moved without suffering damage. The replacement of the original glass windows with copies, an excellent solution for small windows, cannot be considered here, because the museum accommodating the old glass would need to have the dimensions of Cologne Cathedral choir.

3. THE JACOBI METHOD

Professor Willy Weyres, Architect to the Cathedral 1944–1972, realized this long ago, and as early as 1953 he contacted Dr Richard Jacobi, as an expert in glass and plastics of the Deutsche Tafelglas AG in Fuerth, whose successful pioneering work in the field of safety-glass technology is sufficiently well known ('Sekurit'). As early as 1937 Jacobi had, for the first time, conserved a mediaeval stained-glass window in Naumburg with his newly developed method. Under his direction, this process was improved and further refined in Cologne Cathedral.

The principle is to embed the old piece of glass in a soft plastic mass, which is covered inside and outside with a thin piece of modern transparent glass. Simple as the idea is in itself, it is extremely difficult to put it into practice. There are, after all, over 3000 panels to conserve, that is about 1080 square metres of mediaeval glass, altogether approximately 380,000 separate pieces. Only a well-coordinated workshop with economical means of mass production is in a position to cope with such a task.

4. THE METHOD OF WORK

The glass panels are carefully removed from the mullions and tracery, superficially cleaned, and photographed both in colour and in black and white. An exact tracing on tracing paper is made, which serves as a documentary record of the conservation, and on which, as the work proceeds, all forms of treatment on every single piece of glass are recorded. Later on it is possible from this tracing to tell exactly, among other things, which cracks were glued, which gaps were filled in, and where bits of old or modern glass were used in the panel as replacements.

*Based on the original publications of Dr Richard Jacobi, 8470 Nabburg/Opf., Rotbühlring 70, West Germany.

Now the lead framework is cut away on the outside, so that the glass pieces can be separately removed and placed on a soft fibreboard support. For cleaning, no liquid of any sort is used. Dirt and dust and hard edges of putty are removed only by mechanical means. Loosened particles of black paint are fixed with a polymerisable silicone solution, which is applied with a pointed brush. Then the broken fragments, which once formed a single piece of glass in the original design, are provisionally fixed with cellulose tape. A paper stencil, made in accordance with the tracing, helps to reconstruct the original form and size of each piece of glass. For naturally very often the pieces have been broken off at the edges and corners, or have been shortened during earlier repairs in order to fit in a strap lead. These gaps and other missing bits of glass are filled with pulverized glass, larger holes are mended with fragments of mediaeval glass of a similar colour.

The adhesive, which is of an extremely thin flowing consistency, (a product specially developed by Farbwerk Hoechst), is then applied with a glass rod. Penetrating all the cracks through capillary attraction, the adhesive also saturates the pulverized glass. As soon as it has reached the consistency of wax, the surplus adhesive is removed with a razor-blade. In the drying cupboard, the glass pieces harden at a temperature of about 50°C. Now the projecting surplus edges of the pulverized glass, which has been used to replace the missing bits of glass, can be marked according to the paper stencil made from the tracing and worked away on the grinding wheel to the desired form.

5. MAKING THE MOULDS FOR CURVING THE COVERING PIECES OF GLASS

Two covering pieces exactly matching each of the two sides of the original piece of glass are now cut from a sheet of window glass, 1.3 mm thick. Since the surfaces of the old glass pieces are not even but undulating or even strongly warped, the surfaces of the covering pieces have to be bent to fit those of the old glass. To achieve this, several pieces of original glass — the number depending on their sizes — are laid next to one another and a very thin plastic foil is then spread over them. A thin iron ring, 2.5 cm high and about 20 cm in diameter, is now laid around the whole lot. Into the ring is poured a doughy mass of plaster and pounded fire-clay mixed in water, which hardens in a few hours. The resulting mould is then lifted off, and the foil removed from it. It is dried first in the air and then in the oven at a temperature of 200°C, so that it is freed from all moisture. Only a so-called 'overburnt' and granulated fire-clay must be used, since otherwise the moulds warp and no usable curvatures can be obtained. The impressions in the mould made by the old pieces of glass are scraped away about 1 mm at the edges, so that the covering pieces can fall freely into the mould during the bending process. In the kiln used for bending the glass, the covering pieces adapt themselves fully to the surface of the mould at a temperature of about 720°C. If the surface is badly warped, it may be necessary to assist the bending process with an iron rod.

6. JOINING THE COVERING PIECES TO THE ORIGINAL GLASS

Now the methacrylic acid methyl ester in powder form (plexi-powder) is dissolved with the necessary amount of softening agent (phthalic acid ester) in ethyl acetate. After evacuating the air from the liquid, a film, 0.4–0.5 mm thick, is cast, which must be dried until all of the solvent has evaporated. Independently of this, a liquid mixture of the same ingredients is made, which, when heated to a temperature of 80°C, produces the same film, so that any deviations in curvature can be equalized. Some plexi-liquid is now applied and then plexi-film of exactly matching size is mounted on each side of the original pieces of glass. After some more plexi-liquid has been applied over the film, the covering pieces of glass, matching in size and curvature the original pieces, are laid on top, first on one side and then on the other. This process requires considerable skill and there must be no air bubbles in the plexi-liquid. By means of tube clamps screwed on, this assembly is merely held together under very light pressure. Following this, it is heated to a temperature of 80°C in the drying cupboard. The method is so easy for a practised hand that it is possible (depending on their sizes) to join 50 to 130 pieces in one hour. After taking the lamination out of the drying cupboard, the clamps are removed and the assembled pieces left to cool. After one day, the surfaces and edges are cleaned with a razor-blade, and the lamination is now ready to be re-leaded. This is done in the usual way, though for sealing the edges only a glazier's putty completely free of solvent and preferably containing a minimum of pure linseed oil can be used.

7. ADVANTAGES AND DISADVANTAGES

The process described here offers the exposed stained glass paintings the best possible protection available through scientific research today. The ancient glass is protected from every contact with the corrosive outer air and is embedded in the soft, acrylic mass which is absolutely fast to light.

Without loss of the last remnants of patina, that is, the partial darkening of single glass pieces, the windows have been freed from dirt, which cannot now adhere to the smooth surfaces of the covering pieces of glass in such thick layers. The windows now glow again 'like jewels' in their old splendour.

However, the disadvantages cannot be ignored. The old leading cannot be re-used, since the laminated glass is much thicker. But the original leading is being carefully preserved. Then, the process is not suitable in the case of very small pieces of glass, that is, when they measure less than 1 cm across. Finally, the question of costs cannot be left out of account.

An important advantage in comparison with other methods of glass preservation must, however, be emphasized. If a better method of conservation should one day be developed, it is possible, without endangering the old glass or the paint in any way, to take the pieces apart again. This the workshop in Cologne has put into practice on several occasions. One could even restore the windows almost to their present state, since the old lead framework still exists.

However, to those responsible for the Cologne Cathedral workshop, no other method of conserving mediaeval stained glass is known which has been able to solve the special problems of saving the large areas of the high clerestory windows in the Cathedral choir: relatively large single pieces, 95% of which are still the original glass but all in a badly corroded state and with innumerable cracks.

There must still be a large number of precious mediaeval windows all over Europe with similar problems to those in Cologne. For many of them the Jacobi method of lamination should at least be considered.

REFERENCES

Jacobi, R., Ein neues Verfahren zur Erhaltung alter Glasmalereien, in 'Zeitschrift für angewandte Chemie', 1940, p. 452.

Jacobi, R., Ein neues Verfahren zur Erhaltung alter Glasmalereien, 'Deutsche Kunst und Denkmalpflege' 1 (1952), 50.

Rode, H., Zur Wiederherstellung der Obergadenfenster des Domchores, 'Kölner Domblatt' 8/9 (1954), 173.

Jacobi, R., Das Konservierungsverfahren für die Obergadenfenster des Kölner Domes, 'Kölner Domblatt' 10 (1955), 122-130 (with 12 illustrations).

Jacobi, R., Die Konservierung alter Glasmalereien, 'St Lucas' 11 (1957), 186-192 (with 22 illustrations).

Jacobi, R., Fehlurteile über die Restaurierung der Domfenster, Entgegnung auf einen Aufsatz von G. Frenzel, 'Kölner Domblatt' 18/19 (1960), 167-170.

Jacobi, R., Ein Konservierungsverfahren für mittelalterliche Glasfenster auf der Basis der modernen Sicherheitsglastechnik, 'Glas-Email-Keramo-Technik' 5 (1971), 172-174 (with 7 illustrations).

Jacobi, R., Zur Frage der Erhaltung alter Glasmalereien, 'Maltechnik/Restauro' (München), 2 (1973), (with 14 illustrations).

Wolff, A., Sicherheitsglastechnik rettet die Domfenster, 'Kölner Technische Mitteilungen' 11 (1974), 2-5 (with 16 illustrations). (German original of the present article).

Rode, H., Die mittelalterlichen Glasmalereien des Kölner Doms, in 'Corpus Vitrearum Medii Aevi', Vol.IV,1, Berlin 1974, 236 pp., 756 illus., 16 colour plates.

Figure 1.   Clerestory of Cologne Cathedral Choir. Light streams into the oldest part of the Cathedral through 1080 square metres of mediaeval stained glass.

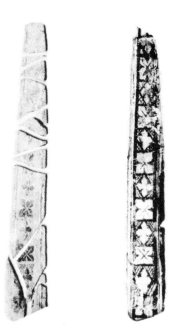

Figure 2.   A piece of mediaeval glass, broken into 13 fragments, before and after being glued together.

Figure 3.   Corrosion and conservation of a piece of mediaeval glass (section through the assembly).

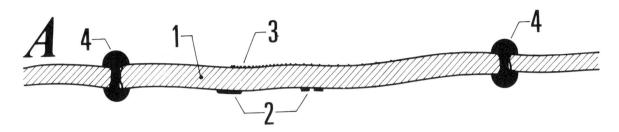

A. Mediaeval assembly, original condition: 1. piece of mediaeval glass; originally 4-6 mm thick; 2. painted contour on the interior; 3. painted shading on the exterior; 4. strip of lead.

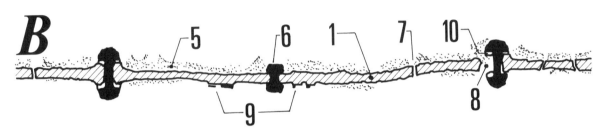

B. Mediaeval assembly today: 5. corroded glass and dirt; 6. strap-lead; 7. crack; 8. broken-away edge; 9. paint, loose or weathered away; 10. hardened putty.

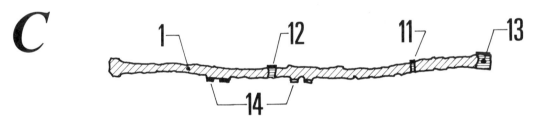

C. Piece of mediaeval glass removed from the lead framework and glued: 11. glued cracks overpainted with black; 12. gap left by the strap-lead, filled in and painted black; 13. broken-away edge restored with pulverized glass; 14. loosened paint on the glass, fixed, or repainted black over visible traces.

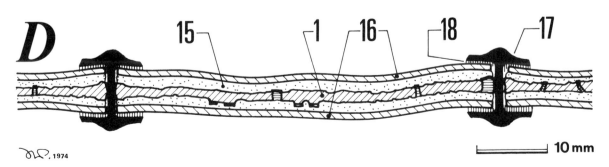

10 mm

D. Assembly after conservation: 15. soft acrylic film; 16. covering-pieces of modern glass, 1.3 mm thick, bent to correspond with the mediaeval glass; 17. modern strip of lead, 8-10 mm wide; 18. linseed-oil putty.

Figure 4.

Figure 4. The lead framework of a mediaeval panel with the head of a King, showing cracks (thin lines) and strap-leads (double lines). No modern replacements. The panel, measuring 82 x 58 cm, consisting originally of 121 pieces of glass, had broken into over 450 pieces.

Figure 5 and 6. Cologne Cathedral: head from one of the Windows of the Kings, dated about 1305-1310 (lead framework shown in Figure 4). Panel before and after restoration. Only soot and dirt have been removed in the cleaning process. The so-called patina — that is, the darkening of single pieces of glass through very old age — has been preserved, as the face and neck of the King show. Thanks to the absence of the strap-leads, the composition has been restored to its original clarity of form (see neck of the King).

Figure 5.

Figure 6.

CRIZZLING – A PROBLEM IN GLASS CONSERVATION

Robert H. Brill, The Corning Museum of Glass, Corning, N.Y. 14830, USA

1. INTRODUCTION

Crizzled glasses are familiar to all curators or collectors who have handled much early English or European glass, the word 'crizzled' being used to describe the appearance of certain glasses which have a diminished transparency owing to very fine surface crazing. A typical example is illustrated in Figure 1. Under the microscope, a network of fissures can be seen clearly on the surfaces of such glasses, as shown in Figure 2. On those glasses which are most severely afflicted, small bits of glass may have spalled away. The effect is the result of unstable chemical compositions which render the glasses susceptible to chemical attack by water, usually in the form of water adsorbed from the atmosphere.

Crizzling is most often associated with glasses made in the seventeenth and eighteenth centuries, but earlier examples may exist, and nineteenth century examples are by no means rare. The glasses come from rather widespread areas encompassing England, Western Europe (including Venice), Scandinavia, North America, and China. There are numerous pieces, which are known to have been crizzled for a long time, throughout all of the large collections dealing with glass of this period.

Crizzling is one variant of what has often been called 'sick glass' – a persistent, but not very precise term referring to various forms of surface deterioration. These range from a slightly cloudy or dulled appearance, to crizzling, to occasional occurrences of 'weeping glasses' or 'sweating glasses', which repeatedly generate slippery surface films or droplets if exposed to humid conditions. All are related in that they are manifestations of hydrolytic attack by atmospheric water, but we will be concerned here primarily with the crizzling phenomenon.

Perhaps the best known crizzled glasses are those made by George Ravenscroft, the English glassmaker credited with being the first to capitalize on the properties of lead glasses. During his early experimentation, Ravenscroft made some pieces which crizzled within a few months of manufacture, a deficiency which he quickly attempted to correct [1].

Several treatments have been suggested for crizzled glasses. Most of these involve impregnations with polymeric materials which consolidate the surface and restore transparency and a glassy reflectance. The first application of this type of treatment known to the author was that by Professor J. Arvid Hedvall of Uppsala University [2]. Actually, however, none of the treatments we have seen have yielded entirely satisfactory results. Because storage under proper conditions and careful handling seem to forestall further damage to already crizzled glasses, the outlook of The Corning Museum has been to postpone treatment until a completely safe and satisfactory treatment has been perfected. This is still our outlook as far as already crizzled glasses are concerned, since these objects seem to be stable for the present.

However, it has recently become known that there is a related and most urgent problem concerning crizzling [3]. There exists a category of glasses in early stages of crizzling, which have taken up water over the centuries but which do not exhibit very obvious signs of deterioration. Only when they are handled and turned around under correct lighting conditions can the telltale silvery rays of beginning crizzling be seen. These glasses are of the same general origins and dates as the already crizzled glasses. They have become hydrated and 'equilibrated' over the centuries with humid environments. When brought into centrally-heated galleries or apartments, they may be subjected abruptly to very dry conditions during the winter months. For example, in our galleries the relative humidity frequently drops into the 20 – 30% range during midwinter, and upon occasions has even fallen below 15% on extremely cold days. Under such conditions these hydrated glasses become dehydrated, and the crizzling fissures, which were not very evident to begin with, open up and propagate a network of hairline cracks across the surface. Thus, these glasses can become severely crizzled – and this may happen in the course of only a few months. We have observed one serious example of this effect in our museum and suspect that a half-dozen or so other objects have deteriorated to a less marked degree over the years. In addition, we have heard several reports of similar occurrences throughout North America, Europe, and Britain.

While most of the occurrences of this accelerating deterioration which have come to our attention involve vessel glasses, the author has examined one roundel of fifteenth century German glass (a glass bearing painting and silver-stained regions) which has developed an effect akin to crizzling over the past decade or so. Since it had hung adjacent to a heating register during that period, it seems very likely that a dehydration process was the cause of its accelerated deterioration.

By way of definition we have coined the term 'incipient crizzling', to describe this dangerous metastable state of deterioration. It designates glasses which are hydrated and in the initial stages of crizzling (the damage being apparent only under careful inspection) and which are susceptible to a rapid surface deterioration should they be exposed to dehydrating conditions. The object of the research which follows was to arrive at recommendations for the safe storage of glasses with incipient crizzling so as to prevent their disintegration into a severely crizzled state. We are less concerned for the moment with already crizzled or 'weeping' glasses.

Based mainly upon intuition and a few preliminary observations, we recommended earlier that glasses which show incipient crizzling should not be exposed to low relative humidities, that the temperature and humidity should be maintained at relatively constant levels, and that localized high temperatures, such as could result from installations with dramatic lighting, should be strictly avoided. Since then, some further progress has been made towards making firm suggestions as to safe exhibition and storage conditions based upon actual laboratory studies. The general approach to this research has been:

1. To obtain fundamental chemical information on susceptible glasses.

Table 1. Analyses of some crizzled glasses

		Venetian(?) c. 1709 colourless 457	Venetian(?) c. 1709 colourless 461	French c. 1750 colourless 449	French 1600-50 grayish 1050	French 1725-50 colourless 1498	Silesian* 1710-30 colourless 4011	American 1790-1810 colourless 1487	American 19th C. colourless 1488	American late 19th C. light blue 1630	Jamestown* 1971 green 1823
SiO_2	d/g	≈ 76	≈ 67	76.0	70.7	≈ 74	≈ 73.5	≈ 69	≈ 77	≈ 81	≈ 67
Na_2O	a	0.13	0.99	0.89	17.7	0.29	0.39	2.62	5.00	12.7	17.5
CaO	a	1.30	0.30	0.22	1.53	2.87	1.61	3.19	2.72	1.96	4.66
K_2O	a	18.7	18.4	18.7	3.42	19.9	16.6	24.2	12.7	2.24	6.82
MgO	a/s	0.04	0.06	≈ 0.1	≈ 0.1	0.22	0.03	0.20	0.32	0.12	0.10
Al_2O_3	a/s	0.1	0.05	≈ 0.5	≈ 0.5	1.95	1.03	0.55	1.51	0.44	2.61
Fe_2O_3	a/s	0.05	0.1	≈ 0.05	≈ 0.1	0.03	0.002	0.05	0.01	0.03	0.28
MnO	a/s	0.01	0.05	0.45	0.38	0.51	0.04	< 0.01	0.00X	0.00X	0.01
PbO	q/s	2.22	12.8	0.002	0.01	nf	5.88	< 0.01	nf	1.5	0.05
As_2O_5	q	1.66	0.24	--	--	--	--	--	≈ 0.5	0.2	--

Notes:

*All glasses except 1823 and 4011 are heavily crizzled. 1823 is hygroscopic but uncrizzled; 4011 shows incipient crizzling.

Analyses by R. H. Bell and C. A. Jedlicka of Lucius Pitkin, Inc., NYC, and P. B. Adams of Corning Glass Works.

a – atomic absorption.
q – quantitative, various methods.
s – emission spectrography.
g – gravimetry.
d – SiO_2 by difference.
≈ – denotes spectrography.
nf – sought but not found.

Also found in varying trace levels: TiO_2, CuO, CoO, Ag_2O, BaO, SrO, Li_2O, Rb_2O, B_2O_3, $ZrO_2 \cdot P_2O_5$ contents uncertain but generally less than 1.0%. Where no As_2O_5 given, values are uncertain but less than 1.0%.

2. To characterize the crizzling process physically and chemically.
3. To evaluate the chemical durability of the susceptible glasses relative to other types of glass.
4. To duplicate crizzling in the laboratory on both synthetic glasses and actual pieces of early glass.
5. To identify the primary factors controlling the chemical mechanism of crizzling. (Although it would be desirable to establish the details of the mechanism in the sense of a true reaction and kinetic study, this is not feasible just now.)
6. To arrive at recommendations as to how to prevent susceptible glasses, those showing incipient crizzling, from deteriorating into severe crizzling.

2. CHEMICAL COMPOSITIONS OF CRIZZLED GLASSES

It has generally been held that crizzling is caused by the attack of atmospheric water, possibly augmented by the uptake of carbon dioxide, and that the susceptibility of the glasses to hydrolysis is the result of a deficiency in lime, the most common stabilizer in glasses. While we also held that view — and still do — it seemed worthwhile to confirm it by chemical analyses. Therefore, chemical analyses were made of several early crizzled glasses, eight of which are reported in Table 1. To simplify the table, only major and minor constituents are reported. Data on trace elements have been excluded. Also included in the table are an example of a glass showing incipient crizzling (no. 4011) and one of a modern glass (no. 1823). Both of the latter were used in experiments aimed at duplicating crizzling in the laboratory. (Descriptions of the glasses analysed are given in the Appendix.)

For working within the system $Na_2O:CaO:SiO_2$ (soda-lime-silica glasses), a lime content of less than about 4% by weight would be regarded as very unstable by present-day standards. Even among ancient glasses, lime contents are ordinarily greater than 5.5–6.0%, and many of them are heavily weathered. It will be seen, however, that only two of the early glasses in Table 1 (nos. 1050 and 1630) are actually soda-lime glasses. The others are in the $K_2O:CaO:SiO_2$ system (potash-lime-silica glasses) or are glasses containing some lead (PbO). The minimum concentration of lime required to stabilize a potash glass may not be just the same as the 4% level cited above for the soda-lime glasses, but it is certainly not very different from that level.

It is quite apparent from the table that all of these glasses are indeed seriously deficient in lime and should be expected to be prone to hydrolysis. Only nos. 1487 and 1823 might be judged to have borderline lime contents and these both have such excessively high total alkali contents that they would also be expected to be very unstable. (A total alkali content of 20% or greater would not be tolerated by modern commercial standards, and ancient glasses with that much alkali are usually very heavily weathered.) Nos. 461 and 4011 are the only glasses of this group which really qualify as lead glasses, and while we have not yet completed our literature search on durabilities within the system $K_2O:PbO:SiO_2$, the potash levels are substantially greater than would be used in modern manufacture.

The explanation of the compositional imbalance of these glasses is of some interest to the historian of chemical technology. Whenever glassmaking is in an ascendency, the glassmaker seeks technological means for improving the quality of his wares. In attempting to make more nearly colourless glass, 'cristallo' in the case of Venice, it was recognized that the purification of raw materials would have a beneficial effect. When leaching and recrystallization processes were introduced for the purification of plant-ash alkalis, this would have had the effect of lowering the concentrations of calcium, magnesium, and aluminum in the resulting alkali, because these elements have a tendency to be present in less soluble chemical forms than the soda and/or potash. Consequently, when purified alkali was used for making glass, the resulting product would have been deficient in lime, magnesia, and alumina. Such glasses then would have unstable compositions until the glass technologists of the day became aware of this effect and compensated for it by adding additional lime in the form of some other ingredient. The net result in the interim would have been the production of purer and possibly more nearly colourless glass, which would have been susceptible to crizzling in the years to follow. There is ample evidence, in fact, that this is just what did happen in the descriptions of Neri regarding the purification of alkali as well as in the story of Ravenscroft's perfection of his lead-glass compositions [4]. We have under way some experiments with barilla plant ashes to verify this.

This effect would have been magnified if a greater percentage of alkali were used in the basic formulation, as might have been done in Venice in an effort to produce a glass with a longer working range, that is, a glass which would remain softened for a longer time and allow the glassmaker to perform the more elaborate manipulations required to make complicated decorative forms.

In connection with the chemical compositions, it is worth commenting upon a common misunderstanding. One often hears the remark that it is the pink glasses which tend to crizzle, and there are, indeed, a great many crizzled glasses which have a pronounced pinkish colour. However, this pink colour is confined to the crizzled surface of the glass and the objects were initially colourless. Since manganese was often used as a decolorant, or might even have been present in some of the plant ashes, many early glasses contained manganese. When these glasses are attacked by water and alkali is leached out, the structures are opened up and the manganese becomes oxidized, yielding a pink colour in the crizzled layer. That this is true has been verified by the fact that when a crizzled layer is removed from one of these pink objects, the remaining glass is perfectly colourless.

3. ELECTRON MICROPROBE ANALYSES

Electron microprobe analyses of five of the glasses appearing in Table 1 were carried out by W. T. Kane and T. W. Bierweiler of Corning Glass Works. The analyses were made on small samples of glass removed from each of the objects. The samples were mounted in cross-section so that both the crizzled layer and the unaffected glass were exposed for analysis. Individual analyses of both regions on all samples were made for silicon, sodium,

123

potassium, calcium, and lead (where present). Concentration maps for each element on each glass were obtained so that it is possible to see how the concentration of each element varies over an area including the glass, the crizzled layer, and their interface. The maps covered areas of about 100 x 25 μm. Profiles for each element were also constructed to see how their concentrations varied along a continuous path from the unaffected glass out through the crizzled layers. The concentration maps and profiles established the following points, to which are added our interpretations.

1. In the four glasses which were heavily crizzled (nos. 449, 461, 1050, and 1498) the sodium and potassium were very greatly depleted in the crizzled layer, indicating that these two elements had been thoroughly leached out of the glasses and probably removed to a large extent from the surface by washing in the past.

2. The silicon appears somewhat richer on a percentage basis in the crizzled layer than in the unaffected glass. The enrichment is the result of the depletion of the alkali, and it is likely that the total quantity of silica present was about the same before and after the crizzling attack took place.

3. The calcium and lead contents appear to have been unaffected by the leaching process because they, as within the silica, are less soluble than the alkalis. (It would have been difficult, however, to detect changes in the calcium level because the concentration was low to begin with.)

4. A void space could be detected in the four crizzled specimens which clearly marked the separation of the crizzled layer from the glass beneath. The analysts likened the appearance of the profiles to a 'step function', showing extensive depletion of the alkali outside the fissure in the crizzled layer. In two instances a second fissure was revealed beneath the crizzled layer, but this underlayer does not show complete depletion of alkali, only a tendency towards lower concentration. This indicates that the hydration and leaching reactions have proceeded onward into the glass beyond the first fissure separating the depleted layer from the glass. This serves as a reminder that we are dealing with a dynamic system, and that the process does not stop when a flake of crizzling products appears.

5. In a few places, highly localized concentrations of alkali showed up indicating that alkali had redeposited within the fissures. We believe we have also seen such deposits during microscopic examinations of various crizzled glasses. This would be the fate of alkali which had been exchanged by water but had never been washed off the glass during its history of human handling.

6. In sample no. 4011, a glass which showed only incipient crizzling, the alkalis have not been entirely removed from the glass, and the profile does not show the step-like appearance of the crizzled glasses. The alkali concentration shows a gradual depletion gradient sloping down from the unaffected glass to the surface. The profile has the character of a diffusion front. There is some evidence of the beginning of a fissure within the hydrolysing layer. (In anticipation of suggestions which might be prompted by the demonstrated presence of some alkali within this layer, we regard it as doubtful that the process could be reversed successfully and the glassy structure of the layer reconstituted by reintroducing alkali.)

7. The overall thicknesses of the reaction zones as seen through a light microscope measure between 45 and 100 μm, but the microprobe profiles yield additional information. From the spacing of the fissures in the profiles, the thicknesses of the separated layers (the crizzled layers) can be estimated. They range from 25 to 55 μm. In three of the four 'already crizzled' glasses, the layer which had separated is totally depleted in alkali. In the fourth glass, the front of the reaction zone is still within the crizzled layer, and the undersurface of the crizzled layer is quite rich in alkali. In the three instances where the reaction zone had advanced beyond the fissure separating the crizzled layer, the depletion/hydration fronts had penetrated between 40 and 80 μm from the 'original' surface. On the piece showing only incipient crizzling, the depletion/hydration front had penetrated 23 μm into the glass.

If one takes the thicknesses of the crizzled layers and ages of the glasses at face value, the hydration/alkali depletion rate of these five glasses averages out to about 0.3 μm per year. Compared to ancient glasses which are heavily weathered (those suitable for layer-counting), this is not as rapid a rate of hydration. The latter glasses hydrate at a rate of about 0.5—3.0 μm per year. However, lightly weathered ancient glasses, such as those showing iridescence, hydrate more slowly than the crizzled glasses. Iridescent Roman and Islamic glasses hydrate at a rate of only about 0.1 μm per year or less.

4. SYNTHETIC CORROSIBLE GLASSES

In order to learn more about the crizzling process a series of synthetic glasses was prepared. The compositions of the glasses, which are given in Table 2, were patterned like those obtained from the chemical analyses of four of the early glasses reported in Table 1. The glasses were prepared by A. A. Erickson of Corning Glass Works and his co-workers. The compositions given in Table 2 are theoretical values calculated from batch compositions, but chemical analyses of the glasses match them closely. These glasses were used for several types of experiments.

Table 2. Compositions of synthetic early glasses

| | Glasses susceptible to crizzling | | | | |
	XS	XT	XU	XV	PP
SiO_2	73.5	75.5	75.0	65.0	75.8
Na_2O	22.0	––	––	––	0.1
K_2O	––	20.0	20.0	20.0	18.7
CaO	2.0	2.0	1.0	1.0	1.30
MgO	1.0	1.0	––	––	––
Al_2O_3	1.0	1.0	1.0	1.0	0.2
PbO	––	––	3.0	13.0	2.25
MnO	0.5	0.5	––	––	––
As_2O_3	––	––	––	––	1.65
Prototype	1050 (French)	449 (French)	457 (Venetian)	461 (Venetian)	457 (Venetian)

Table 3 contains compositions of synthetic mediaeval stained glasses also prepared by Dr Erickson. There are seventeen such glasses in the table. Their prototypes were groups of glasses, analysed by the author, from York, Nürnberg, and the Zerek Camii [5]. Series were also prepared to test various compositional effects on properties related to durability and weathering characteristics. The glasses represent variations in concentrations of Na_2O/K_2O, P_2O_5, MgO, and CuO; the effects of colour on both stable and durable glasses; and the duplication of an extremely interesting group of lead-containing mediaeval glasses. Some of these glasses have been used by Mr Bettembourg* in his research. We have carried out weathering and durability tests on several of these synthetic stained glasses, but they will not be discussed here, since they are beyond the scope of this paper.

5. WEATHERING AND DURABILITY TESTS

Samples of the synthetic corrosible glasses (XS, XT, XU, and XV) were subjected to three types of testing. These were a miniature powder test, weathering cabinet exposure and autoclaving. All the testing was carried out by P. B. Adams, H. V. Walters, and M. L. Nelson of Corning Glass Works using their routine testing procedures.

Since the details of the individual tests are rather complicated, we shall only outline the procedures here, but further information can be obtained by writing to Mr Adams.** The powder test consists of a water treatment of powdered glass at 90°C for four hours. The weight of alkali extracted is then determined by chemical analysis. The weathering cabinet test consists of exposing small pieces of the glass to an environment of 98% relative humidity at 50°C, and making periodic inspections for surface damage, which is then expressed in a standard terminology. The autoclaving was carried out at 121°C, at 15 psi, for various lengths of time, with the glasses immersed in the liquid phase. Small polished plates of the glass were used for autoclaving. (Other variations of the conditions for the tests were also used for exploratory purposes.)

The first two tests were used for evaluation of the durabilities of the glasses. The conditions parallel standard glass-testing procedures, so the results can be used for comparison with more familiar types of glasses.

The autoclaving was undertaken to look for chemical cracking and for the investigation of hydration— dehydration effects. For the latter purpose, autoclaving served to introduce water into the glasses. Different samples of the glasses were then stored under different relative humidity conditions (at room temperature), to see what levels of relative humidity might successfully inhibit the dehydration which produces crizzling. (As will be shown below, this hydration—dehydration treatment produces a kind of deterioration which is indistinguishable from the crizzling seen on actual early glasses.) The results of the tests are summarized in Table 4.

Some of the findings of the tests are listed below, accompanied by our interpretations.
1. In the powder test, glasses XS and XU, the soda glass and the potash glass with the light lead concentration, showed very poor resistance to hydrolysis. Glass XV, the more heavily-leaded glass, shows a considerably better resistance; and XT, the potash-lime glass, is still better. In fact, the durability of XT approaches that of some of the poorer present-day commercial glasses. It is somewhat surprising that XT holds up as well as it does, but it indicates that the addition of even the small increment of CaO (from 1.0 to 2.0%) over XV brings about a marked increase in stability. In comparing the durabilities of XS and XT, it should be noted that although the concentrations of soda and potash are not very different on a weight-percentage basis, in terms of mole percent the alkali content of the potash glass is markedly less (13.7% vs. 21.5%). This undoubtedly accounts for much of its increased durability. The glasses appear to rank as follows, in order of increasing durability: (very poor) XS ≈ XU ≪ XV < XT (fairly stable).
2. In the weathering cabinet exposures, XS was by far the poorest, and XT again the best. While some commercial bulb glasses do not fare much better than XS in this test, container glasses are much more durable. The glasses appear to rank as follows in order of increasing durability: (very poor) XS < XU < XV < XT (fairly stable).

*Laboratoire de Recherches des Monuments Historiques, Château de Champs/Marne, France.
**Corning Glass Works, Corning, NY 14830, USA.

Table 3. Compositions of synthetic stained glasses

	QQ	QR	QS	RC	RD	RE	RF	VS	VW	VX	VY	VZ	FE	FF	FG	FH	FI
SiO_2	58.5	55.5	66.0	60.0	54.0	48.0	48.0	63.0	63.0	56.7	56.7	56.7	50.0	48.4	63.0	61.0	69.5
K_2O	8.5	18.5	1.5	20.0	18.0	16.0	16.0	18.0	—	16.2	16.2	16.2	17.0	16.4	12.5	12.0	1.5
Na_2O	3.0	0.5	14.0	—	—	—	—	—	18.0	—	—	—	3.0	2.9	1.5	1.5	14.0
CaO	16.0	19.0	10.0	20.0	18.0	16.0	16.0	18.0	18.0	16.2	16.2	16.2	16.0	15.4	12.0	11.6	12.0
MgO	7.0	2.5	1.4	—	—	—	—	—	—	—	10.0	—	7.0	6.9	4.0	3.9	—
Al_2O_3	1.0	1.0	2.0	—	—	—	—	—	—	—	—	—	1.5	1.5	1.5	1.5	1.5
P_2O_5	4.0	1.0	—	—	—	—	—	—	—	10.0	—	—	4.0	3.9	4.0	3.9	—
Fe_2O_3	1.0	1.0	1.0	—	—	—	—	1.0	1.0	0.9	0.9	0.9	0.5	0.5	0.5	0.5	0.5
MnO	1.0	1.0	1.0	—	—	—	—	—	—	—	—	—	1.0	1.0	1.0	1.0	1.0
CuO	—	—	3.0	—	—	—	3.0	—	—	—	—	10.0	—	3.0	—	3.0	—
CoO	—	—	0.1	—	—	—	—	—	—	—	—	—	—	0.1	—	0.1	—
PbO	—	—	—	—	10.0	20.0	17.0	—	—	—	—	—	—	—	—	—	—
Prototype	York	Nürn-berg	Zerek Camii	K_2O base glass	PbO effect	PbO effect	PbO effect	K_2O base glass	Na_2O-K_2O subst.	P_2O_5 effect	MgO effect	CuO effect	Un-stable	Un-stable, blue	Durable	Durable, blue	Na_2O-K_2O subst.

126

3. The autoclaving produced chemical cracking [6] in XS even after only short durations. XU and XV developed a surface haziness, while XT showed no apparent change. The glasses appear to rank as follows, in order of increasing durability: (very poor) XS < XU < XV ≪ XT (apparently stable).

Table 4. Results of durability tests

	XS	XT	XU	XV
Powder test*				
Alkali extracted				
(Wt −% of glass)				
Na_2O	0.48	––	––	––
K_2O	––	0.057	0.71	0.16
Alkali extracted				
(Mmole/100 g glass)				
Na_2O	7.7	––	––	––
K_2O	––	0.61	7.5	1.7
Weathering cabinet exposure**				
Time required to breakdown	2 wks	8 wks	4 wks	6 wks
Chemical cracking***				
Days required	1	none occurs	≈8	≈15

* Sample wt ≈1 gram, adjusted to constant surface area from density;
   −40 to +50 mesh; 5 ml H_2O. Run for 4 hours at $90°C$.
** 98% RH, $50°C$. Breakdown = Obvious damage under inspection without magnification.
*** 2.5 x 2.5 x 0.1 cm polished plates in 285 ml H_2O, $95°C$, 15 psi, for varying times.

6. INFRARED ANALYSES

Infrared reflectance and transmission spectra were taken for several samples of autoclaved glasses and their untreated counterparts. The spectra were run by H. Hoover and B. Butler of Corning Glass Works.

Reflectance spectra in the 8-12 μm region established clearly that the autoclaved glasses had been depleted in alkali because they showed a sharper reflectance peak than the anhydrous glasses. The shift indicates less disturbance of the Si—O—Si bonds by alkali or other modifiers. It is noteworthy that this was true even of the glass XT, which showed no visible evidence of alteration after the autoclaving.

Infrared transmission spectra in the 2-5 μm region indicated the presence of large quantities of beta-hydroxyls, or loosely-bound water. A sample of glass XV which had been hydrated through autoclaving was crizzled by heating it to $135°C$ for 1½ hours. A spectrum of the crizzled glass fell in between the spectra for the hydrated glass and an anhydrous control, indicating that although a significant amount of the beta-hydroxyl was removed, a significant amount still remained after the crizzling was induced.

Infrared spectra of an autoclaved sample of XV (30 minutes at $121°C$) were taken progressively as the hydrated surfaces were polished away. By this means it was possible to estimate that this particular hydration process had hydrated this glass to a depth of approximately 20 μm, somewhat less than the thicknesses of the crizzled layer on early glasses.

Further infrared work is being conducted in an attempt to identify the different states of binding of water within the hydrated glasses [7].

7. HYDRATION—DEHYDRATION EXPERIMENTS

Several experiments have been carried out with a view to duplicating crizzling in the laboratory. Among these were preliminary experiments which demonstrated that by heating certain types of actual historic glasses (but not all types) to temperatures between $100°$ and $150°C$, severe surface crizzling can be produced. These glasses were of diverse origins, including Roman glass from Karanis, some specimens of mediaeval stained glasses and eighteenth century vessel fragments. Other investigators have had similar experiences [8]. With this in mind, several pieces of synthetic glasses having corrosible compositions were held over water or immersed in water at $85°C$ for varying times and then dehydrated. It was found that the dehydration could be accomplished either by warming the glass to $50-65°C$ or by placing it in a desiccator. By various combinations of experimental conditions, several such glasses developed surface crizzling identical to that observed on early objects of crizzled glass. It might be added that some of the synthetic mediaeval stained glasses behaved similarly under these treatments.

We next set out to determine what levels of relative humidity, at room temperature, would inhibit the dehydration of hydrated glasses so as to arrest the development of crizzling. Experiments were carried out with the four synthetic glasses XS, XT, XU, and XV. In addition, two actual early objects were sacrificed for this experiment. These experiments were carried out by M. L. Nelson and H. V. Walters. A similar series of experiments was conducted by the author in the Museum.

Small polished plates of the four synthetic glasses were hydrated by autoclaving at 121°C and 15 psi with total immersion in water. Various autoclaving times were used. After drying in air, the hydrated glasses were placed in glass chambers (actually desiccator jars) which maintained constant internal relative humidities established by saturated salt solutions in the bottoms of the chambers. The relative humidities were monitored with an electric hygrometer. The humidities were: 1%, 25-30% (ambient laboratory conditions), 40%, 72%, and 100%. (The samples in the 100% chamber soon became covered with droplets of condensed water.) Although the samples selected for the experiment were autoclaved for different times, all were similar in that after the autoclaving they showed no surface damage detectable by the unaided eye. After varying intervals of time, extending from a few days up to several weeks, many of the glasses developed crizzling. At the time of writing (March 1975), some samples still have not crizzled. The results are summarized in Table 5. .

Table 5. Effect of storage conditions on hydrated glasses

Glass	Percentage of glasses which ultimately crizzled*				
	1%RH	25-35%RH	40%RH	72%RH	100%RH
XS	100%	17%**	0	0	0
XT	100	40	40	0	0
XU	100	100	100***	50***	0
XV	100	100	12	0	0
% crizzled irrespective of composition	100%	65	38	12	0

Duration of experiment to date: 11 Sept. 1974 — 17 Jan. 1975
Total number of samples used: ≈110

* The times required to develop crizzling varied widely. Some samples crizzled within a few days, others required several weeks.
** Of the balance, they might not all have been hydrated.
*** Hydration might have been excessive.

Glass	Some other experiments	
	Treatments	Results
XS	1. Imm. water, 85°C, 78 hrs	Little surface change
	2. Storage at: 0%RH	Crizz. after few days
	31%	No change after 35 mos.
	75%	No change after 35 mos.
	100%	No change after 35 mos.
	3. Storage at: 0%	All show crizz. after 9 hrs
XS, XT, XU, XV	1. Imm. water, rm temp., 35 mos.	XS, XU — Incip. crizz.
		XT, XV — No change
	2. Storage at: 0%RH	XS, XU, XV — Crizz. after 9 hrs
		XT — Start crizz.(?) after 2 wks
1823	1. Imm. water, rm temp., 35 mos.	No change
	2. Storage at: 0%RH	Start crizz. after 90 min.
		Crizz. after 16 hrs
	12%RH	Start crizz.(?) after 2 wks
1823	1. Storage at: 100%RH	
	Rm temp., 35 mos.	No change
	2. Second storage at: 0%	Crizz. after 16 hrs
4011	1. No laboratory hydration	
	2. Storage at: 0%RH	Crizz. within 24 hrs
	12%	Start crizz.(?) after about 4 wks
	21%, 34%, 52%,	
	70%, 100%	No change yet after 11 wks

A similar set of hydration — dehydration experiments was started in 1971, but most of the apparatus, glasses and records were destroyed in the flood which struck the Museum in June 1972. Fortunately, there were some survivals which now show interesting results. Samples of glass XS were hydrated by immersion in water at 85°C for 78 hours. The samples showed little change after the hydration step. They were then stored for eleven days at humidities of 0%, 31%, 75%, and 100%. The piece stored at near-zero percent crizzled severely; the others did not show much change. They were left in the same chambers for 35 months and little further damage occurred. They were then transferred to a near-zero humidity chamber and within nine hours all developed crizzling.

In another experiment, pieces of glasses XS, XT, XU, and XV were given no high temperature hydration, but just left to hydrate in distilled water at room temperature for 35 months. XS and XU developed some chemical cracking and incipient crizzling, respectively; but XT and XV showed no surface alteration at all. However, when placed in a near-zero humidity, all except XT developed severe crizzling within nine hours. (XT again proved to be surprisingly durable, as it did in certain other experiments.)

The experiments carried out on the two early glasses, nos. 1823 and 4011, offer a different approach to the problem and avoid the difficulties posed by the use of autoclaving to hydrate the glasses.

Glass no. 4011 is an engraved Silesian goblet made in about 1710-30. The piece shows typical incipient crizzling (Figure 3). The foot of the goblet had been broken in the distant past, and the piece was not considered to be of outstanding historical importance. Therefore, Mr Jerome Strauss, who owned the object for some years, donated it to the Museum for use in our experiments, feeling that the information to be gained from sacrificing parts of the glass would prove to be more valuable than the glass itself. Samples were sawed from the rim above the engraving. They were carefully photographed under reproducible lighting conditions, and photomicrographs were taken to record the original state of the incipient crizzling. One small piece was used for chemical analysis, and several of the others were placed in chambers for storage at known humidities.

Once again the humidities of the chambers were controlled by saturated salt solutions, except for a desiccating chamber employing silica gel for a near-zero humidity, and one containing distilled water for 100% humidity. No attempt was made to control the temperature. Instead, ambient room temperatures prevailed. The humidities, as measured with an electric hygrometer, are: ≈0%, 12%, 21%, 34%, 52%, 70%, and 100%.

It was found that the piece of object no. 4011 placed in the chamber at near-zero humidity became severely crizzled within 24 hours (Figures 4 and 5). The piece in the chamber at 12% seems to have begun to show signs of developing crizzling at the time of writing, which corresponds to an elapsed time of about four weeks at 12%. None of the samples at other humidities have changed.

Glass no. 1823 is a small green bottle made in 1971 at the Jamestown, Virginia, factory. It was sent to the author for examination because it developed a slippery surface feeling shortly after manufacture. After a chemical analysis showed an excessive alkali content to be the cause, parts of this bottle were also sacrificed for hydration—dehydration experimentation. Fragments were stored for four months at ambient conditions in Corning and then stored in a 100% humidity chamber for 35 months. Another fragment of the same glass was immersed in distilled water for 35 months. Neither glass showed any visible signs of surface deterioration at the end of these hydration steps. Samples of these same fragments were then placed in a near-zero humidity chamber, and others in a 12% chamber. Within 90 minutes of being placed in the near-zero chamber, the samples showed beginning stages of crizzling. They were left overnight in the chamber and had become severely crizzled by the next morning after a total of 16 hours at near-zero humidity. One of the samples in the 12% chamber appears to be developing slight crizzling after about two weeks, at the time of writing.

It is conceded that the logic which is about to be followed is weakened by a few significant defects, but even with these in mind it is worth pursuing. In some of the experiments outlined above, the hydration conditions were chosen arbitrarily and were not always the same for each glass, so care must be exercised in comparing the behaviour of one glass with another. Moreover, the autoclaving used to hydrate the glasses was a rather drastic treatment. It can be argued that the hydrated state induced by autoclaving might not be the same as that brought about by the slower 'natural' hydration produced by the action of atmospheric water vapour over centuries at room temperature. But nonetheless, these are the only data we have, and in effect this same defect marks the interpretation of any accelerated ageing test, so it is familiar to all conservators.

From the results in the first part of Table 5, it could be concluded that hydrated glasses of this type will crizzle rapidly if stored at near-zero humidity, but will not dehydrate (not rapidly) at humidities of about 70% or greater. In the range of 25-40%, many such glasses will crizzle; between about 40-70%, some glasses will crizzle.

The findings presented in the second part of Table 5 represent longer term experiments and different hydration processes, some of which eliminate the onus of accelerated ageing. From the results of these experiments, it can be inferred that glasses hydrated by exposure either to hot water for short times or to cool water for a matter of years will retain their moisture for long periods when stored at humidities between 30-100%, but that they rapidly give up that moisture and become severely crizzled if transferred to a near-zero humidity environment.

The experiment most closely simulating actual museum conditions, that involving the Silesian goblet, demonstrated unequivocally that storage of a glass showing incipient crizzling at a near-zero humidity will provoke severe crizzling within a matter of hours. The data on the Jamestown glass substantiate this finding. It remains to be seen whether relatively rapid crizzling can also develop on susceptible glasses in the range of about 25-40% relative humidity, and we have set up long-term experiments to answer this question.

8. STORAGE CONDITIONS AND CASE DESIGN

From all of the foregoing, it is apparent that dehydration is the cause of the advancement of incipient crizzling into full crizzling, and it is obvious that very low humidity conditions must be avoided if susceptible glasses are to be protected. The next point to be established is just what constitutes an optimum range for safe storage.

It is somewhat disquieting that dehydration occurs at relative humidities as high as 40-60% and that only levels of 70% or greater appear to hold hydration water in the experimental glasses. It is likely, however, that this is because the water had been driven into the glasses under rather drastic conditions. It is doubtful that early glasses with incipient crizzling dehydrate significantly in the 40-60% range. After all, such glasses must already have spent much of their existence in humidities within that range and have not gone over to full crizzling. We are prepared to assume, then, that the 40-60% range is safe.

Storage at very high humidities with a view towards keeping water in might then accelerate the hydration of the glasses and contribute to their ultimate deterioration, to say nothing of the impracticalities posed by possible mould growth, condensation, etc. We conclude, therefore, that from the viewpoint of protection against dehydration:

1. The 70-100% range is unnecessarily high and undesirable.
2. The 40-60% range is safe.
3. The 25-40% range remains open to question and should be studied in terms of years-long storage experiments on actual early glasses.
4. The 0-25% range is dangerous, in fact very dangerous at the lower end.

The situation, then, can be reduced to questioning whether there is anything else that can go wrong in the 40-60% range.

In 1959 Organ and Bimson [9] dealt with a related — but not identical — problem to that being discussed here. They recommended that for safe storage unstable glasses should be kept dry, specifying that by dry they meant at a relative humidity below 42%. The reasoning was that at humidities below 42%, potassium carbonate (the ultimate form of alkali leached out of potassium glasses) is not hygroscopic. This reasoning is certainly sound for the types of glasses they were considering, that is, 'weeping' or 'sweating' glasses, and the validity of their recommendation seems to have been borne out by actual experience. In the intervening years, large numbers of 'weeping' glasses from the collections of the British Museum were stored in cases where the humidity was kept at or below 42%. In a recent visit to the British Museum, the author accompanied Ms Bimson and Mr Hugh Tait on an inspection of the glass involved. It was found that few of the glasses in the cases had the slipperiness to touch which characterizes 'weeping' glasses. (Those examples which were found to be somewhat slippery were Venetian glasses which might have been soda glasses instead of potash glasses.)

A troublesome question then arises as to whether the dehydration rate of glasses with incipient crizzling might become fast enough to provoke full crizzling if they are stored at humidities below 42%; or, indeed, could the same thing happen to 'weeping' glasses? It is probably artificial to treat these as two entirely different kinds of glasses. Mr Tait and Ms Bimson did not recognize among the glasses in the British Museum cases any which they could say had become more deteriorated during the years of storage in those cases. However, since so many glasses were involved, and since no photographic records of the original states of the objects were at hand, it could not be determined with certainty whether or not any of these glasses had become more crizzled.

With this in mind, we can turn to the practical problem faced by The Corning Museum of Glass, the protection of glasses which show incipient crizzling. There are perhaps 50 such objects in our collections. Our primary object is to arrest any further deterioration brought on by dehydration and, if possible, to minimize the continued uptake of moisture. (It is recognized that improving storage conditions will not correct the damage already inflicted upon the glass.) Ideally, one would assume the safest condition to be a humidity level where a steady state could be established under which neither the hydration nor dehydration reactions would progress. Since it is not likely that we could now arrive at a single level which would satisfy steady-state conditions for so many different glasses, we have elected to err on the side of hydration, feeling that this offers less hazard to the glasses than dehydration. It might further be guessed that, to ensure that dehydration will not occur, the humidity should be in approximately the range to which the glasses had become accustomed in their early histories.

For these reasons, we have decided to aim initially for case control at the 45-55% relative humidity range, with provisions for sufficient adaptability to allow the humidity level to be shifted somewhat in either direction. (For example, if persistent slipperiness developed upon the surfaces, we might want to drop slightly below the 42% level.)

A committee of conservators was convened to offer advice on our system design and case construction. The committee consists of Robert Feller, Lawrence Majewski, Susanne Sack, and Nathan Stolow. The designs have not yet been completed, but several pivotal decisions have been made. The resultant system contains three main components: the cases, controlling devices, and a regenerating unit.

The cases themselves will be sealed, with access through one door. One face, at least, will be glass or plexiglas for exhibition purposes. Proper gasketing will be very important. The case will contain some humidity-buffering material to offset variation caused by changes in temperature. Since the temperature of our galleries can be controlled, no special temperature control will be introduced in the cases.

Special care will be given to lighting the cases. The lighting will be external and properly situated so as not to cause a heat build-up, and infrared absorbing shields will be used. The deleterious effects of spotlighting objects for dramatic exhibition are appreciated by conservators but not by all curators or collectors. The effects of heat build-up can be very serious on certain types of glass, for example, glasses with incipient crizzling, painted surfaces, or weathering products. In an experiment conducted in our museum, flat plates of glass were placed on a wooden pedestal painted black and lit with two 12-volt automobile lamps at a distance of about one metre. The temperatures of the glasses were measured by thermistor probes placed in hollowed-out depressions in the glasses. At one point within a piece of glass, a temperature of $67°C$ was measured. Temperatures of this level could seriously endanger glasses of the sorts mentioned and should never be tolerated.

The cases will be connected to controlling units containing trays of silica gel which will have been equilibrated previously to the target relative humidity, perhaps 45% to start with. It was decided that silica gel would be used as the controlling medium because of its inertness, low sensitivity to temperature change, regenerative qualities, and adaptability to different levels of humidity control. Circulating devices with proper safety controls will be used to assure adequate circulation between the control units and the cases. A remote recording thermohygrograph will monitor the relative humidity and temperature through sensing probes. A separate re-equilibrating unit in our workroom will be used to regenerate the silica gel as required.

It is expected that, if the sealants are good and the cases are not opened frequently, the system will remain stable for some months at a time. One of our major goals is to install a system which will operate with a minimum of maintenance and will be as free as possible of annoyances caused by failures of mechanical or electrical parts. For this reason, which may appear paradoxical to some readers, the Museum has elected not to install a fully-automated system. Our belief is that the more elaborate a system becomes mechanically, the more things there are to go wrong.

It is hoped that, through proper design and construction of these cases, our glass with incipient crizzling will be safely preserved throughout the coming years while we attempt to devise treatments which will restore chemical stability to these glasses, instead of just maintaining a delicately-balanced metastable state.

ACKNOWLEDGEMENTS

The author thanks all of the persons cited in the text for their contributions of experimental work. In particular, P. B. Adams, H. V. Walters, and M. L. Nelson have devoted much time to the planning of the work and interpretation of results. Special thanks are due to those who donated glasses which could be used in our experiments. D. P. Lanmon, Curator of European Glass at The Corning Museum of Glass, and P. N. Perrot and K. M. Wilson, both formerly of the Museum, are especially thanked for their concern and assistance over the course of several years. This research was partially funded by a grant from the National Endowment for the Arts.

REFERENCES

1. There are numerous accounts of Ravenscroft's early experimentation. One is: Hartshorne, A., 'Antique Drinking Glasses', Brussel and Brussel, New York, 1968, pp.240-241. The term 'crizzle' was applied to glasses as early as Ravenscroft's time. The common usage of the word was to describe roughening of surfaces, or the crackling of sunburnt skin on the face or hands, an apt parallel to the appearance of these glasses.
2. Hedvall, J. A., Jagitsch, R. and Olson, G., Uber das Problem der Zer-Störung antiker Gläser, 'Transactions of Chalmers University of Technology' No.118, Gothenburg, Sweden, 1951. We are not attempting here to compile a complete bibliography on this subject.
3. Brill, R. H., The scientific investigation of ancient glasses, in 'Proceedings of the Eighth International Congress on Glass', London, 1968, pp.47-68; Incipient crizzling in some early glasses, 'Bulletin of the American Group of the International Institute for Conservation of Historic and Artistic Works', 12 (1972).
4. There are many editions of Antonio Neri's 'L'Art Vetraria'. The first edition was printed in Florence in 1612; the first English translation, by Merrit, was in 1662. R. M. Organ has also described this chemical effect [9].
5. Brill, R. H., Scientific studies of stained glass, 'Journal of Glass Studies', 12 (1970), 185-192.
6. Adams, P. B., Crack propagation of annealed glass during exposure to water, in 'Tenth International Congress on Glass', No. 11, The Ceramic Society of Japan, Kyoto, 1974, pp.16-23.
7. Other experiments have also been attempted or are as yet incomplete, so they are not discussed here. These include various approaches to determining water contents, and electron microscopy.
8. Bimson, M. and Werner, A. E., The danger of heating glass objects, 'Journal of Glass Studies', 6 (1964), pp.148-150.
9. Bimson, M. and Organ, R. M., The safe storage of unstable glass, 'Museum News', 46 (1968), pp.39-47.

449   Wineglass, French, c. 1750.
Colourless glass, pink surface, heavily crizzled.

457   Beaker, Venetian(?), c. 1709.
Colourless glass, heavily crizzled.
Donated by Gudmund Boesen; Rosenborg Collection, Inv. no. 109.

461   Cut pendant from candelabrum, Venetian(?), c. 1709.
Colourless glass, heavily crizzled.
Donated by Gudmund Boesen; Rosenborg Collection, Inv. no. 27-43.

1050 Wineglass, French, 1600-50.
Grayish glass, heavily crizzled.
Donated by William J. Young.

1487 Pane in bookcase, American, 1790-1810.
Colourless glass, heavily crizzled.
Donated by Dwight Lanmon.

1488 Pane from frame of painting, American, nineteenth century.
Colourless glass, heavily crizzled.
Donated by the Henry Francis duPont Winterthur Museum.

1498 Wineglass, French, 1725-50.
Colourless glass, pink surface, heavily crizzled.
Donated by the Henry Francis duPont Winterthur Museum.
(Figure 1 in text.)

1630 Rim fragment, petal and loop design, American, late nineteenth century.
Light blue, heavily crizzled.

1823 Reproduction of early bottle, Jamestown, Virginia, 1971.
Green glass, 'weeping'.
Donated by James Haskett.

4011 Engraved goblet, Silesian, 1710-30.
Colourless glass, incipient crizzling.
Donated by Jerome Strauss. (His no. S538)
(Figures 3, 4, and 5 in text.)

Figure 1.	Typical example of early crizzled glass. French, 1725-50, no. 1498 in this study.

Figure 2.	Photomicrograph of surface of wineglass in Figure 1. Magnification approx. 6X.

Figure 1.

Figure 2.

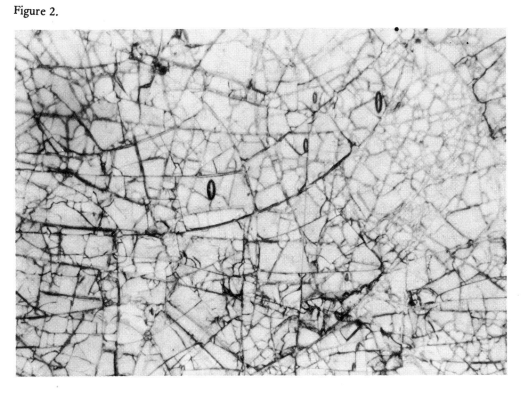

Figure 3.

Figure 3. Typical example of glass with incipient crizzlin Silesian, 1710-30, no. 4011 in this study. Donated by Mr Jerome Strauss for experimentation.

Figure 4. Rim sample of glass in Figure 3. No hydration treatment. Traces of incipient crizzling can be seen along lower left edge.

Figure 5. Same sample as in Figure 4. Severe crizzling wa produced by room-temperature storage at near zero RH within 24 hours.

Figure 4.

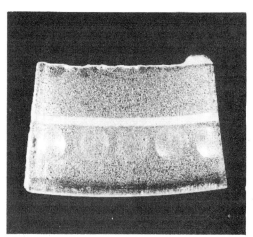

Figure 5.

REACTION MECHANISMS OF CORROSION OF MEDIAEVAL GLASS

J. C. Ferrazzini, Kristallographisches Institut der ETH, Sonneggstrasse 5, CH-8006 Zurich, Switzerland

Under normal conditions in equilibrium with the environment, corrosion of glass only happens if the thermodynamic conditions for the occurrence of a chemical reaction on the surface are met. Mediaeval methods of glass manufacture were primitive in comparison with today's technology. In some cases, the glass was badly melted at a low temperature, often with imperfections such as cords, and also burned-in surface impurities such as ashes and grains of sand. During the centuries, additional defects of physical origin will have occurred on the surface in the form of scratches, fractures, cracks, etc. These heterogeneous regions of chemical, technical or physical origin are more susceptible to attack by weathering than a homogeneous glass surface, because these zones are thermodynamically different. The effect of these zones may only penetrate to a few layers of atoms. Although the attack always starts at a specific location, we are not in a position to recognize it in advance with our present analytical methods. Therefore we can only study the corrosion as it appears.

On the other hand, deeper layers of the glass surface have also to be taken into consideration. It is most important to investigate the structural modifications of the glass with increasing depth, because any physical destruction of the glass lays bare material from the interior of the body. In his dissertation at the Technical University of Berlin (1973), R. Corbach published the concentration profiles of the alkali ions in glass. If a glass is heated thoroughly during a technologically normal process, it shows a reduction of the alkali ions and an increase of water in the combined and molecular state towards its surface. The concentration profiles stabilize at a depth of 7 to 10 μm at a value corresponding to the effective composition of the glass. A natural protective coating prevents an exchange reaction between protons from the environment and alkali ions of the glass in such a way that the initial step of the corrosion reaction cannot take place. The more thoroughly the glass is heated, the more effective is this protective skin. Different thermal treatments on mediaeval glass carried out at our own laboratory at temperatures of about 400°C to 900°C, followed by quick cooling to room temperature, noticeably diminished the concentration of alkali in the covering layers. In addition, scratches and small fissures could be removed by melting in this process. The application of even higher temperatures cannot be recommended; diffusion in the melt becomes so fast that the ions evaporated from the surface can be immediately substituted from the interior. Therefore there is an insufficient concentration gradient towards the surface and the glass lacks the natural protective coating. Consequently such a glass is more susceptible to corrosion.

The question arises as to what sort of reaction the alkali ions engender. It has to be considered that sulphur oxides are very soluble in water and form acids. The protons of these acids can easily enter into an exchange reaction with the alkali ions of the glass. The protons enter into the glass and replace the escaped metal ions. This process is intensified by rain and condensation water which wash away the metal ions or their compounds from the surface. Since sulphur oxides are constantly present in the atmosphere, their concentration can be used as a constant in the reaction equation and the equilibrium can be influenced in favour of the exchange reaction. The alkali ions escaping from the glass quickly react to form sulphates.

The replacement of alkali ions by protons facilitates the diffusion of larger ions in the glass (the 'tunnel effect'). Therefore the calcium ions are able to escape and to react with the sulphates or with the sulphur oxides present. The main products of these reactions are syngenite and gypsum, which form the deposits which are known as 'weathering crusts'. Below and partly within these, there remains a loose, porous lattice of silica with bad mechanical properties.

Water plays an important role in the corrosion reactions. This knowledge is extremely important in considering the possible inhibition of corrosion. The destruction of mediaeval glass by the sulphur oxides of the environment can be stopped by keeping the water of the surrounding atmosphere below a critical level. For reaction temperatures between 0°C and 30°C this value lies at 60% relative humidity. Several experiments are in progress to find the best method of controlling humidity. In one method, an outer protective glass is used. The air between this glass and the stained glass is heated to keep the relative humidity at a tolerable level. Resistance heaters, like the defrosters in motorcars, are being used for this purpose.

The question is continually raised as to whether radical cleaning methods will influence corrosion. By radical cleaning is meant the use of air abrasive tools, cleaning with hard brushes with metal bristles, grinding and polishing of surfaces, etc. Theoretical studies and laboratory tests have shown that the total removal of old corrosion layers, involving damage of the natural protective surface, will encourage and even accelerate a new phase of weathering. The whole phenomenon of corrosion depends on diffusion processes. Whenever the active ions of the surface are exposed through improper cleaning, diffusion of the ions through the glass is no longer inhibited. Restorers applying such cleaning methods should consider that they are killing the glass. They not only seriously damage the natural protective coat of stained glass but remove most of the whole skin. A conscientious restorer only removes loose and porous weathering products from the surface. He never indiscriminately removes compact, patently genuine, glass layers as is to be expected using radical cleaning methods.

ETUDE DE MASTICS ELASTOMERES – LE MASTICAGE
DES PANNEAUX DE VITRAUX ANCIENS

J. M. Bettembourg, Laboratoire de Recherche des Monuments Historiques,
Château de Champs-sur-Marne 77420, France

L'emploi de mastic traditionnel à base de carbonate de calcium (blanc de Meudon, blanc d'Espagne . . .) et d'huile de lin pour le masticage des panneaux de vitraux anciens peut être à l'origine de dégradations importantes:
- durcissement du mastic ôtant toute souplesse au réseau de plombs entraînant ainsi le bris de pièces de verre sous l'effet des pressions du vent.
- attaque et transformation en sulfates du mastic par les agents atmosphèriques conduisant à une élimination progressive des joints plombs-pièces de verre. La chute de pièces de verre, l'infiltration de l'eau de pluie en sont le résultat.
- en présence d'humidité, ce mastic peut favoriser la croissance de mousses et de lichens participant à l'altération du verre.

Ces faits ont amené le L. R. M. H. à entreprendre l'étude de mastics élastomères susceptibles de remplacer le mastic traditionnel pour le masticage des panneaux.

Des éprouvettes, constituées de quatres verres d'épaisseur différente sertis de plombs, ont été préparées par les Ateliers Gaudin et mastiquées à l'aide de 11 mastics différents. Ces mastics ayant une viscosité beaucoup plus élevée que celle du mastic traditionnel ne peuvent être appliqués par la méthode habituelle de masticage des panneaux. La faible dimension de l'espace situé entre l'aile des plombs et les pièces de verre ne permet pas une bonne infiltration du produit dans cet espace au moyen d'un pistolet, moyen utilisé pour la pose de joints à l'aide de ces mastics dans le bâtiment. La pose à la spatule de ces mastics se révèle long et l'infiltration du produit reste difficile. En vue d'abaisser la viscosité de certains des mastics étudiés pour pouvoir les appliquer à la brosse, nous avons essayé de les diluer dans différents produits organiques. Les solvants utilisés sont donnés dans le tableau 1. Les résultats du vieillissement accéléré de ces mastics portent donc sur des mastics élastomères modifiés de façon à pouvoir être utilisés pour le masticage des panneaux.

Ces éprouvettes insérées dans des porte éprouvettes métalliques ont été soumises à des cycles de vieillissement artificiel par le Laboratoire National d'Essais.

Chaque cycle d'une durée de 24 heures comprenait les alternances suivantes:
- une heure d'immersion dans l'eau distillée à 20°C
- deux heures dans une ambiance humide à 50°C et 95% d'humidité relative.
- 17 heures dans un appareil Weather Ometer Atlas réglé de manière à avoir:
  - 102 minutes de lumière
  - 18 minutes de lumière avec arrosage d'eau.

Dans cet appareil le rayonnement lumineux riche en ultra-violets est produit par deux lampes à arc de carbone sous globe de verre pyrex.

L'atmosphere dans l'appareil est saturée d'humidité à la température de $35 \pm 5°C$.

La température aux emplacements des éprouvettes mesurée avec un thermomètre à corps noir, atteignait $65° \pm 5°C$ en absence d'arrosage.

La durée de l'essai a été de quarante cycles.

Le tableau nous permet de donner une classification des mastics suivant leur résistance aux tests de vieillissement accéléré.

Ref.	Nom commercial	Composition	Mode d'application	Comportement du mastic au vieillissement
A	GUTTA G 137	Caoutchouc	Dilution dans l'alcool Brosse	S'effrite mais reste souple. Eprouvettes perméables à l'eau.
B	Seurasil 1503	Silicone	Dilution dans le White Spirit Brosse	S'effrite mais reste souple. Eprouvettes imperméables à l'eau.
C	Sécoflex	Caoutchouc	Dilution dans White Spirit	S'effrite. Eprouvettes imperméables à l'eau.
D	Enke Thiokol	Thiokol	Dilution dans Primer Thio Joint. Brosse	Durcit et s'effrite. Eprouvettes imperméables à l'eau.
E	Guttaterna G 40	Caoutchouc	Dilution dans White Spirit Brosse	Eprouvettes imperméables à l'eau. Durcit et s'effrite.

F	Silygutt	Silicone	Dilution dans White Spirit Brosse	Bonne tenue, reste souple Eprouvettes imperméables à l'eau.
G	Mastic traditionnel		Brosse	Durcit et s'effrite Eprouvettes perméables à l'eau.
H	Thio-Joint	Thiokol	Brosse	S'effrite mais reste souple. Eprouvettes imperméables à l'eau.
I	Weatherban Sealant	Caoutchouc	Spatule	Perd de la souplesse et s'effrite. Eprouvettes imperméables à l'eau.
J	M.S.W.2A	Silicone	Dilution dans White Spirit Brosse	Bonne tenue et reste souple. Eprouvettes imperméables à l'eau.
K	Rhodorsil 3 B	Silicone	Spatule	Bonne tenue et reste souple. Eprouvettes imperméables à l'eau.

1. Mastics conservant une bonne tenue et restant souples:
   J — K — F : mastics silicones
2. Mastics restant souples mais s'effritant:
   B : mastic silicone
   H : mastic thiokol
   A — C: mastics à base de caoutchouc
3. Mastics durcissant et s'effritant:
   D : mastic thiokol
   I — E : mastics à base de caoutchouc
   G : mastic traditionnel

Silicones > Thiokol ≥ Caoutchouc > Mastic traditionnel

Ces résultats montrent que les mastics silicones sont les plus appropriés pour remplacer le mastic traditionnel

Les mastics F (Siligutt: Société Guttaterna-Séres, 89 rue Victor Hugo, 92-Courbevoie) et J (MSW 2A: Société Vetter et Fils, 3 rue Christian de Wett, 69609-Villeurbanne) peuvent être dilués dans le White Spirit pour pouvoir être appliqués à la brosse. D'après les résultats des essais, cette dilution n'a pas affecté la qualité de ces mastics.

Le mastic K (Rhodorsil 3B : Rhône Poulenc, Avenue Montaigne, Paris 8) a une viscosité trop élevée pour pouvoir être appliqué à la brosse et ne peut être dilué. Le joint ne peut être posé qu'à la spatule, travail trop long pour le masticage des panneaux importants.

La souplesse de ces joints, leur imperméabilité, permettra de les utiliser pour le masticage des panneaux de vitraux exposés dans des conditions néfastes pour le mastic traditionnel : pollution importante, écarts importants de température, climat humide . . . Après application des mastics J et F à la brosse, la surface des verres peut être nettoyée au moyen d'un chiffon et de White Spirit. Les dernières traces de produit sont éliminées avec de l'acide acétique dilué. Des essais en cours permettront d'autre part d'étudier les propriétés physiques de panneaux de vitraux mastiqués au moyen de ces mastics élastomères. Ils porteront sur l'étude des déformations des réseaux de plomb sous l'action de différentes pressions.

USE OF LASERS IN THE CONSERVATION OF STAINED GLASS

J. F. Asmus, University of California, San Diego, P.O. Box 1529, La Jolla, California 92037, USA

1. INTRODUCTION

Laser radiation provides a versatile and convenient means of depositing spatially and temporally localized energy in a material. The lateral extent of such energy deposition is controlled by the convergence or divergence of the beam. The deposition depth can be controlled through the radiation wavelength, as virtually all substances possess a spectral dependence in their optical absorption coefficients. Finally, possibly deleterious heat conduction effects may be minimized through the use of arbitrarily short laser pulses.

The above conditions obtainable with pulsed laser radiation are routinely employed in science and industry for a wide variety of materials-processing applications. Among these are [1] hole piercing in exotic materials, welding, scribing, trimming, surface hardening and alloying, selective vaporization, cutting and contouring. Whereas numerous other methods are able to perform these functions, lasers are often utilized because they provide a non-contact process, permit the use of a wide range of cover gases, and can deliver high powers rendering virtually all materials susceptible to processing. Most decisions concerning the implementation of a laser technique are based on economic considerations and the degree of ancillary damage to the material during the laser interaction.

There are numerous problems that beset antique stained glasses. In the investigation reported here the emphasis is on the treatment of deteriorating surface flashing on these materials. This appears to be a plausible starting point as past investigations [2] have shown that surface features are more readily accessible with laser radiation than are interior problems. With badly decomposed stained-glass flashing, two possibilities for laser treatment suggest themselves. First, it may be possible to remove the surface mineralization so that light can pass through the glass again. (This may be followed by recoating with paint or re-flashing if desired.) Alternatively, it may be possible to revitrify the surface through laser-induced surface melting.

2. THEORETICAL ANALYSIS

In order to determine whether it is possible in principle to divest surface mineralization from stained glass or to revitrify this material, it is desirable to have theoretical guidance. This can be helpful in deciding upon the propitiousness of an experimental programme and in designing the experiments. It would be desirable to learn from such an analysis if the thermal and optical properties of the decomposed flashing and glass are such that self-limiting removal of only the mineralization is possible. Further, will there be significant thermal gradients in the glass that can induce local crazing? In addition the thermal diffusion distance will be calculated to reveal the appropriate laser pulse length for the vitrification of a given thickness of decomposed flashing.

For a one-dimensional model of a plane glass surface the heat flow equation [3] yields the solution (1):

$$T(z,t) = \frac{2F_0(kt)^{1/2}}{K} \text{ ierfc} \left[\frac{z}{2(kt)^{1/2}} \right] \qquad (1)$$

In this equation F_0 is the laser flux absorbed at the surface ($z = 0$), $T(z,t)$ is the temperature as a function of position z and time t, k is the thermal diffusivity of the material, K is the thermal conductivity of the material, and the function ierfc(y) denotes the integral of the complementary error function.

It can be seen from the argument of the error function in equation (1) that the distance a thermal wave will travel into the material as a function of time has the form

$$z = 2(kt)^{1/2}$$

For typical minerals

$$k \cong 10^{-2} \, cm^2/sec$$

Consequently,

$$z = 0.2 \, t^{1/2} \qquad (2)$$

Thus, if one desires to revitrify a mineralized layer of flashing that is 0.1 mm in thickness, a pulse length of 2.5×10^{-3} sec should be used. If the layer has a thickness of 1 mm, then 250×10^{-3} sec are required. On the other hand, if the intent is to remove these layers through laser-induced vaporization, then a pulse length substantially shorter should be employed to minimize thermal conduction into the underlying glass.

Returning to equation (1), let us calculate the incident laser flux needed for vaporization and vitrification. On the surface $z = 0$ this solution has a parabolic form given by

$$T(o,t) = \frac{2F_0}{K} \left(\frac{kt}{\pi} \right)^{1/2} \qquad (3)$$

The relationship between the absorbed laser flux F_0 and the incident laser flux I_0 is

$$F_0 = (1-R) \, I_0 = AI_0$$

where R is the surface reflectivity and A is the surface absorptance. With this substitution equation (3) becomes

$$T(o,t) = \frac{2AI_0}{K} \frac{kt^{1/2}}{\pi} \qquad (4)$$

Equation (4) may be rewritten as

$$I_0 = \frac{K}{2kt^{1/2}} \; \frac{T}{A} \qquad (5)$$

and used to estimate the temperature rise of highly absorbing layers of surface mineralization. Two typical cases are plotted in Figure 1. There, the relationship between incident laser energy flux and surface absorptance required to yield a specified temperature rise is given. Assuming that a 500°C temperature rise will yield surface vitrification and that a relatively long 0.1 sec pulse is needed for conduction through the mineralization leads to the curve labelled 500°C. For the other curve 1000°C is assumed to produce surface vaporization and a short 10^{-3} sec heating time is selected. In principle, if the surface absorptance of the decomposed flashing is measured it should be possible with the aid of Figure 1 to determine the laser flux needed either for divestment or revitrification.

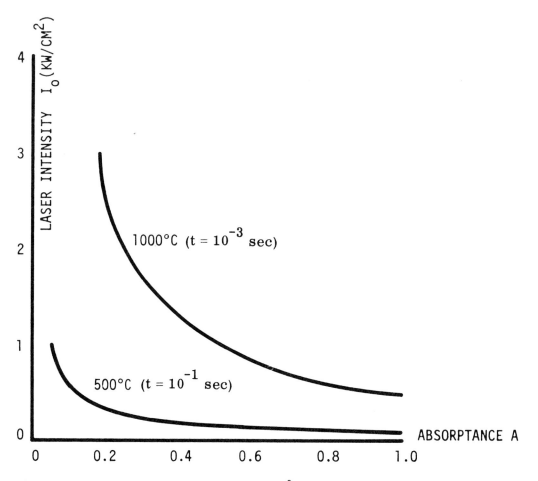

Figure 1.   Contours of constant temperature rise (°C) showing the relationship between incident laser power density and the surface absorptance needed to reach that temperature. A laser pulse duration of $t = 10^{-3}$ sec was used to calculate the 1000°C curve and $t = 10^{-1}$ sec was used for the 500°C curve.

3.   EXPERIMENTAL RESULTS

Probative laser irradiation tests have been performed on samples of painted and enamelled glass* from Great Britain. The goal of these first tests centres around determining the prognosis for the removal and/or vitrification of superficial materials without damaging the stained glass itself with the laser radiation.

With the aid of Figure 1 the flux from a ruby laser with a 10^{-3} sec pulse duration was adjusted so as to vaporize glass-like materials having an absorption coefficient of 0.5 or greater. Figure 2 shows the results for a blue glass with a dense opaque layer (seemingly badly darkened ancient enamel). This dark enamel was encrusted with a superficial brown deposit or layer of decomposed material. In Figure 2 the laser beam was centred at the lower right portion of the picture. There, the light-appearing flat regions are the glass surface. Scattered vitrified coagula are visible in this region. Moving toward the upper left and lower laser intensity, a band emerges where the brown deposit has been stripped away. Under it is crust material that has evidently been partially revitrified and balled-up, but not as completely as at the bottom right-hand corner. Then, at the extreme left and top, is the unaltered brown material.

The surface of some badly weathered glass of a green colour is shown in Figure 3. As received, it had a frosted appearance due to a thin superficial encrustation. Near the lower centre of the surface shown in Figure 3 a dark

*Courtesy, Dr Roy G. Newton, formerly Director of Research, The British Glass Industry Research Association.

region is visible. This resulted from a single pulse from the ruby laser. Evidently, the surface scattering has been substantially reduced, due either to the removal or vitrification of the encrustation.

The final experimental example illustrates a quite different type of condition. A piece of enamelled glass that has been coated with a clear plastic film is shown in Figure 4. The dark irregular oval near the centre shows the laser removal of this film. There is no visible evidence of damage to the smooth vitreous surface where the coating was removed. It appears that the irregular fragments of plastic residue within the oval could be easily brushed or blown away.

The ruby laser presently used in this work is not able to produce pulses as long in duration as indicated optimum for surface revitrification. Consequently, it seems desirable in the future to investigate the possibility of modifying it through substitution of a Neodymium YAG rod for the production of longer pulses.

4. CONCLUSIONS

These first exploratory experiments have shown that superficial layers can be removed from fragile glass surfaces with the aid of pulsed laser radiation. As there are no indications of copious surface damage, it may be possible safely to clean relatively large areas where variations in material properties would suggest variations in the optimum laser flux.

Although we have calculated the flux level that should lead to surface revitrification, our present laser is incapable of producing the appropriate pulse length in its present configuration. Further work is planned to modify the laser for longer pulses for revitrification tests and to determine energy thresholds for incipient damage to the glass. The identification of the compositions of the encrustations is planned in order to evaluate the selectivity of the cleaning process.

REFERENCES

1. Ready, J. F., 'Effects of High-Power Laser Radiation', Academic Press, New York, 1971.
2. Asmus, J. F., Murphy, C. G., and Munk, W. H., Studies on the interaction of laser radiation with art artifacts, 'Proceedings of the Society of Photo-Optical Instrumentation Engineers' 41 (1973), 19-27.
3. Carslaw, H. S., and Jaeger, J. C., 'Conduction of Heat in Solids'. 2nd Ed., Oxford Univ. Press, 1959.

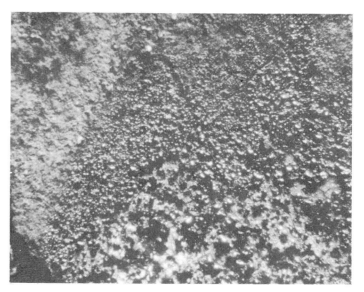

Figure 2. Laser test cleaning spot on mineralized stained glass surface layer. The centre of the laser spot is at the lower right. (Magnification, 60X)

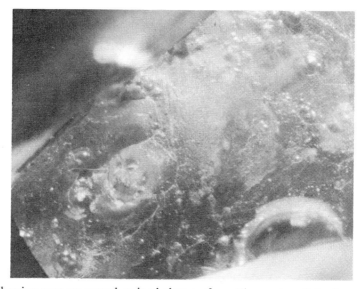

Figure 3. Laser test cleaning spot on crazed stained glass surface. The centre of the laser spot is near the lower centre of the picture. (Magnification, 60X)

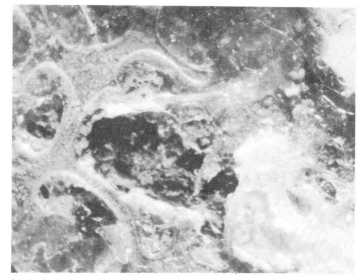

Figure 4. Laser removal of plastic coating on stained glass. The laser-cleaned spot is the irregular oval near the centre of the picture. (Magnification, 60X)

THE LIFTING OF MOSAIC PAVEMENTS

W. E. Novis, Carter & Co. London Ltd., 159 Clapham Road, London SW9 0PU, England

The discovery of an ancient pavement is an exciting event, but very soon in most cases comes the sobering question of what to do with it, a decision which will influence every action from that point. Naturally there must be temporary protection and further archaeological investigation which will have a bearing on the ultimate decision. But for this paper we must assume that removal of the pavement from its present position is required. The re-siting of the pavement, the possibility of later changes, and the means of access must be taken into account as these factors vitally affect the method of carrying out the work. The simplest division of methods can be described as between taking up the pavement in small sections or as a rolled 'carpet', either of the whole mosaic in one or in several large parts.

The advantage of the first simple method — taking up the pavement in small sections — is that progress can be made without great preparation. If the site is wet, small areas can be dried out to provide working time so much more easily; if the site is inaccessible, as in the middle of woodland, it needs only a footpath, no major plant or facilities are necessary, transport is simple, the sections can be taken into any location for ultimate reassembly or display, and the risk of loss is minimal [1]. The disadvantages are that, being in small sections, greater care and skill is required in reassembly to avoid joints between the sections remaining visible, and that the relaying must be carried out from the face, restricting the methods, or preventing some advantages in method being utilized.

The risk of loss is of fundamental importance. My company has carried out a great number of commissions in recent years for various authorities and museums — St. Albans, Winchester, York, Cirencester, Chichester, for the British Museum and the London Museum, and on pavements such as those at Woodchester, Bignor and Banbury; and in undertaking this work all elements of risk must be avoided [2]. Consequently we have not been greatly tempted to lift any pavement by the single carpet method, in spite of the success which has been achieved elsewhere. Actually it is difficult to recall any of our work on which this could have been easily employed, taking into account not only the original sites but also the intended new homes. However, I propose to deal with this in some detail later, basing my words on the published accounts by Mr John Bartlett, formerly of Kingston-upon-Hull Museums and now Director of Sheffield City Museum. I must, before going on, admit that I had heard of a certain failure (I believe it to be true) where the 'carpet' became a heap of loose tesserae and the pavement a total loss. I have felt it right not to court the risk of such a disaster.

It is against the background of these thoughts that I shall now describe how my company, which also incorporates Art Pavements & Decorations, has lifted pavements in small sections. The method differs from that which we used around 1930 at St. Albans and at Bignor and described by Mrs T. V. Wheeler in 1932 [1], in that modern materials afford more predictable and reliable lifting of the pavement, with less disturbance to surrounding and underlying parts of the site.

The first step is to make a scale drawing detailing the main elements of the design, on which the various sections can later be recorded, and to ensure that there is a photographic record of the whole pavement before it is disturbed. A wooden batten is then placed around the perimeter and marked at intervals of 1 ft (30 cm) setting out from centre lines of the design in order to establish a grid pattern.

The mosaic then needs to be thoroughly cleaned on the face and all loose material removed from the joints between the tesserae. If the mosaic dries out after cleaning then all is well but if not, equipment is required to assist in the drying process. It will be appreciated at this stage that a temporary roofing over the area will be of the greatest benefit. No work should be undertaken on exposed sites without protection from the rain, for much has been lost at the bottom of water-filled excavations.

The next stage is to glue over the whole surface a layer of tough flexible material, having an open weave, through which sufficient detail of the pattern may still be seen. Scenic gauze is a very satisfactory material for the purpose, lending itself to being pressed down into local irregularities of the surface and having sufficient strength to withstand considerable strains. But before applying the glue to the surface of the stones, isolated tests should be made to see that the glue will not have any ill effects on the stones themselves. Some materials can cause severe staining and this must be avoided. At one time, ordinary commercial animal glue was used and, being easily soluble in water, was ideal on a dry site during lifting, and simple to remove later, on reassembly. But fortunately we now have PVA emulsion adhesives which are invaluable on the wetter sites. They can be diluted with water to any required degree and there are the appropriate solvents to use for their final removal.

Having covered the surface with the gauze one should then mark the grid lines across the floor, using a different colour marking in opposite directions. This completed, one can proceed with the lifting of sections of any reasonably convenient size. The size and shape of the section is determined and the gauze on the face is cut through with a razor knife blade along predetermined lines, following the lines of the tesserae and if possible at a joint where stones of different colours abut one another, such as between rows of white and black cubes.

The blade of a long masonry trowel is then inserted beneath the stones at the outer edge and gradually worked under the mosaic. As the edge becomes freed from the bedding mortar, it can be curved upward, and the trowel blade taken still further under this sheet of mosaic. As progress is made, it is valuable to slip a piece of hardboard below the loosening sheet, and the trowel cutting is pursued under this protective support. The mortar will normally be found to be soft and perished, enabling the blade of the trowel to cut through it, and part from the mosaic by a careful levering action of the blade. A tool formed from a forged roofing tool known as a slate ripper, with a cutting edge at the tip, is also most useful for this work.

So one has a sheet of mosaic resting on the piece of hardboard. Place another piece on top, hold them together and turn the 'sandwich' over. The mosaic will now be lying face down on a hardboard panel, the back can be cleaned off, any stones that have become displaced can be refixed in their original position and the sheet is ready for placing in a shallow box or tray for storage and transport. The sheet requires to be numbered, the size and shape of the section marked on the scale drawing, and the given number recorded. The process can be carried out steadily across the floor until all are safely in the trays, and recorded.

This covers a fairly simple operation which, however, requires to be carried out with great skill and care, making sure, as the work proceeds, that the gauze is securely adhering to every stone and investigating most carefully every obstacle that hinders the simple progress. Should any stones become detached they should be bagged, marked and stored, for replacement in their original sections. And all of the time it is valuable to search for indications as to whether the mosaic was laid to a design scratched into the bedding mortar, a single stone at a time, or whether some parts were preassembled on some form of sheeting and laid in sheeted form. Some evidence has been found to support this submission.

It will be asked how to decide the size and shape of each section of the mosaic to be lifted. It is best to restrict the size, for ease of handling both in lifting and relaying. Regarding shape, it is wise to divide the work along the pattern lines, preferably between rows of differing colours, black and white, etc., so that when the work is reassembled any minute differences in the thickness of joints between the disturbed tesserae at the joint between the sections is further minimized by the colour contrast.

Later comes the actual reassembly, sometimes for the mosaic to be relaid on a new concrete bed or in some panel form. Here again, it is convenient to revert to the traditional art of the mosaic layer and bed the sheets into a mortar bed. The backs of the sheets will have been thoroughly cleaned, and satisfactory and lasting stability is secured with modern fixing mortars. As each succeeding section is beaten into place, the craftsman can bring the pieces into exactly their original relationships. The cleaning of the gauze from the face, the refixing of any displaced stones and the making up of any voids with a textured infill mortar where the original mosaic has disappeared, complete the whole operation.

If it is desired to prepare the mosaic in panel form, it is convenient to commence with a resin-bonded waterproof ply-board, treated on the surfaces with epoxy resin and covered with expanded metal or other suitable reinforcement key securely fixed to the board. The mosaic can then be laid on this surface with suitable adhesive mortar in the way already described. If a number of panels are necessary to carry the whole pavement these should be cut to suit sections of the design and fitted together first before laying the mosaic and then a thin polythene strip suspended between the mosaic and bed of adjoining sections so that no adhesion occurs yet the whole pavement appears as one. When all is set, the sections can be drawn apart and transported separately to the desired point for display.

The following drawings illustrate panel arrangements:

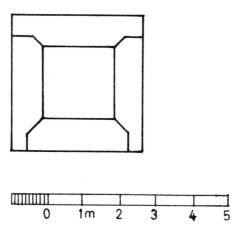
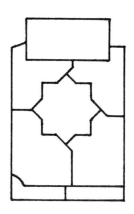

The Sparsholt Pavement
City Museums, Winchester (1970)

The Hare Pavement
Corinium Museum, Cirencester (1974) [2]

Such panels can be made up to thicknesses of not less than 2″ and will weigh approximately 15 lbs per square foot.

An exceptionally interesting task was the floor of Room 20 of the North Wing of the Fishbourne Roman Palace, discovered in 1961 [3]. This room contained a polychrome mosaic of geometric pattern, the foundation of which had subsided to a considerable degree, particularly into the post-holes of the earlier post building which had preceded the later structure now exposed. The mosaic was almost undisturbed around these circular subsidences yet, because of the expanding area, the joints had widened and, as drying out took place, the stones were loose and in danger of falling out. It was decided to lift the mosaic, to relay a new foundation to the existing contours and to relay the mosaic.

This was most successfully carried out by first recording the exact contours at 12″ centres from a level grid formed above the floor, with additional recordings at 6″ centres at the areas of acute displacement, then the careful lifting of the mosaic, the further excavation (with its own intrinsic interest), the laying in of a concrete base to the recorded levels and the relaying of the mosaic, all as already described. Not a single stone is thought to have been lost and the evidence of the earlier building is thus preserved together with its successor.

These are the methods mainly employed in our work undertaken over a number of years, with the method of lifting matching the ultimate requirement, but we must also consider the very different and more sophisticated way of lifting the pavement in a single 'carpet' form [4]. This has been carried out most successfully at Rudston and Brantingham in Yorkshire by Mr John E. Bartlett, then Director of Kingston-upon-Hull Museums and now Director of Sheffield City Museum [5]. With the permission of Mr J. Bradshaw, Curator of Museums and Art Galleries, City of Kingston-upon-Hull, I now quote from the Museum's Bulletin No. 9, dated October 1972, written by Mr Bartlett:

Method of lifting
The method used is that developed by the present writer and his assistant, Mr T. H. Southern, for the previous removal of pavements from Rudston in 1962.

Briefly, the operation went as follows. The first pavement to be tackled was the Second Geometric. Five days (100 man-hours) were spent in preparing the pavement for lift, cleaning the surface, drying the tesserae out with Calor gas hot-air blowers, cutting a key for the plastic adhesive by removing surplus mortar from between the stones, applying two or three coats of plastic adhesive and incorporating a loose-weave material in the plastic coating. The various sections of the pavement to be lifted were then rolled on to specially strengthened cardboard drums whilst at the same time the Roman mortar was cut away from the base of the tesserae with the aid of specially made tools.

The principal lesson learned from this first and easier stage of the operation was that more time was really needed to ensure that the pavement was thoroughly dried out before rolling was attempted.

Two borders of the Charioteer mosaic were next removed in the same fashion and gave no difficulty. The Leopard panel was also taken up as a separate piece. This left the figured portion of the Charioteer and one border, a rectangle measuring 10 ft x 15 ft, to be rolled up as the final stage of the operation. Twelve days (200 man-hours) were spent in the preparation of the pavement and this proved barely sufficient in view of the very hard and resistant texture of the Roman mortar between the tesserae, which made cutting a key for the plastic extremely difficult. A new cardboard tube 2 ft in diameter and 16 ft long was once again obtained from T.P.T. Limited, Romiley, Stockport, Cheshire and strengthened internally with Hull Telephone Department cable drums. The City Engineer provided a lorry equipped with a crane capable of taking the estimated weight of about 1 ton, and at the prearranged time, with television and film crews in attendance, rolling and undercutting commenced. It was soon evident that this pavement presented tougher problems than any previously encountered elsewhere. The underlying Roman mortar, like the pavement itself, was excellently preserved, and neither wished to part company with the other. Moreover, the tesserae were nearly everywhere still tightly bonded together so that there was a danger of the pavement coming up on to the tube in flat plates about 1ft wide instead of rolling on to it smoothly and tightly. This danger was overcome by suspending the rolling until the surface of the pavement had been thoroughly pounded with a heavy hammer, using a short plank as a buffer. Whilst not damaging the tesserae this essential operation successfully loosened the Roman mortar and enabled the rest of the pavement to be rolled up without trouble. Dust sheets and corrugated cardboard were incorporated in the roll to prevent one layer of tesserae being crushed against the next.

Rough estimates suggest that the cubes of stone making up the Charioteer pavement and its borders numbered in all about 105,000. Of these less than 200 or 0.2%, came off or were displaced during the removal. The tesserae that did become loose were either immediately replaced in position using modelling clay to fix them or placed in a recording tray according to a numbered grid. A quick and easy method such as this of ensuring that the right tesserae can be put back in the right holes saves endless time and trouble later on. Equally important, in our experience, is the tight trussing up of the total parcel once rolling on to the tube is finished. This was done by inserting a long spindle through the centres of the cable drums and getting the crane on the lorry to take the weight, whilst ropes were passed beneath. With the various tubes safely bedded down on bales of straw, the Charioteer and the Second Geometric were dispatched, at 10 mph towards Hull.

The next day, in the Museum warehouse, the Charioteer mosaic was unrolled, taking it off the top of the jacked-up roll so the pavement could be slid upside down on to a prepared inclined base. This makes it possible thoroughly to clean the back of the pavement and to restore missing parts of the general design. In a few weeks' time a new back, made up of fibre glass and Araldite stiffened with a stainless steel grid, will be cast on to the back. It will then be possible to turn the complete slab over and to begin the lengthy process of removing the plastic adhesive from the front.

These mosaics are now on display at the Kingston-upon-Hull Museum.

It is also of value to note that a similar technique was used in Germany in lifting the great Dionysos mosaic at Cologne Cathedral about 15 years ago [6]. The combined method of cutting and rolling in smaller sections was employed at Low Ham, Somerset [4]. Similar preparations for display have been carried out by ourselves with every success, making use of light alloy framings bonded together with the mosaic using epoxy resin with vermiculite fillers over intermediate reinforcements, but care must be exercized to ensure that these large panels can be handled through existing openings to the point of exhibition.

If the original site is reasonably dry, and reasonably accessible, and the workshop and the final display point have suitable entrances through which the large panel can be transported, the method has much to commend it. But as with the simpler, more traditional form it is vital that the greatest care is taken that materials used are tested for their suitability and compatability before general application. Every task seems to bring a new situation and each must have the fullest attention.

ACKNOWLEDGEMENTS

I am greatly indebted to Mr Bartlett for his permission to quote from the Bulletin, and to Mr K. Painter, Deputy Keeper in the Department of Prehistoric and Romano-British Antiquities of the British Museum, for checking and assisting with the references shown. We were closely associated in the lifting of the Hinton St. Mary Pavement in 1965 and in subsequent work for the British Museum [7]. Also to Mrs Margaret Rule, Curator of The Roman Palace at Fishbourne, Chichester, for her assistance regarding the references to our work on the mosaics at Fishbourne.

REFERENCES

1. The method was described by Mrs T. V. Wheeler: Wheeler, T. V., Experiment in removing a fragment of Roman pavement, 'The Museums Journal' 33 (1933), 104-106; reprinted in Wheeler, R. E. M., 'Archaeology from the Earth', Oxford, 1954, pp. 111-113.

2. Cirencester: McWhirr, A. D., Cirencester, 1969-1972; ninth interim report, 'Antiquaries Journal' 53 (1973), 190-218.
   Woodchester: Smith, D. J., 'The Great Pavement and Roman Villa at Woodchester, Gloucestershire' Woodchester Roman Pavement Committee, 1973.

3. Cunliffe, B. W., 'Excavations at Fishbourne, 1961-1969, Vol. I, The Site', Reports of the Research Committee of the Society of Antiquaries of London, No. XXVI (1971), 198-201.
   Cunliffe, B.W., 'Fishbourne Roman Palace and its Gardens', Thames & Hudson, 1971.

4. This technique was employed at Low Ham. Dewar H. S. L. and Radford, C. A. R., 'Journal of Roman Studies' 36 (1946), 142.
   Radford, C. A. R. and Dewar, H. S. L., 'The Roman Mosaics from Low Ham and East Coker', Somerset County Museum Publications, No. 2, 1954.
   Radford, C. A. R., 'Journal of Roman Studies' 44 (1954). (Further information was kindly communicated by Dr Radford. The work was carried out using Italian workmen from Friuli, who had previously applied the technique in Italy.)

5. See also: 'Araldite in the Restoration of Roman Mosaics', CIBA Technical Notes, July 1965;
   Bartlett, J., Lifting the pavements, in Richmond, I. A., 'The Roman Pavements from Rudston, East Riding', Hull Museum Publication No. 215, 1963;
   Smith, D. J., in Liversidge, J., Smith, D. J. and Stead, I. M., Brantingham Roman Villa, 'Britannia' 4 (1973) 84-106, especially 90;
   A definitive monograph on Rudston Roman Villa by Dr I. M. Stead is in the press.

6. Fremersdorf, F., 'Das Römische Hans mit dem Dionysos-Mosaik vor dem Südportal des Kölner Domes', Berlin 1956.
   Parlasca, K., 'Die Römischen Mosaiken in Deutschland', Berlin. 1959, pp. 75-80.
   Doppelfeld, O., 'Das Dionysos-Mosaik am Dom in Koln', 1964 (3rd edition 1970). (The work was carried out by Stefano Locati of the Istituto Centrale del Restauro of Rome.)

7. Painter, K. S., The Roman site at Hinton St. Mary, Dorset, 'British Museum Quarterly' 32 (1967), 15-27 especially 21-23.

SOIL SECTION TRANSFERS IN ADVERSE CONDITIONS

C. E. S. Hett, Conservation Division, National Historic Parks and Sites,
Parks Canada, 1570 Liverpool Court, Ottawa KIA OH4, Canada

1. INTRODUCTION

The transfer of soil sections was published by Voigt in 1933 [1]. In Voigt's method a cellulose lacquer was used to consolidate the surface, affix a gauze backing, and remove the consolidated soil surface. A more recent account of Voigt's method, and its application in special conditions was published by Hahnel in 1961 [2]. Shorer [3] published the transfer of soil sections onto a flexible support using natural rubber latex in 1964: his procedure has advantages in that larger transfers can be made in one piece, readily rolled up and transported with ease. The demands of work in Canada favour this latter approach, because of the very large distances through which a soil section transfer may have to be shipped. Using natural latex a wider range of soils can be lifted than with the use of cellulose lacquers described by Voigt; damp and even very wet soils with peat and clay can be lifted. The difficulties of lifting these materials using Voigt's method are well described by Hahnel [2]. As Shorer notes [3], natural rubber latex has a short life expectancy; this short life can be a problem if the transfer is destined for prolonged museum exhibition, or for reference purposes. Tests were carried out to find a material as effective as natural latex in wet and difficult conditions, but which would have a longer life span.

2. USES FOR SOIL SECTION TRANSFERS

Soil section transfers can be used for different ends which, together with the availability of materials, will often determine the choice of materials and methods to be used. In archaeology there is commonly a need to record in great detail features of soil sections: drawings and photographs alone are not always completely adequate as documents. In field work, where complex problems arise in the understanding of natural or artificial features, soil specialists are often not available, but evidence will be destroyed in the course of excavation. In narrow trenches photography of profiles may be impossible, and drawing difficult; to overcome this a transfer can be made, and other recording carried out more conveniently. In these cases no great permanence is required, but for display and reference purposes a maximum possible life should be aimed for. These factors were borne in mind when planning field work for the 1974 season at the presumed Norse site at L'Anse aux Meadows, situated across the strait from Labrador on the northern peninsula of Newfoundland. Conditions there are extremely wet, with soil materials which are intrinsically difficult to transfer. The choice of lifting materials is therefore limited since many resins will not function at all in these conditions.

3. FIELD CONDITIONS

At the site of L'Anse aux Meadows there are two principal areas of archaeological excavation. The first is the habitation area which consists of a series of house remains. These structures originally had turf walls, and were built on an old, raised beach situated between two peat bogs, one inland and one to seaward. This raised beach is well drained, and the soil in summer, though damp, is not waterlogged. In this area soil section transfers were requested to record and display the appearance of these structures during excavation. The second area of archaeological excavation is the bog to seaward which existed at 1000 A.D. and has continued to develop since. In this bog objects made of organic materials might well be preserved and discovered. Soil sections were to be made to record natural features in soil profiles in this area whose interpretation presented problems. The climate at the site could be described as adverse, although the site is not situated very far North; the latitude is similar to that of Amsterdam. The climate is modified by the Labrador current and compares unfavourably with that of the European Atlantic seaboard. Humidity and precipitation are high and temperatures low. The peat bogs are frozen near to the surface as late in the year as the end of July. Permafrost is found on higher land nearby. The soils to be transferred include peat and clay, two of the more difficult materials to lift. Compressed degraded turf, sand, humus gravel and stones were also present.

4. MATERIALS TESTED

When planning the field season allowance was made for tests and experiments with materials which previous experience had shown to be useful, or whose known stability offered interesting possibilities. The materials tried were: Rhoplex AC 33 (acrylic emulsion), Bulldog Grip 20-minute white glue (PVA emulsion), Moisture-Cure Polyurethane, Flexible Mold Facing Compound (natural latex), Vultex 3–A–5029 (neoprene latex), Polysar Caulking Compound (butyl rubber solution).

5. TESTS

Preliminary tests were made at an early stage. It was found that the butyl rubber solution was quite ineffective as an adhesive in wet conditions and that the vinyl and acrylic emulsions did not dry satisfactorily. The moisture-cure polyurethane seemed very promising as an adhesive, but was not useful for attaching the backing fabric because it produced a rigid and uneven result. Butyl rubber proved quite satisfactory for attaching the backing, since it adhered to the moisture-cure polyurethane, and remained flexible. However, it was slow to dry,

Column numbers: 1–34

1ST COAT
- 1–3: RHOPLEX AC 33 (50/50)
- 4–5: P.V.A. EMULSION LATEX
- 6–7: NATURAL LATEX
- 8–9: NEOPRENE FLEX AC 33
- 10–12: RHOPLEX AC 33
- 13–15: P.V.A. EMULSION
- 16–18: NEOPRENE LATEX
- 19: NATURAL LATEX
- 20–22: M.C.P.U. 50/50 SOLV.
- 23–25: M.C.P.U. 50/50
- 26–28: M.C.P.U. 50/50
- 29–31: M.C.P.U.
- 32–34: M.C.P.U.

2ND COAT
- 1–3: NEOPRENE LATEX AC 33
- 4–5: RHOPLEX EMULSION
- 6–7: P.V.A. LATEX
- 8–9: NATURAL LATEX
- 10: NEOPRENE (none)
- 11–13: RHOPLEX AC 33
- 14–16: P.V.A. EMULSION
- 17–19: NEOPRENE (none) / NATURAL LATEX
- 20–22: M.C.P.U. 50/50 SOLV.
- 23–25: M.C.P.U. 50/50
- 26–28: M.C.P.U.
- 29–34: M.C.P.U.

ADHESIVE USED FOR BACKING
- 1–3: NEOPRENE LATEX AC 33
- 4: EMULSION
- 5: EMULSION
- 6–7: LATEX
- 8–9: LATEX
- 10: RHO-FLEX AC 33
- 11: RHO-FLEX AC 33 EMULSION
- 12: P.V.A. EMUL. LATEX
- 13: NEO-PRENE LATEX
- 14: NAT-URAL LATEX
- 14–16: NEOPRENE LATEX
- 17–19: NATURAL LATEX
- 20–21: NEO-PRENE LATEX RUBBER
- 22: M.C.P.U.
- 23–24: NEO-PRENE LATEX RUBBER
- 25: NAT-URAL LATEX RUBBER
- 26: BUTYL
- 27: F.S.
- 28: NEO-PRENE LATEX RUBBER
- 29: BUTYL
- 30: M.C.P.U.
- 31: NEO-PRENE LATEX RUBBER
- 32–34: BUTYL / M.C.P.U.

SURFACE
- 4–5: POOR
- 6–7: FAIR
- 8–9: FAIR
- 10: FAILURE
- 11–12: POOR POOR
- 13: OK (NON SATIS.) / POOR
- 14–16: SATISFACTORY
- 17–19: SATISFACTORY
- 20: MOD.
- 21: MOD.
- 22: LOSSES
- 23: MOD.
- 24: MOD.
- 25: MOD.
- 26: POOR
- 27: POOR
- 28: POOR MODERATE
- (TOO THIN NOT VISIBLE — THIN —)
- 32–34: POOR

BACKING
- 1–3: FLEX
- 4: RIGID
- 5–7: FLEXIBLE
- 8–9: WASHED OUT
- 10–11: RIGID
- 12: RIGID
- 14–16: FLEXIBLE
- 17–19: FLEXIBLE
- 20: FLEX-IBLE
- 21: FLEX-IBLE
- 22: FLEX-RIGID
- 23: MOD.
- 24: FLEX-IBLE
- 25: FLEX-RIGID
- 26: FLEX
- 27: FLEX BRITTLE
- 28: FAIR MOD.
- 29: RIGID
- 30: FLEX-RIGID
- 31: FLEX-IBLE
- 32: FLEX-IBLE & BRITTLE

OBSERVATIONS
- MODERATE — BALD SPOTS — WASHED OUT
- LOSSES — FAILURE MATERIAL — MATERIAL WASHED OUT
- (Flexibility / Flexibility notes)
- "LIGHTER IN TONE ⟷ DARKER IN TONE"

KEY:- SATISFACTORY | BALD = FAILURE OF ADHESION OF 1ST COAT
      MODERATE | LOSSES = FAILURE OF ADHESION OF BACKING
      FAIR
      POOR

COVERED DURING RAIN / I.R. HEATER APPLIED / LESS DRYING TIME and remained tacky for several days. In practice the butyl rubber was applied as a very viscous solution directly from the tin using a trowel.

St. Anthony, the port nearest to the site, was ice-bound until late June, which delayed the arrival of many of the materials to be tested. When the final shipment arrived a larger scale test was carried out to compare the materials under similar field conditions. The test was carried out on a prepared south-facing length of a trench cut through the peat bog to seaward, which included some layers of peat and other materials: sand, clay and fine gravel. The lower levels of peat were very much more compact than those at the surface. For three days and nights previous to the test there was continuous rain, and the peat bog was oversaturated, to an extent uncommon even there. During the period of the test drying, conditions were good for the area: only light rain fell for a few hours.

The test was carried out as follows: over a 3.5 m length of trench the profile was cleaned, lines were plumbed at 10 cm intervals over 3.4 m of the length, and strings fixed to nails along the plumbed lines, and the delineated areas were numbered. Different combinations of the chosen materials were applied either to consolidate the surface or to adhere the backing to the consolidated surface. The materials used and observations on their performance are listed in the Table.

6. TEST RESULTS

As a result of the tests, natural and neoprene rubber latex appear to be the most effective materials for transferring soil sections. Neoprene latex has several advantages over natural latex:

1. The life expectancy of a neoprene rubber transfer has not yet been determined, but can be expected to be several times greater than that of one made from natural rubber latex [4].
2. Mould growth on the natural rubber backing of soil sections had been a problem encountered on several occasions when these were stored and shipped in humid conditions. This problem has not yet been found on neoprene-backed soil sections, probably due to the presence of zinc oxide included in the neoprene latex formulation.
3. Neoprene latex was considerably cheaper than natural latex at the time of testing.

In preliminary tests, moisture-cure polyurethane appeared very satisfactory when tried out in the same trench as the large test described, particularly when the adhesive used for backing was butyl rubber. The relative failure of this material in the later testing described was probably due to the excessive saturation of the trench at the time of the test, impeding penetration of the polyurethane which therefore cured on the saturated surface without the adhesion. The combination of polyurethane and butyl rubber solution should still be considered potentially useful. The tackiness of the butyl rubber backing could be overcome by dusting the back with talc (suggested by R. M. Organ). Shorer [5] has successfully made fairly small rigid transfers with Quentglaze 531/31, a polyurethane [6], simply using a greater number of coats of Quentglaze without any cloth backing at all.

The greatest cause of failure in soil section transfers is the failure of the first coat of consolidant to cure adequately. This first coat is also the slowest to dry. Once the first coat has dried out and is impermeable, other coats will dry relatively easily.

Aqueous dispersions of vinyl and acrylic resins largely disappeared into the soil surface, or were washed out by the oozing water. Transfers made with these materials are largely bald.

Artificial drying was planned, with infra-red heaters and high-powered fans; but the AC current was not installed in time. A power source was provided for the IR heaters using a DC inverter from the truck alternator, but without the fans no appreciable gain in drying was noted.

7. SOIL SECTION TRANSFERS MADE

Ten soil section transfers were successfully made at the site during the course of excavations, mostly with neoprene latex. On some of the sections across turf walls on the well-drained terrace (referred to earlier) moisture-cure polyurethane was used for the first coat, and backed with neoprene latex. When the polyurethane was used, a thicker layer of soil was removed than when neoprene latex alone was used, but definition of the profile was less perfect. The polyurethane-consolidated sections backed with neoprene latex are less flexible, and feel more brittle than those backed with butyl rubber in the trial transfers.

8. PROCEDURES USING NEOPRENE LATEX

In late September 1974 a soil section transfer was requested from the iron foundry village site at Trois Rivières, Quebec. This measured 3.35 m x 2 m, and had to be completed in two days. The soil was basically a pale-coloured sand, containing a lot of rubble filling, and was covered by layers of slag, humus and turf. The profiles of sand-casting moulds, filled in by a dark grey sand, were clearly visible within the section. In this case a shelter was already provided, and at our request two space heaters were rented in advance to allow a forced rapid drying of the neoprene latex used. These heaters provide a horizontal blast of hot air, requiring a source of gasoline fuel and AC current for the fan.

			Quantity used
Wednesday:	1.	photography	
	2.	16.00 hrs: spray 1st coat neoprene latex, with nozzle adjusted to deliver a very fine 'mist' spray to avoid disturbing the sand	9,000 m
	3.	dry till 20.00 hours	
Thursday:	4.	8.00 hrs: dry 1st coat; base still very damp	
	5.	9.30: apply 2nd coat neoprene latex: drying continued	1,425 m
	6.	11.00 hrs: second coat dry; apply 1st coat neoprene latex with gauze	2,250 m
	7.	15.30 hrs: dry; apply 2nd coat neoprene latex with gauze	3,650 m
	8.	17.55 hrs: apply final coat neoprene latex; dry till 19.30 hours.	1,450 m
		Quantity of neoprene latex/m^2 = 2.6 l	17.775
		dry for 2 hours	
Friday:	9.	plumb vertical line on surface, and paint line with acrylic emulsion paint	
	10.	hammer over area of slag layer (see note below)	
	11.	cut 5 cm-deep incision behind transfer at top edge to cut through roots, which may otherwise pull soil from the transfer	
	12.	raise carefully, starting from the base; gently ease transfer away from soil surface whilst assistants hold the top, until it is freed	
	13.	lay flat and roll over a drum-shaped form.	

Certain of the procedures need some elaboration:

2. The Vultex 3–A–5029 neoprene latex has a near 50% solids content but is considerably less viscous than natural rubber latex and can be sprayed undiluted.

6. For a soil section of this size a heavier backing than gauze would be preferred, but scrim was not available at short notice.

9. In the final mounting procedure it has been found very useful to have a vertical or horizontal line painted on the back of the transfer to help align the axis correctly within rectangular borders. The timbers along the top of the section described by Hahnel can only provide this alignment if the top surface chosen is flat and horizontal. Acrylic emulsion paint is used for this purpose; the pressure of a wax crayon could dislodge material and leave bald spots on the face, and 'magic marker' dye can easily migrate to the soil surface and stain it.

10. The slag layer contained some large pieces which would not normally be lifted with the transfer. After the final coating was applied, hammering of the surface broke up the large lumps of slag, allowing the complete slag layer to be removed, albeit in smaller fragments. A similar procedure is described by Hahnel for certain rocks.

9. NOTES ON EQUIPMENT

Spray equipment:

1. Latex: on most soils the first coats are best applied by spray. Many spray units will become blocked very rapidly when using latex; therefore the unit chosen must above all be simple to dismantle and clean. This must be done immediately after use. Two types of spray unit have been found useful and easy to clean: a large agricultural hand-pump sprayer, the 'Chapin' Funnel Top, was used with few problems. The principle of this mechanism is described by Organ [7]. Shorer [8] uses with equal effect a garden syringe, with a single action pump which is filled from a bucket.

2. Polyurethane: moisture-curing polyurethanes are extremely resistant to solvents when set and will ruin delicate spray equipment. The most useful spray for this material is the common 'Flit' spray, or similar simple spray. The principle of these is also described by Organ [9]. They are inexpensive, trouble-free, and can eventually be discarded should they become clogged.

Other equipment:

1 large pair of scissors, 1 knife, string, backing material (gauze or scrim), 1 line level and line, 1 plumb bob and line, nails, disposable polyethylene gloves, acrylic emulsion paint and fine brush, polyethylene beakers and bucket, 2.5 and 5 cm brushes. Barrier cream, and a respirator with an organic vapour cartridge should be included if polyurethane is used.

10. MATERIALS, SUPPLIERS, PRECAUTIONS

Neoprene latex: Vultex 3–A–5029

Composition:

Neoprene latex No. 842 (Dupont)	
(approx. 50% solids dispersed in water)	100 pts
Aquarex WAQ (surfactant)	1 pt
Zinc oxide	5 pts
Wingstay L (anti-oxidant)	2 pts

Characteristics:	As with most aqueous dispersions, limited shelf-life: best used when freshly prepared; self-curing.
Supplier:	General Latex 20 Ibsen Place Candiac, Quebec J5R 8G9 Canada

Natural latex: Characteristics:	Flexible Mold Facing Compound As above; more expensive than Vultex 3—A—5029; shorter life span.
Supplier:	General Latex

Moisture Cure Polyurethane

Characteristics:	Short shelf life (very short, once opened); must be diluted with its own solvent; offensive smell. The resin will cure on skin and cannot be removed: it must be sloughed off. Expensive; unpleasant to use.
Supplier:	Canus Equipment Ltd 340 Gladstone Ottawa, Ontario Canada

Rhoplex AC—33

Composition:	Acrylic emulsion co-polymer ethyl acrylate and methyl methacrylate
Characteristics:	As with most emulsions, limited shelf life; stable.
Supplier:	Rohm and Haas of Canada Ltd 2 Manse Road West Hill, Ontario Canada

'Bulldog Grip' 20-minute adhesive

Composition:	Relatively pure PVA emulsion with a di-butyl phthalate plasticizer
Supplier:	Canadian Adhesives Ltd 420 Marien Montreal, Quebec Canada

Caulking Compound

Composition:	Butyl rubber solution in mineral spirits
Characteristics:	One of the more permanent elastomers available to date. Supplied as solution of 40% solids in mineral spirits; viscous solution; inoffensive to use.
Supplier:	Polysar Vidal Street Sarnia, Ontario Canada

ACKNOWLEDGEMENTS

I would like to acknowledge the help kindly given by Mr P. H. T. Shorer and Miss E. T. G. Mibach, and suggestions from Mr R. M. Organ.

REFERENCES

1. Voigt, E., Die Ubertragung Fossiler Wirbeltierleichen auf Zellulose-film, eine neue Bergungsmethod fü Wirbeltiere aus der Braunkole, 'Palaont Zeitsche' **15** (1933).

2. Hahnel, W., Die Lackfilmethode zur Konservierung geologischer Objecte, 'Der Präparator Jahrgang' **7** (1961 243-261.

3. Shorer, P. H. T., Soil-section transfers: a method for the transfer of an archaeological soil section on to flexible rubber backing, 'Studies in Conservation' **9** (1964), 74-77.

4. Skeist, I., 'Handbook of Adhesives', Van Nostrand Reinhold Co., New York, 1962, pp.209, 268.

5. Private communication.

6. IIC-UKG Meeting, June 1967.

7. Organ, R. M., 'Design for Scientific Conservation of Antiquities', Butterworths, London, 1968, p.118, fig.5.6C

8. Private communication.

9. Organ, R. M., op. cit., p.116, fig.5.56.

Also:

Schurman, J. J. and Goedewoagen, M. A. J., A new method for the simultaneous preservation of profiles and roo systems, 'Plant and Soil' **VI** (1954).

SOME FIELD EXPERIMENTS IN THE REMOVAL OF LARGER FRAGILE ARCHAEOLOGICAL REMAINS

J. G. Price, Ancient Monuments Laboratory, Directorate of Ancient Monuments and Historic Buildings, Department of the Environment, 23 Savile Row, London W1X 2AA, England

1. INTRODUCTION

Field trials show that it is possible for the archaeological conservator to remove intact larger fired or unfired clay structures using relatively basic techniques. Local archaeological facilities are not always sufficient to resolve the problems presented by the occasional need to move large, well preserved, but fragile antiquities from the excavation site. This report discusses some basic principles involved in the safe transfer of a large 'mass liable to disintegration' (MLD), and outlines some techniques used in recent field experiments on the lifting and removal of structures in the 300–20,000 Kg range. Problems of lifting at short notice are mentioned.

Recent years have witnessed a remarkable increase in the worldwide threat of total destruction to many areas of archaeological interest. In the United Kingdom, extensive urban renewal, road construction schemes and the use of modern agricultural techniques have generated a large programme of archaeological excavations designed to recover information from a selection of the more important sites, which would otherwise vanish without a record of scientific investigation [1, 2]. Many thousands of artifacts are recovered in the course of these operations and undergo the normal laboratory examination and treatment procedures evolved for dealing with such material.

Certain artifacts, of course, need special care, and lifting techniques for their removal from the field are well established [3, 7]. Larger objects present difficulties. Examples typifying the problems involved are small structures such as kilns or metal working furnaces. By virtue of their construction, usage or age, few survive relatively undamaged [4, 8]. The greater majority yield useful archaeological information and, after systematic recording and documentation, will be destroyed. However, a minority of cases may warrant permanent preservation. On certain sites this could be highly impracticable in situ because of impending building construction or civil engineering works. In the rescue context of many current excavations it is therefore necessary to consider what rapid removal techniques are available if preservation is desired. Archaeological importance, rarity or completeness may indicate a case for relocation. However, when faced with the proposed transfer of a large crumbling mass, built perhaps of fired clay or unmortared stonework, the excavator may be forgiven if he initially regards the idea as impracticable. The occasional transfer of unstable material, of larger dimensions than those normally encountered, is usually achieved by sectioning into smaller fragments in order to facilitate removal. We have thought it useful to assess the difficulties involved in lifting subject matter as one intact mass, normally weighing up to 1500 Kg. A recent project has, however, involved preparation of a block of about 20,000 Kg.

At the lower end of the scale much may be achieved with basic resources but it is likely that a number of potential projects are never considered because of the apparently insurmountable problems involved. These are not always of a technical nature. The conservation techniques required are essentially straightforward and the main problems resolve themselves into questions of available finance, time and staff. Nowadays remarkable achievements are possible and house, temple or palace may be moved using the resources of modern technology. These large projects must be carefully preplanned by the architect and civil engineer and backed by suitable and formidable technical means. Events in what may be termed 'rescue archaeology' cannot always be pre-determined, and the archaeological conservator, who may be called upon at infrequent intervals to assist at field operations, generally has little more than basic equipment to deal with urgent cases. Nevertheless, even with limited resources, it is possible to remove successfully what we will define here as the larger 'mass liable to disintegration' (MLD). There are, of course, problems: certain soil and rock formations, the geometry and proximity of other vital archaeological features, and the shortage of time.

It has been mentioned that certain structures may be dismantled and lifted in sections which are of manageable proportions [3, 5]. In some circumstances, such as restricted access to the proposed museum display area, this may be the only solution. Subsequent reassembly and reconstruction will provide an acceptable compromise. Problems arise when handling certain structural fabrics, which may be so weak after prolonged burial that sectioning can produce serious losses or possible total disintegration. In these cases, total lifting techniques are advisable.

There is no real substitute for actual fieldwork and the experience gained from recent projects has been invaluable in assessing:

1. What can be achieved using basic equipment and materials.
2. Requirements for successful rapid operations.
3. Problems arising from compatibility of lifting work with any surrounding archaeological remains.

2. LIFTING – PRELIMINARY DETAILS

Work should preferably only go ahead after a close site examination and discussions with those responsible for the archaeological aspects of the area and those concerned with the after-care of the material. Conservation work resolves itself into three distinct phases:

1. Insertion of a rigid base under the MLD.

2. The boxing in and internal support of the MLD (in order to minimize vertical and lateral movement during transportation).

3. Detachment and removal of the boxed mass and its subsequent transport.

Major technical problems, if encountered, will probably occur in phase 1 and a flexible approach must be adopted to deal with unexpected soil conditions or methods of construction. Before work is started, it is of course important to consider the factors that will affect the progress of the operation. These include:

1. Condition of the structure (or object).
2. Time available for completion of work.
3. Type of rigid frame to be inserted.
4. Type of boxing and packaging required.
5. Soil conditions; methods and space available for introducing framework.
6. Space available to work in.
7. Access to site and availability of suitable transport.
8. Removal intact? or in sections? Availability of lifting equipment.
9. Liaison with site archaeologist and possible conflict with remaining current archaeological activities or remains.
10. Availability of suitable skilled team.
11. Consolidation requirements.
12. Weather; is a shelter required?
13. Final resting place; how and where will it be displayed?
14. Funds available.
15. Safety measures [9].

On urgent projects it is wise to consider these points at the earliest possible stage. Experience has shown that what may appear at first sight to be of minor importance may seriously affect the time required for completion of work.

Archaeological investigation naturally takes precedence on the site and, ideally, should be completed before the area is subjected to possible disturbance by the lifting operation. In practice, this is not always feasible. Archaeological evidence may still remain beneath, or close to the MLD, and if subsequent excavation is planned to continue on these levels, particular care must be taken whilst working in these areas. Normally, little conflict exists when the lifting of small subjects is undertaken, but with those of larger dimensions, greater caution must be exercized in preventing unnecessary disturbance of neighbouring archaeological features.

3. SOME BASIC METHODS

3.1. Insertion of a rigid base or platform

This is perhaps the most interesting phase of the operation. A large MLD must have a strong non-distorting base placed underneath it before any attempt at removal takes place, and it is evident that means must be provided to retain the mass intact whilst this work is undertaken. For a heavy subject it is obvious that an adequate base must be built up from a strong material capable of supporting the potential stresses and loading that will occur (one cubic metre of sandstone may weigh 2200 Kg). Concrete, steel and wood are possible choices. The need for a strong rigid section, capable of bearing high loads with minimal deformation, is perhaps best met by the use of steel plates or sections, preferably of a size that may be handled with relative ease. These supports must, of course, be introduced in a horizontal plane, beneath the MLD, through previously bored openings or small tunnels; or, if soil conditions permit, by driving them underneath the mass using a small hydraulic ram or screw jack. The areas around the structure may have to be fully or partially excavated before this operation. In due course the unstable mass will be supported on a carefully built-up platform of solid plates, the ends of which may rest on steel girders placed either side of the MLD. These girders can be subsequently raised up by jacks, thus detaching the mass from its original ground support. If suitably bolted or welded together, the main frame may be used as a cradle when the boxed mass is finally raised and transported.

Soil conditions will vary considerably from site to site and will often change beneath the structure. For this reason each project requires a very careful examination of the foundation layers together with an assessment of the capacity for survival of the material structure. If faced, for instance, with foundations of relatively soft sand, it would be preferable to attempt a complete underpinning, using an unbroken area of supporting steel plates. Where, however, the sub-structure comprises an interlocking, tightly-knit mass of stone rubble, it may be possible to insert steel plates only at irregular intervals, but in such positions that the total block is capable of being safely raised. Simple jacking equipment, widely available, is most useful under certain conditions in helping to insert the horizontal platform, especially when it is important to avoid damaging underlying levels.

3.2. Consolidation and internal support

Although well supported at its base, the MLD, when isolated from its surrounding soil matrix, will have a natural tendency to collapse because of its weight and size, especially if it is subjected to vibration and lateral stresses. This potential disaster may be averted by a certain amount of surface consolidation, and the subsequent application of a rigid reinforcing material capable of protecting the structure from complete degradation or serious erosion during transit. What is required in practice is the application of a rigid outer skin or box around the mass, and its encapsulation in a material capable of:

1. providing suitable protection and support;
2. being readily removable in the final reconstruction phase.

We have used strong plywood (18-25 mm thickness) for the exterior skin and, primarily for reasons of speed and weight-saving, have investigated the use of polyurethene foam systems as the embedding agent. Other materials, such as plaster of Paris or well-packed sand, soil, sawdust or lightweight cements, could possibly be utilized with effect, but the properties of polyurethane foams offer certain advantages, which in practice are difficult to resist.

The foam system adopted was Bibbithane RM 118*, a fluorocarbon blown, diphenyl methane di-isocyanate based, room temperature curing, rigid formulation, suitable for bucket-mixing operations. The material is resistant to fungal growth and has good load bearing capacity. Its use in the field has been found very acceptable although the desired physical properties are not fully attained at temperatures under 20°C. It is essential to use a barrier or release agent as polyurethanes have extremely good adhesive properties. Aluminium foil has been found to be most suitable. Some shrinkage may be expected in the final setting stage and must be allowed for. The warmed foam product produced in the exothermic reaction contracts as it cools and solidifies, often leading to the formation of a thin cavity between the face of the material and the protective foam filling. For this reason we have found it advisable to build the foam packing up in layers, allowing the previous mix to cool and contract, and then filling in the thin 2-5 mm gap, caused by contraction, with fresh foam.

Consolidation of the friable surface fabric is often essential, but this cannot always be fully achieved under field conditions. The foam, in addition to desirable weight saving characteristics, provides a material which can be removed at later stages with relative ease causing minimal damage to the fabric. For this reason it is of great value when areas of somewhat doubtful stability cannot be fully impregnated on site. Experience has shown that there is a need for the application of foam support at various periods throughout the duration of the removal operations. Difficulties in underpinning may necessitate the protection and embedding of a particularly weak section of the structure in order to prevent collapse during the work; any unwanted cavities appearing are readily and effectively filled with this rigid foam.

3.3. Detachment and lifting

Lifting is normally a straightforward operation and should present no particular problems providing that local lifting equipment is obtainable, and good access to the site has been arranged. In areas where no specialized plant is available, some improvisation may be required; hoists and many willing hands may be the answer. If lifting cannot be achieved in time for subsequent building operations to start, it may be possible to move the boxed structure horizontally to a temporary safe area by winching or towing on smooth ramps. The larger and heavier the final load, the more important it is to seek the advice of a lifting specialist who will be concerned with the last stages of the operation. Large cased structures will require specially sited lifting points incorporated into the design of the basic steel framework, and this must be under consideration at an early stage.

Our main concern, however, is with the initial detachment of the MLD from its site. It will have been protected on at least four sides by the wood outer shell and inner foam support, and it will be resting on the inserted platform. Several options are now open:

1. The large boxed mass and its platform could rest on a framework of steel joists which are joined together. Provided that the box is strapped or bolted in some way to this framework to prevent sideways slip, it will be possible to lift the whole in one complete operation.

2. Smaller subjects can be dealt with in a similar manner to 1 but problems arise if the two supporting girders on either side of the box are not firmly joined together by bolted linking sections.

The simplest approach is to lift the two side main supporting girders by means of jacks placed under each end. In this way the whole MLD is raised, on its platform, about 5 to 8 cm and is thus totally detached from its original matrix (Figures 13a-d). Through the gap created at the base, it will be possible to insert the wooden bottom of the containing box, lower the jacks and, finally, withdraw very carefully the plates of the inserted steel platform. Using this technique, it is possible to encase the MLD completely in a wooden shell. The wooden base thus inserted may be screwed to the adjoining vertical wooden walls or held firmly to the mass by means of strapping.

In a number of instances, however, it will be found extremely difficult to insert steel supports in a regular horizontal pattern because of underlying rubble foundation (Figure 15). As a result, the insertion of a flat wooden base which will mate to the four wooden sides is impossible. A solution here, after the top lid has been attached and the box totally filled with polyurethane protection, is to strap the metal plates of the platform firmly to the boxed mass after it has been jacked up. The total package can then be lifted and completely reversed. The subject will then be completely inverted but will rest on a solid bed of rigid foam, ready for transport.

Another solution is to raise the boxed mass with its firmly strapped base plates and to lower it onto the transporting vehicle, making sure that any rubble which adheres firmly to the boxed structure is well clear of the floor of the vehicle. A further possibility is to raise the MLD by jacking, to insert the wooden base and fill any spaces with foam before lowering (Figures 16, 17).

Varying site conditions will call for the judgment of the conservator in selecting the best approach. Most of the above techniques helped to provide solutions in the following field projects, which are discussed in detail.

4. EXAMPLES

4.1. Seventeenth-century glass furnace, central segment

The author first became acutely aware of the practical problems to be solved when asked to investigate the feasibility of removing, for public display, the remains of an early coal fired glass furnace [6]. It was understood

*Information on Bibbithane polyurethane foam systems is obtainable from Bibby Chemicals Ltd, Accrington BB5 2SL, England.

to be of a type hitherto unknown and first reactions were to use twentieth-century technology to lift and transport it intact. This optimism was soon tempered by the realization that there were a considerable number of formidable problems involved in such an undertaking. In 1971 archaeological investigation continued, revealing structure with substantial surviving dry stone walling and an overall length of about 9 metres. With the resources and time available to the excavation team, it was decided that the best course of action was to record fully and dismantle the stone walling and archways for future reconstruction at the museum. This method of removal appeared to provide a most acceptable procedure for future rebuilding of the structure in the confines of the display gallery.

Although dismantling and crating of the stonework could go ahead, one embarrassing and unwieldy section which existed in the centre of the structure pointed to the need for an approach based on normal techniques of lifting smaller archaeological objects. Our problem was a siege platform upon which the crucible vessels had rested in the furnace. A large proportion had survived and it was essential to retain it in its entirety. The brief, therefore, was quite simple: means had to be devised to detach and protect the siege core for transport to the museum 30 miles away. First thoughts were not encouraging, as this part of the structure was composed of a fused and partly friable mass of sand, slag, stone and crucible remains which were 'welded' on to the central stone flue.

In the event, the main part of the operation proceeded smoothly in a matter of days, the actual time span being about four weeks as a consequence of the unavoidable archaeological investigation required. This is a matter which cannot be overstressed. The interaction of lifting operations and the detailed careful excavation of nearby areas may be complex, and close liaison and planning at the outset is essential. If an intricate removal exercise is planned during primary excavation, a rigid timetable may be rendered quite inoperative by fresh archaeological discoveries. The scheme adopted followed the pattern:

1. Initial surface consolidation of soft and powdered areas using a solution of polyvinyl acetate in an ethanol/acetone mixture.
2. Application of aluminium foil to all exposed surfaces (Figure 1).
3. Construction of a strong wooden box around the central siege mass and application of polyurethane foam to fill all interior cavities.
4. A series of holes were made using conventional masonry drills with extension pieces, at the boundary (interface) of the fused base of the siege mass and the upper surface of the flue stone walling. These circular openings served as guide channels for a series of horizontal steel channel support sections (5 cm by 2.5 cm), which were sharpened to a V-profile at one end and driven in by simply tapping the other end (Figure 2).
5. At this stage, the solid mass was protected at the sides and partially severed at its base by the steel inserts. Detachment was achieved as follows. The surrounding areas of trenching were carefully filled, using soil and wood planks, to a level where it was possible to place two small steel girders under and either side of the inserted steel channel supports. These girders were then raised by jacks placed underneath, resulting in the lifting of the steel supports and hence the boxed, protected siege mass.
6. The wooden base of the box was inserted into the newly created gap caused by the upward displacement of the siege mass. The box was then surrounded by slings and lifted by a mobile crane.
7. The metal channel supports were now easily extracted, and the packaged mass then inverted with the aid of crane and manual effort, so that the previously attached lid now became the base. Our original intention was to encapsulate the siege platform completely with the polyurethane foam but in the final stages of filling the wooden casing we discovered the supply of the material was exhausted. A relatively small space remained to be filled and this was therefore packed with fine soil before the lid was positioned.

4.2. A second-century Romano-British pottery kiln

In 1973, archaeological investigations prior to the implementation of a major road improvement scheme were undertaken on part of a Roman settlement near Ipswich, Suffolk. Amongst the features revealed was second-century pottery kiln which, being reasonably complete, had some claim to preservation, preferably for public display. At a short site meeting, two weeks before the road construction unit was due to commence operations, it was decided that an attempt would be made to remove the kiln intact in one swift operation.

An intense period of activity then began. Careful measurements and estimates were made and a steel raft constructed which could be inserted in sections under the structure (Figure 3). The main frame was designed so that it could be bolted together in situ. Because of the limitations of space inside the chamber, there being just sufficient room for a single person to work, it was reluctantly decided to remove a small surviving central clay pedestal by conventional boxing, and lifting it vertically through the top of the kiln. Once completed, this operation enabled us to obtain the improved access that was required for the subsequent treatment of the inner surface of the structure. It also helped to provide space for the insertion of the central steel H-beam, the two outer girders being positioned in two side tunnels which were excavated carefully in the clay and sandy gravel soil (Figures 11a, b). Across these longitudinal side girders, short steel plates (10 cm wide, 1 cm thick and 75 cm in length) were inserted, with their ends resting on the top of the outer girders and the main central beam. The plates were placed in this position by using screw jacks which were located horizontally on both sides of the kiln.

The firing chamber had been constructed of clay and it was clear that certain areas required some form of consolidative treatment. As little time was available and much work could be completed at a later restoration phase, it was decided to spray the most affected areas, which were in danger of becoming detached, with solution of polyvinyl acetate in ethanol. This provided reasonable short-term protection. The interior surfaces were covered with aluminium foil and the whole cavity filled, in several operations, with polyurethane foam. The stabilized structure was enclosed in a strong wood box, all remaining cavities being filled with foam (Figure 4

The whole was then strapped by a small steel frame to the main steel lifting platform. This was necessary in order to counteract the results of any possible sideways tilt during the lifting and unloading operations. On the final day of the project, the whole mass was raised swiftly and uneventfully, loaded and transported six miles in two hours to the museum store (Figure 5).

4.3. A small early iron furnace

Excavations at a large ironstone quarry in Northamptonshire, extending over a period of years, had revealed an Iron Age settlement, Roman agricultural activities and numerous remains of iron smelting furnaces. These structures, set in pits dug in the natural bedrock, provided evidence of iron-working activity that had continued into the Roman period. Out of a group of about 30, one small furnace was found in a reasonably complete condition towards the final stages of the 1974 excavations, and it was decided to attempt to raise it in one complete operation.

The site was situated on a bed of Upper Lincolnshire Limestone. Surface soil conditions were variable. The area we were concerned with consisted of limestone rubble, marly clay and sand mixture with a large unsuitable natural cavity existing beneath the structure, although this was not discovered until the latter stages of the operation.

One of the objects of this exercise was to assess the practical aspects of removal from a matrix such as the limestone rubble in which the structure was embedded (Figure 6). The clay fabric of the small firing chamber was friable and liable to complete disintegration after its prolonged burial. Its base was soft and appeared poorly fired. A brief visit to the site a month before the main work was planned to commence indicated what equipment was required and also provided an opportunity for first aid treatment. As there were doubts regarding the stability of the circular clay walling, it was protected by lining the interior surface with thin aluminium foil and then filling the chamber with polyurethane foam (Figure 7).

On our return to the site, the main problem appeared to be the insertion of a rigid base. There was, in fact, no alternative but to excavate small tunnels beneath the mass and remove the rubble (fragments up to 30 cm in diameter) by levering, chiselling and trowelling. This somewhat crude but vital exercise was happily completed in a shorter period than originally estimated. Each tunnel was started from both sides of the structure. When completed, metal support plates (120 cm by 10 cm by 1 cm) were inserted and held in position by wooden chocks (Figure 8). Any interspace between the base of the structure and top of the steel plate was filled with polyurethane foam placed in a polythene bag. It was thus possible to place the mixed liquid components in relatively inaccessible 'cells' which became potential load-bearing columns after the foam had reacted and solidified.

In this way the block containing the furnace was finally supported on several steel plates, as well as resting on some isolated rubble 'pillars' which still remained uncut. The plates themselves were carried on two steel box sections (10 cm by 5 cm). The total mass was then encased in a 2.5 cm plywood shell, filled with foam, and raised by the action of hydraulic and screw jacks placed under the two main box sections. Final detachment was achieved by passing ropes around the base steel plates and the box, and then lifting onto the ground surface using a mobile quarry crane with the assistance of its maintenance team (Figure 9). We then reviewed the next phase of the operation. Time was short and there was a 100 mile journey to the museum store. Examination of the furnace base showed that it was going to be an extremely tedious procedure to insert a wooden base, as was the original intention. There was, in fact, no real need to box completely. If the mass were reversed, time would be saved on site and a concrete base could be constructed at a later date when the display stage was reached. It would also afford an opportunity in the meantime for an examination of the furnace base if this was required. Accordingly the boxed structure was inverted, loaded and transported with remarkably little difficulty (Figure 10).

4.4. Prehistoric burial mound

Lifting techniques in archaeological investigation are not necessarily confined to subjects destined for permanent preservation. Soil blocks containing complex assemblages of highly deteriorated artifacts are occasionally sent to the archaeological laboratory for more detailed examination. A recent field exercise (currently under way) illustrates both the preservation and the investigation aspects that may be involved.

The central grave pit of a prehistoric burial mound in Lincolnshire had been located during excavation and the laboratory was asked to provide aid for the removal intact of a rare and interesting planked wood structure preserved as a friable mass of charred wood. Our two main objectives were:
1. To preserve the remains intact for possible future display.
2. To examine the lower surface for further information on methods of construction and use.

Soil conditions appeared to be excellent for a routine lifting operation but the plan had to be abandoned when it was realized that the wooden structure overlaid a pit containing important archaeological evidence. The next approach appeared to provide a satisfactory solution to the problem of detailed excavation underneath the very fragile wooden remains:
1. A larger soil block would be detached (1.8 by 1 by 1 metre).
2. The soil block would be carefully protected and completely boxed. Once detached it would be inverted.
3. Detailed archaeological excavation could then proceed on the pit remains with recovery of the desired information. The planked structure remaining, and in one piece, could undergo further laboratory examination and conservation.

Figures 14a-c illustrate the proposed approach, which had to be postponed because of extremely poor weather conditions.

5. CONCLUSION

A small number of field trials on difficult subjects has shown that successful results are possible in lifting operations using basic equipment. Further work is required on techniques for rapid completion of work. Recently preparations have been completed for raising a kiln of about 20,000 Kg weight (4 by 2.5 by 2 metres), and it is hoped to report on this exercise later in 1975.

ACKNOWLEDGEMENTS

Throughout these projects, which depend on teamwork, the author has been greatly helped by advice and assistance from many interested individuals. Work on the seventeenth-century glass furnace was undertaken by staff of the North Western Museum and Art Gallery Service, to whom grateful thanks are due. Other projects listed above have been assisted by the Ancient Monuments Laboratory Conservation Section.

REFERENCES

1. Department of the Environment, 'Archaeological Excavations 1973', HMSO, London, 1974.
2. Rahtz, P. H., (editor), 'Rescue Archaeology', London, 1974.
3. Dowman, E. A., 'Conservation in Field Archaeology', London, 1970.
4. Musty, J., Mediaeval pottery kilns, in 'Mediaeval Pottery from Excavations', London, 1974.
5. Butterworth, P., Moving a Roman kiln, 'The London Archaeologist', 4 (1969), 75-79.
6. Hurst-Vose, R., 'Bickerstaffe and Haughton Green Excavations', Extrait des Annales du 5e Congres de l'Association Internationale pour l'Histoire du Verre, Liege, 1972.
7. van der Heide, G. D., Wrecks as ancient monuments, in 'Underwater Archaeology', UNESCO, Paris, 1972.
8. Gibson Hill, J., Notes on lifting a furnace base, 'Journal of the Historical Metallurgy Society' (1974), 50-53.
9. Fowler, P. J., (editor) in 'Responsibility and Safeguards in Archaeological Excavation', Council for British Archaeology, London, 1972.

Figure 1. Remains of a siege platform from an early seventeenth-century coal-fired glass furnace, showing the application of an aluminium foil barrier prior to embedding in a polyurethane foam.

Figure 2. The first two steel channel sections of the supporting stage are inserted at the base of the protected, boxed, siege mass.

Figure 3. Steel platform prior to insertion under the pottery kiln, which is visible in the background. The two main support girders are 220 cm in length. (Photo: Ancient Monuments Laboratory).

Figure 4. The kiln walls, covered with aluminium foil and in a wooden box, are embedded in polyurethane foam. (Photo: Ancient Monuments Laboratory).

Figure 5. Boxed kiln is lifted. Note small steel frame which provides the lifting points. (Photo: Ancient Monuments Laboratory).

Figure 6. Rear of isolated furnace block shows the extent of rubble matrix. Photo: Ancient Monuments Laboratory).

Figure 7. The small iron furnace, after being isolated from adjoining rubble matrix and protected with polyurethane foam, is ready for the underpinning stage. (Photo: Ancient Monuments Laboratory).

Figure 8. Boxed structure rests on inserted steel plates. Note wooden chocks between plates and main steel side supports. (Photo: Ancient Monuments Laboratory).

Figure 9.   Furnace is lifted to ground surface; plates have been strapped to wooden box. (Photo: Ancient Monuments Laboratory).

Figure 10. Boxed structure is carefully inverted before metal plates are removed. (Photo: Ancient Monuments Laboratory).

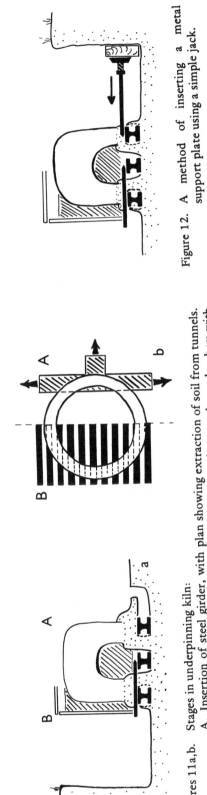

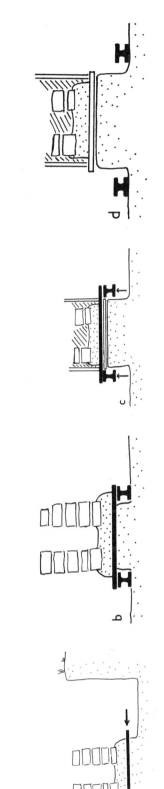

Figure 12. A method of inserting a metal support plate using a simple jack.

Figures 11a,b. Stages in underpinning kiln:
A. Insertion of steel girder, with plan showing extraction of soil from tunnels.
B. Plan of kiln structure, showing polyurethane foam and wooden box with steel underpinning.

Figures 13a,b,c,d Stages in boxing a structure.

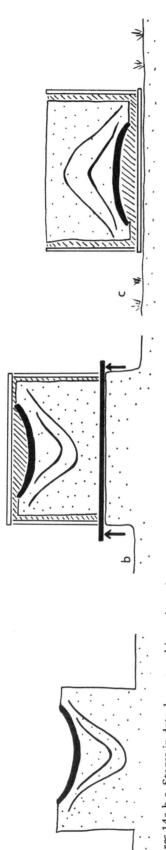

Figures 14a,b,c Stages in detachment and inversion of a soil block.

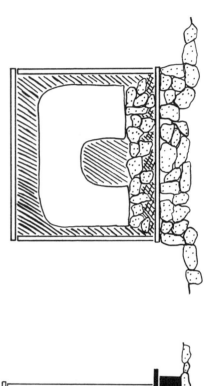

Figure 17. Boxed structure has foam or concrete base inserted in final phase of detachment.

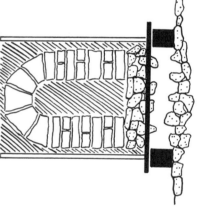

Figure 16. Rubble foundation is difficult to extract and rests between metal plates which support the structure.

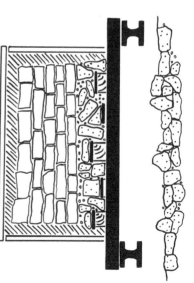

Figure 15. Structure on rubble foundations has been detached. Metal support plates rest on wooden blocks on main side girders.

164

A NEW APPROACH TO ARCHAEOLOGICAL CONSERVATION

C. L. Rose, Anthropology Conservation Laboratory, National Museum of Natural History,
Smithsonian Institution, Washington, DC, USA

1. INTRODUCTION

If one faces the problem of the conservation of archaeological specimens realistically, one soon realizes that the conservation world can in no way currently fulfil the need for 'in-field' conservators to accompany archaeologists, nor are there adequate training programmes in this specific area. If, on the other hand, one waits for the artifacts to return to the 'home' laboratory, the problems are compounded, necessitating remedial treatments rather than preventive ones.

To stabilize archaeological specimens as they are excavated, thereby removing them from their state of equilibrium and subjecting them to a new environment, requires a knowledge of the inherent complexities of an archaeological site which would modify standard conservation techniques. Therefore, it would seem necessary to devise a system whereby any trained conservator could become sufficiently familiar with a given archaeological site to pre-train the archaeologist and his technicians in 'first aid' conservation techniques.

Working with known factors in a predefined pattern of reasoning can aid the conservator in comprehending the variables at the site and the conditions of the artifacts. He should then be able to suggest which conservation techniques would be applicable at a given location and which would be feasible for the archaeologist at his particular site.

2. METHODOLOGY

The site must first be defined according to general data, that of the ecological zone to which specific data of the micro-environment and soil conditions can be added. Correlation and analysis of this information will produce specifications concerning the conditions of the site. Based on this information, fairly accurate assumptions can be made concerning the state of preservation of the artifacts and necessary conservation supplies. Relevant data can be organized as follows:

Ecological zone
Division of the world into biomes based on vegetation and climatic conditions, e.g. tundra, tropical forest, grasslands. (Obtained from texts on earth sciences and climatology.)

Micro-environment
Specific environment in which the artifacts are located, e.g. cave, cistern, under water. (Supplied by the archaeologist.)

Soil conditions (if applicable)
Soil type(s) — organic and mineral content, texture, aeration, pH, etc. (From texts on geochemistry and soil chemistry, geological survey reports, and soil analyses by the archaeologist.)

Depending on the origin of the material culture excavated, the time factor must be considered separately in determining if and when homeostasis with the environment has occurred. Until many more sites have been studied, this factor will be difficult to gauge. We must therefore rely on previous finds of material culture in the same time-span to determine which types of artifacts would be representative.

By estimating the effect that each of these known factors has in promoting physical, chemical, and biological decomposition, one can begin to determine differences in the general states of preservation of organic and inorganic materials at different sites.

Using these deductions, the conservator can prepare himself and/or the archaeologist with conservation supplies better suited to the material culture and in quantities reflecting the number of artifacts to be conserved. Climatic conditions of the area will also determine which chemical solutions could remain stable while specimens are being treated and stored in the field.

3. EXAMPLE

A variety of sites have proved this methodology successful in determining specific treatments for archaeological specimens. At several sites, the archaeologists were pre-trained in conservation techniques by the conservator; at others, the conservator pre-oriented himself in applicable conservation techniques.

An historical site in the sub-Arctic will be detailed with respect to this systematic approach because of the many variables it contained.

3.1. Description of site
Historical Eskimo winter house (outlined to facilitate correlations), Eskimo Island, Labrador.

Ecological zone: forest-tundra (extracted from references on climatology [1])
Summerless Arctic region — long, extremely cold winters — annual mean temperature 30°F (−1°C) — maintains

soil moisture in frozen state until late spring − thawing in first few feet of soil − frozen subsoil − soil seepage
precipitation small − evaporation small − cloud-covered areas − humid soil and atmosphere.

Micro-environment (personal communication with archaeologist [2])
Latitude 54°N − mean winter temperature 0°F (−18°C) − mean summer temperature 50°F (10°C) − hou
made of turf and peat walls − hearth probably present (sea mammal oil fuel) − artifacts buried in peat
approximate date 1650.

'Soil' conditions
Mounds covered with sedges, lichen, mosses − unhumidified peat in upper levels − humidified peat in lower leve
− surface thawing in summer: saturated surface.

Table 1 suggests assumptions which can be made concerning the site. At this point, we are dealing with thr
separate micro-environments: a permanently frozen subsoil; a freezing and thawing surface layer; and probably
hearth where the burning of oil would have taken place. From these observations, one can begin to deduce ho
physical, chemical and biological reactions could have affected the artifacts while they were buried.

Table 1.

	Permanently frozen subsoil	Surface	Hearth (buried in permafrost)
Temperature	below 0° Celsius	low to freezing	freezing
Water	frozen	damp to saturate (25%) frozen (75%)	frozen
Oxygen	free oxygen may be negligible	% higher in cold water dependent on % used up in biotic activity	may be negligible if objects encased in peat and oil
pH	below 7 mostly organic acids	below 7	dependent on % of fat and peat
Pressure	terrestrial pressure negligible at this depth	expansion and contraction as a result of thawing and freezing	

Time: site dated to approximately 1650 A.D.
Climatic fluctuation: two warming periods, one in late 1700s, one in early 1800s [3].

3.2. Deductions
It could be deduced that the artifacts recovered from the surface layer would be poorly preserved. Expansion ar
contraction as the result of freezing and thawing of ice crystals would lead to the disruption of the cellul
structure of organic materials. Water movement, biotic activity, and acid conditions during the summer mont
would have contributed to further deterioration. The two 'warming periods' since the seventeenth century ma
also have influenced an increase in the rate of these reactions.

Organic materials should be well preserved in the permanently frozen subsoil where biotic activity would ha
ceased. Inorganic materials may still undergo chemical reactions, but the rate of these reactions will be great
decreased.
The types of chemical reactions which could have occurred in the hearth area will depend on the percentage
oil, peat, and charred material. If specimens were saturated with oil, oxidation reactions would be minimized.

Representative artifacts
Since the method of excavating the artifacts was to thaw the frozen subsoil layer by layer, one could assume th
all of the specimens would be cold and wet upon recovery.

Bone
Hydrolysis of the ossein, organic decomposition, and breakdown of the inorganic framework could have occurre
on the surface during the summer months. If found, bone would be fragmentary and spongy. Methods of casti
impressions, lifting and impregnating the bone should therefore be discussed. Procedures for cleaning, slow
drying or impregnating well-preserved bone from the permafrost should be outlined.

Wood
Freezing-thawing, water movement, and biotic activity would have contributed to the deterioration of surfa
finds of wood. Since all recovered pieces would be wet, temporary impregnation with a solution of polyethyle
glycol of low molecular weight was suggested.

Tanned skins and textiles

Leather would suffer from reactions similar to those affecting bone and wood. The extent of deterioration may have been minimized by protective tanning agents in the skin, and by slightly acid conditions. It was suggested that these specimens be rinsed with water and sealed in polyethylene bags with a fungicide; then reburied to keep them damp and cool. The same procedure was mentioned for textiles, which should be better preserved if they were protein in origin.

Iron

Iron objects should be in an oxygen-deficient atmosphere, otherwise even those artifacts buried in the frozen subsoil may be completely mineralized. Special precautions should be taken in lifting and packaging the iron; no attempts should be made in the field to remove corrosion layers. Specimens should be rinsed and sealed, wet, in plastics.

3.3. Results

Based on these deductions, provisions could be made for the preservation of specific materials in the field. The variables modifying standard treatments could then be taken into account: excavation could only be accomplished by thawing the frozen subsoil, therefore specimens would be cold and wet upon recovery; low arctic temperatures would limit the types and molecular weights of impregnating solutions that could be used in the field; the rate of chemical reactions such as those involved in casting materials would be greatly decreased; humid conditions may necessitate the use of fungicides and insecticides.

In addition, variables such as time, funds, availability of conservation materials, space, facilities, energy sources, means of transportation, and number of workers are vital considerations in determining conservation procedures at all archaeological sites.

4.   IN SITU STABILIZATION

A conflict of interests often arises at an archaeological site. The conservator might be anxious to remove and stabilize the specimens, while the archaeologist might prefer them to remain in situ long enough to examine their cultural context and implications. Stabilization of specimens in situ may again modify conservation techniques, consolidation materials, their molecular weights and concentration. Modification in this case would be directly dependent on local environmental conditions, especially humidity, temperature, and precipitation.

The stabilization of large archaeological structures has too often been neglected or has been postponed until excavation has been completed. Although it would obviously be difficult to predetermine the exact steps which should be taken in the preservation of structures before excavation, the conservator and the archaeologist should both be aware that temporary stabilization is often vital between excavation seasons. The factors determining necessary protective measures are again the variables of the local environment, available materials, and location and accessibility of the site.

5.   CONCLUSION

In view of the number of variables involved, one realizes that this is still a preliminary proposal for a method with which to approach 'in-field' conservation. The problems may seem overwhelming, but the advantages to be gained from preventive conservation measures will far outweigh them. Working with the archaeologist in a methodology such as this should alleviate many of the unexpected difficulties in archaeological conservation.

6.   FURTHER APPLICATIONS OF THIS METHODOLOGY

There are at least two other beneficial effects which would become apparent if conservators were to adopt a system such as this in studying archaeological sites. The first involves determining the origin of undocumented archaeological specimens by examining their corrosion and decomposition products. By comparing these factors with micro-environmental conditions of likely sites, it may be possible to provide information regarding the specific origin of a specimen.

The second result could only be accomplished after adequate data had been assembled on the rates of decomposition of materials under various conditions. Understanding how and where rates of decomposition vary can aid the archaeologist in modifying conclusions about the excavated culture such as diet, technology, and cultural comparisons, which are based on artifact remains.

REFERENCES

1. Strahler, A. N., 'The Earth Sciences', New York, 1963.
2. Fitzhugh, W. W., Associate Curator of Archaeology, Smithsonian Institution (personal communication).
3. Fitzhugh, W. W., 'Environmental Archeology and Cultural Systems in Hamilton Inlet, Labrador', Washington, DC, 1972.

[Parts of this paper are reprinted from: Rose, C. L., Notes on archaeological conservation, 'Bulletin of the AIC', 14 (1974), 123-130.]

CORROSION AND CONSERVATION OF IRON

Lars Barkman, Wasavarvet, Djurgårdsbrunnsvägen 24, 11527 Stockholm, Sweden

1. SOME GENERAL ASPECTS OF CORROSION

Most metals do not occur as pure elements in nature but must be extracted by the application of energy. According to the laws of nature a system strives to attain the lowest possible state of energy, which for metals usually means that they tend to return to their oxidized state and hence to their stable energy form. That iron corrodes under certain conditions is therefore as natural as that a stone falls to the ground.

The extent of corrosion is to a high degree dependent on the environment. In archaeological contexts a distinction must be made between corrosion in a maritime environment, in air and in soil. A metal corrodes if it is exposed simultaneously to oxygen and water. Corrosion takes place electrochemically, as the corrosion medium is an electrolyte. The dissolution of the metal is an anodic process occurring simultaneously with a cathodic process in which oxygen, and sometimes hydrogen ions, are consumed. Examples of the amount of corrosion in $\mu m/10$ years for unprotected steel in different environments are shown in the Table below.

Air			Water			Soil		
Industry	City	Rural area	River water	Sea water	Tap water	Very corrosive	Medium corrosive	Little corrosive
1000	500	100	500	1000	100	1000	300	50

Corrosion proceeds in the soil at different speeds due primarily to differences in its specific electrical resistance. The lower the resistance, the greater the quantity of water and salts. Measurement of the resistivity, as it is called, therefore gives a good idea of the corrosive effect of a soil. Another factor affecting corrosion is the presence of oxygen, in accordance with the reasoning above. If the content of oxygen diminishes at greater depths in the soil, the speed of corrosion diminishes correspondingly. The amount of corrosion in soils thus varies according to whether, among other factors, they were formed in salt water, fresh water, or through weathering, and is much higher below than above the marine limit. In judging the corrosion of an object, therefore, it is important to find out whether it has been buried and in which marine deposit. As is evident, sea water is very corrosive. Of fresh waters, river water is more corrosive than, for example, hard tap water, in which the relatively high content of calcium provides some protection against corrosion.

Many of the findings from the 'Wasa', from wood, iron and other materials, have attracted the interest of scientific researchers. Here the corrosion and the conservation of the iron findings will be dealt with. The iron objects constitute the second largest group of artifacts after wooden objects.

The conditions for corrosion of the 'Wasa' are known, and therefore the corrosion can be studied under known premises. It is also of interest to study where the iron that rusted away has gone and, finally, how the remaining iron objects should best be treated in order to be preserved.

Of more than 5000 one-inch bolts — many more than one metre in length — fragments remain of only two. All iron nails in the decks had rusted away. The original number of nails was even greater than that of bolts. Other parts which have practically entirely disappeared are the forgings for the 64 gun carriages and also for the 52 gunports.

Examples of analysis for the compact iron core from forgings and castings are given below.

	% C	% Fe$_{tot}$	Si	Mn	P	S
Bolt 1" (20083)	1.06		<0.1	0.01	0.02	0.015
Iron support in main mast (22014)	0.6		<0.1	0.01	0.03	0.010
Cannon-ball, 24 lb (13698)	3.58	95	1.21	0.07	0.04	0.05

Example of analysis of the rusty cast iron:

	% C	% Fe$_{tot}$	Si	Mn	P	S
Cannon-ball (13698), porous material	12.4	ca.43	5.35	0.09	0.06	0.02

Cl-determinations show contents of 0.7–1.2%

For some reason, apart from the high carbon concentration, the percentage of silicon has risen. This may be an additional contributory reason why the cast-iron finds have retained their volume despite corrosion. The main element in the iron salts is Fe_2O_3. The low sulphur content shows that there are no sulphates or other sulphur compounds in the corroded layer. The analyses show high chloride contents, which is one of the main reasons for the breakdown of the finds if they are not properly treated.

The iron dissolved from the metal objects in the corrosion process has to a large extent been precipitated on material in the vicinity, mainly because of the virtual absence of water-flow. When, therefore, the 'Wasa' was raised to the surface and the investigations started, the planking was resplendent with all manner of yellow, brown, black and red shades. Stalactite deposits of up to half a metre in length hung from the ship's sides in the hold and on the orlop deck, usually down to a knee or strake of ceiling. An investigation of the stalactites shows that the stalactite formation consists of an inner core of magnetite, siderite and pyrrholite. The outer varicoloured fine powder appears to consist of oxidation products of these compounds — iron, sulphate, iron hydroxide, goethite and lepidocrocite. The formations have an extremely light and porous structure and appear to be caused by the fact that the precipitation of iron took place on timber. This is confirmed by the presence of organic carbon. From the geological aspect, the crystallization of magnetite is of interest through this 333-year-old 'laboratory experiment'.

2. CONTINUED CORROSION

The cannon from the 'Riksäpplet', which foundered in 1676, was salvaged in 1953. It was scraped, brushed and treated with anti-rust oil, and placed in the museum in 1954 (Figure 1). After 18 years the corrosion had proceeded so far that all ornamentation had disappeared (Figure 2).

The large iron pot from the 'Wasa' was rusted to different degrees at the time of salvaging. Part had rusted through, while other parts had their iron core intact. Attempts at stabilization were made by rinsing it with water, extracting the water with acetone, drying in vacuum, and vacuum impregnation with acrylic lacquer. The result was unsatisfactory, and continued corrosion was observed within a few weeks.

3. THE REDUCTION FURNACE

Hydrogen gas reduction of iron oxides has long been used in industry and was described, inter alia, in Chemiker-Zeitung XI of 1887, under the name Hartwich'sches Reduktionsverfahren. It did not come into wide use in museums, however. As a result of investigations made by Olof Arrhenius and Erik Sjöstrand at different Swedish industrial enterprises and at the National Maritime Museum and the Warship 'Wasa' Research Laboratory, the method was developed for practical use for museum objects. An electrically-heated 'soaking pit' was constructed in consultation with Max Sievert AB, Stockholm, and was brought into use on 26 November 1964. It was designed for 'Wasa' findings, but has since come into wide use for conservation of valuable finds from other places, mostly from prehistoric times.

3.1 Cannon-ball, object no K6

This test consisted of reduction followed by anticorrosive treatment. The reduction time in this case was 18 hours at $800°C$ and 5 hours at $1060°C$.

3.2 Analysis of cannon-ball K6
(Sample no 1 from surface)

Before reduction

No	Sample weight g	Fe %	Fe met %	C %
1	5.0	23.6	no trace	30.2
2	5.0	24.9	no trace	27.7
3	6.0	28.9	no trace	24.3
4	7.0	32.9	no trace	20.1
5	7.0	30.5	no trace	22.6
6	10.0	28.0	no trace	25.8

After reduction

No	Sample weight g	Fe %	Fe met %	C %
7	4.5	39.0	39.0	33.3
8	6.0	38.5	38.5	36.2
9	7.0	50.2	47.0	29.2
10	7.0	50.9	47.5	29.1
11	6.0	47.2	45.5	31.0
12	4.8	42.8	42.0	32.7

As is seen, a fully satisfactory reduction of the object has taken place. To prevent continued rusting, it was treated with paraffin wax. The anti-rust agent was 2% VPI (Shell patent). Accelerated rust-prevention tests in a climatic chamber with admission of air during 10 months showed that the object had acquired a fully satisfactory protection against corrosion.

In addition to vacuum treatment of the reduced objects with molten paraffin wax, the aim of which is as far as possible completely to fill the pores in the entire object, anti-rust agents with solvent can be used. The degree of filling for the anti-rust agent in question is proportional to the concentration in the solution. This implies that one attains a degree of filling of 25-35%. This method is used when requirements of increased mechanical strength of the objects are not unduly strict.

No drying is done in the present reduction processes. After being cleaned, the objects can be laid directly in the retort for drying in a protective atmosphere, and subsequently reduced. A normal schedule for, say, 24-pound cannon-balls, up to a total weight of 60 kg, can be run in a week as follows:

Heating to 200°C for 8 hours
Maintenance at 200°C approx. 16 hours
Heating to 400°C for 8 hours
Maintenance at 400°C approx. 16 hours
Heating to 600°C for 5 hours
Maintenance at 600°C 18 hours
Heating to 800°C for 5 hours
Cooling to room temperature for 48 hours

The cost of the conservation work consists primarily in salaries. The furnace cost was 24,500 Skr, which results in a depreciation of 30 Skr per charge.

NOTE

This paper is an abridged version of 'Conservation of Old Rusty Iron Objects. Reduction of Rust with Hydrogen Gas' by O. Arrhenius, L. Barkman and E. Sjöstrand, published by the Swedish Corrosion Institute (as Bulletin No 61E) in 1973.

Figure 1. Cannon from 'Riksäpplet', foundered 1676, salvaged in 1953.

Figure 2. Same cannon with severe corrosion damage in 1972. All ornamentation has disappear

INVESTIGATIONS INTO METHODS FOR CONSERVING IRON RELICS RECOVERED FROM THE SEA

N. A. North and C. Pearson, Department of Material Conservation and Restoration, Fremantle Branch, Western Australian Museum, Finnerty Street, Fremantle, W.A.6160, Australia

1. INTRODUCTION

The majority of iron objects prior to the 20th century were fabricated from either wrought or cast iron. These were used for everyday utensils and tools, also for ship's fittings including cannon and anchors. The majority of shipwrecks contain the remains of these iron relics and it is well known that they are probably the most difficult to conserve of the different metals recovered from a wreck.

2. CORROSION OF IRON IN THE SEA

Iron is more susceptible to corrosion than any other metal normally found on a shipwreck. Silver, copper, gold, lead and their alloys are all cathodic to iron [1] and if in contact with it will create a galvanic couple increasing the corrosion rate of iron. The water salinity, oxygen content, temperature and movement of sand and water will also play an important role in the deterioration of iron objects and it is therefore very difficult to predict how well such an object will survive on the sea bed. On the same wreck some iron objects have been found in an excellent condition while others have completely corroded [2].

Wrought iron is essentially pure iron which contains small amounts of refining slag. During the working of the iron the slag is formed into fibrous inclusions running through the grains of iron. In sea water, chloride ions penetrate into these inclusions and are subsequently difficult to remove. Corrosion occurs rapidly along the slag inclusions and produces a creviced or wood-grain appearance on the surface. The corrosion products formed on the outer surfaces of wrought iron are non-adherent, flake off readily and although still reflecting the general shape of the original object, all surface markings are usually missing (Figures 1 and 2). However, the preferential corrosion along the slag inclusions often shows the manner in which the object was built up from individual pieces of wrought iron, which is of importance to the historical archaeologist (Figure 2).

Early cast irons usually contain 3-5% carbon by weight and, depending on the quality of the iron, varying amounts of other impurities, principally silicon, phosphorus, sulphur and manganese. Most of the carbon is present in the form of graphite flakes distributed throughout the iron matrix. As this is cathodic to the iron it is immune to corrosion whereas the surrounding iron is convereted into oxides and hydroxides, some of which are transported away from the surface of the object [3]. The presence of the carbon flakes maintains the original shape and surface details of the object even though there may be very little or none of the original solid metal remaining (Figure 3). This process is known as graphitization [1]. The graphitized material is soft, relatively easily damaged, and, we have found, may contain up to 60% by weight of iron and 13% by weight of chloride. The remaining central core of uncorroded iron is very reactive; in the presence of oxygen, water and chlorides, rapid formation of corrosion products at the metal surface will occur, causing the outer graphitized layers to exfoliate.

3. AIMS OF CONSERVATION

When considering a system for stabilizing marine iron artifacts it is important to consider which characteristics of the iron object it is desirable to retain. Generally these characteristics fall into three categories:

3.1 Shape and surface markings

These characteristics are used to identify the artifact. At the simplest level they show what the artifact was, e.g. a cannon, and at the best, as in the case of inscriptions, can provide information concerning the date and place of manufacture, original dimensions, etc.

3.2 Chemical composition of the metal

In the early irons the only intentional constituents were iron and carbon. All other constituents of the iron entered accidentally from the ores and materials used in the smelting process. Consequently the chemical composition of the iron can provide information on ore bodies and iron-making methods at the time of manufacture [4].

3.3 Metallurgical structure of the metal

In both wrought and cast iron the metallurgical structure can provide valuable information on manufacturing processes. This is particularly noticeable in the case of wrought iron where the slag inclusions, or the crevices produced from them, show how a large object, e.g. an anchor, was built up by working together a number of smaller pieces of wrought iron (Figure 2). At the microscopic level, processes such as cold working and tempering in the wrought iron, and chill casting and annealing in the cast iron, all affect the final structure of the iron.

The ideal method of iron conservation should be able to preserve these three characteristics of the object and, in addition, should do so quickly, simply and cheaply. For those iron objects which are completely corroded, points 3.2 and 3.3 are irrelevant, and when conserving such objects the only consideration is retention of the shape and surface markings, if any, of the original object. This can sometimes be achieved by taking a cast of the hollow left in the surrounding concretion or marine debris [2, 5] as shown in Figure 4.

4. STABILIZATION

The corrosion of iron, both in the sea and after recovery, is governed by the pH, electrochemical potential (Eh) and chloride content of the solution in contact with the iron. The electro-chemical potential of a solution is a measure of its oxidizing ability and is usually determined from the potential of a platinum electrode immersed in the solution. The effects of pH and Eh for iron in both pure water and 1 M NaCl are shown in Figure 5a and 5b [6]. The passivation of iron in oxidizing solutions (high Eh) is due to the formation of a protective oxide film on the surface of the metal. Chloride ions (Figure 5b) lessen the protective characteristics of this film and allow corrosion to occur over a wide range of pH and Eh.

Corrosion will not occur in the absence of water but, as iron chlorides are deliquescent, any dried artifact containing chlorides will extract moisture from the atmosphere and so form a very corrosive solution with a high chloride content. If the chlorides are absent from the corrosion products, then the remaining iron will be stable (passified) over a wide range of pH and Eh, and in addition, once the object is dried, there will be little tendency for atmospheric moisture subsequently to form solutions in contact with the iron. Consequently, the problem of stabilizing marine iron is basically one of removing the chloride and water contents without damaging or otherwise altering the object.

4.1 Role of chloride ions

The maximum concentration of chloride ions in the corrosion products which can safely be tolerated without producing decay of the remaining iron is not known. This maximum chloride level will depend on the temperature and humidity of the storage conditions. Analyses of treated iron by Eriksen and Thegel [10] indicate that chloride levels of 0.01% by weight (100 p.p.m.) or less are not detrimental to the stability of the artifact; but in a hot, humid climate these chloride levels may be too high.

In discussing treatment procedures for marine iron it is important to know the nature of the chlorides found in the corrosion products, as different chlorides have different chemical properties. If the chloride content of the corrosion product is sufficiently high, the crystal structure and chemical composition of the chloride can be determined by X-ray diffraction techniques. Using a sample containing 13% by weight of chloride from the corroded section of a cast iron cannonball we were able to identify the chloride phase as being ferric oxy-chloride (FeOCl). The properties of FeOCl are well known [7, 8], and two of these are of particular importance to marine iron conservation.

Firstly, at room temperatures, FeOCl will slowly convert to $FeCl_3$ and FeO(OH) in the presence of water; the rate and extent of this reaction appear to depend on the pH and chloride content of the water. Secondly, FeOCl is thermodynamically stable in air at temperatures between 94 and $430^{\circ}C$ [7, 8]; at $430^{\circ}C$ the volatile $FeCl_3$ is formed. In inert atmospheres, even higher temperatures are needed for complete volatilization of the chlorides due to the partial formation of $FeCl_2$ (m.p. $675^{\circ}C$) [8]. The thermal behaviour of FeOCl in a reducing atmosphere, e.g. H_2, has not been studied, but the formation of $FeCl_2$ appears likely. Consequently the temperatures required for the complete volatilization of chlorides from corrosion products are well above the temperatures at which changes in a metallurgical structure of iron will readily occur.

A further factor which has to be considered is the effect which the method of chloride removal will have on the other corrosion products. Our X-ray diffraction analysis of untreated wrought and cast iron corrosion products show that the iron is present predominantly as a mixture of magnetite (Fe_3O_4), iron oxy-hydroxide (FeO(OH)), iron oxy-chloride (FeOCl) and, in the case of cast iron, iron carbide or cementite (Fe_3C). If corrosion occurs under anaerobic or reducing conditions, the major product is magnetite and the chloride content is relatively low (approx. 0.3% by weight at 35% salinity). Under more oxidizing conditions the proportions of both iron oxy-hydroxide and iron oxy-chloride are higher. Both FeO(OH), s.g. approx 4.2 g/cm^3, and Fe_3O_4, s.g. approx. 5.2 g/cm^3, are less dense than metallic iron, s.g. approx. 7.5 g/cm^3. Consequently any treatment which involves a reduction of FeO(OH) to Fe_3O_4, or to metallic iron, will cause a reduction in the volume occupied by the corrosion products and an increase in the void space. If this increase in void space is concentrated in a particular area of the corroded region then cracks will develop in the object and exfoliation of the corroded layers may occur. This problem can be alleviated by either not reducing the corrosion products or by containing the reduction to the formation of magnetite.

Finally, a warning on chloride analysis. Many stabilization methods involve the transfer of chlorides from the solid corroded iron phase to an aqueous solution, e.g. by electrolysis. The extent of chloride removal from the iron is generally monitored by following the concentration of chloride in the liquid; when this remains low and constant, the treatment is assumed to be completed with all chloride removed from the corrosion products. This assumption is not necessarily correct and it must be proved for each treatment method. This can be done by treating an object until no further chloride release is found and then analyzing the remaining corrosion products for chloride ion content, right down to the original metal/corrosion product interface.

4.2 Role of water

In the absence of moisture, iron corrosion will not occur. If moisture is present corrosion may occur, depending on the composition of the solution formed (Figure 5). Consequently it is desirable, after chloride removal, to dry the iron artifacts thoroughly and to treat them so that they remain dry. This can be carried out by drying the artifact with either acetone or a dewatering fluid, and then applying a protective coating in the case of wrought iron, or filling the pore spaces with micro-crystalline wax in the case of cast iron.

5. TREATMENT METHODS

The treatment of any marine iron object must commence the minute it is recovered from the sea bed. The conservation procedures can be divided into three categories: recovery, storage and conservation. Recovery includes the process of physical removal of the object from the sea bed until it reaches storage or conservation facilities. Storage can be defined as producing an environment in which the iron does not react further, whereas conservation consists of altering the iron in such a manner that it does not react with the normal atmosphere.

5.1 Recovery

The extreme reactivity of iron objects recovered from the sea and exposed to the air is well known. Cannon balls have been known literally to explode, hemp wadding from the bore of a cannon to commence smouldering [3], and we have recently observed strong exothermic reactions during the excavation of iron tools and nails from concretions. This reaction is caused by the combined effects of moisture, chlorides and a plentiful supply of oxygen.

It is therefore essential to retain as much of the concretion or marine growth as possible on the excavated object and to keep the object wet. In this manner the entry of air into the corroded regions is minimized and the chloride solution in the corroded region is prevented from becoming even more corrosive through concentration by moisture evaporation. The objects can be kept wet by total immersion in water or an alkaline solution, by continual hosing with water or by wrapping in wet canvas and sealing with polythene. Just a few minutes' exposure to fresh oxygen, especially on the hot exposed deck of a work boat, may be sufficient for fresh, vigorous and irreversible corrosion to occur.

5.2 Storage

A delay of a few hours to several months, depending on individual circumstances, generally occurs between the time an iron object is recovered from the sea and the time the conservation treatment commences. During this time the object must be stored in a stable environment and there are three methods of storage which appear to be satisfactory:

5.2.1 Alkaline environment

In the pH range 10 to 13 (0.5 M Na_2CO_3 or 0.1 M NaOH), the corrosion rate of iron is very low even at high chloride concentrations (Figure 5). The solubility of the corrosion products is low in this pH range and the corroded regions are also safe from attack. When fresh water is not available to prepare these solutions, as is often the case with wrecks off the West Australian Coast, we have found that the solution formed by the addition of 20 grams of NaOH per litre of sea water is a satisfactory medium for iron storage. This storage method is simple, relatively inexpensive and requires very little maintenance. In addition, this method also removes some of the chloride from the corrosion products, even in alkaline sea water (provided the concretion is removed). The reaction is given in Equation 1 (see below).

5.2.2 Dehydration

Corrosion cannot occur in the absence of moisture. Consequently an untreated marine iron object which is stored in a dry environment, e.g. in a closed container with a silica gel dessicant, will remain stable for an indefinite period. We have tested this method with samples containing up to 10% by weight chloride and, even with frequent exposure to the atmosphere for inspection purposes, no deterioration of the samples has been noted in twelve months. This storage method is particularly suited to small, fragile specimens. If a glass container is used which is closed and sealed, the specimen will be stable as long as the seal remains intact. To guard against ineffective seals, the use of a self-indicating silica gel is recommended.

5.2.3 Inert gas

An inert gas, such as dry nitrogen, may possibly be used for storing marine iron objects. As with the dehydration method, this is particularly suitable for small fragile objects. We are at present experimenting with this technique to determine the relative importance of oxygen, nitrogen and water for this storage method.

For all storage methods, it is important to remove any concretion or marine growth from the iron object. In storage method 5.2.1 this will facilitate chloride ion removal, and in the other two methods it is necessary because such a concretion would tend to harbour moisture, chlorides and oxygen. When concretion removal is not feasible due to the fragile nature of the iron artifact, storage in an alkaline environment is the only method we can recommend.

With cast iron materials, in particular, the main feature to be avoided during storage is the partial dehydration of the corrosion layer. In the presence of oxygen this produces a very corrosive medium at the metal/corrosion layer interface. If left, this may cause exfoliation of the corroded layers or, at best, leave a weakened layer between the metal and these layers, which can cause serious problems during the subsequent treatment process.

5.3 Conservation treatment

Over the years, a number of methods for stabilizing marine iron have been proposed. We have examined most of these methods and, for various reasons, have found none of them to be completely satisfactory. These methods, and their difficulties, are as follows.

5.3.1 Acid pickling

This involves the removal of the corrosion products, and the included chlorides, by treating a sample with an inhibited mineral acid, usually phosphoric acid (H_3PO_4). This treatment necessarily results in the loss of surface layers and cannot be used for cast iron as it would remove the graphitized layers and therefore any surface markings. It would also be very difficult to remove all traces of the acid from the porous surface of cast iron. With wrought iron, although the corrosion products are generally non-adherent, complete removal of this corrosion is difficult to achieve, as some spots are very resistant to acid attack, particularly in the crevices formed from slag inclusions. These remaining areas form a centre for subsequent corrosion attack.

5.3.2 Sandblasting
This method removes the surface layers of the object down to the base metal and cannot be used if the corrosion layer is thick or if the surface markings would be destroyed, as is the case for cast iron or for fragile objects. We have also found this method to be ineffective with wrought iron, as the corrosion products in the crevices are not removed. The shiny metal surface produced by sandblasting is very reactive and if protective paint is not applied immediately after sandblasting, the surface rapidly corrodes.

5.3.3 Protective coating
The application of a protective paint or sealant to a corroded iron surface without prior removal of the chloride is not successful as no paints are completely impermeable to moisture (which the chlorides will attract). As the only insoluble chloride salts, $AgCl$ and Hg_2Cl_2, are unstable in the presence of metallic iron, it is not possible to fix the chloride ions as an unreactive insoluble solid as, for example, is done in the case of SO_4^{2-} ions by the use of a $Ba_3(PO_4)_2$ containing paint. In addition, painting over crevices which still contain moisture and chloride ions will very often aggravate corrosion by the formation of differential oxygenation and pH cells.

5.3.4 Cold alkaline washing
When a marine iron object is placed in a alkaline aqueous solution, the chloride ions in the corrosion product are replaced by hydroxide ions. This process,

$$FeOCl + OH^- \rightleftharpoons FeO(OH) + Cl^-$$

is an equilibrium, and the amount and rate of chloride release into the solution increases with the pH and decreases with the Cl^- content of the solution. Consequently the Cl^- content of the solution has to be monitored (quantitatively) and the solution changed when necessary.

As tested in this laboratory, the following washings were successively used:
1. 0.5 M Na_2CO_3 (technical grade) in tap water (130 p.p.m. Cl^-)
2. 0.1 M NaOH (L.R) in tap water
3. 0.1 M NaOH (L.R) in deionized water (3 p.p.m. Cl^-)
4. 0.1 M NaOH (A.R) in deionized water

The final wash lasted for eight weeks. This method has proved successful, to date, for some wrought iron metal working tools (Figure 6) from a 17th century wreck ('Vergulde Draeck') [2]. However, if the artifact is heavily corroded, this method is not successful as the wash solution has poor penetrating powers and consequently leaves chloride ions in the inner corroded regions.

5.3.5 Hot alkaline — reduction washing
If hot (60-80°C) alkaline washing is carried out, the rates of reaction are increased and the viscosity of the wash solution is lowered, thus increasing its penetrating powers. However, corrosion products are not stable in hot hydroxide solutions and loose FeO(OH) forms rapidly. This can be prevented by using a solution of 0.5 M Na_2SO_3 and 0.5 M NaOH. This solution is strongly reducing and the following reactions occur:

$$3FeO(OH) + e^- \longrightarrow Fe_3O_4 + OH^- + H_2O \tag{2}$$
$$FeOCl + 2FeO(OH) + e^- \longrightarrow Fe_3O_4 + Cl^- + H_2O \tag{3}$$

During treatment, the iron in the corrosion products is completely converted to Fe_3O_4, which we verified by X-ray diffraction studies. As Fe_3O_4 is denser than FeO(OH), its production increases the porosity of the corrosion products and this further improves the penetration of the wash solution. As in all washing techniques, the solution has to be monitored for Cl^- content and changed when necessary. After treatment, the excess $SO_3^{2-} + SO_4^{2-}$ are removed firstly by washing, at room temperature, in deionized water, and then in 0.1 M $Ba(OH)_2$ to fix any remaining SO_3^{2-} or SO_4^{2-} as the insoluble barium salts.

The major disadvantage with this method is that hot SO_3^{2-} solutions react rapidly with atmospheric oxygen, hence the reactions must be carried out in a sealed container. For this purpose we use a sealed 200-litre drum and remove any residual oxygen by nitrogen purging. At present this method is still at an experimental stage but the results, to date, appear very promising. Retention of shape and surface markings is good and, at the temperature used, there is no danger of altering the composition or structure of the metal. It would seem to be particularly useful for fragile iron objects which cannot be treated by the electrolysis method (5.3.7).

5.3.6 Heat treatment
When marine iron is heated sufficiently, the chlorides are expelled as HCl, $FeCl_3$ or $FeCl_2$ (section 3.1). If the heating is carried out in air then spalling of the surface layers occurs [10], causing the loss of surface markings and, if extensive, much of the shape. This problem can be alleviated by heating in an inert or reducing atmosphere [9] but difficulties can still occur due to loss of graphite (decarbonization) or shrinkage of the corrosion product through reduction to the denser metallic iron. In addition, metallic iron and corrosion products have different thermal expansion coefficients and the heating and cooling cycle will physically weaken the bond between the two. The temperatures required in all these heat treatments are such that changes can occur in the metallurgic structure of any uncorroded iron which is in the object. Hence any information which could be determined from the structure of the iron, now or in the future, is destroyed or, at best, rendered suspect.

5.3.7 Electrolysis

By making the iron object the cathode in an electrolytic cell, the Cl^- ions can be removed from the corrosion products by the combined effects of iron reduction and applied electric field [3]. This reduction is generally carried out in sodium hydroxide or sodium carbonate solutions.

With this method it is essential that all corroded regions have an approximately equal current flow; this can be achieved by placing the anodes at approximately equal distances from the surface of the object. Care must also be taken not to allow pockets of gas to form in contact with the cathode as these will stop current flow through the area in contact with them.

The major problem in electrolysis is that nearly all the current is used in the generation of hydrogen and very little is used in the reduction of the corrosion products or in chloride removal. In the initial stages of electrolysis, the main reaction at the cathode is the redution of $FeO(OH)$ to Fe_3O_4 (Equation 2). Once this reduction is complete, the main reaction becomes hydrogen generation through:

$$H_2O + e^- \rightleftharpoons \tfrac{1}{2} H_2 + OH^- \tag{4}$$

This reaction is favoured by the presence of graphite, as the hydrogen over-potential on this is much less (at least 200 mV) than on metallic iron [1, 11]. The applied current is used mainly to generate OH^- ions at the cathode, carry these through the solution and then destroy them at the anode (by oxygen production). Consequently, very long treatment times are necessary for satisfactory chloride removal. In addition, we have found that hydrogen evolution at the cathode may cause damage to the graphitized surface layers of cast iron objects, especially if weaknesses, caused for example by poor storage conditions, exist in the corroded layer prior to electrolysis. This method should not be used for fragile objects or for objects which do not contain a substantial metal core.

5.4 Washing, drying and coating

For all chloride extraction methods carried out in aqueous solutions it is necessary subsequently to remove all reagents from the corroded regions and to dry the object thoroughly. This is generally accomplished by first washing in inhibited distilled or deionized water, then in acetone and finally drying at room temperature. For large objects, such as cannon and anchors, it is more convenient to wash in tap water and then remove excess moisture by using a commercial de-watering fluid. During this washing process any loose or extraneous surface matter can be removed by careful brushing.

After a wrought iron artifact has been dried, the only additional treatment which we have found necessary is the application of a suitable protective paint system. The procedure we have used is the initial application of two coats of a zinc phosphate based anti-corrosion primer ('KEPHOS', manufactured by Dulux Paints, an ICI subsidiary) which is clear drying. These coats are brushed on and are approximately 12 μ thick. The primer coats are then followed by six coats of a high durability acrylic lacquer diluted 2:3 parts with thinner. The acrylic itself is a clear, matt polymethyl methacrylate, with approximately 12% solids. This mixture gives good adhesion and is transparent, provided the thickness is not too great. This paint system has been found to provide adequate protection to the wrought iron for indoor exposure and is aesthetically pleasing.

Cast iron artifacts, after treatment and drying, retain a porous and relatively soft surface (graphitized zone). To increase the strength of this layer and to prevent moisture penetration, we impregnate the cast iron objects with a high melting point micro-crystalline wax. This process is carried out by submerging the object in a wax bath at approximately $120°C$ [3]. After impregnation, any excess wax is removed from the surface with petroleum spirits.

6. CONCLUSIONS

The choice of storage and treatment methods for the stabilization of marine iron objects will depend on local conditions, the nature and quantity of material, the expertise and facilities available and, naturally, the sources of finance. In the preceding sections we have attempted to summarize the advantages and disadvantages of the various methods. We acknowledge the fact that due to lack of suitable facilities, etc., any individual person or institute may have to resort to the least satisfactory of these methods; however, at least he will be aware of the possible shortcomings of the method and can keep a watch for further corrosion outbreaks.

Of these methods we can recommend only two: for large, mechanically-sound iron objects and those where a solid metal core remains, electrolysis, and for fragile iron objects, the washing in a hot alkaline reduction solution. However, marine iron conservation is still at an experimental stage and no method can be regarded as being entirely satisfactory for all artifacts.

ACKNOWLEDGEMENTS

We wish to thank the Australian Research Grants Committee for the provision of a maintenance grant for one of us (N.N.), and M. Owens for assistance with the experimental work.

REFERENCES

1. Uhlig, H. H., 'The Corrosion Handbook', John Wiley and Sons, New York, 1966.
2. Pearson, C., The Western Australian Museum Conservation Laboratory for marine archaeological material, 'Int. J. Naut. Archaeol. and Underwater Archaeol' 3 (1974), 295-305.
3. Pearson, C., The preservation of iron cannon after 200 years under the sea, 'Studies in Conservation' 17 (1972), 91-110.

4. Simpson, B. L., 'History of the Metal-Casting Industry', Amer. Foundrymen's Soc. Inc. Publication, 1969.

5. Katzev, M. L. and van Doorninck, F. H., Jr, Replicas of iron tools from a Byzantine shipwreck, 'Studies Conservation' 11 (1969), 133-142.

6. Pourbaix, M., Significance of protection potential in pitting, inter-granular corrosion and stress corrosi cracking, 'J. Less Comm. Met.' 28 (1972), 51-69.

7. Schafer, H., Wittig, F. E. and Jori, M., Die Thermochemische Bestandigkeit des Eisenoxychlorids FeOCl, ' anorg. u. allgem. Chem.' 287 (1956), 61-70.

8. Pechkovskii, V. V. and Voreb've, N. I., Thermochemical transformation of iron chlorides, 'Russ. J. Inor Chem.' 9 (1964), 6-10.

9. Arrhenius, O., Barkman, L. and Sjostrand, E., 'Conservation of Old Rusty Iron Objects', Bulletin No.61 Swedish Corrosion Institute, 1973.

10. Eriksen, E. and Thegel, S., Conservation of iron recovered from the sea, in 'Tojhusmuseets Skrifter Copenhagen, 1966.

11. Booth, G. H., Tiller, A. K. and Wormwell, F., Ancient iron nails well preserved in an apparently corrosi soil, 'Nature' 195 (1962), 376-7.

Figure 1. Wrought iron Bower anchor from the 'Investigator' (1803). Treated by electrolysis.

Figure 2. Fluke of 'Investigator' (1803) Bower anchor. Cleaned of concretion but not otherwise treated. Fluke height 63 cm. Note built-up structure of fluke.

Figure 3.   Cast iron cannon, untreated, with graphitized surface from the 'Vergulde Draeck' (1656).

Figure 4.   Piece of concretion containing cavity left by a totally corroded iron lock. Below is a plastic replica
the lock cast from upper concretion. 'Batavia' (1629).

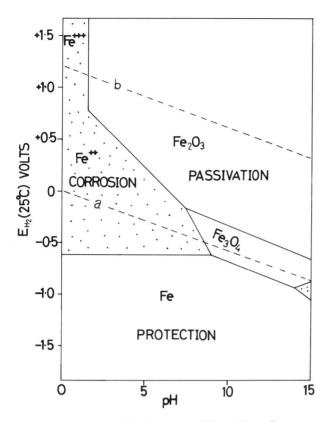

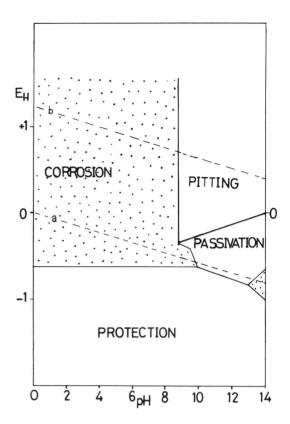

Figure 5a. Equilibrium potential — pH, or Pourbaix diagram, for iron — pure water system at 25°C.

Figure 5b. Pourbaix diagram for iron — 1M NaCl system at 25°C.

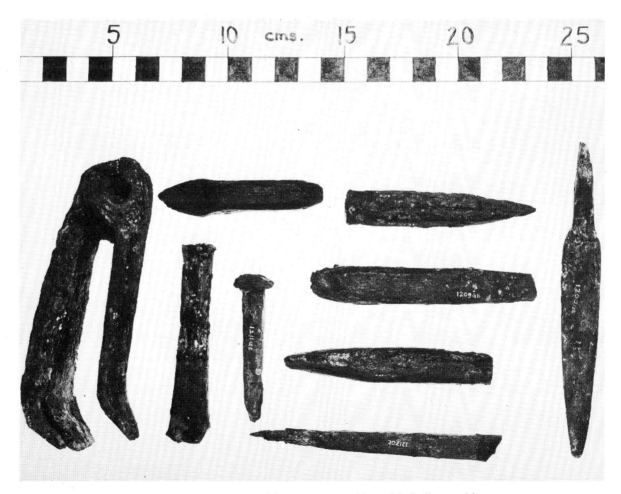

Figure 6. Iron tools from the 'Vergulde Draeck' (1656), treated by cold alkaline washing.

CONSERVATION OF CANNON RECOVERED FROM THE BRACKISH SEA

Ora Patoharju, Tehtaankatu 8A1, SF-00140 Helsinki 14, Finland

1. INTRODUCTION

The Baltic Sea is one of the world's largest bodies of stagnant water. Natural processes, aided by pollution, are exhausting the oxygen dissolved in its depths. While the surface layers continue to support fish, the sea's capacity to absorb and degrade sewage and waste is clearly limited. Stagnation periods are turning the entire deep-water area of the Baltic into a large oceanic desert without any kind of life except anaerobic bacteria.

The anaerobic sewage sludge which slowly filled the inside of the mighty 'Wasa' after she sank in the harbour of Stockholm in 1628 might be the main reason for the excellent preservation of the artifacts found on her decks. Thus, the only people who may take advantage of the pollution of the Baltic are the marine archaeologists, who expect to find the estimated 80,000 shipwrecks along our shores in an excellent state of preservation.

But in at least one case the anaerobic conditions in the depths do not favour the preservation of objects found on the sea-bed: cast-iron cannon. Old cast iron contained a considerable amount of graphite. Particles of graphite and iron form electrolytic cells in sea water. A crust is formed from the corrosion products and sand, etc., and this crust helps to create anaerobic conditions inside the crust. Iron dissolves in soluble and movable ion-form due to the electric potential between iron and graphite. The Fe^{++} ions wander towards and into the crust, and the iron percentage of the cast iron itself is diminishing. This, however, does not increase the dimensions of the objects, and they may retain to the smallest details their shape and dimensions while on the sea-bed.

But when the object — such as a gun — is brought to the surface and cleaned, it is directly exposed to the oxygen in the air, and corrosion of the iron compounds still left in the graphite layer proceeds at a rate depending upon the degree of moisture and the chlorides present. The increasing volume of rust, which can no longer be transported outside in movable ion-form, blows up — 'explodes' — the object, and the eventual result is a powdery product of rust and graphite, if no (or insufficient) conservation is applied.

2. CORROSION SPEED

Corrosion specialists estimate the speed of graphitization in sea-water to be approximately 0.02 to 0.2 mm per year (0.1 to 0.8 inches in a hundred years); both cast iron and steel are corroded at the same speed. Corroded parts contain only a fraction of the original iron, and metallic iron is no longer present. Graphitization begins from the surface and proceeds inwards, the results depending on the time of submersion and the salinity of the water. As an example, the guns from the frigate 'Nicholas' in the Finnish battleground Ruotsinsalmi (Svensksund) have less than one inch of graphitized layer after 160 years in the Gulf of Finland; underneath is solid iron. Some hand-grenades dating back at least to the Crimean War, found off Helsinki, also more than 120 years in the sea, have the ½-inch shell thoroughly corroded, but some other grenades nearby remained intact.

A cast-iron gun from one of our oldest wrecks, 'Jussarö I', approximately 400 years underwater, is almost pure graphite, as are the guns of the frigate 'Lossen', 250 years on the sea-bed in the salty ocean in Oslofiord, where the author dived as a guest of the local club in 1964.

Steel differs from cast iron by corroding away so that the original outlines disappear. Sometimes the crust formed around the object retains its outline, and should therefore be carefully preserved. If all metal is gone, the crust can be sawed in two and used as a mould.

Some examples of the composition of the graphitized surface layers, where no metallic iron was left, are given in Table 1.

Table 1.

Sample	Density	Iron	% of original Fe
'Wasa' (1628), cannon balls [1]	2400 kg/m^3	25%	
'Moskva' (1713), cannon	2200 kg/m^3	40%	12%
'Nicholas' (1790), cannon	2300 kg/m^3	46%	15%
Hand-grenades (≤ 1855), shell	1200 kg/m^3	20%	3.3%

3. CONSERVATION

There are two methods of conservation of cast-iron objects found in the sea but, in both cases, it is of the utmost importance that the chlorides of the sea-water are removed from the porous layer before the final treatment. Hygroscopic salts in the rust layer keep the object moist and, in presence of chlorides, the formation of ferrous chloride as a by-product of corrosion greatly favours the decomposition of the object, even if it is kept under controlled conditions in a museum. However, very often in museums one recognizes the tell-tale $FeCl_3$-droplets under the artifact; the conservation has not been successful.

The two methods are, in principle:

1. porous metal objects can be dried out in the absence of oxygen and then allowed to absorb a conservation fluid, which gives mechanical strength and seals the porous layer;
2. the substance can be reduced back into its original metallic state. Reduction can be effected electrochemically, chemically, or in a reducing atmosphere at elevated temperatures. In this case also, the reduced layer is porous and needs strengthening and sealing to avoid further corrosion.

The question of reduction does not arise where only little or no iron is left in the shell. However, a strong enough mineral frame holds the artifact together, and the shape and the size of the original object is preserved. The structure of the graphitized layer needs more research; this could improve conservation techniques.

4. CONSERVATION RESEARCH

Reduction at elevated temperatures and in gaseous phase has been applied to cannonballs in the Wasa-Museum [1]. The reduction took place in a specially constructed hydrogen oven at temperatures of 800–1060°C. The result was very successful; the balls kept their original dimensions and neither shrinkage nor cracks were observed. A great advantage of this method is the elimination of chlorides, which are volatilized. After the reduction, the somewhat porous but soon firm object is sealed against moisture with a paraffin wax or epoxy resin impregnation. Some doubts are, however, entertained about the high temperature, which may cause loss of carbon, and, in order to give time for studies of adequate reduction temperatures and times, the beginning of 'full scale' reduction has been postponed. According to preliminary information [2], similar trials have taken place in England with two whole cannon from the 'Mary Rose' (1545), in autumn 1972.

Cannon conservation without actual reducing processes is reported from Northern Ireland [3]. Cannon from the Spanish 'Girona' (1588) were first soaked with water; then the remaining iron surface and corrosion products were impregnated in a vacuum tank with a 20% solution of orthophosphoric acid, to inhibit further corrosion. Finally, the object was dried in air at approximately 110°C and the surface was sealed with nitrocellulose lacquer.

Reports of the careful removal of chlorides from the wrought-iron artifacts found in the 'Cog of Bremen' [4] describe treatment with ammonium salts and the removal of the ammonium chloride thus formed at a temperature of 150°C under vacuum. Bresle [5] has developed a washing solution with lithium hydroxide in an organic solvent, which effectively removes chlorides from a rust layer. This method is used both for conservation and protection of antique iron objects, and to prepare a good ground for metal painting in industry.

5. ORIGINS OF THE FINNISH GUNS

Two major Russo-Swedish sea-battles in 1789 and 1790 took place in the basin of Ruotsinsalmi (Svensksund in Swedish), well known today as the modern seaport of Kotka. In 1948, mapping and sounding activities in the entrance to this commercial port located the wreck of a big wooden vessel, a man-of-war sunk in the second battle of 1790. The wreck has been assigned the working name of the 'Great Nicholas'. During the following years, deep-sea divers raised some 20 cast-iron guns complete in their carriages, wine bottles and numerous small artifacts and objects. Ericsson [6] comments on the local proceedings in a recent report. When brought to the surface, the frigate's guns, which are displayed on a nearby island which serves as a museum, were freed from the surface layer of rust and brushed with paraffin wax after drying, as no better methods of preservation were known or considered necessary at that time. These guns are now deteriorating, and seem to be changing into powdery rust. It seems evident to the divers who have seen the guns still left below in the wreck that these are the only ones which will last. For this reason, divers have refrained from raising any more iron objects from the ship.

Late in 1967, three remarkable cast-bronze guns of Swedish manufacture from the 16th century were found in the eastern entrance to the Jussarö anchorage. These are the first bronze guns found in Finnish waters. Jussarö was once the point of departure for the Hanseatic city of Reval (Tallinn), and the sheltered anchorage was of considerable importance. Finally, an iron gun fused with its wooden carriage was raised. After storage underwater, the guns have now been treated chemically. A new wreck, located at the western inlet to the same anchorage, was found late in 1968: a well-preserved two-masted hull (brig?) with her maindeck, bowsprit and rudder intact, and four small guns still mounted in carriages.

Information was received by chance about a number of cast-iron guns and some short-barrelled swivel-guns, to the east of the Porkala headland, west of Helsinki. In June 1968, a group of eleven iron guns and two pivoted swivel-guns was located on the rocky bottom. The guns belong to the late 18th century, possibly to the Napoleonic era. These guns are now in the possession of the City Museum of Helsinki.

6. FINNISH TRIALS

6.1 Wet reduction

In 1963, wet electrolytic treatment was carried out as a conservation experiment on two Ruotsinsalmi guns, with the support of a local company [7]. One gun was brought to the surface years ago and allowed to dry in the open air; the other was found the same summer and deliberately kept under water until the treatment could be started immediately. The original purpose of the treatment was to reduce the surface rust to spongy iron which could easily be brushed off, revealing the uncorroded iron underneath. The electrolysis was carried out in a 10% Na_2CO_3 solution, using stainless steel sheets as anodes. The process was first continued for one month at 20 amperes DC and then at 150 A for five months, at a voltage of 4 V. This meant an amount of electricity equal to 8 GJ (2.2 MWh) or 2 million coulombs at 4 V. After treatment, the guns were cleaned with a steel brush, washed in fresh water and finally coated with varnish. Evaluation of the results is founded on visual observation. The 'dry' gun seems to be in the same condition as before electrolysis, and it flakes after drying as it did before. The 'wet' gun was believed to have retained its metallic surface, a little rough but with the original surface forms and reliefs preserved. However, in winter 1969/70 a name and date were drawn with some sharp tool on the 'wet' gun, which is stored in the open air with only a roof to shield it against direct rain, and thus revealed that the surface was not metallic iron.

The Porkala guns, in the possession of the City Museum of Helsinki, were treated by the same method, as there were neither funds nor methods for other cheap treatments – only time. All the guns were first kept for one year in fresh water in order to remove the chlorides; the first two guns were electrolyzed for 2 years 9 months with 4 V, 24 A, because no more power was available. The treatment served mainly to remove the chlorides from the porous layer. However, the electrical energy used, 8.25 GJ (2.3 MWh) or 2.1 MC at 4 V, is slightly more than that used in the treatment of the two Ruotsinsalmi guns (8.0 GJ).

6.2 Hot reduction

Reduction at elevated temperatures in the gaseous phase has been applied to cannonballs in the Wasa-Museum. In autumn 1970, an industrial plant in Finland offered a suitable reduction oven for experimental use with a privately owned gun, probably originating from the wreck-site of the Russian flag-ship 'Moskva' (1713).

The atmosphere in this 2 x 60 kW oven was 12% hydrogen and 88% nitrogen. Owing to the low partial pressure of hydrogen, a first trial was made with a cannonball, with good results. After that, one cannon of 413 kg was reduced during approximately 12 hours up to 500°C and 8 hours at 800°C. The result (Figure 1) was a spongy, porous, but iron-rich surface, which was impregnated by brushing it several times with an epoxy-resin solution. The final success of the treatment will be verified after many years' observation of the object, which is also stored in the open air, but sheltered against snow and rain.

6.3 No reduction

In Finland, trials are being carried out to conserve fully or deeply graphitized artifacts after water-soaking, by drying them out with alcohol and then sealing the porous layer with resins. Polyester was used initially for the resin-impregnation trials, but its poor wetting ability on iron or rust surfaces brought about a change to epoxy resins. The objects were first dipped in the resin, or it was applied by brushing. The attempts to conserve the Ruotsinsalmi guns by brushing them with undiluted polyester and epoxy resins did not lead to the desired results. The treatment of some cannon was carried out in summer 1963 but, after the winter and snow had gone, not much of the resin was left on the surface. A far better method, however, was the impregnation of the objects with a 10-20% solution of the resin in a toluene-butanol mixture. This method allows the resin to be absorbed on the inner parts of the porous rust before polymerization.

A totally graphitized gun, the oldest found in Finland, was conserved by epoxy impregnation ('Vita Falken', 1563?). In lifting and transportation operations, the fragile gun-barrel broke in two and the knob fell off. After preliminary cleaning, the piece was soaked in tap-water for 32 days, distilled water for 25 days and alcohol for 69 days. When the cannon was air-dry, the remaining shot was skilfully and carefully removed and a steel tube was placed inside to strengthen the broken point. Thinned epoxy resin was applied to the cannon until it ceased absorbing the liquid. During later transfers, the cannon has broken several times, revealing that the resin solution had not been absorbed more than 15-20 mm deep in the porous surface. However, in the author's opinion, this does not correspond to a misfortune in conservation but only to the impossibility of introducing mechanical strength to the fragile structure. Impregnation in a vacuum chamber seems to be necessary in order to strengthen the pieces thoroughly.

Eighteenth century light guns from the Jussarö island (1780?) are preserved after water-soaking and alcohol-drying in plastic bags, which are kept dry inside with silica gel. Further corrosion is prevented with small amounts of vapour phase inhibitor (Shell VPI 260). Despite over three years' storage with this temporary shield, no sign of continuing corrosion is observed. The Jussarö guns are awaiting funds and time for vacuum-chamber impregnation.

Barkman [1] reports unsuccessful trials to leach out the chlorides and claims that hydrogen-oven reduction is the only right method. However, the 'poor man's' experiments mentioned above seem to confirm that the removal of chlorides from the corroded layers can be achieved by a prolonged leaching in water baths.

7. EXAMINATION OF THE CORROSION LAYER

7.1 Frame research

Hand-grenades, found off Helsinki [7] and dated back at least to the Crimean war, 7 cm in diameter and with a wall-thickness of 1 cm, provide excellent material for conservation studies due to their great number and varying degree of corrosion. Chemical analysis and microscopic examination of one of the lightest (d∿1200) of the grenades have revealed practically no iron; the shell is held together by a mineral frame. It was first assumed that the graphite lamellae formed the frame. In order to clarify the structure, small pieces were dissolved with boiling 'aqua regia' to remove the remaining metal compounds. After this operation, the pieces retained their original dimensions and their radial needle-like character was very clearly visible. In microscopic examination, black crystals, probably graphite, appeared between the needles or lamellae. The graphite crystals were accumulated in the inner surface of the shell. After careful ignition at 1000°C, the loss of ignition was approximately 78% and the black crystals had disappeared, but the fragile frame was left nearly intact. The residue had a silica content of 83% SiO_2. This, calculated as silica, is approximately 1% of the weight of the original cast-iron shell. Studies on the 'Wasa' cannon-balls reveal similar silica contents: 1.2%. The Finnish Pulp and Paper Research Institute (Oy

Keskuslaboratorio) has kindly aided the author in collecting data and releasing stereoscan electron micrographs of the structure of the graphitized shell (Figures 2 and 3).

ACKNOWLEDGEMENTS

The author wishes to thank Prof. Waldemar Jensen, Messrs Keskuslaboratorio for their kind permission for help in studying the structure of the grenades and cannon, Mr P. E. Ahlers for the preparation of the samples, and Mrs Marja-Sisko Ilvessalo-Pfäffli for the stereoscan electron micrographs.

REFERENCES

1. Arrhenius, O., Barkman, L. and Sjöstrand, E., Konservering av gamla rostiga järnföremål (Conservation of old, rusted iron artifacts), 'Swedish Corrosion Inst. Bulletin' 61 (1973).
2. Sixteenth century cannon gets shot of corrosion, 'New Scientist' 56 (1972), p. 575.
3. Rees-Jones, S. G., Some aspects of conservation of iron objects from the sea, 'Studies in Conservation' 17 (1972), 39-42.
4. Ladeburg, H., Konservierung der Eisenteile der Bremer Kogge (The conservation of the iron artifacts from the Cog of Bremen), 'Der Präparator' 19 (1973).
5. Bresle, Å., Nya metoder för konservering av antikvariska järnföremål (New methods to conserve antiquarian iron artifacts), 'Kemia-Kemi' 1 (1974), 227-229.
6. Ericsson, Ch., A sunken Russian frigate, 'Archaeology' 25 (1972).
7. Patoharju, O., 'Corrosion problems in marine archaeology', paper presented at Scandinavian Corrosion Congress, Helsinki 1964.

Figure 1. Finnish cast-iron gun after hydrogen-oven reduction 8h 800°C 12% H$_2$.
Photo: Pekka Lindfors.

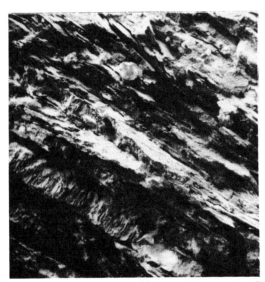

Figure 2. Stereoscan electron micrograph of low-iron (3% tot. Fe) hand-grenade shell, magnification 500X.

Figure 3. Same sample as Figure 2, iron removed, magnification 500X. (Both pictures courtesy Messrs. Keskuslaboratorio).

ELECTROLYTIC DESALINATION OF ARCHAEOLOGICAL IRON

R. Wihr, Rheinisches Landesmuseum, Trier, West Germany

1. INTRODUCTION

Many iron objects which have been 'conserved' in the past with their layers of corrosion intact are today in a poor state of preservation because their treatment was carried out without the knowledge of scientifically-based principles of conservation. Figure 1 illustrates a piece of iron of the late La Tene period which has been out of the ground for about nine months. It has a blister formation, typical of these finds, which has a hard skin filled either with a dry powder or with a pale yellow clear liquid. These blisters always contain large quantities of chloride. Figure 2 shows a similar corrosion formation on a piece of iron which was treated by immersion in water, drying at 120°C and then soaking in paraffin. The blisters formed after three years' storage. Figure 3 illustrates an untreated piece of late La Tene iron after three years' storage in the Museum repository. The iron has split into many pieces.

In 1882 Krause came to the conclusion that the small, but always measurable, chloride content was the main cause of further corrosion of iron finds [1, 2]. The first step in a successful treatment of heavily corroded and chloride-rich iron must be the removal of the chloride. The processes of normal electrolytic reduction or of strongly heating the iron [3] are out of the question, as the aim of these treatments is to remove the corrosion products from the uncorroded iron. If the iron has been heavily corroded these methods of treatment will alter it out of all recognition and render it useless for archaeological purposes. A method of treatment must be found which preserves the iron together with its adhering rust so that after the chlorides have been removed any necessary mechanical cleaning can be carried out.

Four methods of removing chlorides from corroded iron have been compared on a group of late La Tene iron finds from Wederath, Kreis Bernkastel/Mosel, which were assumed to have comparable amounts of chloride contamination. These four methods are:

1. Washing at normal and raised temperatures.
2. Washing with a fluctuating temperature (intensive washing [4, 5]).
3. Desalination by ionophoresis [6].
4. Cathodic desalination [7].

2. WASHING AT NORMAL AND RAISED TEMPERATURES

Washing at a temperature of 16 to 18°C was tried as a method of chloride removal. After 816 hours, a comparatively low chloride content was achieved in the wash water, but the objects were corroding and flaking so much that the treatment had to be stopped at this stage before all the chlorides had been removed. The experiments were repeated at a temperature of 35–40°C and the same level of chloride was reached after 620 hours, but again the treatment had to be abandoned before the objects were free of chloride because of the extensive flaking.

3. INTENSIVE WASHING

This is a development from a simple boiling technique. Alternate baths of water are used at 98°C and room temperature respectively in order to improve the penetration of the water into the pores of the corroded iron. After 16 cycles of treatment no chloride was detected in the wash water, although subsequent treatment by the electrolytic desalination process proved that these objects were not free of chloride.

4. THEORY OF THE ELECTROLYTIC DESALINATION PROCESSES

It was hoped, by electrolysis, to carry out complete desalination of iron finds more quickly than by any other method. Matti Kenttämaa carried out and published the first experiments in the 1930s [6] and Bercé has more recently worked along similar lines [7]. Our experiments have shown that neither of them achieved a satisfactory removal of chlorides, but we have developed an improved technique based on their work.

Two different circuit arrangements are possible: the first in which the objects are suspended between the anode and cathode in a bath of distilled water without forming part of the circuit; and the second in which the object is connected as the cathode and suspended in the bath between two anodes. Calculations suggest that removal of chlorides from deep inside the corrosion layers is more likely to take place using the second arrangement, known as cathodic desalination. The first technique is known as ionophoresis.

The following observations can be made:

1. Up to a certain point, increasing the bath temperature accelerates the dissociation of the salts.
2. The resistance of the bath decreases as the salt concentration in the bath increases.
3. An alteration of the applied DC voltage can increase or decrease the movement of the ions to the electrodes.

These factors must be taken into account and for a rapid desalination process it is necessary to optimize the bath temperature, the periods of time between changes of the water and the value of the DC voltage.

5.   THE IONOPHORESIS TECHNIQUE

Two stainless steel plates are suspended in the bath and used as cathode and anode respectively. The objects are hung between them carefully so that they are not in actual contact with the electrodes. If there are a number of small iron finds they may be packed in boxes made of perforated stainless steel (see Figure 4).

This technique considerably speeds up the desalination process as opposed to simple washing. Further improvements result from increasing the bath temperature to $35-40^\circ$C, but no advantage is gained by any further increase. Increasing the current also accelerates the desalination process, but not in the same proportion as an increase in the bath temperature. The intervals of time between changing the solution will depend on the amount of salts being removed, but there is nothing to be gained from too frequent changes of the solution. Normally the water should be changed about once every 24 hours, although in the initial stages of the desalination of iron finds with a high chloride content, such as those found in the vicinity of the sea, the solution must be changed more frequently. The ratio of volume of iron to volume of water in the bath must be about 1:10. The ionophoresis technique will not damge any organic remains (such as wood or textiles) which are adhering to the iron, but it is not possible to effect a complete removal of chloride by this process alone.

6.   THE CATHODIC DESALINATION TECHNIQUE

Two stainless steel electrodes are suspended in the bath, both being connected to the anode of the power supply. The objects are hung between them, or packed in perforated stainless steel boxes which are placed between them, and connected to the cathode. This arrangement of the circuit brought about a further removal of chlorides from objects which had already been treated by the ionophoresis technique. With finds which have a high chloride content and/or organic residues adhering to the surface, this circuit arrangement can result in some damage to the object as a result of the evolution of hydrogen on its surface.

From the results of these experiments it has been concluded that the most satisfactory method of chloride removal is to alternate between ionophoresis and cathodic desalination.

7.   APPARATUS FOR ELECTROLYTIC DESALINATION

Suitable materials for the bath are stoneware or plastic and it must be fitted with an inlet and outlet for water, and with a lid. The DC supply of electricity should be at 5 to 10 volts and up to 60 amps. The water temperature should be controlled with a thermostat connected to the ceramic or stainless steel immersion heater. If the bath and its lid are well insulated against loss of heat, considerable savings in electricity will result. Initially tap water may be used as the electrolyte, but after the first week distilled or de-ionized water must be used.

The finds are treated either singly or in groups, according to their size. For treating large quantities of small finds it is advisable to pack them in perforated stainless steel baskets (see Figure 4) which can be stacked vertically in the centre of a large tank. The lowest basket should stand about 5 cm clear of the bottom of the bath on glass or ceramic supports. For the treatment of large numbers of finds which have a high salt content, the process of water changing could be made automatic by means of time switches and electrically operated valves. The labour factor in this desalination process is small, being merely daily changes of water and light brushing of the electrodes, and is negligible when set against the effective conservation of the finds.

8.   PREPARATION OF THE FINDS FOR DESALINATION AND THE TECHNIQUE OF THE PROCESS

The initial experimental work was carried out on iron finds from the same La Tene grave which had chloride contents in the region of 0.5 to 1%. The objects had, for the most part, only small metallic cores which were surrounded by extensive layers and blisters of corrosion products. To facilitate chloride removal, blisters were pierced, either with a pointed tool, or with a grinding wheel on a flexible shaft or with an air abrasive apparatus. The process of chloride removal is followed by observing changes in the current flowing in the solution by using an ammeter. The amount of chloride removed can be determined by titration of samples of the wash water with 1/10 N silver nitrate solution using potassium chromate as the indicator [8]. Naturally, conductivity meters can also be used to follow the chloride removal and to determine when the process is complete.

Based on 10 years' experience, the most effective electrolytic desalination technique seems to be to start by using the ionophoresis method for the first week at a temperature of $40-50^\circ$C with a voltage of 10 V DC, with normal tap water in the bath. The water should be changed daily. At the end of this time most of the chlorides will have been removed and the process is changed to cathodic desalination, in which the iron objects become the cathode. The same bath temperature is used, but distilled water now replaces the tap water, and the process is carried out for two weeks with daily bath changes. This is followed by three more days of ionophoresis and three days of cathodic desalination, by which time analysis usually shows that the wash water is free from chloride.

9.   FINAL TREATMENT

After removal from the bath the finds should be rinsed in distilled water and dried at 150°C for 24 hours. They can then be impregnated in a bath of a high melting point synthetic wax [9], or in an epoxy resin [10], preferably under a partial vacuum. The latter gives excellent results, especially for those objects which require mechanical cleaning or which have silver inlay which requires restoration.

Electrolytic desalination is suitable for treating iron finds which are in any condition and at any stage of corrosion. Using this technique, iron which has been stripped either chemically or electrolytically may be rendered chloride-free in less than one day. Iron finds which have been impregnated with paraffin wax in the past without being de-salted may be treated by the addition of a wetting agent to the bath, which should have its temperature raised to 60–70°C. Provided that the ionophoresis technique is always applied before cathodic desalination, no damage will be caused to any traces of organic remains. This method for removing chlorides from iron may be regarded as a big improvement on simple washing with water, which should now be regarded as belonging to the past.

REFERENCES

1. Krause, E., 'Zeitschrift für Ethnologische Verhandlungen' **14** (1882), 533-538
2. Rathgen, F., 'Die Konservierung von Altertumsfunden', Berlin, 1926.
3. Rathgen, F., op. cit., pp. 50 et seq.
4. Organ, R. M., The washing of treated bronzes, 'Museums Journal' **55** (1955), 112-119.
5. Plenderleith, H. J., 'The Conservation of Antiquities and Works of Art', London, 1956, pp. 198 et seq.
6. Kenttämaa, M., Das elektrolytische Reinigungsverfahren bei der Konservierung von im Boden gefundenen Metallgegenständen, 'Suomen Fornminnesföreningens Tidskrift' **42** (1938).
7. Bercé, ?., Die Metallkonservierung in Museen im Lichte de Korrosionsbekämpfung, 'Archäologia Austriaca' **18** (1955), 1-15.
8. Rathgen, F., op. cit., p. 89.
9. Montanwachs BJ, manufactured by Farbwerke Hoechst, Werk Gersthofen, 8900 Augsburg 1, and obtainable from Farbwerke Hoechst, Verkaufskontor, 68 Mannheim M 1,5, Postfach 941.
10. Araldite MY 757 with 10% of hardener HY 992. Manufactured by and obtainable from CIBA who have agencies in many countries.

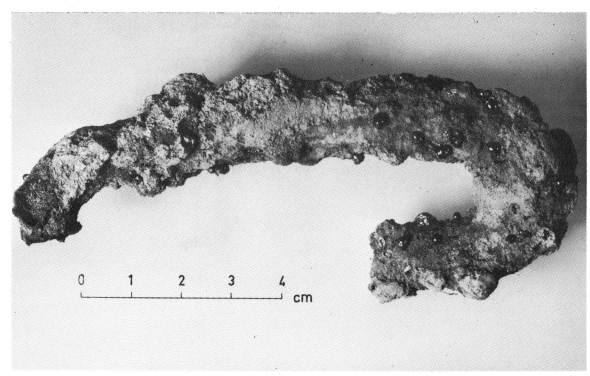

Figure 1.

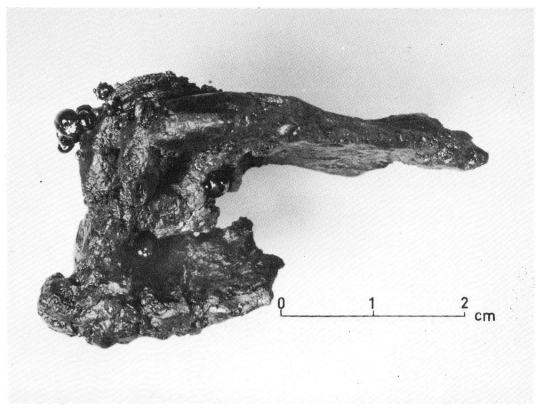

Figure 2.

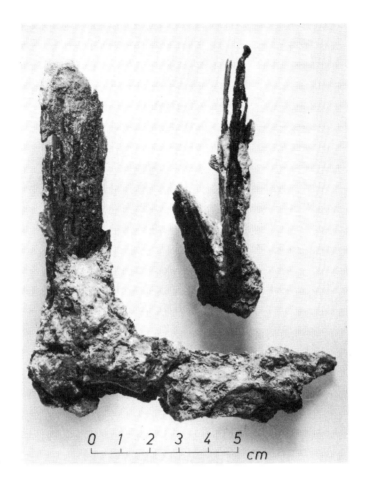

Figure 3.

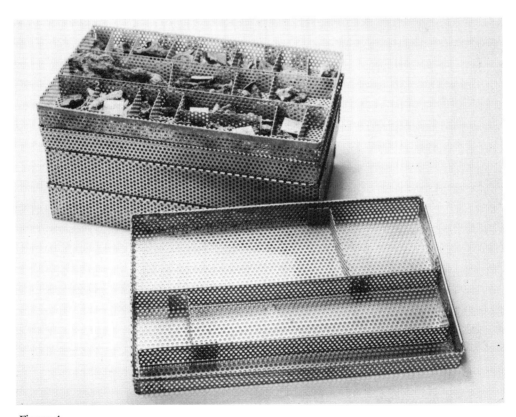

Figure 4.

PASSIVATION OF IRON

J. D. Fenn, British Museum Research Laboratory, London WC1B 5DA,
and K. Foley, Lincoln Archaeological Trust, Lincoln, England

1. INTRODUCTION

For some time it has been realized that the traditional method of conserving archaeological and historic iron by selective removal of rust, washing, and the application of a protective surface coating, does not necessarily stabilize an iron artifact unless it is subsequently kept in a carefully controlled environment. Where this is not possible corrosion often breaks out again within a few years, resulting in further expenditure of time and labour in dealing with the inevitable further deterioration of the object. Other methods of treatment have been tried, such as the removal of chlorides by high-temperature annealing [12] or the vacuum sublimation of the chlorides [4], but these processes require special equipment which is not available to most conservation laboratories.

One of the major problems in treating iron artifacts successfully is their variability. Comparatively small inclusions of different minerals in the iron have a disproportionately important effect on the rate and manner of corrosion. Variations in structure resulting from manufacturing processes, and stress resulting from use, also influence the behaviour of each artifact. Cast iron and wrought iron, for example, have very different properties and corrode in entirely different ways (even when they are of comparable chemical composition). These existing variables are complicated even more, depending on whether the deterioration of the artifacts occurred in the atmosphere, under water, or during burial in the ground, and also to what corrosive substances they were exposed in these environments.

When this disparate nature of iron is considered it is not really surprising that there are intermittent failures from a regime of treatment which does not take such differences into account. It is obvious that the whole system of treatment needs to be investigated more closely to see how it can be improved. At present it consists of four main stages:

1. Restoring the appearance of the artifact as far as possible by selective rust removal, using such methods as electrolytic and electrochemical reduction, mechanical stripping, or by means of chemical reagents.
2. Washing out aggressive salts and any residues from the stripping agents.
3. Drying the artifact either by heat, or by fluid displacement of water.
4. Providing some sort of physical barrier against re-contamination, such as lacquers or non-acidic waxes.

The theory behind this treatment is based on the assumption that each of these stages can in fact be successfully carried out, but since there are so many failures it seemed necessary to examine some of these stages in more detail in an attempt to ascertain the cause of failure.

2. WASHING

Soluble salts are probably never completely removed from an object no matter what washing procedure is used. Of 30 Roman nails washed by ionophoresis, or by ionophoresis alternating with soaking in alkaline solutions until the wash solutions were consistently free of chloride, 18 nails produced yet more chloride after rigorous boiling in distilled water, or after a few minutes in an ultra-sonic tank. Of six further objects boiled from the outset in distilled water, only two achieved a chloride-free reading. This was after 135 and 1400 minutes respectively. Of 60 nails subjected to continuous washing in de-ionized, de-aerated water until the wash water was free of chloride, six were selected at random and made the cathodes in the cathodic desalination process [13]. There was a further leaching of chlorides and a rise in the registered current. After five days, when the current had fallen and the wash water was again consistently free of chlorides, the nails were pulverized and boiled in distilled water. All six were still noticeably contaminated, three of them very heavily.

This seems to indicate that there is no means of telling when an object in solution is really free of chlorides.

3.   DRYING

Since it is probable that soluble salts will not have been completely removed it is imperative that the object be properly dried.

After removal from an aqueous medium, iron artifacts are very vulnerable to rapid rusting because the surface is covered by a comparatively thin film of water to which oxygen has much readier access; there is a sharp acceleration in cathodic activity. Heat drying at the low temperatures normally used (approximately 90°C so that the structure of the iron is not changed) accelerates this rusting while the artifact dries. This newly formed rust may act as a poultice [8] retaining some moisture, and this is even more likely to occur on heavily rust-encrusted iron which is too fragile to strip completely. Moreover, some laboratories do not have a filtered atmosphere so there is always the danger that an artifact could be re-contaminated while it is drying. Therefore it seems that this method of drying is not satisfactory. The alternative to heat drying is the use of a liquid which has the properties of dewatering fluid, which is discussed later in this paper.

4.   ORGANIC PROTECTIVE COATINGS

Industrial research has been carried out on paints, lacquers, waxes and oils, and it is thought that although the coatings used on museum iron may prevent direct re-contamination during handling, they are not impervious to oxygen and water vapour [2]. Since iron reacts with oxygen and water even in the absence of salts, it is obvious that no matter how well the artifacts are washed, dried and lacquered, this form of treatment alone is not sufficient to protect any iron which is inherently unstable as a result of surface inhomogeneity.

Since environmental conditions cannot always be controlled to suit iron, some means is needed to make the metal itself less reactive, if possible, by using some form of corrosion inhibitor.

5. INHIBITORS

An inhibitor is a chemical substance which, when added in small amounts to a corrosive environment, effectively decreases the corrosion rate of a metal or alloy. Inhibition is closely related to the mechanism of corrosion, so the action is limited to specific environmental conditions. Any significant change in that environment, such as an increase in the concentration of aggressive ions, changes in pH, elevated temperatures and decrease in available oxygen, can change the effective range of inhibition [10].

There are several types of inhibitor: passivators such as phosphates and chromates, etc, long-chain polar organic compounds collectively known as slushing compounds, for example petroleum sulphonate; and the vapour-phase inhibitors, e.g. cyclohexylamine carbonate and some nitrites. These particular types of inhibitor all have some properties which may prove useful in preserving iron antiquities.

6. PASSIVATING INHIBITORS

Passivatory inhibitors have the effect of altering the galvanic potential of a metal to a more noble value. The way they achieve this is under dispute but it seems that most passivated surfaces are attributable in some degree to a protective film [11]. There are at least two opinions about the nature of these films. Firstly that it is a diffusion barrier caused by reaction products which separate the metal from its environment and stifle galvanic action. Secondly that it is a chemisorbed film, usually of oxygen, its inertness being attributed to the satisfaction of secondary valence forces.

Certain aggressive ions, especially chlorides, sulphates and nitrates, break down passivity. It is not certain whether they diffuse through gaps in the film, or cause colloidal dispersion of the film thus increasing its permeability, or whether they adsorb onto the surface of the metal in competition with adsorbed oxygen. Whatever the actual mechanism, the result is the formation of tiny anodes of active metal resulting in severe local pitting, even perforation. The presence of such ions demands increased concentration to maintain passivation which is dangerous if the inhibitor is as toxic as the chromate inhibitors.

Passivating inhibitors of various kinds are already being used in conservation treatment, for example by using phosphoric acid rust-removers in an attempt to leave a phosphated surface on iron. However it should be emphasized that corrosion can actually be accelerated by indiscriminate use of such inhibitors. Incomplete passivation encourages severe local corrosion as the unpassivated areas become anodic to the rest of the surface. Unless the whole surface can be successfully passivated it is better not to use this type of inhibitor, especially on archaeological iron which usually has incalculably large surface areas with inaccessible crevices blocked by soluble salts and corrosion products. Such a surface is not conducive to the formation of a continuous passive film.

Historical iron suffers from similar defects but the metal surface is sometimes more compact so that in certain cases it might be possible to passivate such material. For this purpose a number of rust-removing preparations commonly used by conservators were tested to determine their performance as passivators. The samples used were pieces of rolled iron sheeting which had been exposed to the London atmosphere for approximately three years. Each sample was prepared so that it had three types of surface: an area of high polish, an area from which the rust had been removed by sand-blasting, and the original rusty surface. In this way it was hoped to ascertain whether the passivation effect would extend across the different types of surface. After being treated with the stripping reagents, the samples were hung in the open air but protected from the rain.

The results were very disappointing because they were so inconsistent. Of the 40 samples treated with phosphoric acid preparations, only three were completely passivated. All the others began to show pitting corrosion within a week. Fourteen of the twenty samples stripped in a 5% solution of the disodium salt of ethylene diamine tetracetic acid remained resistant to corrosion for five weeks before beginning to corrode around the edges. The remaining seven pieces began to pit during the second week. Twenty samples stripped in ammonium citrate showed consistently patchy passivation while 20 samples soaked in sodium hexa-metaphosphate resulted in one completely passivated sample, six partly passivated samples and 14 which showed absolutely no sign of passivation at all but rusted in exactly the same manner as the control samples.

Tannic acid is reputed to stabilize rusty iron surfaces [6]. Preliminary experiments using this treatment on sheet iron were not very successful. Six out of ten samples showed pinpoints of rust three weeks after treatment, which was no advantage over the control samples; the remaining four samples are still unrusted after two months. A variation of this treatment which consists of a mixture of tannic acid and phosphoric acid [9] has protected ten samples for two months.

Another approach to stabilizing metal surfaces is the incorporation of inhibitive substances such as sodium benzoate or zinc chromate into the undercoat of a lacquer. The theory is that water vapour which condenses as liquid on the surface of the metal will dissolve some of the inhibitor and become less corrosive. Some experiments with triethanolamine in polyvinyl acetate on both new mild steel nails and archaeological Roman nails were not encouraging but other combinations may prove more successful.

Some of the passivating inhibitors, such as potassium chromate or sodium hydroxide, prevent the corrosion of iron in an aqueous medium and consequently have been used to protect iron during washing processes requiring long periods of soaking. It is important to prevent rusting during this type of washing for two reasons: firstly because of the inevitable damage to the object, and secondly because of the swift formation of gelatinous corrosion products which precipitate on the metal surface blocking the crevices and retarding the diffusion of the salts. Comparatively small losses of iron result in a precipitate of this kind. A new 3.5 cm mild steel nail was immersed in 250 ml of distilled water in a covered beaker. Within 24 hours it was completely covered by a thick, slimy, orange deposit even though rusting was taking place only at the head and the point. The weight loss from the nail during this period was 0.0006 gm.

Although alkaline inhibitory solutions are successfully used to protect modern mild steel, it is possible for an alkaline inhibitor such as sodium hydroxide to react with dissolved ferric chloride in solution in the pores of archaeological iron to form colloidal ferric hydroxide:

$$FeCl_3 + 3NaOH \longrightarrow Fe(OH)_3 + 3NaCl$$

In this way, the use of the wrong type of inhibitor during washing could have a detrimental effect on subsequent attempts to passivate the metal by causing an unnecessarily high concentration of salts to be retained in the metal.* It remains to investigate the use of inhibitors other than alkaline solutions in this context.

In view of the limited use and very real risks in using passivating inhibitors with archaeological iron, it was hoped that other types of inhibitor such as slushing compounds and vapour-phase inhibitors might be of more use in connection with these particular problems.

7. SLUSHING COMPOUNDS

Some long-chain polar organic compounds such as glyceryl mono-oleate and basic barium dionylnaphthalene sulphonate act as temporary corrosion inhibitors. Unlike passivating inhibitors they do not have a very significant effect on cathodic or anodic polarization but they wet the metal surface preferentially displacing the water molecules. Such compounds are used in commercial dewatering fluids.

Any dewatering fluid has an inhibitory effect in the broadest sense because it removes one corrosive agent from the metal, i.e. water. Commercial dewatering fluids consist of compounds such as butanol which displace the water from the metal surface and small concentrations of an inhibitor which covers the metal with an adsorbed hydrophobic mono-layer and prevents the re-spreading of the water.

It was hoped that dewatering fluids might provide a better means of drying than the use of heat. The following experiments were made to explore the possible use of commercial dewatering fluids on archaeological iron. After receiving an account of the problem of salt residues in archaeological iron, the B.P. Energol Development Laboratory sent four products to be used after the excess of the corrosive salts had been washed out. All four products were described as leaving corrosion-resistant films.

Eight groups of samples each consisting of 36 new mild steel nails and 12 Roman nails were washed by the continuous washing process until the readings on the wash water were consistently free of chlorides. Each group was then dried by a different method and half of each group was lacquered with 10% polyvinyl acetate in acetone. Afterwards all the samples were exposed to a corrosive environment with a high variable humidity for two months.

Table 1   Drying methods on mild steel nails

Treatment	Total number of mild steel nails	Total number uncorroded	Number lacquered uncorroded	Number unlacquered uncorroded
heat dried	36	0	0	0
acetone	36	10	5	5
Ferromede	36	9	5	4
CPD 34	36	3	3	0
BP X	36	18	10	8
CPD 32	36	25	14	11
CPD 4	36	32	18	14
control	42	0	0	0

Table 2   Drying methods on archaeological nails

Treatment	Total number of Roman nails	Total number uncorroded	Number lacquered uncorroded	Number unlacquered uncorroded
heat dried	12	5	5	0
acetone	12	7	5	2
Ferromede	12	6	4	2
CPD 34	12	6	4	2
BP X	12	5	4	1
CPD 32	12	11	6	5
CPD 4	12	8	5	3
control	9	1	1	0

It will be seen from the Tables that all samples dried through a dewatering fluid performed better than those which were heat dried, or than the controls.

*Results of experimental work by K. Foley suggest that where the integrity of the object is preserved in the corrosion products, methods of washing involving prolonged immersion may weaken it. Weight losses, although not consistent, appear to relate to the length of immersion.

Since the earliest batches of these samples were processed only two months before this paper was written it too soon to say what the long-term effects may be. Nor is it certain whether the resistance to corrosion is chiefl attributable to superior drying action or to the residual effect of the inhibitors. Further experiments are bein conducted to investigate this aspect.

8. VAPOUR PHASE INHIBITORS

Another group of inhibitors which may be relevant to a museum situation are the vapour phase inhibitors. Thes are compounds such as cyclohexylamine carbonate which afford some protection to ferrous metals. The vaporize and deposit on the metal surface as an adsorbed film displacing and resisting the existing water molecule and possibly the oxygen as well. The protection lasts only as long as there is a sufficiently high vapou concentration in the immediate vicinity of the metal surface. Such inhibitors have been used when transportin exhibiting or storing wrought iron artifacts. It is probable that, being in vapour form, such inhibitors penetrat the crevices in corroded iron more successfully than inhibitors in a liquid medium. The disadvantage of thes inhibitors is that they attack some non-ferrous metals such as copper and that they are reputed to be less effectiv with certain types of cast iron. It is also not always convenient to keep artifacts in sealed containers to preven the inhibitor from dispersing too quickly. Their toxicity is still a matter of dispute.

It is clear that the structure of the surface of corroded iron has an important bearing on the successful use o inhibitors. In particular the presence of inaccessible fissures may impede the removal of salts, the process o drying and the formation of inhibitive films. Therefore an essential preliminary to research on inhibitin archaeological and historic iron will be to find out more about the kind of surfaces which are left by the method of rust removal normally used by conservators: for example, whether electrochemical reduction of rust leave deposits of zinc or aluminium in the pores of the artifact. It is also hoped that if enough is learnt about the actior of chemical stripping reagents it will be possible to avoid actually creating a surface which is physically impossibl to stabilize, especially on historic iron. For example, an acid from which hydrogen is not readily displaced by iror might create a more fissured surface than a more aggressive reagent because of a tendency towards preferentia attack along slip lines and grain boundaries, thus aggravating the already fissured nature of the surface. Whereas a reagent that readily reacts with iron would attack the whole surface, especially the projecting areas, because o their greater exposed surface area. With such a reagent the degree of attack at weak points is minimized becaus of the rapidity of the overall attack. The result can be a smoother surface with shallower crevices. Although th overall loss of metal would be greater by using a reagent of this kind, the remaining metal might have a better chance of stability and survival than the metal suffering from intergranular fissures.

9. CONCLUSION

The experimental work described above suggests that none of the existing methods of treatment of iron i completely satisfactory. It would seem, however, that their weaknesses may be remedied by a careful use o inhibitory substances. For example, dewatering fluids with inhibitive additives are seen as a potentia improvement on existing means of drying by the use of heat or acetone. Further work will be carried out or archaeological material to confirm this observation.

Some of the dangers of using these inhibitory and passivating substances have been pointed out and no firm recommendation for their use can be given until further investigation has been carried out.

It remains to acknowledge that work in this field for archaeological material is in its infancy, and to continu the search for an effective combination of dewatering fluids, inhibitors and lacquers.

REFERENCES

1. Baker, H. R., Leach, P. B., Singleterry, C. R. and Zisman, W. A., Cleaning by surface displacement of wate and oils, 'Industrial and Engineering Chemistry' **59** (1967), 29-40.
2. Burns, R. M. and Bradley, W. W., 'Protective Coatings for Metals', Reinhold, New York, 1962.
3. Gwathmay, A. T., Effect of crystal orientation on corrosion, in 'Corrosion Handbook', ed. H. H. Uhlig, Johr Wiley and Sons, New York, 1948, pp. 33-35.
4. Ladeburg, H., Konservierung der Eisenteile der Bremer Kogge, 'Der Präparator' **19** (1973).
5. Mayne, J. E. O., Current views on how paint films prevent corrosion, 'Journal of Oil and Colour Chemists' **40** (1957).
6. Pelikan, J., Conservation of iron with tannin, 'Studies in Conservation' **11** (1966), 107-115.
7. Pompowski, T., Klenowicz, Z. and Jakobs, J., The influence of polar inhibitors and the electrochemica properties of temporary corrosion preventatives, 'Corrosion Science' **7** (1967), 665-672.
8. Rosenfeld, I. L. and Zhigalova, K. A., 'Investigation of processes of corrosion', research report.
9. Stambolov, T., 'Corrosion of Metallic Antiquities and Works of Art', Central Research Laboaratory, Amsterdam, n.d.
10. Uhlig, H. H., 'Corrosion and Corrosion Control', 2nd ed., John Wiley and Sons, New York, 1971.
11. Uhlig, H. H. and Mears, R. B., Passivity, in 'Corrosion Handbook', ed. H. H. Uhlig, John Wiley and Sons, New York, 1948, pp. 20-33.
12. Eriksen, E. and Thegel, S., Conservation of iron recovered from the sea, 'Tøjhusmuseets Skrifter' **8** (1966).
13. Wihr, R., Elektrolytische Metallentsalzung, 'Arbeitsblätter für Restauratoren' **5** (1972).

AIR POLLUTION AND POSSIBLE EFFECTS ON
ARCHAEOLOGICAL OBJECTS BURIED IN THE GROUND

B. Ottar and S. E. Haagenrud, Norwegian Institute for Air Research, P.O. Box 115, 2007 Kjeller, Norway

1. INTRODUCTION

The continuous expansion of production and consumption in modern society is accompanied by a steadily increasing emission of air pollutants of different types. Combined with a concentration of population in cities and urban areas, this has in many places led to serious air pollution problems during the last two to three decades. The extensive use of fossil fuels for heat and energy production, with added pollution from specialized industries and a major contribution from motorized transport, are the main elements in this development. In order to limit local air pollution levels, cleaning of stack gases has been applied when a practicable technique was available, while in other cases emissions through tall chimneys, as well as dispersed siting of polluting industries, have been used in the belief that adequate dispersion takes place naturally and that all pollutants have a comparatively short life in the atmosphere. This has led to a wider dispersion of pollutants, and increasing background levels in regions beyond the urban industrialized areas.

There is growing concern about this development. The increasing acidity of the precipitation in large parts of Europe was first discussed by Odén in 1968 [1]. Data collected by Granat in a case study prepared by Sweden for the UN Environment Conference in 1972 [2] are illustrated in Figure 1. It shows how a central region with highly acid precipitation has been expanding through the years. This development has been further studied in a cooperative research programme, organized within the frame work of the OECD. According to our present knowledge, considerable concentrations of air pollutants, such as sulphur dioxide, nitrogen oxides and airborne particulate matter, may remain in the atmosphere for periods of one to several days. Clearly, therefore, air pollutants may have effects far outside the source regions. Under certain meteorological conditions, significant amounts of air pollutants emitted from the urban industrialized areas in Europe can be transported over distances of several thousand kilometres. Striking demonstrations of this are observations of grey layers of snow containing soot and fly ash, and the acidification of the precipitation which in Scandinavia has caused extensive damage to freshwater fisheries.

At the 1972 meeting the question was raised, could this development possibly affect the life-time of archaeological specimens buried in the ground? This is a complicated question to which no simple answer can be given at present. But it may be of some use to examine the various factors involved, in order to give the archaeologist some background for making his own judgments.

In order to answer the question, information is needed concerning the emission, the atmospheric dispersion, and the deposition of the pollutants in the various geographical areas. Further, one has to identify the aggressive chemical components which may possibly be present in sufficient amounts to have an effect on the archaeological samples. Finally, the extent of such effects will depend on the type of specimens and how deep in the ground and in what type of soil they are buried.

2. THE EMISSIONS

The main components emitted are sulphur dioxide, nitrogen oxides, particulate matter and organic compounds. On a large geographical scale, only sulphur dioxide and nitrogen oxides give rise to the formation of aggressive chemical compounds in amounts sufficient to have an effect. On a local scale, other aggressive components may be considered, such as hydrochloric acid originating from waste incineration and hydrofluoric acid from various industrial processes.

In Figure 2 an emission survey for sulphur dioxide is shown for Europe [3]. The major source areas are situated in a heavily industrialized belt across Europe, from England through Germany into Poland and Czechoslovakia. This is the region where the large coal deposits originally formed the basis for industrial development.

The emissions of nitrogen oxides largely originate from two types of source: the emissions from stationary sources, the distribution of which will be largely the same as for sulphur dioxide, and an addition of approximately 50% from motorized traffic. No emission survey for nitrogen oxides has so far been made.

3. ATMOSPHERIC DISPERSION AND DEPOSITION

Measurements of air pollution from aircraft and by other means in the European region have shown that most of the time the majority of the air pollutants are found below a height of 1-2 km above the ground. A few hundred kilometres downwind of large urban industrialized areas, the pollutants become evenly distributed within this 1-2 km thick layer, but the concentration of the pollutants may still be considerable. During the subsequent movement of these polluted air masses to remote areas, the main processes which serve to change the concentrations are dispersion on the synoptic scale (> 500 km), deposition on the ground, and chemical changes of the composition of the pollutants in the atmosphere.

The main processes by which deposition on the ground takes place are gas absorption in moisture and vegetation, dry deposition of particulate matter by impaction, and deposition by precipitation. Absorption and dry deposition at the ground may dominate near the source areas, while wet deposition may become the most important sink at a greater distance. The wet deposition is enhanced when polluted air masses are forced upwards by higher terrain or mountain ranges (orographic precipitation). Thus, a large part of the sulphur dioxide emitte in the highly industrialized part of Europe is deposited on the slopes of the mountain ranges surrounding t more central part, for instance the exposed sides of the Scandinavian mountains and the Alps, etc. On occasio the polluted air masses may move out over the Atlantic Ocean and days later give rise to highly acid precipitatio in Scotland, Iceland, or on the northern coast of Norway.

The importance of orographic precipitation is illustrated in Figures 3 and 4. Figure 3 shows the mean annu precipitation in Europe. In Figure 4 the amounts of precipitation and precipitated sulphate ($\sim$ 70% sulphur acid) are shown for Southern Norway. In this case, air which is coming in over the sea from Europe is mo polluted than air from the Atlantic area, and the maximum deposition of sulphate therefore does not coincic with the maximum for the precipitation.

During movement in the atmosphere, the pollutants undergo chemical transformations. Sulphur dioxide gradually turned into sulphuric acid, part of which is neutralized by various cations. These may be metal-ior present in the particulate matter emitted from the same or other sources, but the most common cation observe with acid particles and precipitation is ammonium. This originates from ammonia emitted as a result of the deca of organic material originating from the natural environment and agricultural activity. Very little is known abou the magnitude of these emissions, and they are generally assumed to be evenly distributed over the land area: When ammonium sulphate particles come in contact with soil and plants, the ammonium is extracted by th plants. Therefore the total acidity deposited is best estimated by the total content of sulphate ions.

The nitrogen oxides are oxidized somewhat more slowly than the sulphur dioxide and they end up as nitri acid and nitrates. Most of the acidity in the precipitation is due to sulphuric acid, but under special weathe conditions equal amounts of nitric acid have been found. As a first approximation the addition due to nitrate ior may, however, be neglected in this relation.

It is difficult to determine the contribution of sulphates deposited in the form of particulate matter an gaseous sulphur dioxide relative to precipitation. Various estimates indicate that the contribution is considerabl In dry areas it will obviously be the dominating factor. In areas with much precipitation, its influence will b relatively less, but still a significant part. Estimates can be made by multiplying the air concentration with deposition of 0.8 cm/sec for sulphur dioxide and p.2 cm/sec for particulate matter. If the area is covered wit snow these values will be much smaller.

4. GROUND CONDITIONS

The effects of the deposited pollutants on the ground depend on the composition of the soil, and the run of conditions. Part of the precipitation will pass on top of the soil and more or less directly into rivers and lake: Another part will pass through the soil and mix with the ground water before it contributes to the rivers an lakes. This latter part will be affected by chemical reactions in the soil, and change its composition. If the terrai is flat, most of the water may pass down into the soil. In steep terrain, rapid run-off may dominate. During winte the pollutants may be stored in the snow cover. As most of the pollutants are situated on the surface of the snov crystals, the first thaw in the spring will contain a proportionally larger part of the pollutants. On occasion th effect has led to the poisoning of fish in rivers and lakes.

In principle, most soils would be able to neutralize the acidity brought down by precipitation if the acid wate was left in contact with the soil for a sufficiently long period of time. But the rate of neutralization differs greatl for the various types of soil. In the Scandinavian area, where the soil consists largely of granitic materials, the rat of neutralization is very slow, and in practice the soil has a very limited ability to neutralize the acidity. This ha had a devastating effect on fish and other biological life in rivers and lakes. It is also feared that the acic precipitation will increase the leaching of calcium and other nutrient ions from the soil, and thus cause reduction of the forest growth. In other parts of Europe, a high content of carbonates in the ground ha prevented such effects.

Archaeological samples may be situated at depths down to a few metres in the soil. What part of the acic precipitation will be able to find its way down to the archaeological specimens will depend on the porosity of th soil, its neutralizing capacity and the inclination of the terrain. On this basis one might expect that possibl effects would most likely be found in horizontal terrain with a porous acid type of soil.

5. EFFECTS OF THE ACID PRECIPITATION

When entering the soil, the polluted precipitation normally enters a highly buffered system. In general, th amount of acidity brought down far away from the major emission areas will be too small to have an effect o archaeological samples buried in the ground, and effects can only be expected in particularly exposed areas.

The amount of acidity in the precipitation depends on the geographical position of the area. Near the major source areas, as for instance in the Netherlands, the average value of pH in precipitation is close to 4, and almost all precipitation is acid. In some remote areas, highly acid precipitation with a pH between 3 and 4 may occu 10-30 times a year, while the precipitation in between is more neutral. This difference may be of som importance.

As far as the type of archaeological specimen is concerned, the discussion will be limited to samples of iron, o mild steels. The diagram in Figure 5 shows how the rate of corrosion varies with the pH-value of the water [5] . Ir acid solution, steel dissolves freely with evolution of hydrogen. With increasing pH the corrosion rate decrease: regularly until a pH-value of about 4.0 is reached, when the influence of the oxygen reduction at the cathode begins to be appreciable. In the pH range 4.0-9.5 the rate of attack is nearly constant. This is generally attributed to the buffering action of the products formed on the metallic surface, which gives a pH at the metallic surface ir the range 8.5-9.5. In most natural waters the corrosion rate will therefore be very similar as far as the pH is concerned. Although the overall attack may be reduced by increasing the pH, there is a real danger that the attack will be concentrated at a limited number of areas, and the depth of pitting may become very severe, particularly in the presence of aggressive ions such as chloride and, to some extent, sulphate ions.

Chloride and sulphate ions interfere with the development of protective films on many metals and will break down existing passive films. Although, under certain conditions, the overall amount of metal lost may not be markedly influenced by the concentration of chloride and sulphate, the attack differs from that in, say, distilled water. In particular the attack is more localized and as a result pits are deeper. In natural waters corrosion is further complicated by the presence of other ions, e.g. calcium and bicarbonate, which reduce the corrosion rate by the formation of an adherent carbonate-containing rust. The pattern of corrosion is governed by a combination of all these factors and may vary with time.

We may, however, try to make some rough estimates in order to see what the magnitude of the various effects could be. That is, we may consider some theoretical cases which would be worse than any case experienced under real conditions. As a starting point we may assume an area with a yearly precipitation of 5 g H_2SO_4/m^2. This corresponds to 1000 mm precipitation and an average pH equal to 4, a situation which is reached, for instance, in the Netherlands. It also corresponds to the area with maximum deposition of acid precipitation in Southern Norway, with 2000 mm precipitation and an average pH of 4.3. In this area the actual pH is 3-4 during periods which altogether bring down less than 50% of the total yearly amount of precipitation. Further, we will assume that all the acid reaches the specimen, and no reactions with the soil are considered. This means that the amount of acid which reaches a piece of iron is given by its horizontal projection and the amount of precipitation per unit surface area.

If anaerobic conditions are assumed in the ground, the maximum amount of iron dissolved can be estimated on the assumptions given. The result is a removal of about 0.3 μm/year from the surface of the sample, that is to say it will take 1000 years to remove 0.3 mm from the surface. The acidity due to the deposition of particulate matter may be assumed to double this value at most. Also, a doubling of the acidity as a whole may take place in the next 10 years. With these assumptions, the attack would far exceed real conditions, and it may be concluded that this type of attack would hardly be of importance for the archaeological sample.

On the other hand, the acid precipitation with high sulphate concentration may possibly affect the corrosion from sulphate-reducing bacteria, operating under anaerobic conditions. The total redox equation for this process is:

$$4Fe + H_2SO_4 + 2H_2O \rightarrow 3Fe(OH)_2 + FeS$$

The total effect of sulphuric acid precipitation under anaerobic conditions will be complex and very difficult to predict. On the one hand, the above corrosion reaction is enhanced by increased sulphate concentration; on the other hand the sulphate-reducing bacteria grow best between pH-values from 5.0 to 9.0 [6]. If the acid precipitation is assumed to retain its normal content of oxygen, the damage determined by the rate of corrosion will increase in amounts corresponding to the oxygen reduction. Incidents of highly acid precipitation will be more important than the yearly average. An increase in the yearly rate of corrosion by a factor of 2 will probably be in excess of what would be observed in a real case.

So far we have considered a general attack on the whole sample. We should also take into account the possibility of pitting. Generally it may be said that pitting is caused by concentration differences in the medium surrounding the sample. If the concentration of ions at the surface of the sample is larger at one place than another, a concentration cell will be established and one can obtain a high local corrosion rate. There are many ways in which such a system can be established. The presence of sulphate and chloride ions may break down the protective film or protective oxides covering the surface and thus release a pitting process maintained by a concentration cell. The concentration cell will be due to differences in the concentration of salts, hydrogen ions and in particular oxygen. For such pitting processes the rate of corrosion may be 10-100 times faster than the general corrosion. This type of attack is easily established in the presence of chloride ions and to a lesser degree by sulphate ions. An indication of the importance of this effect is obtained by comparing the condition of samples buried near the coast or below the marine level, with those from further inland, as the former are exposed to different amounts of chloride ions from sea salt.

6. CONCLUSION

It may be concluded that it is difficult to say definitely whether archaeological samples can be damaged by acid precipitation in remote areas. A more detailed study of certain typical areas would be required in order to do this. Generally, one would not expect such effects unless the area is heavily exposed to acid precipitation, and a general idea of these areas can be obtained from Figure 2. In addition the buffering capacity of the soil must be low, and the surface run-off must be limited.

One should, however, be aware that in areas closer to the large source areas the conditions may be entirely different. In these areas the deposition of acid materials by particulate matter and absorption of gases may contribute 10 times as much to the soil acidity as the precipitation. Also in these cases other chemical components may be deposited in sufficient amounts to have an effect and this will complicate the situation.

REFERENCES

1. Odén, S. and Ahl, T., 'The acidification of air and precipitation and its consequences on the natural environment', Ecology Committee, Bull.1, Nat. Sci. Research Council of Sweden, 1968.
2. Sweden's Case Study for the United Nations Conference on the Human Environment, Stockholm, 1971.

3. Eliassen, A., and Saltbones, J., Decay and transformation rates of SO_2, 'Atmospheric Environment' 9 (1975) 425-9.
4. Schjoldager, J., Svovelforurensninger i luft og nedbør ved norske bakgrunnstasjoner, NILU Teknisk Notat N 65/73.
5. Whitman, G. W., Russel, R. P. and Altieri, V. S., Effect of hydrogen-ion concentration on the submerge corrosion of steel, 'Ind. Eng. Chem.' 16, 665-670.
6. Rosenqvist, I. Th., 'Biochemical processes in corrosion of steel in soils', private communication.

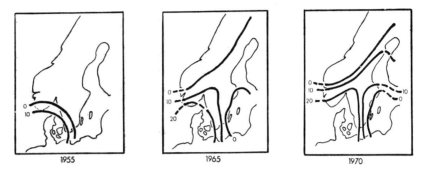

Figure 1. Acidity in precipitation (millimol/m^2/year) (L. Granat [2]).

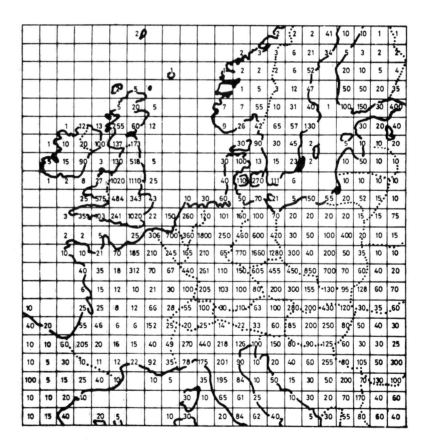

Figure 2. Calculated emissions of sulphur dioxide 1972 [3].
Unit: 10^3 tons So$_2$/year.
Grid: 127 x 127 km.

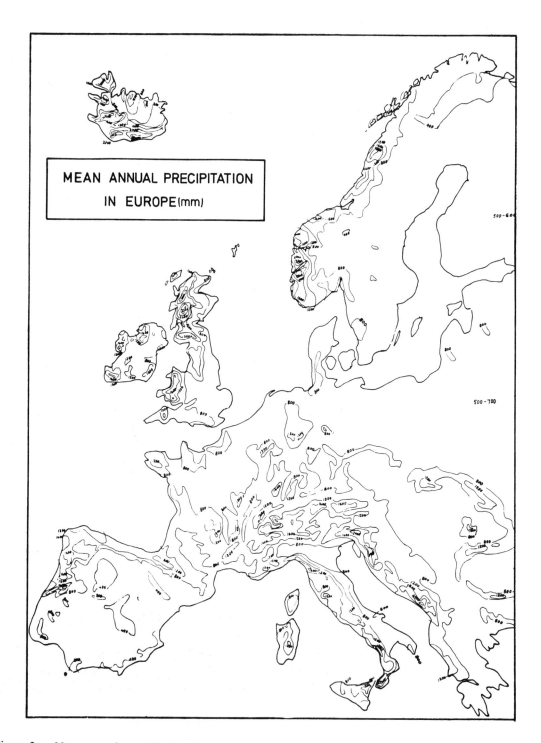

Figure 3.   Mean annual precipitation in Europe (mm) (WMO Climatic Atlas of Europe, Vol. I, Geneva, 1970).

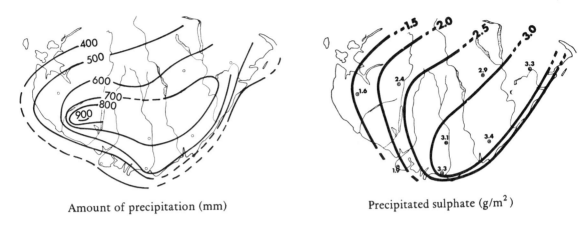

Amount of precipitation (mm)   Precipitated sulphate (g/m^2)

Figure 4.   Amount of precipitation and precipitated sulphate 1 January—30 June 1972 in Southern Norway [4].

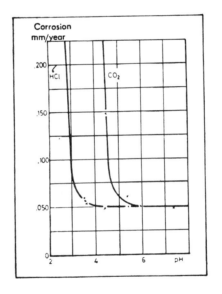

Figure 5.   Corrosion of iron in Cambridge water at different pH [5].

THE DE-ALLOYING OF COPPER ALLOYS

T. S. Weisser, Walters Art Gallery, Baltimore, Maryland, USA

1. INTRODUCTION

The de-alloying, or selective corrosion, of copper alloys has until recently been the concern mainly of engineers trying to determine the materials which are best suited for specific jobs. Some conservators have been concerned with this problem in relation to antiquities, but the majority are unaware of its importance. The reason for this unawareness may be that de-alloying very often is not obvious in the way general corrosion is. An alloy that has undergone de-alloying is basically unaltered in size and shape, although the residual metal may be less dense than the original alloy. The colour of the residual metal may be different, but this fact is often obscured by corrosion products from simultaneous general corrosion.

My intention in writing this paper is to discuss particular forms of de-alloying in copper alloys and to survey the literature available on this topic. I also hope to make the practising conservator aware of the importance of avoiding treatments which cause de-alloying when working with copper alloys. The results of a preliminary experiment on de-alloying in a solution generally used for treating bronzes will be discussed.

2. DEZINCIFICATION

The most familiar form of de-alloying seems to be dezincification, i.e. the preferential removal of zinc from brass (a copper-zinc alloy). Brasses of more than 15% zinc are susceptible to this form of corrosion and the tendency for it to occur generally increases with zinc content. (However, in a report by J. C. Rowland [76] it was shown that gamma brass grains in samples containing 61% Cu, 1% Sn, less than 1% Pb, balance zinc, were unattacked, while alpha and beta grains containing less zinc were dezincified. This result may be determined by the additions to the alloy.) A brass which has undergone dezincification is characterized by areas in which the zinc has disappeared from the alloy leaving behind 'spongy' copper. This spongy copper is inherently weak and stresses cause cracking through it.

Dezincification may be general and occur in a layer over the surface of the brass or be local in the form of a deep plug of residual metal at an angle roughly perpendicular to the surface of the alloy (Figure 1). Often a combination of the two forms is seen on the same piece.

2.1 The mechanism of dezincification

Dezincification was first reported in 1866 [20]; however, the mechanism by which the phenomenon occurs is to this day controversial. Two main hypotheses have been put forth:
1. the entire alloy corrodes and the copper is re-deposited to form a porous outer layer;
2. the zinc is selectively removed from the alloy leaving a copper-rich residue.

In the engineering literature, various results of experiments and observations have been reported on the mechanism of dezincification — many of them conflicting. The researchers can be divided into three main camps: those who support the first mechanism mentioned above [1, 6, 14, 21, 35, 39, 40, 54, 58, 64, 68, 73, 78, 85, 87, 90]; those who support the second mechanism [4, 7, 8, 29, 56, 69, 83, 84]; and those who believe both mechanisms occur [12, 16, 23, 27, 45, 49, 66, 81].

In an article published in 1972, Robert H. Heidersbach, Jr. and Ellis D. Verink, Jr. [37] reported results of their experiments on the dezincification of alpha and beta brasses. Taking into consideration the conflicting evidence over the mechanism of dezincification, they attempted to choose test methods which would not bias their results and thereby avoid the criticism levelled at other experimenters. Heidersbach and Verink used several techniques: x-ray diffraction, electron microprobe, metallographic, atomic absorption, and electrochemical. They gave rather convincing evidence that both disputed mechanisms are 'operative under certain conditions of potential and pH for both alpha and beta brasses'.

In the same article Heidersbach and Verink developed an electro-chemical explanation for the occurrence of de-alloying using Pourbaix Diagrams. They wrote that 'Potential vs pH plots (Pourbaix Diagrams) of regions of chemical stability of elements, their ions, and their salts in aqueous environments, present one possible way of providing a basis for predicting the tendency for de-alloying'.

2.2 Conditions influencing dezincification

Dezincification has been reported to occur under diverse conditions. In fact, the factors influencing dezincification may be so numerous that it is impossible to say exactly what conditions will cause it.

Much depends, first of all, on the composition of the alloy. For example, a brass containing less than 15% zinc may not be susceptible to dezincification at all. C. F. Nixon [64] says less than 10% zinc. Particular additives to the brass, whether intentional or accidental, may act as inhibitors of dezincification in alpha brass under conditions where dezincification might ordinarily occur. Such additives include arsenic, antimony and phosphorus. These additives must be in certain proportions or they may stimulate corrosion.

The mechanism of inhibition by arsenic (and it is assumed to be the same for the other additives) was reported by F. W. Fink [27] to be anodic in character. He showed that while arsenic undoubtedly has some effect at the cathode, it acts chiefly as an anodic inhibitor forming a film which creates a barrier for selective corrosion. Thus, the main mass of metal undergoes corrosion. G. Masing and L. Koch [57] believe that inhibition from arsenic is due to the re-deposition of metallic arsenic on the brass surface. This re-deposited arsenic has a lower overvoltage than brass. Hydrogen is deposited in preference to copper ions.

The environment surrounding a copper-zinc alloy to a large extent determines the possibility of attack. Brass has been shown to dezincify readily in acid solutions, but the process also occurs in alkaline media.

The ions present also affect dezincification. Chloride ions are well-known for stimulating attack. Other highly ionic non-oxidizing environments may have a similar effect. Several authors specify the presence of copper ions in dezincifying solutions [16, 76].

The amount of oxygen present can determine the resistance of a brass to dezincification. In situations where oxygen supply is low, e.g. under a porous surface film, in pits or crevices, in stagnant water, dezincification is favoured. However, dezincification has been reported in atmospheric tests where oxygen is plentiful, by S. C. Britton [12].

Differential aeration cells also stimulate dezincification. These cells are caused by a lesser amount of oxygen reaching the metal surface in one spot than another. This may be due to local deposits of foreign bodies, corrosion products, or water. It may also be due to cracks in a once protective surface film, or to any other phenomenon causing local differences in oxygen supply.

The development of anodic and cathodic areas in a brass can lead to dezincification or general corrosion in a conducting medium, depending on what areas become anodic.

Langenegger and Callaghan [49] have developed an empirical potential shift method for predicting accelerated dezincification rates in various media. They show that 'dezincification rates may be correlated to this potential shift, irrespective of the oxidizing reagent or external current used to achieve this shift in potential'. Thus, it is possible 'to predict and compare dezincification in various media under widely different conditions of exposure'.

3. DESTANNIFICATION

Destannification, the selective removal of tin from a tin bronze (a copper-tin alloy), has not been noted as frequently as dezincification (Figure 2). Consequently, it has not been studied as thoroughly. Heidersbach and Verink [37] mention that it has been reported in practice, but have nothing further to offer on the subject.

W. D. Clark [14] in an article on the selective corrosion of phosphor-bronze in hot-water service concluded that '... the attack is by selective solution analogous to dezincification and that solution and re-deposition is almost certainly involved'. The environment causing destannification in this instance was alkaline.

In a discussion of Clark's paper, R. A. U. Huddle* questioned Clark's conclusion on the mechanism involved in destannification. He felt that selective removal of the tin leaving residual copper lakes should not be overlooked, and that Clark's evidence was not conclusive enough to rule out this alternative.

In 1951 P. Trautzl and W. D. Treadwell [86] showed that tin could be selectively removed from tin-rich bronze in an acidic environment. They found that from powdered bronze samples containing 8.8% and 47.6% tin, the tin could be removed practically quantitatively as $SnCl_2$ by a stream of HCl gas in a temperature range of 350-400°C without noticeable attack on the copper.

4. OTHER FORMS OF DE-ALLOYING

Other forms of de-alloying of copper alloys which have been observed include the preferential removal of aluminium [14, 36], nickel [14, 51], and copper. Only the preferential removal of copper will be discussed in detail here since it plays an important role in the conservation of antiquities.

4.1 Decuprification

The preferential removal of copper from a copper alloy, or decuprification, is rarely mentioned in the engineering literature. (It has been reported to occur in brass under certain conditions, according to Heidersbach [36].) However, it has been reported as a curiosity in the conservation literature.

In an article by C. G. Fink and E. P. Polushkin [26] on the microscopic study of ancient bronzes, the attack of copper-rich alpha is listed as the initial stage of corrosion in a Chinese bronze containing 12-15% tin. Fink and Polushkin give the following order of attack in this case:

1. '... copper-rich alpha is corroded first, with deposition of metallic copper. Eutectoid, or at least its white constituent delta, remains unaffected. The resistance of eutectoid to corrosion is so strong that it can be found even in the remote layers of cuprite and malachite, where the rest of the metal has long been mineralized.
2. In the next stage, metallic copper is oxidized.
3. Corrosion of tin-rich alpha takes place during stage (2) or later.
4. Corrosion of eutectoid is the final stage of the process.'

In an article written in 1934, R. J. Gettens described the surfaces of several high-tin bronzes. One of these bronzes, a small Chinese mirror of the Han period in the Hoyt Collection at the Fogg Art Museum, was smooth with a metallic lustre. On microscopic examination it was found that the dendrites were pale blue-green and somewhat translucent, while between the dendrites was a dark grey lustrous material which reflected light strongly and seemed to be metallic. This structure showed up without intentional etching. What Gettens described here may be a case of the selective corrosion of the copper in a high-tin bronze.

Examples of bronzes with the dendrites naturally etched and the tin-rich interdendritic areas unattacked have also been reported by H. H. Coghlan among some Bronze Age tools and weapons in the Newbury Museum, Berkshire.

In 1969 Gettens again mentioned the peculiar corrosion of high-tin bronzes. He described the patina as a smooth, grey-green patina usually with a layer of hydrous tin oxide which results from the leaching out of the copper constituent of the alloy and its replacement by the tin alteration product without apparent volume change. The green colour he attributed to a stain from the copper salts. This type of patina has been found not

*Metallurgy Division, Atomic Energy Research Establishment, Harwell, England.

only on Chinese bronzes, but also late Bronze Age European bronzes and Etruscan bronze mirrors.

One possible explanation for this phenomenon may be that inter-metallic compounds of copper and tin (which may be found in the area richest in tin in a cast bronze containing over a certain percentage of tin) can be cathodic to the copper-rich phase [50]. Another possible explanation is that the common salts of copper — the chlorides, sulphates and carbonates — are more soluble in soil waters than the corresponding salts of tin, and thus are more readily carried away from the metal surface. A third possibility is that the copper can be selectively removed from bronze by solutions containing certain ions which form complex ions with copper, for example, solutions containing ammonia or cyanide. The possibility should not be excluded that solutions containing ions which form complexes with copper were applied to bronze during manufacture as a tin surface-enrichment technique.

5.   IMPORTANCE TO PRACTISING CONSERVATORS

The examples of de-alloying in copper alloys cited above occurred in antiquity, during burial, or in industrial use. It is the responsibility of the practising conservator to ensure that he does not create the conditions which may cause de-alloying while caring for or treating objects.

First of all, he must be informed on the composition of the alloy he is treating. Is it a copper? a brass? a bronze? a high-tin or low-tin bronze? etc. He should not assume from a catalogue identification (unless identification was made in a reliable scientific fashion) or from general appearance or colour what the composition is. In my own experience many 'bronzes' I have received for treatment were brasses. A 'copper' object may be a dezincified brass.

The conservator must be aware of the conditions which may cause de-alloying in the object he is treating. Treatments intended for one alloy may be detrimental to another. I have seen a yellow-brass object changed to pink by the use of an alkaline treatment intended for low-tin bronze.

Once the conservator knows the composition of his object and what conditions may be detrimental to it, he must then peruse the treatments available and choose the safest treatment for his particular case.

6.   A PRELIMINARY EXPERIMENT

In the past, not enough attention has been paid to de-alloying in the selection of treatments for copper alloys, especially where bare metal may be exposed. Many recommended treatments need to be reviewed with respect to de-alloying. and some may need revision to be safe for certain alloys.

With this problem in mind, I decided to test the recommended treatments for bronze disease on various compositions of copper alloys by a metallographic-section examination technique, followed up by analysis of the solutions for metallic ions.

The following is a preliminary report of the effects of sodium sesquicarbonate on a high-tin bronze. Sodium sesquicarbonate has been recommended for the treatment of bronze disease which often requires soaking a bronze in a 5% solution for over a year.

The sample: 78.76% copper, 19.41% tin, trace of manganese.*

The test solution: 5% sodium sesquicarbonate in distilled water, pH 9.5 (approx.).

Procedure: The bronze sample was cut on a low-speed saw with a diamond blade so that distortion and heating would be minimized. The sample was polished to a mirror finish on one surface, photographed, degreased, and placed in the solution. The sample was removed from the solution periodically to take photomicrographs of the polished surface.

Observations: After only 6 hours in the solution, the polished surface had been etched making the dendritic pattern very visible, even to the unaided eye. Part of the eutectoid between the dendrites had been attacked while other parts had not, creating a dendritic-looking pattern in the eutectoid. A fringe of highly reflective, unattacked metal surrounded every dendrite and appeared to be the same as the unattacked constituent of the eutectoid. This fringe of unattacked metal may be the tin-rich delta-fringe which is mentioned in metallographic literature. It is the part of the eutectoid closest to the dendrites; the copper constituent from this part of the eutectoid has been absorbed into the dendrite, leaving only tin behind (Figure 3). After 2 days the solution began to turn blue. After 7 days the dendrites began to be attacked. This attack appeared to start in one spot in several dendrites simultaneously and spread from these spots. The highly reflective metallic fringe and the previously unattacked constituent of the eutectoid continued to be unattacked. The solution was bluer than before (Figure 4). This experimental work is still in progress.

I performed this same experiment in London a year ago with the same observations listed above. However, I was able to conduct the experiment for a longer period of time. These are the further results of that experiment. Observations: After 20 days in the solution, the dendrites were almost entirely corroded away. Only the metallic fringe and part of the eutectoid were unattacked (Figure 5). The solution was very blue.

Conclusions: The sequence of events of corrosion of this high-tin bronze in 5% sodium sesquicarbonate seems to be that listed above by Fink and Polushkin, i.e. the alpha or copper-rich phase is corroded while the delta or tin-rich phase is highly resistant to corrosion. The blue colour of the solution after 2 days also suggests that there are copper ions going into the solution. This was confirmed by atomic absorption analysis. The most probable reason for this selective attack of the copper is that the tin products are not soluble in a cold solution of sodium sesquicarbonate at a pH of 9.5. However, copper forms a complex, intensely blue-coloured ion in a double carbonate solution. Thus, the selective attack of the copper is favoured.

This experiment may or may not be a fair representation of what occurs in sodium sesquicarbonate on a patinated object since there are other factors involved, but it should be borne in mind that, by soaking a copper

*Cast by Windsor Metalcrystals, Inc., Westminster, Md., and analysed by Arnold Greene Testing Laboratories, Inc., Natick, Mass.

alloy in such a solution for a year or so, one is taking a chance on its safety. And certainly a copper alloy with exposed metal may be seriously affected over such a period of time. This does not mean, however, that sodium sesquicarbonate should be abandoned as a treatment. It simply means that we must consider ways of making it safer. For example, a way of protecting the copper in the object while it is undergoing treatment, without affecting sodium sesquicarbonate's ability to remove the dangerous chlorides, could perhaps be devised.

7. CONCLUSION

The de-alloying, or selective corrosion, of copper alloys has been observed in industrial metals and in antiquities. It is the responsibility of the practising conservator to be aware of the damage that may be caused by de-alloying in treating copper alloys, and to avoid treatments that may initiate such attack.

8. ACKNOWLEDGEMENTS

I would like to thank E. C. G. Packard, Director, Conservation Department, Walters Art Gallery, and W. T. Chase, Head Conservator, Freer Gallery of Art, for their assistance and encouragement.

REFERENCES

1. Abrams, R. B., 'The dezincification of brass', American Electrochemical Society Advance Paper, 21-23 September 1922.
2. Aleikina, J. K., 'Russian Journal of Physical Chemistry' 38 (1964), 7.
3. Bartonicek, R., Holinka, M. and Lukasovska, M., Die Korrosion von Messing in Ammonium-chloridlosungen, 'Werkstoffe u. Korrosion' 19 (1968), 1032-42.
4. Bassett, W. H., 'Chem. Met. Eng.' 27 (1922), 340.
5. Baudo, G. and Giuliani, L., Korrosionskennzeichnung von Kupferlegierungen, 'Werkst Korros.' 21 (1970), 332-5.
6. Bengough, G. D. and May, R., 'Seventh Report to the Corrosion Research Committee of the Institute of Metals', Institute of Metals Advance Paper No. 3, 8-11 September 1924.
7. Bialosky, J. M., Anodic corrosion of brass, 'Corrosion and Materials Protection' 4 (1947), 15-16.
8. Bird, D. B. and Moore, K. L., 'Materials Protection' 1 (1962), 70.
9. Booth, N., Davidge, P. C., Fuidge, G. H. and Pleasance, B., Corrosion of water heaters, 'Gas World' 125 (1946).
10. Borgmann, C. W., Larrabee, C. P., Binder, W. O., Burghoff, H. L. and Dix, E. H., Jr., Corrosion of metals, 'American Society for Metals' (1946), 181.
11. Brandon, D. G., 'Modern Techniques in Metallography', 1966.
12. Britton, S. C., 'Journal of the Institute of Metals' 67 (1940), 119.
13. Chaplet, A., Résistance à la corrosion du cuivre et de ses alliages, 'Cuivre et Laiton' 12 (1939).
14. Clark, W. D., Note on selective corrosion of phosphor bronze in hot-water service, 'Journal of the Institute of Metals' 73 (1947), 763-767.
15. Coghlan, H. H., 'Sibrium' 8 (1964-66). (Publ. by Centro di Studi Preistorici ed Archeologici Varese, Musei Civici di Villa Mirabello).
16. Colegate, G. T., 'Metal Industry' 73 (1948), 483, 507, 531.
17. Craievich, A. and Guinier, A., Cavités submicroscopiques dans le laiton dezincifié, 'Acta Metall.' 21 (1973), 1327-1333.
18. Czochralski, J. and Schreiber, H., Korrosion von Messing infeuchter Ammoniak-Atmosphaer, 'Korrosion u. Metallschutz' 13 (1937), 181-3.
19. Derge, G. and Markus, H., 'Studies upon corrosion of tin. II. Effects of other anions in carbonate solutions', American Institute of Mining and Metallurgical Engineers Tech. Publ. (Metals Technology), 1938.
20. Desai, M. N., Talati, J. D. and Trivedi, A. M., 'Journal of the Indian Chemical Society' 38 (1961), 565.
21. Dixon, E. S., 'ASTM Bulletin' 21 (1940).
22. Elder, T. and Kendoel, F., Normbronzen und Schwefelsaeure, 'Korrosion u. Metallschutz' 15 (1939), 85-6.
23. Evans, U. R., 'The Corrosion and Oxidation of Metals', 1960.
24. Evans, U. R., The corrosion of copper and copper alloys, 'Chemistry and Industry' 43 (1924), 127T-131T.
25. Fallerios, I. G. S. and Pieske, A., Consideracoes sobre a dezincificacao do ligas cobre-zinco, 'Met. ABM' 26 (1970), 21-6.
26. Fink, C. G. and Polushkin, E. P., 'Microscopic study of ancient bronze and copper', American Institute of Mining and Metallurgical Engineers Tech. Publ. (Metals Technology), 1936.
27. Fink, F. W., Dezincification of alpha brass, with special reference to arsenic, 'Electrochemical Society Transactions' 75 (1939), 441-6 (discussion 446-8).
28. Flatt, R. K. and Brook, P. A., Effects of anion concentration on the anodic polarization of copper, zinc and brass, 'Corrosion Sci.' 11 (1971), 185-96.
29. Gastev, S. S., 'Izvest. Akad. Nauk. SSR Metally' 3 (1965).
30. Gettens, R. J., 'Technical Studies in the Field of the Fine Arts' (1934-35), 29.
31. Gettens, R. J., 'The Freer Chinese Bronzes', 1969.
32. Greaves, R. H. and Wrighton, H., 'Practical Microscopical Metallography', 1967.
33. Haas, M., Beitrag zur Korrosion des Messings, 'Korrosion u. Metallschutz' 5 (1929), 26-35.
34. Harrington, R. H., 'The Modern Metallurgy of Alloys', 1948.
35. Hashimoto, K., Ogawa, W. and Shimodaira, S., 'Journal of the Japanese Institute of Metals' 4 (1963).

36. Heidersbach, R., Clarification of the mechanism of the de-alloying phenomenon, 'Corrosion' 24 (1968), 38-43.

37. Heidersbach, R. H., Jr. and Verink, E. D., Jr., Dezincification of alpha and beta brasses, 'Corrosion' 28 (1972), 397-418.

38. Heyn, E., A study of the micro-structure of bronzes, 'Journal Fr. Inst.' (1899).

39. Hollomon, J. H. and Wulff, J., Corrosion of copper and alpha brass — chemical and electrochemical studies, 'American Institute of Mining and Metallurgical Engineers Transactions (Inst. Metals Div.)' 147 (1942), 183-200 (discussion 201-4).

40. Horton, R. M., New metallographic evidence for dezincification of brass by re-deposition of copper, 'Corrosion' 26 (1970), 160-3.

41. Hudson, J. C., Atmospheric corrosion of metals, 'Faraday Society Transactions' 25 (1929), 475-496.

42. Hume-Rothery, W., 'Electrons, Atoms, Metals and Alloys', 1955.

43. Itoh, I., Togashi, M. and Hikage, T., Dezincification rate of beta-brass in vacuum at high temperature, 'Journal of the Japanese Institute of Metals' 38 (1974), 294-300.

44. Kehl, G. L., 'The Principles of Metallographic Laboratory Practice', 3rd ed., 1949.

45. Kenworthy, L. and O'Driscoll, G., 'Corrosion Technology' 21 (1955), 247.

46. Kroehnke, O. and Masing, G., 'Die Korrosion von Nichteisenmetallen und deren Legierungen', 1938.

47. Kufferath, A., Die neuzeitliche Mikroskopier technik im Dienste der Korrosionforschung, 'Korrosion u. Metallschutz' 12 (1936), 171-5.

48. Ladeburg, H., Untersuchnungen von Entzinkungserscheinungen an Fittings aus Kupferlegierungen, 'Metall' 20 (1966), 3342.

49. Langenegger, E. E. and Callaghan, B. G., Use of an empirical potential shift technique for predicting dezincification rates of alpha beta brasses in chloride media, 'Corrosion' 28 (1972), 245-254.

50. Leidheiser, H., Jr., 'The Corrosion of Copper, Tin and their Alloys', 1971.

51. Lennox, T. J., Jr., Peterson, M. H. and Groover, R. E., De-alloying of copper alloys and response to cathodic protection in quiescent sea water, 'Materials, Protection and Performance' 10 (1971), 31-7.

52. Lord, J. O., 'Alloy Systems', 1949.

53. Lucey, V. F., 'British Corrosion Journal' 1 (1965), 7.

54. Lynes, W., 'Proc. ASTM' 41 (1941), 859.

55. Mandran, G., Exemple de corrosion interne du laiton, 'Aciers Spéciaux Métaux et Alliages' 6 (1931), 293-4.

56. Marshakov, I. K., Bogdanov, V. P. and Aleikina, S. M., 'Russian Journal of Physical Chemistry' 38 (1964).

57. Masing, G. and Koch, L., Studien über die Entzinkung von Messing bei der Korrosion, 'Wissenschaftliche Veroffentlichungen aus dem Siemens-Konzern' (1925), 257-273.

58. Mitchell, N. W., Corrosion resistance of copper alloys, 'Metal Progress' 28 (1935), 38-41.

59. Moore, E. W., Corrosion of brass in water subjected to pH correction, 'New England Water Works Association' 48 (1934), 47-51 (discussion 51-58).

60. Mor, E., Scotto, V. and Trevis, A., Dissolution anodique de quelques alliages de cuivre dans l'eau de mer, 'Corros. Trait. Prot. Finition' 18 (1970), 67-74.

61. Nagasaki, K., Haruyama, S. and Kaneko, I., Dezincification rate of alpha brass in vacuum at high temperature, 'Journal of the Japanese Institute of Metals' 33 (1969), 1218-24.

62. Nielsen, K. and Rislund, E., Comparative study of dezincification tests, 'British Corrosion Journal' 8 (1973), 106-116.

63. Niskanen, E. and Franklin, U. M., Atmospheric corrosion of copper and some copper alloys, 'Canadian Metals Quarterly' 9 (1970), 339-44.

64. Nixon, C. F., 'A further study of the dezincification of brass', American Electrochemical Society Advance Paper No. 3, 24-26 April 1924, pp. 29-41.

65. Outerbridge, A. E., Jr., A study of the microstructure of bronzes, 'Journal Fr. Inst.' (1899).

66. Piatti, L. and Grauer, R., 'Werkstoffe u. Korr.' 14 (1963), 551.

67. Piontelli, R. and Peyronel, G., Un tipico caso di dezincificazione dell'ottone, 'Chimica e l'Industria' 22 (1940), 161-5.

68. Poetzl, R. and Lieser, K. H., Radiochemische Untersuchungen uber die Korrosion des Messings, 'Z. Metallk.' 61 (1970), 527-34.

69. Polushkin, E. P. and Shuldener, H. L., 'Corrosion of yellow brass pipes in domestic hot-water systems', American Institute of Mining and Metallurgical Engineers Tech. Publ. 1742, 1945.

70. Rawdon, H. S., 'Some types of non-ferrous corrosion', paper presented to the 39th General Meeting of the American Electrochemical Society, 21-23 April 1921, pp. 73-79.

71. Rawdon, H. S., Typical cases of the deterioration of Muntz metal (60:40 brass) by selective corrosion, 'AIMT' (1917).

72. Reedy, J. H. and Feuer, B., The corrosion of brass in dilute electrolytes, 'Journal of Industrial and Engineering Chemistry' (1920), 541-547.

73. Rhodes, F. H. and Carty, J. T., 'Ind. Eng. Chem.' 17 (1948), 909.

74. Roetheli, B. E., Cox, G. L. and Littreal, W. B., Effects of pH on corrosion products and corrosion rate of zinc in oxygenated aqueous solutions, 'Metals and Alloys' 3 (1932), 73-6.

75. Rothenbacher, P., Zur Entzinkung von Rekristallisierten und Statisch Belasteten Kupfer-Zink-Legierungen mit 30 At-% Zink, 'Corrosion Science' 10 (1970), 391-400.

76. Rowland, J. C., in 'Proceedings of the 2nd International Congress on Metallic Corrosion NACE', 1903, p. 795.

77. Schuekher, F., Zinkverlust beim Glühen von MS 61, 'Metall' 26 (1972), 1143-1148.

78. Scully, J. C., 'The Fundamentals of Corrosion', 1960.

79. Shams El Din, A. M. and Abd El Wahab, F. M., Behavior of copper-tin alloys in alkaline solutions upon alternate anodic and cathodic polarization, 'Electrochimica Acta' 10 (1965), 1127-40.

80. Smythe, J. A., Corrosion of tin and lead-tin alloys, 'Industrial Chemist' 17 (1941), 17 and 21.

81. Stillwell, C. W. and Turnipseed, E. S., Mechanism of dezincification, 'Indus. and Eng. Chem.' 26 (1934) 740-3.

82. Syett, B. C. and Parkins, R. N., Effect of Sn and As on stress corrosion of Cu-Zn alloys, 'Corrosion Science' (1970), 197-210.

83. Tabor, L. E., 'American Water Works Association' 48 (1963), 239.

84. Taylor, F. and Wood, J. W., 'Engineering' 149 (1940), 58.

85. Thompson, D. B., 'Australasian Engineer' (1954), 48.

86. Trautzl, P. and Treadwell, W. D., 'Helvetia Chemica Acta' 34 (1951), 1723.

87. Uhlig, H. H., 'The Corrosion Handbook', 1948.

88. Unni, V. K. V. and Rama Cher, T. L., Anodic dissolution of brass in acids, 'Anti-Corrosion Methods and Materials' 17 (1970), 5-7.

89. Wurstemberger, F. V., Selektive Korrosionen und Entzinkung erscheinungen an Messingteilen, 'Zeit. für Metall Kunde' 14 (1922), 23-29 and 59-69.

90. Zender, A. R. and Bulow, C. L., 'Heating, Piping and Air Conditioning' 16 (1944), 273.

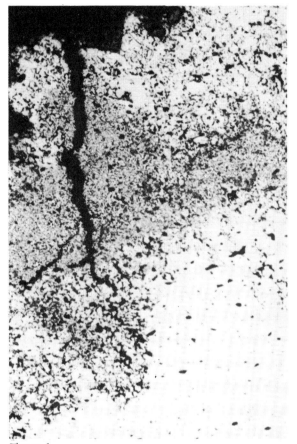 

Figure 1.   Figure 2.

Figure 1.   Dezincified brass wire (see below). Magnification X400. Plug-type dezincification. Light areas are unattacked brass. Medium grey areas are residual copper. Black line is crack through residual copper. (Brass wire section dontated by W. T. Chase, Head Conservator, Freer Gallery.)

Figure 2.   Destannified bronze (78.76% Cu, 19.41% Sn). Magnification X200. Destannified in 5% sodium hydroxide. Light areas are copper-rich dendrites and alpha part of alpha-plus-delta eutectoid. Dark grey areas are attacked eutectoid.

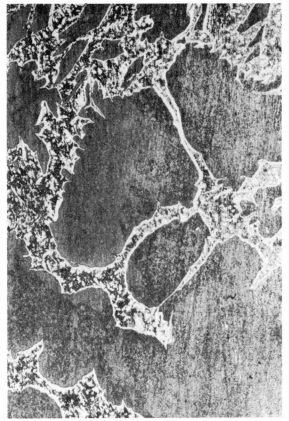

Figure 3.

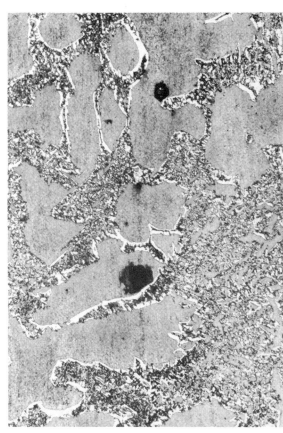

Figure 4.

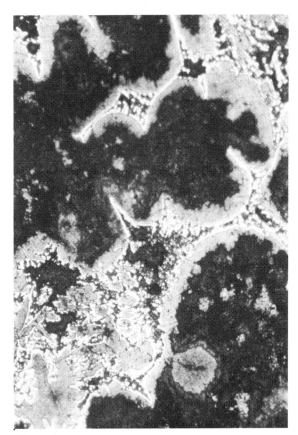

Figure 5.

Figure 3.
Bronze (78.76% Cu, 19.41% Sn) after 6 hours in 5% sodium sesquicarbonate. Magnification X400. Large grey areas are dendrites. White lines around dendrites are tin-rich delta fringes. Eutectoid between dendrites has been attacked (small dark grey areas) leaving behind the white delta constituent.

Figure 4.
Same bronze as in Figure 3 after 7 days in 5% sodium sesquicarbonate. Magnification X200. Large grey areas are dendrites. White lines around dendrites are tin-rich delta fringes. Eutectoid between dendrites has been attacked leaving behind white delta constituent. Black spots are cavities in the dendrites from corrosion.

Figure 5.
Same composition bronze as in Figure 3 after 20 days in 5% sodium sesquicarbonate. Magnification X400. The black areas in the dendrites and eutectoid have been corroded away leaving the white tin-rich delta fringes and delta constituent of the eutectoid.

THE REDUCTION OF LEAD

Hannah Lane, British Museum Research Laboratory, London WC1B 5DA, England

1. INTRODUCTION

The corrosion product most commonly found on lead antiquities is basic lead carbonate, the mineral hydrocerussite [1], which under normal atmospheric conditions forms a thin homogeneous layer on the surface of the lead, protecting it against further corrosion. However, under museum conditions it often forms as a loose powdery mass which does not protect the lead underneath. Lead is normally regarded as a stable metal which withstands corrosion very well, but exposure to the vapour of organic acids in the presence of oxygen, carbon dioxide and moisture causes it to corrode quickly. Unfortunately these conditions are often found in museum storage areas. The organic acids catalyse the corrosion of the lead to produce the powdery lead carbonate, and a very small amount can cause complete destruction of a lead object. In museum storage conditions the commonest contaminant is acetic acid given off by many types of wood, especially oak and pine, often used to make showcases and storage cupboards. It can also be present in cardboard boxes in which many lead antiquities have been stored in the past and this is one of the causes of re-corrosion of treated lead antiquities in the British Museum. All the cases where lead has re-corroded after treatment have been traced to bad storage conditions. Therefore the essential problem is the protection of the cleaned lead against further attack in the presence of the vapour of organic acids.

2. SURVEY OF TREATMENTS

This section compares various methods which have been published and advocated for the conservation of lead.

Lead antiquities may be divided into three types:

1. those that are either so badly corroded or so large that only mechanical cleaning is a feasible method of treatment.
2. those objects which are only superficially corroded and have a solid lead core retaining the traces of any design. These may be treated by removal of all the corrosion products together with any traces of organic acids.
3. objects in which there is a core of sound metal but in which the design is only preserved in the corrosion layer. These objects must be conserved by preservation of the corrosion product in a stable form.

Various methods have been advocated for the removal of lead corrosion products but in some of them problems arise because the reagents will actually attack the metallic lead as well as dissolving the basic lead carbonate, or the chemicals themselves may be difficult to remove completely from the lead after the treatment and may subsequently cause a further outbreak of corrosion [2]. Lead is amphoteric and is readily attacked by both acid and alkaline reagents. This includes distilled water, which has a solvent action on lead, and it should only be used for washing for a very short period, or after it has been boiled to remove any dissolved gases.

Acetic acid has been suggested as a method of removing lead corrosion products but as vapours of this acid are the main cause of lead corrosion in museum environments it cannot be recommended under any circumstances [3]. Although it is volatile it is not always easy to wash the last traces of the acid out of the lead and the smallest remaining trace will lead to serious re-corrosion problems in the future. Acetic acid has also been used as an electrolyte for the cleaning of lead by electrolytic reduction, but it cannot be recommended for use in this context either.

The disodium salt of EDTA [4] has also been recommended for dissolving basic lead carbonate and, although it is very good for this purpose, it also readily attacks metallic lead. For this reason, particular care must be taken if the antiquity is covered by a compact thick layer of soil and corrosion product. The solution of EDTA may penetrate below this compact thick layer and attack the surface of the lead, and it is therefore important to ensure that the solution is regularly agitated and that the surface of the lead is inspected frequently. The lead object should not be left in this solution overnight, but removed and placed in tap water. It is not clear whether traces of EDTA left on the cleaned conserved lead will be harmful in the future, but it is our experience that, in cases where treated objects have been stored in adverse conditions so that the corrosion has re-started, those treated with EDTA have been particularly bad. On the other hand, objects which have been kept in correct conditions have not re-corroded, and in theory EDTA is a very stable compound which should not decompose to leave traces of acetic acid on the object.

Caley's method of treating lead antiquities uses dilute hydrochloric acid and ammonium acetate [5]. This can be very successful on loose corrosion products, but the reaction is very much slower on those objects covered by a compact layer of carbonates and soil. The treatment must be continuously supervised because of the risk that the solution will attack any cleaned areas of lead before all the corrosion products have been removed. Furthermore, the use of hydrochloric acid is not to be advocated in a laboratory where other metal antiquities are treated and on the whole this method of stripping has been superseded by techniques such as electrolytic reduction.

The use of ion exchange resins has also been advocated for cleaning lead [6] but on the whole these methods are not now favoured by conservators. These resins are expensive and have to be regenerated when exhausted. This is time-consuming, and it is difficult to remove all traces of the acid used in the process. The resin itself must be in intimate contact with the surface of the object and the solution needs frequent agitation. It seems likely that there is no particular advantage in using these resins, and the very dilute solution of the acid which was used to regenerate them would be just as efficient as a method of stripping corrosion products from lead.

The electrochemical reduction method using a solution of sodium hydroxide and zinc granules to generate nascent hydrogen is quite a successful way of stripping lead and has the advantage of not requiring an external source of energy, although heating does speed up the process [7]. The main disadvantage of the method is that the zinc is often plated on to the surface of the lead antiquity giving it an unnatural blue-grey appearance which is difficult to remove.

By far the best method for removing basic lead carbonate from lead antiquities is to use the standard electrolytic reduction technique in which the object itself is made the cathode in a suitable electrolyte and current of 2 to 5 amps per square decimetre of surface area is passed at about 12 volts [7]. The electrolyte only needs changing very infrequently and most other disadvantages of the method are fairly easily overcome. This process needs very little supervision, although it is important to check frequently that the current is actually passing, as otherwise the antiquity will start to dissolve. The electrolyte should be one which is harmless to both the antiquity and the operator and for these reasons solutions of cyanide and of acetic acid cannot be recommended. Sodium hydroxide is perhaps the most commonly used electrolyte but adequate ventilation is required to remove the fine alkaline spray which is given off during the process, and a 5% solution of sodium carbonate is more satisfactory. The current should be running before the antiquity is lowered into the electrolyte. A 10% solution of sulphuric acid has also been used, but once again the current must be switched on when the antiquity is lowered into the electrolyte to prevent the layer of basic lead carbonate being converted into sulphate. Sulphuric acid can have the disadvantage of leaching out certain elements from the lead alloy. The main reason for its use is to try and form a chemical layer on the surface of the lead, when the reduction process is complete, to act as a protection against further corrosion attack. At the end of reduction the current is reversed to give a layer of lead peroxide [8].

The material for the anode must be compatible with the electrolyte. Iron anodes may result in the plating of iron on to the lead object when sodium hydroxide is used as the electrolyte, but this is of little importance, since during the final washing it rusts and is easily brushed away. When sodium carbonate and sulphuric acid are used, iron anodes are very quickly attacked and so cannot be used. Stainless steel will tend to become pitted and there is a possibility of chromium or nickel being deposited on the lead. However, it is possible to select a low-carbon steel stabilized with molybdenum which does not suffer from this defect. Platinized titanium is ideal as it needs no cleaning and lasts indefinitely, but it is very expensive. Carbon anodes are quite useless in all electrolytes.

The lead object should be connected up to the supply of electricity with a suitable wire which will support the weight of the object and which will not dissolve in the electrolyte or under the conditions of reduction. Tinned copper wire is normally used and, if the antiquity is very heavy, padding, such as foam rubber, should be inserted between it and the wire at the points where the weight is supported, to prevent marking the soft lead.

Those objects that still retain a metal core with some design visible in the basic lead carbonate layer, but with little or no design remaining in the metallic lead, can only be treated by a technique that will preserve the corrosion layer so as to retain the design, that will at the same time stabilize the lead to prevent further attack, that will allow the object to be handled without loss of the powdery surface, and that will ensure that, after treatment, the object has the appearance of lead. Such a technique was described by Organ as Consolidative Electrolytic Reduction at the IIC Conference in Rome in 1961 [9]. Reduction is carried out at a very low current density, reducing the basic lead carbonate to a compact mass of lead in situ, the lead ions being retained in exactly the same place on the surface of the object instead of being removed into the electrolyte and re-deposited as a loose sludge, which is removed in the finishing process after washing out the electrolyte [8]. In this way all the surface detail is retained and the organic acids are removed, but no further design will be revealed. This is due to the structure of basic lead carbonate which tends to prevent the formation of original surfaces in the corrosion layers as is sometimes the case with some bronze and silver antiquities.

In the original procedure the fragile lead object was connected to the cathode by stainless steel wire, supported by polyurethane foam pads held together by spring-loaded anodes of platinized titanium, iron or stainless steel. The electrolyte was 5% sodium hydroxide and the current density was $100 \, mA/dm^2$. The evolution of minute bubbles of hydrogen indicates that reduction has been completed. It is very important that no bubbles of hydrogen are given off during reduction as these come from the metal surface and would therefore disturb the reduction in situ, causing the lead to deposit elsewhere on the object, resulting in a mass of reduced lead with no resemblance to the original appearance. This will happen at a current density over $250 \, mA/dm^2$. The current must be low enough to prevent this, yet high enough to ensure that the metallic lead is cathodically protected.

Lead anodes should not be used as they quickly deposit lead on the object in an alkaline electrolyte, nor should lead wire be used for the negative connection; tinned-copper wire is recommended. If foam supports are needed they can be held against the object by plastic-covered wire instead of spring-loaded anodes.

Since Consolidative Reduction had been successfully carried out on silver objects [10] using different anode materials and electrolytes, it was decided to carry out further experiments on fragile lead [11]. As 10% sulphuric acid had been used as an electrolyte in normal reduction to give a protective surface layer in the finishing process it was tried out for consolidative reduction [8]. The same current density was used, but the anode and cathode wire must be lead. Other materials such as tinned-copper wire, iron and stainless steel soon disintegrate and plate onto the object. If there are some smooth areas of uncorroded lead on the object, lead foil should be used to connect the cathode rather than lead wire, which tends to mark the smooth surface. The foil can be used to support the fragile lead instead of foam pads and it can be reused. The reduction takes longer than in an alkaline electrolyte, and depends on size and amount of corrosion. Hydrogen gas bubbles are only occasionally observed on the completion of reduction; therefore it is necessary to take out the object and examine it during the course of treatment to determine whether reduction is complete. The reversal procedure at the end of reduction is not used because it is impossible to form a chemically protective coating on the porous lead, particularly at such low current density. The acid electrolyte tends to convert completely corroded surfaces of basic lead carbonate insoluble lead sulphate if the current is dropped below 50 mA/dm^2. Therefore the acid electrolyte should only be used when dealing with small objects having small areas of heavy corrosion, and the alkaline electrolyte for treating objects with large areas of heavy corrosion.

In the case of larger objects a nominal current of 100 mA/dm^2 tends to produce the effect of high current reduction. The heavy lead object will tend to pull down on the wire contact, so that more of the total current output will pass through the object, whereas with small, heavily corroded antiquities most of the current passes straight through the wire. The anode/electrolyte/cathode wire provides a complete circuit, which offers the least resistance to the passage of the current. A corroded antiquity has a high resistance, therefore it is more difficult to get the current to pass through the object when it has an easier by-pass route. Therefore the quoted current density must be used as a 'not infallible' guide. The lead must be regularly observed and, if any bubbles are being produced from the object, the current should be reduced, often by as much as four times for large objects, particularly in the alkaline electrolyte. If an acid electrolyte is used, care must be taken not to decrease the current too much, to avoid producing lead sulphate. Experiments in insulating the wire with either wax or resin to force the current through the lead were not successful [10] because the pitted lead surface and the basic lead carbonate surface are so porous that the insulating coating will flood through the pores under the wire and insulate it from the object so that no electrical contact to the lead object is established. The powdery formation of the basic lead carbonate is easily completely impregnated with the coating which will insulate the molecules of the corrosion, preventing any treatment taking place.

As a result of the treatment of the mineralized silver lyre from Ur [10] the use of partially rectified current was also tried, but no benefits were observed.

Some lead antiquities have areas of corrosion that can be seen to consist of a mass of cracks across an apparently lightly corroded surface penetrating into the centre of the object. In fact this is a sign of intensive corrosion, the whole surface, sometimes the whole object, being formed into separate layers or tiny blocks of corrosion. These cracks are actually filled with soil or dirt, holding all these tiny blocks together, but the surrounding corrosion often masks this fact. If an attempt is made to remove the corrosion or carry out consolidative reduction the soil will fall away and the whole area will disintegrate. Preliminary mechanical brushing will often give an appearance of metallic lead on the surface due to isolated grains of metallic lead in the mass of basic lead carbonate and only mechanical methods of cleaning can be used in these cases.

To test the effectiveness of the consolidative reduction method, specific gravity measurements were carried out both before and after treatment of a series of Indian lead coins. X-ray diffraction analysis showed the corrosion product to be basic lead carbonate, and emission spectrographic analysis revealed traces of silver, copper, tin and iron, with up to 5% tin in the original metal. From specific gravity measurements using toluene as the immersion liquid it could be calculated that from 7 to 20% of the coins consisted of corrosion products. After treatment by consolidative reduction in acid and alkaline electrolytes, specific gravity measurements gave a result of over 99% metallic lead.

It should be noted that after treatment by consolidative reduction the lead is very porous and fragile, and very little final mechanical cleaning can be done, so that the treated lead has a darker appearance than normal. It will also be necessary to strengthen the object by impregnating it with a suitable consolidant.

Consolidative reduction is not an easy treatment because the physical state of each object has to be carefully evaluated and the process monitored, but the resulting success achieved on objects which would otherwise have been left to corrode away, or reduced to an unrecognizable state by other methods, is worth an extra effort by the conservator.

REFERENCES

1. Uhlig, H. H., 'Corrosion Handbook', London, 1948
2. Organ, R. M., 'Current Methods in the Conservation of Lead', text of a lecture obtainable from IIC—United Kingdom Group.
3. Holm, K., Some remarks on lead corrosion and lead conservation, 'Res Mediaevales' 3 (1968), 302-306.
4. Kühn, H., Neue Reinigungsmethode für Korrodierte Bleigegenstände, 'Museumskunde' 29 (1960), 156-161.
5. Caley, E. R., Coatings and incrustations on lead objects from the Agora and the method used for their removal, 'Studies in Conservation' 2 (1955), 49-54.
6. Organ, R. M., Use of ion-exchange resin in the treatment of lead objects, 'Museums Journal' 53 (1953), 49-52.
7. Plenderleith, H. J. and Werner, A. E. A., 'The Conservation of Antiquities and Works of Art', 2nd ed., London, 1971.
8. Werner, A. E., Two problems in the conservation of antiquities, in 'The Application of Science in Examination of Works of Art', published by the Museum of Fine Arts, Boston, USA (1967), 126-144.
9. Organ, R. M., The consolidation of fragile metallic objects, in 'Recent Advances in Conservation', ed. G. Thomson, London (1963), 128-134.
10. Organ, R. M., The reclamation of the wholly-mineralized silver in the Ur lyre, in 'The Application of Science in Examination of Works of Art', published by the Museum of Fine Arts, Boston, USA (1967), 96-99.
11. Lane H., 'Consolidative reduction of lead', text of a lecture obtainable from IIC-United Kingdom Group.

THE 'CONSOLIDATIVE' REDUCTION OF SILVER

D. Charalambous, Conservation Centre, 4 Dioskouron Str, Athens, Greece,
and W. A. Oddy, British Museum Research Laboratory, London WC1B 5DA, England

1. INTRODUCTION

The process of 'consolidative reduction', by which the corrosion products on some extensively corroded metals may be converted back to the metallic state, has been described by Werner for the treatment of lead [1] and by Organ for the conservation of silver [2]. However, although the consolidative reduction of lead has now become a standard method of treatment in the British Museum Research Laboratory, the use of this technique for the conservation of silver is very rarely carried out. In fact it is true to say that since the lyre from Ur was completed [2] only one other silver object has been subjected to consolidative reduction. It seems, therefore, opportune that the results of some experimental work which has been carried out recently on the method of consolidative reduction should be made more widely known.

Organ's experimental work was carried out on fragments of completely corroded silver antiquities, but the work described below has been performed on synthetic silver chloride so that the results are strictly comparable, and it was possible to obtain accurate assessments of dimensional changes which took place during the experiments.

2. THE SYNTHETIC SILVER CHLORIDE

Two forms of synthetic silver chloride were used for the consolidative reduction experiments. One was purchased in strips about 3 mm thick which were then rolled into sheets with a thickness of about 1 mm. The second was made by anodic oxidation of fine silver wire of diameter 0.45 mm. The successive corrosion and reduction of this silver wire enabled the dimensional changes between the original silver and that produced after oxidation and reduction to be measured with great accuracy.

2.1 The 'corrosion' of the silver wire

Lengths of silver wire about 20 cm long were connected as the anode in a solution of 'Analar' sodium chloride, using carbon rods as the cathode, and a current in the range 3 mA/dm^2 to 1 A/dm^2 was applied. The voltage was adjusted occasionally during the course of the corrosion process to take account of the changing electrical resistance of the silver chloride layer as it formed. The corrosion process was carried out at several current densities in the above range using both 2% and 5% solutions of the sodium chloride electrolyte in order to determine whether changing these conditions had any effect on the structure of the silver chloride which was produced. When fragments of the oxidized wires were mounted and sections examined under the microscope, no differences in metallographic structure were observed which could be attributed to variations in the current density during the corrosion process.

The time required for complete corrosion of the wire is inversely related to the current density, and at the lowest current densities it took several days, while at the highest ones it was complete in a few hours. The oxidation process is regarded as complete when the current ceases to pass, which happens when the wire is completely corroded in one part, although the corrosion may not be complete along the whole length and traces of the original silver wire can sometimes be found in the centre of the corrosion products.

Although no differences were visible in the structure of the oxidized silver, the wires which were corroded quickly at the higher current densities were rather more brittle than those corroded slowly. Calculations of the cross-sectional area of the silver chloride produced at different current densities indicate that as the current density increases, the density of the silver chloride decreases.

The changes in structure which take place as the silver wire is corroded to silver chloride are illustrated in Figures 1A to 1C. A cross section of the original silver wire is shown in Figure 1A at a magnification of x 65, which was used for all the photographs which illustrate complete cross sections of the wires so that they are strictly comparable. Figure 1B illustrates a piece of wire after corrosion in 5% sodium chloride solution for 7 days at a current density of 30 mA/dm^2. The diameter of the central cavity is approximately equal to that of the original silver wire, indicating that the corrosion process involves the migration of the silver ions outwards through the thickening layer of silver chloride. Figure 1C shows that at a higher magnification the corroded silver can be seen to consist of a matrix of silver chloride containing some isolated grains of uncorroded silver.

Sometimes the corroded wires have cavities which are far smaller than the diameter of the original silver wire, and this must be attributed to the electrolyte seeping into the cavity during the corrosion process. In such cases the line of the 'original surface' of the silver wire is often visible within the thickness of the corrosion product.

3. REDUCTION OF THE CORRODED SILVER WIRES

The fragments of corroded wire were reduced in electrolytes consisting of either 3% formic acid or 3% sodium hydroxide at current densities of up to 25 mA/dm^2, and the reductions were carried out using both fully-rectified direct current (DC) or partly-rectified current in which the DC:AC ratio varied from 3:2 to 5:1. Carbon rods were used as anodes. The current was drawn from an apparatus of the type described by Organ [2] but the 50 ohm resistances which by-pass two of the silicon rectifiers were replaced with 0 to 100 ohm variable resistances. These two variable resistances were fitted with digital revolution counters so that each could be set to the same resistance and the ratio of AC to DC was measured on a cathode ray oscilloscope connected across the terminals of the reduction cell.

No difference was detected between the metallographic structures of silver produced by reduction in either dilute sodium hydroxide or dilute formic acid, and examples of wires reduced in these respective electrolytes are illustrated in Figures 1D and 2A. In both cases direct current was used and the central cavities in the reduced wires are the same size as the original silver wire, with the result that the diameter of the reduced silver wire is considerably greater than that of the original wire. In fact it is approximately twice the original size and the silver which has been produced is very porous as can be seen from the more highly magnified detail of Figure 1D which is shown in Figure 2B.

The original consolidative reduction experiments which were carried out on fragments from corroded antiquities [2] had not been very successful when 30% formic acid was used as an electrolyte, a certain amount of lamination of the reduced silver having resulted from its use. It is likely that this was due to the presence of residual copper minerals in the corrosion layers and no problem of this type was encountered in the present experiments as fine silver wire was used throughout. However, it was observed that the wires reduced in formic acid were more brittle than those reduced in sodium hydroxide and no explanation can be offered for this phenomenon.

When corroded silver wire was reduced using the mixture of AC and DC, very similar results were obtained to those resulting from the use of DC only and a typical wire is illustrated in Figure 2C. This was reduced in 3% sodium hydroxide solution using a DC:AC ratio of 3:2, and similar results are shown in Figure 2D which illustrates a wire reduced in the same electrolyte but at a DC:AC ratio of 5:1. In this case the initial reduction had not been carried to completion and a considerable part of the original silver wire remains running up the cavity in the tube of corrosion product. Figure 3A shows a detail of Figure 2C from which it can be seen that the silver has the same very porous structure as that found in Figure 2B. It appears that the ratio of AC to DC is not critical for the consolidative reduction of silver, provided that the DC is dominant.

Occasionally rather different results were observed in the reduced silver, and one example is illustrated in Figure 3B. Here the reduced silver has formed three distinct zones, an outer one in which the grains of silver are relatively large, a middle layer with a 'normal' appearance and an inner layer, within what should be the cavity, in which the silver is much more porous. A trace of uncorroded original wire can be seen in the centre of the cavity. Figure 3C illustrates the middle and outer zones in greater detail. No explanation is immediately apparent for the formation of these zones, although they are commonly found when rolled sheet silver chloride is reduced (see below). A good example of the appearance of an 'original surface' after reduction is illustrated by Figure 3D in which the diameter of the original silver wire is marked in the reduced silver by a ring of what appear to be very compact grains of silver, which can be seen in greater detail in Figure 4A.

3.1 Sintering of reduced silver wires

It has been shown above that the reduction of silver chloride by either fully rectified or partially rectified current gives rise to porous silver which has the same dimensions as the corroded test piece. In the case of the conservation of the silver lyre from Ur this was an important aspect of the treatment, as the surface of the corroded silver preserved marks made by the strings of the instrument, and it was important from an archaeological point of view that these marks should be preserved. However, cases may arise in which it is desirable that the thickness of the reduced silver should be equal to that in the original state. The only method of causing the porous reduced silver to shrink is by sintering, which is the agglomeration of solid particles under the influence of heat and/or pressure. It is a solid-state reaction occurring below the melting point of the solid, and the driving force for the sintering process is normally a reduction in surface energy arising from surface tension forces.

Experiments were therefore carried out on the sintering of some of the reduced silver wires in order to see if the diameter could be made smaller until it was equal to that of the original silver wire. The sintering was carried out by heating the fragments of reduced wire in air using an electrically-heated furnace. Previous experiments had shown that porous silver only begins to shrink when heated at temperatures greater than 400°C. Figure 4B illustrates a piece of the same reduced wire shown in Figure 1D after sintering at 500°C for 24 hours. The diameter has been reduced by an average of 4.5% and at a higher magnification, shown in Figure 4C, the structure can be seen to have formed larger grains and larger pores. These larger grains resulted from the coalescence of smaller particles, and at the same time the voids have migrated along the boundaries between grains until they were eliminated at the surface or in the central cavity. Figure 4D illustrates a piece of the same wire after sintering at 800°C for 24 hours. The total change in the diameter is now a shrinkage of 25%, but the wire is still about 44% larger than in the original uncorroded state. At a higher magnification shown in Figure 5A, the grains can be seen to have formed one continuous solid in which a few isolated, but very large, voids occur. In this state the large voids can only be eliminated very slowly by migration of vacancies through the crystal lattice. By the time the silver has been sintered to the state illustrated in Figure 4D the central cavity will be in a similar position to that of the isolated voids, so that further shrinkage will be a very long process. These processes are illustrated even more clearly in Figures 5B and 5C which are cross sections of fragments of another reduced silver wire after sintering at 500°C and 800°C respectively for 24 hours. Severe cracks have been caused by the sintering at 500°C and large isolated voids can be seen in the specimen sintered at 800°C, which has also lost its fairly smooth surface.

4. REDUCTION OF SHEET SILVER CHLORIDE

Some experiments have been carried out on the reduction of rolled silver chloride sheet with a thickness of about 1 mm. Samples measuring about 2 cm square were connected as the cathode in solutions of 3% sodium hydroxide and reduced using a mixture of AC:DC with a ratio of 1:3. Low current densities were used, in the region of 2.5 to 10 mA/dm^2, and some of the samples remained in the electrolyte for periods of up to 100 days, which was considerably longer than was required for complete reduction. In all cases the silver was brittle after reduction.

When fragments from these test pieces were examined on the metallurgical microscope, the structure was usually found to consist of very small globules of silver which often had 'boundaries' running through it as shown in Figure 5D. This sample was reduced for 24 days at a current density of 10 mA/dm^2. These boundaries seem to separate areas with different 'densities' of silver chloride. At first these boundaries were thought to be 'slip planes' resulting from the process of rolling the original silver chloride sheet, but subsequent reduction and examination of samples of silver chloride which had been annealed just below its melting point for one hour revealed that these boundaries are still present. Their origin remains, as yet, unexplained.

A second type of boundary is shown in Figure 6A which is a section of synthetic silver chloride which was reduced for 86 days at a current density of 2.5 mA/dm^2. Along this boundary the silver grains are very large, and these boundaries are sometimes associated with marks appearing on the surface of the silver during reduction, such as those shown in Figure 6B. These 'ripples' spread out from the point of contact of the connecting wire with the back of the specimen and must be a result of the process of reduction. The ripples suggest discontinuities of current during the reduction process, but it is certain that the current remained constant during the whole period of electrolysis. The experiments carried out so far suggest that prolonged electrolysis does result in some grain growth in the reduced silver but more confirmatory work must be carried out.

5. CONCLUSION

This work is very much a preliminary study of the consolidative reduction of silver, but it has confirmed Organ's findings that sodium hydroxide solution is a better electrolyte than formic acid, and it has shown that the ratio of AC to DC does not seem to be critical. In fact, for the fine silver used in these experiments, the use of DC alone was quite satisfactory, although for silver containing some copper it is probable that a mixture of AC and DC would be advantageous. This will be checked by further experiments.

Measurements on the metallographic sections have shown that there are no significant dimensional changes during the reduction process, but the sintering will reduce the volume of the porous silver, although not back to that of the original silver artifact.

Finally, the metallographic structures of the reduced silver have been shown to contain unusual features whose occurrence is not yet fully explained.

ACKNOWLEDGEMENTS

We are grateful to Dr A. E. Werner for his advice and encouragement during this work and to Miss Ann Bugden for printing our photomicrographs.

REFERENCES

1. Werner, A. E., Two problems in the conservation of antiquities: corroded lead and brittle silver, in 'Application of Science in Examination of Works of Art', Boston Museum of Fine Arts, 1971.
2. Organ, R. M., The reclamation of the wholly-mineralized silver in the Ur Lyre, in 'Application of Science in Examination of Works of Art', Boston Museum of Fine Arts, 1971.

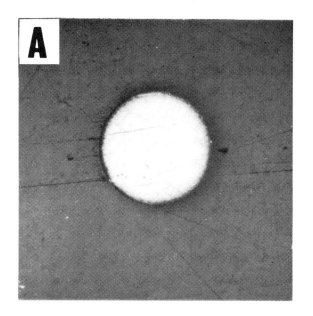
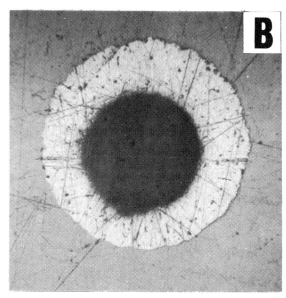
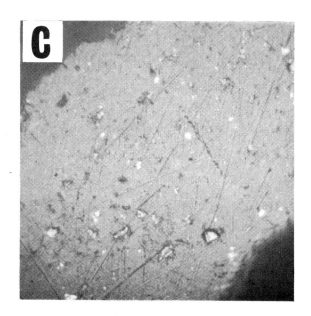
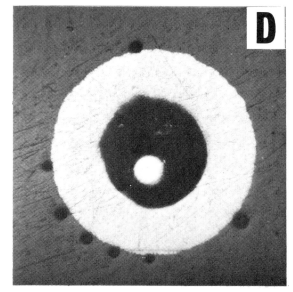

Figure 1A. Cross section of original silver wire (diameter 0.45 mm).
Magnification X65.

Figure 1B. Cross section of silver wire after complete anodic oxidation in dilute sodium chloride solution at a current density of 30 mA/dm^2 for 7 days.
Magnification X65.

Figure 1C. Detail of 1B showing isolated grains of uncorroded silver in a matrix of silver chloride.
Magnification X325.

Figure 1D. Cross section of silver wire after complete anodic oxidation; followed by reduction in dilute sodium hydroxide solution at a current density of 16 mA/dm^2 for 7 days using direct current.
Magnification X65.

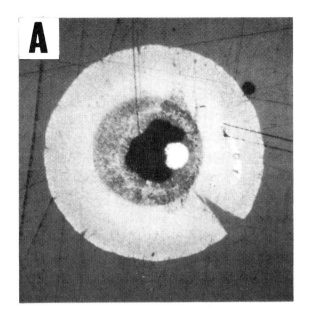
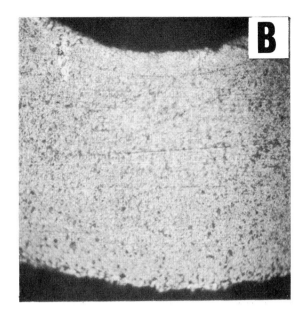
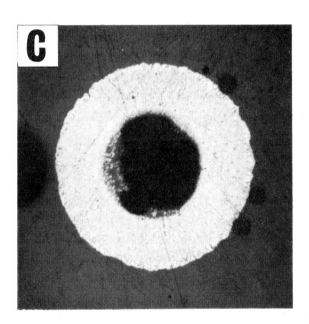
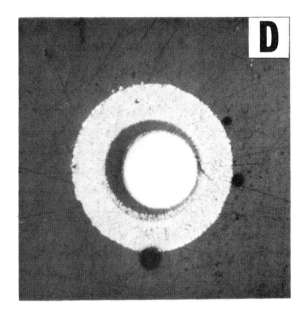

Figure 2A. Cross section of silver wire after complete anodic oxidation; followed by reduction in dilute formic acid at a current density of 15 mA/dm^2 for 7 days using direct current.
Magnification X65.

Figure 2B. Detail of 1D showing porous structure of corroded and then reduced silver wire.
Magnification X325.

Figure 2C. Cross section of silver wire after complete anodic oxidation; followed by reduction in dilute sodium hydroxide at a current density of 10 mA/dm^2 for 8 days using DC/AC current with a ratio of 3:2.
Magnification X65.

Figure 2D. Cross section of silver wire after complete anodic oxidation; followed by reduction in dilute sodium hydroxide at a current density of 25 mA/dm^2 for 7 days using DC/AC current with a ratio of 5:1.
Magnification X65.

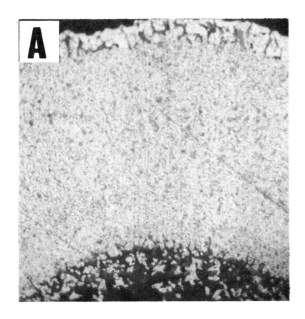
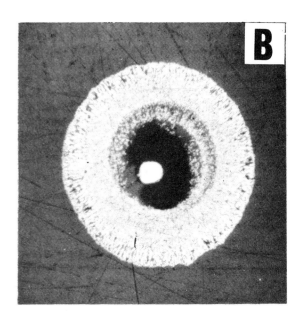
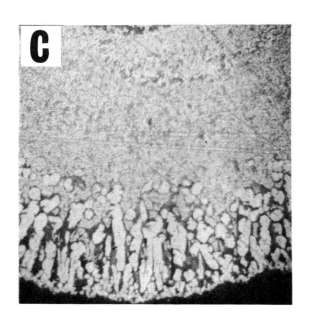
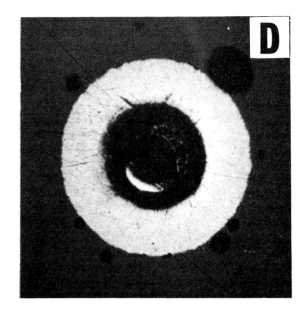

Figure 3A. Detail of 2C showing porous structure.
Magnification X325.

Figure 3B. Cross section of silver wire after complete anodic oxidation; followed by reduction in dilute sodium hydroxide at a current density of 10 mA/dm^2 for 7 days using DC/AC current with a ratio of 2:1. Magnification X65.

Figure 3C. Detail of 3A showing porous structure of middle and outer layers.
Magnification X325.

Figure 3D. Cross section of silver wire after complete anodic oxidation; followed by reduction in dilute sodium hydroxide at a current density of 17 mA/dm^2 for 7 days using DC/AC current with a ratio of 5:1. Magnification X65.

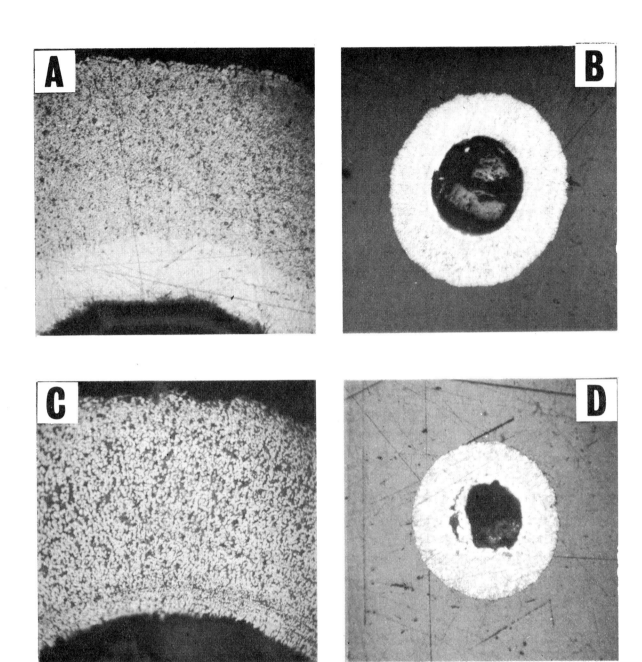

Figure 4A. Detail of 3C showing porous outer layer of reduced silver and more compact inner layer within the line of the 'original surface'.
Magnification X325.

Figure 4B. Cross section of silver wire treated as for Figure 1D and then sintered at $500^{\circ}C$ for 24 hours.
Magnification X65.

Figure 4C. Detail of 4B. See Figure 2B where the voids are much smaller.
Magnification X325.

Figure 4D Cross section of silver wire treated as for Figure 1D and then sintered at $800^{\circ}C$ for 24 hours.
Magnification X65. Etched.

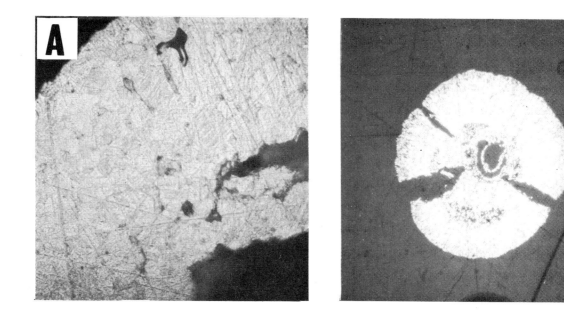

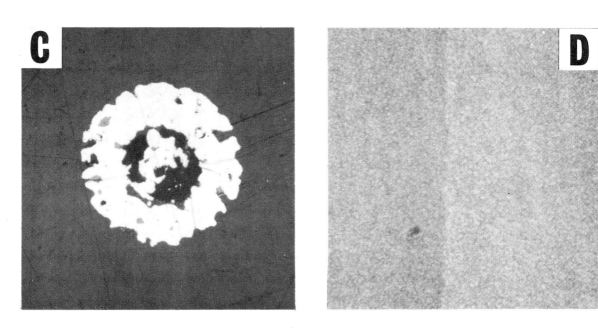

Figure 5A. Detail of 4D. See Figures 2B and 4C. Only a few very large voids remain.
Magnification X325. Etched.

Figure 5B. Cross section of silver wire after anodic oxidation and then reduction in dilute sodium hydroxide at a current density of 10 mA/dm^2 for 7 days using DC/AC current with a ratio of 3:1 and then sintering at 500°C for 24 hours. Note the cracking of the wire and the small central cavity.
Magnification X65

Figure 5C. As for 5B but sintered at 800°C for 24 hours. Note the surface irregularity.
Magnification X65.

Figure 5D. Cross section of synthetic silver chloride after reduction in dilute sodium hydroxide at a current density of 10 mA/dm^2 for 24 days using DC/AC current with a ratio of 3:1. Note the 'boundary' in the structure.
Magnification X720.

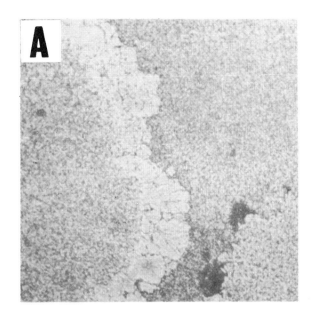 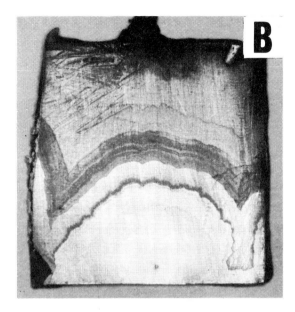

Figure 6A. Cross section of synthetic silver chloride after reduction in dilute sodium hydroxide at a current density of 2.5 mA/dm^2 for 86 days using DC/AC current with a ratio of 3:1. Note the 'boundary' in the structure.
Magnification X850.

Figure 6B. Sample of synthetic silver chloride after reduction to show the 'ripples' on the surface. The sample had an area of 4 cm^2.

CHELATING AGENTS – A REVIEW

W. D. Richey, Chatham College, Pittsburgh, PA 15232, USA

1. INTRODUCTION

Chelating agents are a class of chemical substances characterized by possession of at least two functional groups capable of interacting, in concert, with a metal ion to form a ring structure called a chelate ring. (Chelate is derived from the Greek for lobster's claw [1].) The chemical substances resulting from the interaction of a chelating agent and a metal ion are known as metal chelates.

Metal chelates are a subclass of the very large class of metal coordination compounds. These result when coordinating agents, chemical substances with a functional group which can interact with a metal ion, do so in such a way as to surround it. The term 'ligand' is used frequently in place of coordinating agent (and also to refer to the active site or atom of the functional group). Chelating agents, thus, are a special class of coordinating agent or ligand.

A large number of chelating agents have been studied and many are recognized to have some practical application, particularly in qualitative or quantitative chemical analysis. Essentially all metal ions form metal chelates with one or more families of chelating agents. Most chelating agents will react with quite a number of metal ions, although, in an analytical context, conditions can sometimes be selected so that a given chelating agent will be selective; that is, interact with a limited number of the many metal ion species.

Sequestering agents are the class of chelating agents which, by formation of chelates (but without forming a precipitate), lower the effective concentration of a 'free' metal ion in solution to the point where the solution no longer manifests the characteristic reaction of the 'free' metal ion. When the characteristic reaction is one of analytical significance, e.g. the formation of a colour or a precipitate, the chelating agents are called masking agents.

Unfortunately, the conservator dealing with an object usually cannot draw directly on the many specific or selective chelate reactions. These depend on the complete dissolution of a small sample, followed by freedom to alter pH, or oxidation state, or to add additional reagents and buffers (which may themselves act as ligands).

This review does not attempt to treat in any detail the use of chelating agents in chemical analysis. The conservator interested in the use of chelating agents for qualitative or quantitative analysis will find the literature vast and detailed. Those interested in analytical applications should find the recent monograph by Betteridge and Hallam [2] a useful introduction. Current university texts contain substantial sections on chelates and good introductory bibliographies [3,4]. Both of the major treatises on analytical chemistry [5,6] have substantial monographs on the use of chelates [7,8,9,10] and include chelate methods in the sections on individual elements.

For a general approach to metal coordination compounds, a current university text on advanced inorganic chemistry [11] or coordination chemistry [12] should be consulted. Ferguson [13] covers chelating agents and the chelation process from the point of view of the organic chemist.

The monograph by Martell and Calvin [15] remains a useful point of entry to an understanding of metal chelates and of their uses. The monograph on chelating agents and metal chelates edited by Dwyer and Mellor [1], the two monographs on sequestration and masking by Perrin [15,16], and the monograph on organic sequestering agents by Chaberek and Martell [17] are all well organized and most useful. (All contain a considerably body of material on analysis, but also cover the chelation process and a number of chelating agents in detail.) The best coverage of applications of chelating agents is in Chaberek and Martell [17]. A new comprehensive work on coordination chemistry, edited by Martell [18], is in preparation. The first volume, available currently, is concerned with the determination of structures and solution equilibria rather than specific coordinating agents or uses.

2. NOMENCLATURE

The nomenclature of chelating agents and the metal chelates can be truly vexing. There is, of course, a formal nomenclature system for coordination compounds which is extendable to metal chelates. Fernelius, Loening and Adams [19] offer a useful, brief introduction to the formal nomenclature of coordination compounds, as do the textbooks [11,12], while the 'Red Book' [20] may be consulted for complete details. Chelating agents have formal system names as organic substances, but for those which have been in general commercial use or which are used by chemists as analytical reagents or in extended studies of families of compounds, shortened or popular names (often acronyms) are in common use. Those in commercial use may have additional trade names and those with pharmacological uses have 'drughouse' names. The metal chelates will frequently be referred to as such, i.e. the calcium chelate of EDTA, which would be fine if there were not so many possible variant names for the same substance, e.g. calcium Versenate.

The chelating agents which are polyacids, polybases or can function as both acids and bases are sometimes available in a variety of salt forms, all of which may loosely be referred to as the parent compound. As an extended example, consider N,N'-1,2-ethanediylbis-[N-carboxymethyl] glycine, the aminocarboxylic acid chelating agent known to most of us as EDTA (the acronym for another systematic name, *ethylenediaminetetraacetic acid*), which has four acidic protons. It is commercially available as the parent acid, the mono-, di-, tri-, and tetrasodium salts, and the di-metal salt of some metal chelates, e.g. the disodium salt of the calcium chelate of EDTA. Table 1 gives variant names for EDTA and the sodium salts, starting with the current preferred Chemical Abstracts name, following with other nomenclature system names and then with samples of various alternatives on these names and trade names.

Table 1

Parent acid	Sodium salt	Disodium salt	Trisodium salt	Tetrasodium salt
N,N'-1,2-ethanediylbis-[N-carboxymethyl] glycine	N,N'-1,2-ethanediylbis-[N-carboxymethyl] glycine, sodium salt	---, disodium salt	---, trisodium salt	---, tetrasodium salt
(Ethylenedinitrilo)tetraacetic acid	(Ethylenedinitrilo)tetraacetic acid, sodium salt Sodium (ethylenedinitrilo)tetraacetate	---, disodium salt Disodium ---	---, trisodium salt Trisodium ---	---, tetrasodium salt Tetrasodium ---
Ethylenebis [iminediacetic] acid				---, tetrasodium salt Tetrasodium ---
Ethylenediaminetetraacetic acid	Ethylenediaminetetraacetic acid, sodium salt Sodium ethylenediaminetetraacetate	---, disodium salt Disodium ---	---, trisodium salt Trisodium ---	---, tetrasodium salt Tetrasodium ---
EDTA Edetic acid	Edetic acid, sodium salt Monosodium edetate	E. D. T. A. disodium ---, disodium salt Disodium --- Edathamil disodium Disodium edathamil	---, trisodium salt Trisodium ---	---, tetrasodium salt Tetrasodium ---
Endrate*		Endrate disodium*		
Tetrine acid*		Tetracemate disodium		Tetrine* Tetracemate tetrasodium Tetracemin
Versene acid*			Versene 9*	Versene* Versene-67* Versene-100*
		Sequestrene NA$_2$*	Sequestrene NA$_3$	Sequestrene* Aquamollin* Calsol* Cheelox BF*
		Chelaplex III*		Complexone* Distol 8*
Havidote*				Irgalon* Kalex* Komplexon* Nervanaid B* Nullapon* Questrex* Syntes 12a*
				Trilon B* TST* Tyclarosol*

The names in this table were assembled from the Merck Index [21] and the SOCMA Handbook [22], as an example of the complexities encountered in the nomenclature of a family of materials in common use.

*Registered trademark

In a practical situation, when one has a sample in hand or a reference citing the use of a material and only a trade name is available, what is needed is information on composition or equivalent products. 'The Merck Index' [21] and the 'SOCMA Handbook' [22] have name cross-reference indices which are useful for solving such puzzles. 'The Merck Index' also will give additional information on the substance if a listing is found. When starting from a system name to seek information, the above two references may again be helpful, but the current Chemical Abstracts Index Guide and the Supplements must be consulted if it is a quite recent product that is of interest, or if a comprehensive literature search is contemplated.

3. HAZARDS

Some chelating agents, principally the polyphosphates, the hydroxy acids and the aminocarboxylic acids, have been in commercial use on a relatively large scale for decades. (More than three million pounds of EDTA were manufactured in the United States in 1968 [23].) In conventional use, chelating agents would probably not be considered as particularly hazardous, but a few are quite toxic (oxalic acid, for example), and a number have important pharmacological uses. The use of chelating agents as sequestering agents in foodstuffs and beverages has led in some cases (e.g. EDTA) to the establishment of maximum permissible limits under the United States Federal Food, Drug and Cosmetic Act [24]. Most common commercial chelating agents manifest a limited toxicity from ingestion of small amounts because they are not absorbed from the gastrointestinal tract in their usual solution form as multicharged anions [24]. Shulman and Dwyer [25] have reviewed the metal ions, chelating agents and metal complexes in biological systems, and touch on the toxicity of all three. Williams [26], in a brief review on the possible link between chelated metals and cancer, calls attention to some other reviews in this area.

Since conservators may not use chelating agents in conventional ways, and since the actual manipulations of objects and materials may be carried out by assistants for whom we are responsible, one of Williams' conclusions 'All ligand-users ought to respect their [the ligands] possible carcinogeneity', should be generalized in our context to: all ligand-users should respect their ligands. Preliminary concern about potential hazards is always in order. Remember that the metal ions themselves and the metal chelates can be hazards as well as the chelating agents.

In general, when considering the use of a chemical substance new to you, carefully consult labels and the supplier's literature for warnings of possible hazards. Check a reference source such as the 'Merck Index' [21] for a listing indicating possible medicinal uses, side effects, or indications of toxicity. Always keep in mind that there is a broad range of individual susceptibilities to substances. Some substances quite widely used and tolerated by many people can produce specific reactions in others who prove sensitive to them. When treating an object, large volumes of a chelating agent in solutions may be needed in which the object may be immersed, to emerge dripping; or from which the object may be treated with swabs or cloths. Under such circumstances, large skin areas may be exposed and exposures may be relatively long. This may be a very different sort of exposure from that of an industrial worker tending a semi-automatic process, or of an analyst who may work with small amounts of a reagent for years but rarely have physical contact with it. Always keep in mind when considering a new use that a reagent which may have long been used safely in small amounts in analytical work may actually be a hazard if used in large quantities in an unventilated area. The neutral metal chelates (those formed when the formal charges on the metal ion are offset by charges on the chelating agent) are very much like organic compounds; that is, they are often fat-soluble and are surprisingly volatile [27]. Considering the recognized toxicity of the heavy metals, minimized contact and good ventilation must be recommended.

If the analytical techniques of solvent extraction of metal complexes [15, 16, 28] were to find application in conservation, the possible flammability or hazardous nature of the organic solvent should be considered before large-scale trials were attempted. Again, minimized contact and good ventilation must be stressed.

A potential hazard exists if solutions of heavy metal complexes are allowed to evaporate to dryness. Heavy metal-nitrogen ligand (and other) complexes which are stable in solution can crystallize out in potentially explosive forms. This might seem a remote possibility, yet intermittent but extended use of a tank could produce such a situation.

The precautions of Oddy [29] for the use of benzotriazole may be generalized for chelating agents (and all reagents): take care that fine powders are not inhaled or spilled on the skin or clothing when making up a solution, when an object has dried and is being brushed, or when a spill has dried out; minimize contact of solutions (particularly in alcohol or other organic solvents) with the skin; wear rubber or polythene gloves to handle objects during treatment; carefully clean up all spills and clean all glassware after use.

4. FUNDAMENTAL CONCEPTS

Much of what may be said in a general way about chelating agents and metal chelates is drawn or extrapolated from extended studies on simple metal coordination compounds, those with single atom (ion) or simple group ligands.

Chelating agents are frequently classified on the basis of the number of coordinating groups, called the denticity (or sometimes multiplicity). The simplest chelating agents would be called bidentate, those with three coordinating groups terdentate, and those with a number of coordinating groups would be described as multidentate. (The simple coordinating agents are sometimes referred to as unidentate). Chelating agents with three, four, five and six coordinating groups are in common use. Chelating agents with higher numbers of coordinating groups have been prepared. Not all the potential coordinating groups are necessarily engaged in a given metal chelate [30]. Coordinating groups usually contain an oxygen, nitrogen, sulphur or phosphorus atom, which is referred to as the donor atom, the metal ion being the acceptor atom. The most generally studied (and the earliest studied) class of chelating agents are the bidentates [31]. Examples of chelating agents with higher numbers of coordinating groups have been selectively studied [32], some in great detail, such as the aminocarboxylic acids like EDTA [10, 30].

The 'stability' of a complex is not an easy quantity to specify unambiguously [33, 34]. The most commonly encountered usage refers to mass-action or equilibrium concepts. Stability constants are equilibrium constants, empirically derived measures of the tendency of a metal ion and a given ligand to form a complex. For a given metal and a very closely related family of ligands, or a given ligand and a family of metal ions, such constants may guide judgment about the course of competitive reactions. From the kinetic point of view, stability refers to the frequency with which a given attached ligand exchanges with a free ligand in solution. A ligand which freely exchanges (said to be 'labile' rather than 'inert') may also have a large stability constant, i.e. resist exchange with a competitive ligand. Thermal stability and stability towards chemical attack (oxidation or reduction of the ligand or metal ion) are additional important measures. All of these would be of interest in conservation, but they are definitely not equivalent and are usually not all available.

In solution, positively charged metal ions exist as complexes with solvent molecules. If other neutral species or ionic species are present in the solution, competition for bonding sites on the metal ion will occur and other complexes may be formed. Thus, the conventional chemical shorthand, M^{++}, for an ion derived from the metal M°, may be misleading if it deflects attention from the probable existence of the metal ion in solution in a complexed form, $M(H_2O)_x^{++}$ with the solvent or with anions, $MX_4^=$. A number of complex metal species, positive, neutral and negative, may be present in an apparently simple situation. That is, a solution of copper(II) chloride may contain neutral copper ($CuCl_2$) and negative copper ($CuCl_4^=$) species.

Such a copper(II) chloride solution will also be quite acid, through hydrolysis. Hydrolysis is the general name given to a reaction in which a species releases protons to form an acid solution, or accepts protons from solvent molecules to form a basic solution. Hydrolysis is of concern to us in several ways. First, almost all metal ions are hydrated in water solution and may undergo hydrolysis (often forming complex polynuclear species in the process). The tendency to hydrolysis is most pronounced in the cases of metal ions with relatively high formal charges (Fe^{+3}, Cu^{+2}), which form quite acidic solutions. Hydrolysis can explain the acid condition in corrosion cracks and crevices [35]. Second, a chelating agent may itself be an acid, often a polyacid. A chelating agent may often be used as a metal salt, to overcome the insolubility of the parent acid chelating agent. If the chelating agent is a relatively strong acid, its solution will be acid. If it is a weak acid, its salts will hydrolyze to produce basic solutions. Again using EDTA as an example, the parent acid is a strong acid but relatively insoluble. The mono- and disodium salts are slightly soluble and act like weak acids, the trisodium salt is more soluble and hydrolyzes (the pH of a 1% solution is 9.3) and the tetrasodium salt is very soluble and hydrolyzes to a considerable extent (pH of a 1% solution is 11.3) [21]. Attempts to alter the pH of a solution through the addition of an acid or base, as appropriate, or a buffer may be successful in the limited sense, but may also alter the mode of reaction of the chelating agent, i.e. change the form from ionic to neutral or cause it to precipitate. The added buffer or the counter ions of the acid or base may act as competitive ligands. For a given object to be treated, a careful assessment would need to be made about the possible secondary effects of a given chelating agent. A scale or crust might be satisfactorily removed but at the cost of altering the balance of the patina or etching a surface.

The main set of factors which influence the formation of a metal chelate are the size of the rings and the number formed, the metal ion, the donor atoms on the chelating agent and the basic strength of the chelating agent [34, 36].

Rings of five atoms, i.e. the metal atom, the two donor atoms and two atoms or groups which separate the donor atoms, seem to be preferred, but four- and six-membered rings are well known, and larger rings can be prepared. This, perhaps, is the place to note that there are chemical substances with more than one donor atom (that are, in a sense, bi- or multidentate species) in which the molecular geometry is such that the groups cannot interact with the same metal atom. They may interact with more than one metal atom to form polynuclear or polymeric substances which are metal complexes but not metal chelates in our sense. Trofimenko [37] has suggested the term 'exobidentate' to describe such a circumstance for two donor atoms. Benzotriazole would be an example of such a substance.

In general, for a given type of chelating agent, the greater the number of rings formed (for a bidentate chelating agent, more than one molecule would be involved), the greater the stability of the system. Alternately, the greater the number of coordinating groups engaged (the higher the denticity), the greater the number of rings formed, and the greater the stability of the system in the equilibrium sense. This is quite general and is referred to as the 'chelate effect' [38].

For a closely related series of chelating agents, the greater the experimental measure of basic strength (pK_a), the greater the stability of the metal complex, in the equilibrium sense, unless some structural feature has been added that prevents the closure of a ring or rings [39].

Great effort has been expended across a century in attempts to classify both metal ions and ligands and to organize the information concerning the complexes formed. The hard and soft acid and base (HSAB) concept proposed by Pearson [40] usefully incorporates much of the available information* into a generalized system of classification of reactants as Lewis acids and bases. Hard acids would include the metal ions which are relatively small, have relatively high formal charges or have an inert gas core of non-bonding electrons. Soft acids would include the relatively large, relatively low charged metal ions with non-bonding cores of d-electrons (the transition elements and the immediate post-transition elements). Unfortunately, there is a 'border' classification into which fall many of the species of most interest to us (Table 2). It should be noted that for metals with more than one metal ion (Cu^0, Cu^+, Cu^{++}), the ions may be of different classifications. The classification of bases (here, chelating agents) is based on the observations on metal ions and unidentate ligands. Just as, in the Lewis sense, a metal ion is an acid because it can be an electron acceptor, a base is an electron donor because its groups contain an atom with an unshared electron pair (or pairs). Following the pattern of hard and soft acids, hard bases are relatively small, and have a relatively large negative charge (Table 3). One of the main conclusions drawn from the HSAB approach is that hard acids prefer to bind to hard bases and soft acids prefer to bind to soft bases. This rule does not indicate that the other combination (hard-soft) does not occur, it indicates preferences and the direction of displacement in competitions of ligands. Thus it can be seen that the metal ions of interest to this Congress fall across the classifications, with a plurality in the border class. The usual (and useful) generalization that hard acid metal ions tend to coordinate with nitrogen or oxygen compounds rather than with phosphorus or sulphur compounds and soft acid metal ions with phosphorus or sulphur rather than nitrogen or oxygen compounds

Table 2. Classification of Lewis acids

Hard	Border	Soft
Na^+, K^+		Cu^+, Ag^+, Au^+
Mg^{++}, Ca^{++}	Cu^{++}, Zn^{++}	Hg^{++}
	Pb^{++}, Sn^{++}	
	Fe^{++}, Ni^{++}	
As^{+++}	Sb^{+++}, Bi^{+++}	
Fe^{+++}		Au^{+++}

Table 3. Classification of Lewis bases

Hard	Boder	Soft
H_2O, OH^-		R_2S, RSH, RS^-
RCO_2^-, PO_4^{-3}, CO_3^{-2}		R_3P, $(RO)_3P$
ROH, RO^-, R_2O		
NH_3, RNH_2	$C_6H_5NH_2$, C_5H_5N	

The symbol R stands for an organic group

*The classification schemes of Ahrland, Chatt, Davies [41] and Schwarzenbach [42] are included in the HSAB scheme.

232

holds, but is not very instructive for the border metal ions. Again, it should be recalled that these guide lines were developed from studies on unidentate ligands. When the bi- and multidentate systems are considered, more than one type of coordinating group of a given donor atom may be present and more than one type of donor atom may be present. In such circumstances, neat, concise generalizations are no longer possible, no matter how desirable. Jones [43] offers a concise summary of the vast amount of material collected by Sidgwick [44], with guidelines as to which metal ions will preferentially bond with nitrogen or oxygen.

It should be pointed out here that the Pearson HSAB approach covers a very broad range of materials other than the limited number of metal ions and donor atoms considered in this review. In particular, it does include metal atoms (Hg) and bulk metals (Fe, Cu, Ag, Au) as soft acids. This would imply a preference for interaction of metals with the soft bases, the phosphorus- and sulphur-containing compounds. This seems consistent with observations on corrosion inhibitors, although, again, preferences do not imply exclusions. There are successful oxygen and nitrogen corrosion inhibitors. Trabanelli and Carassiti have recently reviewed the field of organic corrosion inhibitors [45]. Some chelating agents may also function as corrosion inhibitors, although they cannot surround a metal atom on a surface in the sense that they would an ion in solution.

5. USES

Uses of chelating agents other than as analytical reagents are reviewed by Martell and Calvin [14], Chaberek and Martell [17] and Perrin [16]. Most of these uses depend on controlling the level of metal ion concentrations in solution to create or avoid some effect (a colour, a precipitate) or to remove the metal ions from the system.

The use of chelating agents in metal cleaning and scale removal is well established. Chaberek and Martell [46] summarized such uses and Perrin [47] continued the summary through 1969. Frequently mixtures, including hydroxy acids or hydroxy acids and EDTA (or its salts) are used. While there is no real question of the efficacy of such treatments for removal of scales and crusts, there is also no real question that metal will be removed if care is not exercised. Because such applications are often continuous and can be on a very large scale, emphasis has been on commercially available chelating agents and low costs rather than on specialized reagents. The possibility of a specialized treatment for conservation use is quite real, but probably remains to be developed on the basis of a careful match of chelating agent properties to conservation requirements. The limited number of easily recognizable citations of uses of chelating agents in conservation [48] generally involve the use of the EDTA family. These are probably only the tip of an iceberg of actual practical use of chelating agents in conservation.

Brief mention should be made of two interrelated areas which might hold promise for use in conservation. One is solvent extraction, the use of organic solvents to displace aqueous equilibria in a desired direction by selective extraction of neutral metal chelates from an aqueous phase [28, 49]. Solvent extraction might hold some promise for reducing the times involved, reducing the volumes of liquid involved, or possibly, near elimination of water in cases where the object can be damaged by water (and can tolerate the solvent). The second is the relatively recent development of very selective, strong chelating agents for the alkali metals, the macrocyclic polyethers or 'crown' ethers [50]. Crown ethers have been developed that can be used to separate a specific alkali metal ion from mixtures and carry it (with its counter ion) into solution in an organic solvent. They generally show a low affinity for transition metal ions. Almost all work up till now has been on synthesis of new compounds in the series or on understanding the metal binding properties, but applications are beginning to be made. The selective removal of alkali metal or alkaline earth metal salts from objects using a minimum of water is an interesting possibility.

REFERENCES

1. Dwyer, F. P. and Mellor, D. P. (ed.), 'Chelating Agents and Metal Chelates', Academic Press, New York, 1964, p. 3 citing Morgan and Drew, 'Journal of the Chemical Society', 117 (1920), 1456.
2. Betteridge, D. and Hallam, H. E., 'Modern Analytical Methods', The Chemical Society, London, 1972, especially Chap. 3, Organic reagents.
3. Skoog, D. A. and West, D. M., 'Fundamentals of Analytical Chemistry', 2nd ed., Holt, Rinehart and Winston, New York, 1969.
4. Peters, D. G., Hayes, J. M. and Hieftje, G. M., 'Chemical Separations and Measurements: Theory and Practice of Analytical Chemistry', Saunders, Philadelphia, 1974.
5. Kolthoff, I. M. and Elving, P. J. (ed.), 'Treatise on Analytical Chemistry', Wiley Interscience, New York, 1959.
6. Wilson, C. L. and Wilson, D. W. (ed.), 'Comprehensive Analytical Chemistry', Elsevier, Amsterdam, 1959.
7. Ringbom, A., Complexion reactions, in [5], Vol. 1, pp. 543-628.
8. May, I. and Schubert, L., Reactive groups as reagents: inorganic applications, in [5], Vol. 2, pp. 833-916.
9. Holmes, F., Organic reagents in inorganic analysis, in [6], Vol. IA, pp. 210-235.
10. Flaschka, H. and Barnard, A. J., Jr, Titrations with EDTA and related compounds, in [6], Vol. IB, pp. 288-385.
11. Cotton, F. A. and Wilkinson, G., 'Advanced Inorganic Chemistry', 3rd ed., Wiley-Interscience, New York, 1972.
12. Jones, M. M., 'Elementary Coordination Chemistry', Prentice-Hall, Englewood Cliffs, N.J., 1964.
13. Ferguson, L. N., 'The Modern Structural Theory of Organic Chemistry', Prentice-Hall, Englewood Cliffs, N.J., 1963, pp. 62-88.
14. Martell, A. E. and Calvin, M., 'Chemistry of the Metal Chelate Compounds', Prentice-Hall, Englewood Cliffs, N.J., 1952.

15. Perrin, D. D., 'Organic Complexing Reagents: Structure, Behavior, and Application to Inorganic Analysis', Wiley-Interscience, New York, 1964.
16. Perrin, D. D., 'Masking and Demasking of Chemical Reactions', Wiley-Interscience, New York, 1970.
17. Chaberek, S. and Martell, A. E., 'Organic Sequestering Agents', Wiley, New York, 1959.
18. Martell, A. E. (ed.), 'Coordination Chemistry', Vol. 1, Van Nostrand Reinhold, New York, 1971.
19. Fernelius, W. C., Loening, K. and Adams, R. M., Notes on nomenclature: coordination nomenclature I and II, 'Journal of Chemical Education' 51 (1974), 468-469 and 603-605.
20. 'Nomenclature of Inorganic Chemistry, Definitive Rules 1970', 2nd ed., Butterworths, London, 1971, Sect. 7. Also in 'Pure Appl. Chem.', 28 (1971) 39.
21. 'The Merck Index', 8th ed., Merck & Co., Rahway, N.J., 1968.
22. 'SOCMA Handbook: Commercial Organic Chemical Names', American Chemical Society, 1965 (Synthetic Organic Chemicals Manufacturers' Association).
23. Broad, W. C., EDTA − a laboratory chelating agent, 'American Laboratory' 3 (1971), 47-51.
24. Perrin, D. D., in [16], p. 165.
25. Shuman, A. and Dwyer, P. P., Metal chelates in biological systems, in [1], pp. 383-439.
26. Williams, D. R., Metals, ligands, and cancer, 'Chemical Reviews' 72 (1972), 203-213.
27. Frohliger, J. O., private communication to W. D. Richey.
28. Stary, J., 'The Solvent Extraction of Metal Chelates', Pergamon Press, Oxford, 1964.
29. Oddy, W. A., On the toxicity of benzotriazole, 'Studies in Conservation' 17 (1972), 135.
    See also, Oddy, W. A., Toxicity of benzotriazole, 'Studies in Conservation' 19 (1974), 188-189.
30. Garvan, F. L., Metal chelates of ethylenediaminetetraacetic acid and related substances, in [1], pp. 283-333, especially 289-294.
31. Harris, C. M. and Livingstone, S. E., Bidentate chelates, in [1], pp. 95-141.
32. Goodwin, H. A., Design and stereochemistry of multidentate chelating agents, in [1], pp. 143-181.
33. Jones, M. M., in [12], pp. 42-44.
34. Mellor, D. P., Historical background and fundamental concepts, in [1], pp. 1-50, especially 40-42.
35. Pourbaix, M., 'Lectures in Electrochemical Corrosion', Plenum Press, New York, 1973, pp. 264-269.
36. Craig, D. P. and Nyholm, R. S., The nature of the metal-ligand bond, in [1], pp. 51-93.
37. Trofimenko, S., The coordination chemistry of pyrazole-derived ligands, Chemical Reviews' 72 (1972), 497-509; see footnote on p. 497.
38. Mellor, D. P., in [34], pp. 42-43.
39. Mellor, D. P., in [34], p. 45.
40. Pearson, R. G., Acids and bases, 'Science' 151 (1966), 172-177; Hard and soft acids and bases, 'Chemistry in Britain' 3 (1967), 103-107; Hard and soft acids and bases, HSAB, Part I and Part II, 'Journal of Chemical Education' 45 (1968), 581-587 and 643-648.
41. Ahrland, S., Chatt, J. and Davies, N. R., 'Quarterly Reviews' (London) 12 (1958), 265-276.
42. Schwarzenbach, G., 'Experentia' Supplement 5 (1956), 162.
43. Jones, M. M., in [12], pp. 40-42.
44. Sidgwick, N. V., 'The Chemical Elements and Their Compounds', Oxford University Press, Oxford, 1949.
45. Trabanelli, G. and Carassiti, V., Mechanism and phenomenology of organic inhibitors, in Fontana, M. G. and Staehle, R. W. (ed.), 'Applications in Corrosion Science and Technology', Vol. 1, Plenum Press, New York, 1970, pp. 147-228.
46. Chaberek, S. and Martell, A. E., in [17], pp. 335-339 and 396-397.
47. Perrin, D. D., in [16], pp. 165-169.
48. AATA Subject Index for Vol. 1-10, in Special Supplement to 'Art and Archaeology Technical Abstracts' 11 (1974).
49. Perrin, D. D., in [15], pp. 201-235.
50. Christensen, J. J., Hill, J. O. and Izatt, R. M., Ion binding by synthetic macrocyclic compounds, 'Science' 174 (1971), 459-467.

ACKNOWLEDGEMENT

The invaluable advice and assistance of Ms Amy S. Ingraham is gratefully acknowledged.

THE CORROSION OF METALS ON DISPLAY

W. A. Oddy, British Museum Research Laboratory, London WC1B 5DA, England

1. INTRODUCTION

It is well known that the metals of antiquity, with the exception of gold, become tarnished when a clean surface is exposed to the atmosphere. This tarnishing is normally a very slow process which can be retarded by the careful application of a surface protecting agent, such as a tarnish inhibitor or a lacquer. However under certain conditions the tarnishing of museum objects can actually be accelerated by the conditions of storage or display, and in some cases corrosion reactions result which are not usually found in nature. Some of these dangers, such as the storage of lead in oak drawers or cupboards, or the display of silver on textiles which have been treated with sulphur-containing compounds, have been known to museum scientists and conservators for many years [1, 2], but it is only recently that the widespread nature of these and related problems has been more systematically studied.

The development of multitudes of new synthetic polymers in recent years has been of enormous value to the conservator in many aspects of his work, the conservation of waterlogged wood with polyethylene glycol and the protection of friable surfaces with soluble nylon being only two examples, but the use of synthetic polymers has brought with it a host of problems. Firstly their chemical complexity is meaningless to many conservators, and manufacturers sometimes change the formulations of their products without warning, so that a branded product which was ideal for a certain application in one year might not be suitable the next. Secondly the synthetic polymers might have undesirable side effects on the objects with which they come in contact, and they should therefore be tested to see if they do have any deleterious effects before they are used.

2. TEST PROCEDURE

The procedure which has been adopted at the British Museum Research Laboratory for the testing of textiles, wood, adhesives and resins, which are to be used in the construction of showcases, has already been described [3]. It consists of placing the suspect material inside a flask or test-tube closed with a ground-glass stopper, together with a test piece of copper, lead or silver. An atmosphere rich in carbon dioxide is maintained inside the flask containing the lead test-piece, and 'blanks' are run on similar pieces of metal under the same conditions in the absence of the material being tested. Since this test was published various modifications in technique have been evolved, the most important being the inclusion of a few drops of water inside the flasks, since it has been shown [4] that moisture is essential for the tarnishing of silver by traces of hydrogen sulphide. Furthermore the atmosphere in a showcase will almost invariably contain some water vapour, and so the inclusion of water in the test increases its relevance to real conditions. At first the water was added as a few drops in the bottom of the flasks, but corrosion 'tide marks' were left on copper and lead specimens where they had been in actual contact with water droplets and so a small test tube containing moist cotton wool is now added to each flask. When adhesives and textiles are being tested it is important to ensure that they are in physical contact with part of the metal surface.

The normal duration of this test is 28 days during which time the flasks are maintained at a temperature of $60°C$. Any materials which have not caused corrosion during the course of this test may be regarded as safe, as far as copper, silver and lead are concerned. However, the test is quite severe and even the relatively low temperature employed may cause some thermal degradation of organic materials, with the production of undesirable and reactive decomposition products, which would not be formed at room temperature. Hence the occurrence of 'slight' tarnishing of the specimens does not necessarily exclude materials from showcases. Those which give off significant and dangerous amounts of reactive vapours will result in a marked deterioration of the metal specimens.

3. THE TESTING OF MATERIALS OF CONSTRUCTION

Until a few years ago oak and mahogany were the basic raw materials of museum furniture but the enormous increase in timber prices in recent years has resulted in the widespread introduction of veneered blockboard, chipboard or plywood for the construction of showcases and storage cupboards. These 'synthetic' woods are made up using large amounts of adhesives, many of which will give off vapours which are harmful to museum objects. As with the testing of textiles, there is little point in carrying out a systematic programme of testing synthetic timbers because they are made by a large number of different manufacturers, and the materials used are likely to differ significantly from batch to batch.

What is required is the testing of samples of the timber before a showcase or cupboard is constructed. That this is necessary has been proved by the recent experience of one of the national museums in London, which found that silver was tarnishing in a newly built showcase. Three types of timber had been used in its construction, a plywood, a blockboard and solid African mahogany. In this particular case the source of the corrosion was traced to the African mahogany, and it is assumed that it had been treated with some chemical, perhaps an insecticide, before it was used to construct the showcase. In this instance the plywood and blockboard were shown to be safe as far as silver is concerned, but other tests have suggested that copper and lead are likely to be at risk from some of the adhesives which are used to make synthetic timber. Tests on two different types of hardboard resulted in only slight corrosion of the silver specimens but serious corrosion of both copper and lead. However, it cannot be assumed that all hardboards are potentially dangerous to copper and lead, as examples are known of the storage of bronze coins in hardboard trays for many years without any detectable corrosion being reported.

Plastics are also frequently used in the construction of showcases, and recent tests on some strips of plastic 'dust excluder', for use along the edge of sliding glass doors, have shown that copper was tarnished by vapours given off by the plastic at 60°C. Clear plastic sheet is often used for 'glazing' showcases, but it cannot be assumed that it is completely harmless to the exhibits, because although polycarbonate has passed the tests safely, there is a slight suspicion that acrylic sheet may be harmful towards lead.

Two proprietory types of plastic boxes have been tested for their possible corrosive effects on metals, and although the chemical types of the plastic are not known, one of the boxes is designed particularly for the storage of coins. In both cases no harmful effects were recorded towards silver and copper, but slight tarnishing of lead was caused.

The difficulty with compiling information about plastic construction materials arises not so much from the nature of the primary material but from the changes the manufacturers may make from time to time in the minor constituents of the formulation, perhaps to improve certain physical characteristics of the material or simply as a reaction to difficulties in the supply of certain chemicals. Such changes as, for example, an alteration in the type of plasticizer, may well result in a particular product becoming corrosive to metals.

4. THE TESTING OF TEXTILES AND OTHER SHOW CASE LINING MATERIALS

Textiles, paper and paint are the usual materials for lining showcases. Antiquities should not be placed in freshly painted or varnished showcases until the smell of the paint is no longer detectable. No paints have been tested for their long-term effect on metals, but some of the new 'vinyl' paints should be regarded as possibly harmful to lead until they have been cleared by testing.

On the whole, paper would be expected to be harmless, unless it contains soluble salts as a result of the process of manufacture or unless it has been coloured with dyes containing sulphur. However, some poor quality paper and cardboard has been shown to be harmful to lead, and for any long-term display purposes 'acid free' paper should be used.

With the exception of wool, natural textile fibres do not contain any sulphur, and would be relatively inert towards antiquities in their raw state. However, experience has shown that some of the chemicals used in processing and dyeing the fibres will cause corrosion of copper, silver or lead. Experience with the testing of textiles over the past two years has shown that it is impossible to predict whether a textile will be safe or not, and it is essential to test a sample from each batch of cloth before it is used. As an example, the case of two 'shantung' types of textile can be quoted — a green one was found to be safe for the display of silver while a similar blue textile caused the silver to become tarnished. Two different 'hessian' types of textile, a yellow and a blue one, were both found to be safe for the display of silver, but when a series of coloured felts was examined the results were very variable. Dark green, blue/green, dark red/brown and light red/brown felts all tarnished silver very significantly, while a red and a blue sample were quite safe. All of them seemed to have slight effects on copper and lead, but these were probably not significant.

This result is important because felt is a relatively cheap textile for dressing display cases and it can be obtained in a large number of different colours and shades. It is not surprising that several of the felts tested had a corrosive action on silver, because wool and other animal hair is one of the main ingredients of a felt, which often also contains a significant amount of waste and recycled fibres.

Finally, care should be taken with fireproofed textiles. One beige-coloured cloth which was examined recently was found to be fireproofed with disodium phosphate. This was found to be safe as far as lead and silver were concerned, but the textile caused the corrosion of copper at the point of contact. The fireproofing material in this case is not volatile so the textile could be used for the display of copper or bronze objects if they were separated from it by a stand made of a 'safe' plastic or of glass.

Occasionally other materials are used in the bottom of showcases, such as sand, pebbles or vermiculite. In these cases it is essential to test for the presence of soluble salts, which should be removed by washing. Pebbles or sand from a marine shore should never be used for this reason.

5. THE TESTING OF ADHESIVES

A recently published manual [5] has classified adhesives into about 85 different chemical types, many of which are manufactured by several different companies. Hence it will be realized that the number of different adhesives which are available in the United Kingdom alone runs into several hundred. However, many of these adhesives are very specialized in their uses, and would not normally be encountered in showcase construction and dressing.

Basically the aim of the conservator is to be able to advise on which adhesives can safely be used in showcase construction and display work, for most of which a very limited range of glues is required, so that the testing of several hundred different types and brand names is not warranted. The Adhesives Handbook [5] or the Adhesives Directory [6] give classified lists of brand names and chemical types from which a short list of possibly useful adhesives can be selected and tested, and at the British Museum our initial work has concentrated on the chemical types which are commonly in use.

On the whole, polyvinyl acetate emulsions should not be used for showcases where lead will be displayed. The amount of tarnishing produced depends on the plasticizer in the particular brand employed, but for absolute safety it would be better to use a urea/formaldehyde type of glue for building the showcase. Polyvinyl acetate solution adhesives have also given variable results, one brand being harmless to copper, silver and lead while another caused tarnishing of all three.

One well-known impact adhesive which is based on synthetic rubber is very corrosive towards silver but safe for lead, while an adhesive based on latex was harmless to both silver and lead. Special care must be taken with any adhesives containing ammonia, as these will be harmful to lead, base silver and especially copper. Some rubbery adhesives fall into this class, but one acrylic emulsion containing ammonia has also been tested.

Two epoxy adhesives have been tested and were both found to cause tarnishing of silver but not of lead, while two starch-based adhesives were harmful to copper and possibly lead. Finally, both cellulose acetate and cellulose nitrate adhesives, which are widely used in repair work on antiquities, were found to be safe on copper, silver and lead. Sometimes epoxy resins are found to tarnish copper-based alloys. This is almost certainly due to incorrect mixing of the two constituent parts of the adhesive, and careful weighing of the components should eliminate this problem.

Within the showcase it is sometimes desirable to fix antiquities in position with an adhesive, particularly if they are unstable. Plasticine has often been used for this purpose, but many cases are known of corrosion caused by this material, although one type of white plasticine recently passed the tests with all three metals. More recently, several proprietory putty-like substances have come on the market which are designed especially for graphic display work, and there is a great temptation to use them on coins and other small objects. It seems probable that they are a silicone polymer and although one of the brands passed the tests, another has caused tarnishing of coins.

6. CONCLUSION

The experimental results discussed in this paper are rather disturbing, and the stage has not yet been reached where certain adhesives can be specified for use in all situations. However, it is becoming clear that some adhesives must be avoided and at least if the conservator is informed of the problems he can examine the displays in his charge with a new awareness.

One possible remedy in the case of materials which may be slightly suspect is to include a material inside the showcase which will nullify the effects of any dangerous vapours. One such material is now being developed by the 3M company [7]. It is a black powder of very low density, which is chemically a crosslinked polymer with a very large internal porosity resulting in a large specific surface area. Throughout its structure there are a large number of basic sites available for the chemisorption of acid vapours, such as the oxides of nitrogen and the oxides of sulphur, hydrogen sulphide and acetic and other organic acids.

Unfortunately the absorbing power of the 3M product eventually becomes exhausted and the supply in the showcase must be renewed as the material cannot be regenerated. Tests have shown that it has no harmful side effects on copper, silver or lead.

It should also be remembered that vapours generated outside the showcase may well be harmful to the antiquities. The cleaning or laying of new floors may well give rise to oxides of chlorine or of ammonia respectively as a result of the materials used. Furthermore the use of a protective lacquer can have harmful side effects if it is not applied evenly over the whole surface. If small areas of surface are missed when the lacquer is brushed on, these may corrode at an enhanced rate because of the setting up of oxygen concentration cells.

ACKNOWLEDGEMENTS

I am indebted to Mrs S. M. Blackshaw, Mrs J. D. Fenn and Miss F. Halahan who carried out most of the experimental work and to H. Barker and A. D. Baynes-Cope for useful discussion and comment.

REFERENCES

1. Werner, A. E., Conservation and display, (i) environmental control, 'Museums Journal' 72 (1972), 58-60.
2. FitzHugh, E. W. and Gettens, R. J., Calcite and other efflorescent salts on objects stored in wooden museum cases, in 'Science and Archaeology', Cambridge (Mass), 1971.
3. Oddy, W. A., An unsuspected danger in display, 'Museums Journal' 73 (1973), 27-28.
4. Pope, D., Gibbens, H. R. and Moss, R. L., The tarnishing of Ag at naturally-occurring H_2S and SO_2 levels, 'Corrosion Science' 8 (1968), 883-887.
5. Shields, J., 'Adhesives Handbook', London, 1970.
6. Baker, A., 'Adhesives Directory 1972-3', 5th ed., Richmond, Surrey.
7. This absorbent is being developed by Minnesota 3M Research Limited of Harlow, Essex, which is a subsidiary of the Minnesota Mining and Manufacturing Company of St Paul, Minnesota, USA.

PROBLEMS AND ETHICS IN THE CONSERVATION OF METAL OBJECTS

H. W. M. Hodges, Queen's University, Kingston, Ontario, Canada

During the past two decades there have been many contributions to 'Studies in Conservation' and other journals dealing with the problems of conserving metal objects, and since they reflect not only the difficulties that beset us most, but also our changing attitudes to the way in which metal objects should be treated, they must be briefly reviewed.

1. COPPER ALLOYS

Copper and its alloys have evoked a considerable number of papers, most of which deal with a single aspect — the removal or stabilization of cuprous chloride (atacamite). The earlier contributions largely deal with the removal of cuprous chloride by chemical [1] and electrolytic [2] methods, and with methods of testing to ensure that the treatment has been efficacious [3]. More recently, the removal of chlorides by prolonged soaking in sodium sesquicarbonate has been studied [4] while the stabilization of copper alloys using silver chloride [5] and benzotriazole [6] has been discussed. Methods of consolidating heavily corroded and fragile bronze objects have also been advanced [7].

2. IRON AND STEEL

Iron has presented a wider range of problems than the copper alloys, including not only the removal of ferric chloride by chemical [8] and electrolytic [9] means, but also by methods using direct solution in water [10]. The prevention of further oxidation (rusting) has provoked a number of studies including the use of surface coatings [11] and inhibitors applied as liquids [12] or used in the vapour phase [13]. The fact that iron rust is friable and must at times be preserved has given rise to methods by which it may be consolidated [14].

3. LEAD AND PEWTER

The major concerns with objects made of lead appear to have been the removal of basic lead carbonate by chemical [15] and physical [16] methods, and the prevention of further corrosion by the use of suitable coatings [17] and control of the environment in which they are kept [18]. Heavily corroded lead objects which would normally have disintegrated under chemical or electrolytic treatments have been the subject of consolidative reduction by electrolysis [19].

4. SILVER AND ITS ALLOYS

Apart from the removal of the chloride and sulphide products of corrosion by chemical [20] and electrolytic [21] means, the prevention of further tarnishing [22] has been a major issue. As with lead, the consolidative reduction of heavily corroded silver objects has been the subject of a detailed study [23].

5. ALUMINIUM AND ZINC ALLOYS

Objects made of these alloys are beginning to appear in increasing numbers in museum collections, and are certainly presenting problems in their conservation. So far, however, there appear to be few comments published upon possible treatments. Those for zinc alloys have been summarized [24].

In these diverse contributions one can detect some very clear trends. Except in the case of certain classes of ironwork, there has been a steady shift away from electrolytic and chemical methods of corrosion removal as normal procedures, accompanied by an ever-increasing emphasis on methods of stabilization, inhibition and environmental control. In collections of recent materials, however, iron objects represent a large proportion of the objects made of metal, and in these cases electrolytic and chemical methods of removing corrosion appear to be appropriate and continue to be used [25]. Of particular concern has been ironwork recovered from the sea and underwater excavations. Until the development of underwater recovery techniques, massive sulphide corrosion was uncommonly encountered save in the case of silver objects [26]. This, and the other problems unique to metals from underwater excavations, have given rise to a literature of their own [27].

Another trend which appears clearly is a move away from a purely empirical approach to conserving metal objects. It is no longer sufficient that a method used in conserving metals be seen to function: pragmatism has given way to a wish to understand why a method works and to determine its limitations [28].

There is undoubtedly no single explanation for these trends. Of primary importance, however, was the realization by conservators that the removal of all the products of corrosion by chemical and electrolytic means often resulted in a loss of shape of the object under treatment, frequently leaving a surface that was heavily pitted and unsightly. The understanding that, in many instances, the surface that one was aiming at preserving lay within the layers of corrosion implied the use of a more controlled system of corrosion removal than was possible with gross chemical or electrolytic methods. Further emphasis is given to this point of view by the increasing limitations demanded where chemical analysis may be called for at some later date. Thus, in cases where a bronze object has been cleaned by reduction in zinc and sodium hydroxide solution, there may well be a deposit of zinc compounds left on the surface of the object, and this could be sufficient to give a completely false analysis where X-ray fluorescence methods are employed. Equally, chemical methods of corrosion removal may easily leach large quantities of zinc or lead from the surfaces of copper alloys, while the use of phosphoric acid or phosphate solutions to remove iron corrosion may give a false impression of the type of metal on analysis [29]. Furthermore, it is now widely appreciated that the products of corrosion can themselves be highly informative about the past environments to which metallic objects have been exposed [30]. Indeed, in certain cases an indication of the grain structure of the metal is partly retained in the layers of corrosion [31], while the increasing use of metallographic studies [32] and the examination of metallic objects by X-ray diffraction techniques [33] demand that any method of conservation that alters the grain structure of a metal should be used only as a last resort. To this extent there is an increasing emphasis on the concept of keeping a metal object as nearly as possible in the state in which it was found.

In the case of metal objects that are not heavily corroded, generally the materials from historical collections, the main consideration has been how to avoid repeated cleaning which must inevitably result in a loss of metal. In this field the use of surface coatings, many of which contain inhibitors, shows considerable promise [34].

For the future, there seem to be two major concerns to which our efforts will have to be directed. The first is how to deal with those metal objects which outwardly seem quite solid but which have become so embrittled with corrosion that they are in danger of falling apart. Essentially such objects may be seen as small volumes of metal which retain the original grain structure cemented by a network of corrosion. It is to the problem of converting this network of corrosion into one of metal that consolidative reduction is addressed. At the moment neither electrolytic nor gas reduction methods appear to offer an easy solution to the problem.

The other major concern lies with heavily corroded iron objects as typified by those recovered during under-water excavations. In these cases, the layers of corrosion are friable, often laminated or warty, and within them there is no clear evidence of a surface corresponding to that of the original object. At the same time, the sheer depth of the corrosion layers normally makes methods of stabilization difficult or impossible to apply. At the moment, the choice of possibilities appears limited to one of three lines of action. One can remove all the corrosion, either electrolytically or chemically, at the risk of losing entirely the original shape of the object; one can attempt to remove the ferric chloride by solution methods, while at the same time trimming the surface to what one hopes approximates to the original form, and finally consolidate the corrosion with a resin or wax; or one can apply the heating and quenching method pioneered by Rosenberg [35]. Despite two recent laudatory accounts of this method [36], there remains much doubt as to what, chemically or physically, it aims to achieve. A more critical study of this method might show that it is not essential to heat the objects to 800°C, so inviting the production of austenite, nor to quench, thereby making the procedure totally unacceptable to the metallographer.

REFERENCES

1. Plenderleith, H. J. and Werner, A. E. A., 'The Conservation of Antiquities and Works of Art', 2nd ed., London, 1971, pp. 194-197.
2. Plenderleith, H. J. and Werner, A. E. A., op.cit., pp. 197-200.
3. Organ, R. M., The washing of treated bronzes, 'Museums Journal' 55 (1955), 112-119.
4. Oddy, W. A. and Hughes, M. J., Stabilization of 'active' bronze and iron antiquities by the use of sodium sesquicarbonate, 'Studies in Conservation' 15 (1970), 183-189.
5. Organ, R. M., A new treatment for 'bronze disease', 'Museums Journal' 61 (1961), 54-56.
6. Madsen, H. B., A preliminary note on the use of benzotriazole for stabilizing bronze objects, 'Studies in Conservation' 12 (1967), 163.
   Madsen, H. B., Treatment of bronzes with benzotriazole, in 'Conservation, Restoration and Analysis', Stavanger, 1973, pp. 2-7.
7. Organ, R. M., The consolidation of fragile metallic objects, in 'Recent Advances in Conservation', London, 1963, pp. 128-134.
8. Pelikan, J. B., The use of polyphosphate complexes in the conservation of iron and steel objects, 'Studies in Conservation' 9 (1964), 59-66.
   Stambolov, T. and Van Rheeden, B., The removal of rust with thioglycolic acid, 'Studies in Conservation' 13 (1968), 142-144.
9. Plenderleith, H. J. and Werner, A. E. A., op.cit., pp. 197-200.
10. Plenderleith, H. J. and Werner, A. E. A., op.cit., pp. 200-202.
11. Barton, K., The protection of cleaned iron objects, 'Museums Journal' 60 (1961), 284-288.
12. Pelikan, J. B., The conservation of iron with tannin, 'Studies in Conservation' 11 (1966), 109-115.
13. Biek, L., The protection of metals with vapour phase inhibitors, 'Museums Journal' 53 (1953), 110-112.
14. Organ, R. M., The consolidation of fragile metallic objects, in 'Recent Advances in Conservation', London, 1963, pp. 128-134.
15. Caley, E. R., Coatings and incrustations on lead objects from the Agora and the methods used for their removal, 'Studies in Conservation' 2 (1955), 49-54.
16. Organ, R. M., The use of ion exchange resins in the treatment of lead objects, 'Museums Journal' 53 (1953), 49-52.
17. Plenderleith, H. J. and Werner, A. E. A., op.cit., p. 277.
18. Plenderleith, H. J. and Werner, A. E. A., op.cit., p. 274.
19. Werner, A. E., Two problems in the conservation of antiquities, in 'Application of Science in Examination of Works of Art', Boston, 1967, pp.96-104.
20. Plenderleith, H. J. and Werner, A. E. A., op.cit., pp. 227-229.
21. Plenderleith, H. J. and Werner, A. E. A., op.cit., pp. 222-226.

22. Stambolov, T. and Moll, E., 'Reduction of tarnishing of silver and copper with vapour phase inhibitors', ICOM Report, 1969.

23. Organ, R. M., The reclamation of the wholly mineralized silver in the Ur lyre, in 'Application of Science in Examination of Works of Art', Boston, 1967, pp. 126-144.

24. Lewin, Z. Z. and Alexander, S. M., The composition and structure of natural patinas. Part II. Zinc and zinc alloys, 1872 to 1965, 'Art and Archaeology Technical Abstracts' 7 (1968). 151-171.

25. Plenderleith, H. J. and Werner, A. E. A., op.cit., pp. 284-290.

26. Gettens, R. J., The corrosion products of metallic antiquities, in 'Smithsonian Report for 1963', pp. 547-568.

27. Pearson, C., The preservation of an iron cannon after 200 years under the sea, 'Studies in Conservation' 17 (1972), 91-110.
Rees-Jones, S. G., Some aspects of the conservation of iron objects from the sea, 'Studies in Conservation' 17 (1972), 39-43.

28. Oddy, W. A. and Hughes, M. J., op.cit.

29. Lange, H., The occurrence of phosphates in iron objects made from bog iron ore, in 'Conservation, Restoration and Analysis', Stavanger, 1973, pp. 41-45.

30. Gettens, R. J., Mineral alteration products on ancient metal objects, in 'Recent Advances in Conservation', London, 1963, pp. 89-92.

31. Organ, R. M., The examination and treatment of bronze antiquities, in 'Recent Advances in Conservation', London, 1963, pp. 101-110.

32. Gettens, R. J., 'The Chinese Bronzes in the Freer Collection', Vol. 2, Washington, 1970.

33. Chase, W. T., Science in art, in 'McGraw-Hill Year Book of Science and Technology 1972', pp. 10-23.

34. Moncrieff, A., Protecting silver from tarnishing, 'IIC News' 4 (1966), 6-7. Organ, R. M., Remarks on inhibitors used in a steam humidification, 'IIC-AG Bulletin' 7 (1967), 31.

35. Rosenberg, G. A., 'Antiquités en Fer et en Bronze', Copenhagen, 1917.

36. Christensen, B. B., Obsolete method of iron conservation?, 'Archaeologica Lundensia' 3 (1968), 299-301.
Gottlieb, C., Firing of iron objects, in 'Conservation, Restoration and Analysis', Stavanger, 1973, pp. 15-17.

NOTES

NOTES

NOTES